Voice of the Lord

Voice of the Lord

A Biography of George Fox

by Harry Emerson Wildes

Philadelphia
University of Pennsylvania Press

Published in Great Britain, India, and Pakistan
by the Oxford University Press
London, Bombay, and Karachi

Library of Congress Catalogue Card Number: 64–10896

7431

Printed in the United States of America

Preface

THOUGH A MAN OF EXTRAORDINARY INSPIRATION TO OTHERS, AN influence that strengthens steadily, George Fox is personally less known than many leaders of less stature.

Fox's own *Journal* ranks high among spiritual autobiographies, but all too many find it heavy reading. Scholars have assiduously studied his life and works, especially the latter, and they have written skilfully, with insight and, to their great credit, with candor about the founder of Quakerism; but, outside Quaker ranks, their public has been small. Just as in life George Fox subordinated himself to his message so, after his death, his teachings are much better known than his life story. Few, if any, religious leaders of the past three centuries have exerted a stronger impact, but, for all his great vitality, none is more shadowy than he.

The need for a modern biography of this great man has long been recognized. Quaker scholars have written admirably of his personality, but, for one reason or another, have not for more than a generation essayed a "life." My good friend Albert Edward Idell did, in fact, begin such a volume, but, unfortunately, died before completing what would undoubtedly have been a major accomplishment.

In the present endeavor to portray the true and living George Fox, I owe a deep debt to the numerous devoted Friends who have so painstakingly recorded the rise and progress of Quakerism. Their researches proved priceless, not only in supplying necessary data but also in their fruitful suggestions for further investigation.

I am also under obligation to the staffs of various libraries, especially those of the University of Pennsylvania, Swarthmore and Haverford Colleges and the British Museum, as well as the New York Public Library. Edward Millikan, of Friends House, Euston Road, London, and Frederick B. Tolles, of Friends Historical Association, Swarthmore, gave far greater assistance than they can ever possibly realize. To the latter, in particular, who labored earnestly, unselfishly and efficiently to further publication, my gratitude is boundless.

During those periods of depression unavoidable by writers, Oliver G. Swan gave unfailing counsel and encouragement. By no means last in importance is the gratitude I feel toward those who listened patiently for those many months when I could think or speak of nothing else than George Fox, his life and works.

HARRY EMERSON WILDES

Philadelphia.

Contents

Voice of the Lord

1

Drayton-in-the-Clay

HE WAS A STRANGE LAD, THIS SAD GEORGE FOX WHO wandered lonely in the woods and fields of the Leicestershire hamlet which we call Fenny Drayton but which, in Fox's early Stuart time, was known as Drayton-in-the-Clay.

Other boys scuffled, wrestled or played games; young George had no companions nor any heart for youthful trivialities. He could run, apparently a little faster than his fellows, but he wasted no time on useless competition. Other youngsters roamed, dogs at their heels, over the wide grass meadows, but George was not among them. His associates and friends were not his human neighbors nor did he admire their heroes, whether lordly cavaliers or strait-laced Puritans. He lived, not in Fenny Drayton's mundane world of farming, shepherding and cottage industry but in an idealistic private realm whose satisfactions were sweeter, and more lasting, than the finding of birds' nests or the starting of rabbits from their lairs.

He was unusual but not unique. Stuart England knew many men and women, even boys and girls, who, to escape the confusion swirling about Charles I and his unruly Parliament, sought peace and happiness in the hereafter. Because to attain Utopia the Scriptures were unfailing guides, the

11

promises of prophets, the writings of apostles and, far above all else, the teachings of the Lord transcended anything that kings or legislators might decree.

Actually, George Fox was less a Stuart Englishman than an odd mixture of Biblical Hebrew and future dweller in the skies. He could not have foreseen that conflict between revealed precept and current British law would bring him into serious difficulties with the civil authorities; had he known, he would nevertheless have kept his course. The big-boned, broad-faced lad was strong willed and tenacious; once convinced that his beliefs were right no human power ever changed him. Critics called him obstinate and opinionated, but his sincerity was never questioned.

From the little village green at Fenny Drayton, George Fox's sharp eyes looked far beyond the marsh grass and the waving wheat of the surrounding fields. To him the narrow paths that led from the giant yews of St. Michael's church-yard pointed not to the neighbor town of Mancetter nor to the purple-shadowed foothills but toward a bright Heaven where the Lord awaited. The score of grass-roofed cottages clustered about the gray-brown church, the mansion of the squire upon the rising ground, even the stubby, octagonal tower of Atherstone in the distance were but outward vanity, reflecting nothing of God's glory.

It was a doleful period. Puritans preached that mirth was sinful, that earthly life was dreary; but George was even more pessimistic about man. The world he early considered to be folly, shot through with pretension and deceit, caught in the darkness of sin; only in Heaven was there true reality, a life eternal and a neverending peace. Hypocrisy, he thought, reigned everywhere. Men forgot on weekdays the psalms they sang so loudly at the Sunday services. He watched horsemen riding those paths across the fens. Why could they not understand that just as one false step would sink their horses' bellies deep in mire so careless sin was fatal to their souls? He heard the heavy carts rumbling down the Roman road, bringing fruits that to worldly idlers were savory and sweet. But to George Fox the only savor was the honey of the Word of God; all else was bitter ashes.

Neither George nor most others in Drayton knew much of what was happening more than ten or a dozen miles beyond the settlement. Take, for instance, that great house only three miles away, Hartshill, as it was called. A man had lived there, not too long ago, a man named Michael Drayton, whom the squire said was a scribbler; he had not read the poems but he said that this Michael Drayton had fallen into evil ways, drinking in London with an actor named Will Shakespeare. But who, to George, was Shakespeare?

Possibly George Fox heard legends of how man had lived in the neighborhood for many, many years, but it is doubtful if he knew that a rude ridge near the church outlined a mud-walled fort of very ancient times or that a mound less than half a mile away marked the grave of some pre-Christian warrior who may have been King Lear. He must have been ignorant of the fact, nor in his scorn of non-Biblical history, would he have cared to know, that St. Michael's giant yews had flourished in Edward the Confessor's reign or that at the nearby well young Henry of Richmond paused while on his way to snatch the crown at Bosworth Field not quite four miles northward.

More than half the families, George's among them, lived in one-hearth houses, for, in those days, government imposed a two shillings tax upon each fireplace or chimney pot. To raise so much hard cash placed heavy burdens on the hundred residents of Drayton-in-the-Clay.

Not that Drayton was poverty stricken. If poor in ready

money, the hamlet was rich in other resources. It shared the general prosperity of the woolen industry, excelling in hosiery manufacture; it also made good boots and shoes for local purchase. For most residents, though not for George's family, the livelihood was farming, particularly bean growing. "Shake a Leicestershire man," outsiders jeered, "and you can hear the beans rattling inside him." The carousing Michael Drayton told his cronies that he came from "Bean-Belly Leicestershire." Even to this day a nearby settlement glories in the name of Barton-in-the-Beans.

Most Leicestershire folk being "as loike as two peasen" in their speech, George doubtless spoke the local dialect; if it were suggested that he change his diction a Draytonite would swear "Ay wouldn't nivver do naught o' the sort." He knew the odd custom of substituting "have" for the verb "to be"; he could not have avoided hearing neighbors explain when someone inquired about their health, "Ah, ah heven't not quoit so well todee". This was proper talk in Drayton where each man considered himself "as reight as may leg and street as a poike." George himself used other odd turns of speech, words such as "thataways," "thereaways" or "noways," distortions such as "riz" for "rose," "rid" for "ride" and "writ" for "wrote." Now and then, indeed, he also unconsciously employed a local dialect studded with survivals of ancient Celtic or more recent Danish tongues.

Drayton's great man, when George Fox was a boy, was Colonel Sir George Purefoy, Bart., the squire who held what remained of medieval feudal rights. A man of no great prominence, though relatives were influential in the county, Sir George was a Puritan, but one who swayed so gently in the cross winds of politics that he stayed friends with everyone. Purefoy dropped in often at the little Fox home set among the fruit trees. Here, in what was called the Dog Yard, near the church, lived Christopher Fox, the weaver, with his wife, the former Mary Lago, and their children. The visits were enjoyable. Unlike most Drayton people, both parents were literate and well able to talk with some measure of authority upon the political and religious questions agitating England. Christopher expressed his strong opinions with excessive vehemence, but evidently the squire enjoyed the arguments.

Except with Purefoy, Christopher and Mary Fox may not have been too popular in Drayton. They were relatively late-comers to the small community and English rural hamlets were notoriously slow in accepting strangers. True, their immediate ancestors were apparently of Leicestershire stock, there being many Lago yeomen within a dozen miles of Drayton, but a dozen miles is a considerable distance to walk across the fields, and Christopher's people seem to have lived much farther off, forty or fifty miles away. Such areas, in early Stuart times, were far-off lands where people were as alien as foreigners, especially when, as was probably the case with the Fox family, they came from other shires.

Mary's personality, as well as Purefoy's patronage, broke down such isolation as existed. Apparently one of those women whom tombstones were wont to describe as "upright and amiable," she may have been a more or less distant Purefoy relative; instead of the Christophers and Thomases so common in Fox genealogy, she gave her boys the same names as were common on the Purefoy family tree. Whether or not sprung from the same stock as the squire, she believed implicitly that certain of her forebears had been martyred in Mary Tudor's reign, one at Lichfield, sixteen miles from Drayton, perhaps another at Mancetter, only two miles west of St. Michael's Church. If the latter were the case, she, unlike Christopher, was virtually a Draytonite.

Sometime in July, 1624, when Christopher and Mary were

still in their twenties, their first son, George, was born. Four other children followed within ten or a dozen years; the dates are not definite, the early records at St. Michael's being most imperfect.

To his parents, George must have been something of a trial. Christopher certainly looked forward to help from his children in raising the family income, but George showed no aptitude for weaving. The boy was anything but idle nor did he shirk responsibility; he simply had small skill with his hands. Believing, as did his father, in the rightness of his own convictions, as firm as was Christopher in arguing for them, George and his father must have clashed often in argument. If so, it might explain why, in later years, George repressed much personal information about his adolescence.[1] Nor, for that matter, had he comments about his brothers or sisters, unless a casual reference here and there to "my relations" applied to them. From youth he was a solitary, one who loved men in the aggregate but who strongly disapproved of them as individuals. Mary taught him "to walk to be kept pure," but early he discovered that others did not follow these high principles. His intolerance with them may be traceable to overrigid standards or to resentment at the aloofness of older residents, but certain neighbors disgusted the small boy; he would have said that their laziness, their drunkenness and their loud-mouthed roistering "struck at his life." For his fellow man, George Fox had love and charity, but none whatever for the filthy wretch who cherished opposing religious views.

At eleven, he formed an earnest resolution never to behave

[1] In his *Journal,* for example, his reminiscences written long after the events described, he mentioned his father only twice, once in referring to his birth and again, thirty years later, when Christopher, with characteristic intensity, defended his son's right to speak the truth as he saw it. George did not even mention his father's death.

improperly. He kept his vow. "I knew pureness and righteous-ness," he said. At twenty, he remarked, simply and without boastfulness, "I never wronged man or woman." Looking back in his old age, he prided himself on having lived a sinless life. George was thoroughly sincere, but it is not surprising that more fallible folk suffered much discomfort in his presence. Lads thought him unbearably priggish; girls giggled at his inability to laugh and play. In later years, grown men, resenting his calm assumption of perfection, would stone and beat him.

To certain members of the family—George did not identify them—it seemed obvious that if such a paragon would not become a weaver he should enter the ministry.[2]

However Christopher may have felt about the project, he could not afford to send his son to school and university. Instead, and probably with much reluctance, his father "put" him to a neighbor—not one of the ungodly crew whose mis-deeds offended George, but a man of higher quality who lived across the fens at Mancetter, another tiny village much like Drayton. Precise details are lacking, but, by every indication, the master was George Gee, a man of varied interests, all of them small scale and seasonal. Gee was a shoemaker in a country village, a cattle dealer at a time when it was the custom to buy and sell only at the annual autumn fairs, a wool merchant on a part-time basis, a stock raiser with a few

[2] George himself gave no inkling that he was reluctant to do so, but it is an interesting speculation as to what might have happened had he taken holy orders. With such a temperament and such compulsion to speak his mind, no matter to whom or on what subject, he would prob-ably have never taken his degree; before graduation he would have quit the university in disgust or been expelled for incorrigible heresy. Had he been graduated, what kind of minister would he have made? A forceful and inspiring preacher, without a doubt, but what of his obedience to church officials set above him? The only certainty is that he never would have been a servile routineer nor a time-serving hypocrite. George Fox would always have been himself. No one could ask for more.

sheep pastured on the meadows. A businessman whose customers were scarce and whose range was minor had small need for an assistant, but he could use a herdsman-shepherd. He might, at odd moments, teach cobbling and the elements of shoemaking.

Whether young George was formally apprenticed, as he himself implies, is open to some question. Under the provisions of the still valid Elizabethan law, he must, in such event, be bound to labor for at least seven years, not only without pay but under an obligation to give a more or less substantial sum of money in return for being taught the trade; a further provision of that Statute of Artificers could have held George Fox in service until he reached twenty-four. The actual agreement must have been quite different from indenture in the strictest sense; a part-time business man like Gee would scarcely qualify as a master guildsman of a major craft, and Fox worked under far less onerous conditions.

Fox himself recalled, much later in life, when details were much less sharp in memory, that he early carried serious responsibilities ("a great deal went through my hands") and that he was incredibly efficient. A sort of business manager while still in his teens, he so conducted his master's operations that George Gee "was blessed"; but when Fox left, at nineteen years of age, before the expiration of a minimum seven years, Gee "broke and came to nothing."

While thus performing business miracles, the lad took time for other, more important, matters. As he matured he meditated on the Bible stories which he knew so well, on prophecy and revelation and on New Testament injunctions. All these divine revelations he took literally; like many other Englishmen he applied them as an acid test for current law and conduct. One so well versed in the Bible and so sure of his gift of seeing truth clearly would seldom find himself in doubt;

but if certain passages were difficult to understand, aid was always close at hand, almost next door, at St. Michael's vicarage.

2

George Grows Up

IN 1638, WHEN GEORGE WAS FOURTEEN, THE HOLDER OF THE living at St. Michael's fell critically ill. Sir George Purefoy chose as curate, and eventual successor, an earnest preacher, Nathaniel Stephens, holder of an Oxford arts degree.

Stephens sought to know the truth by delving deep into the hidden meanings of the Book of Revelation. A minister's son, a student at Magdalen at sixteen, and restive under High Church ritual, his studies, his postgraduate service as his father's curate and his observations of current politics carried him ever deeper into criticism of the King and Cavaliers. Though a recent rector of St. Michael's believed him dictatorial, Stephens' biographer declared that, in contrast to the general temper of Stuart times, Nathaniel Stephens argued with "good sense and good feelings—seeking neither to please nor to displease any party." If so, it was a policy of which Squire Purefoy undoubtedly approved.

Oddly enough, so did the strong-willed Christopher, now a churchwarden—the only one, in fact, who was able to read and write. He, too, like Purefoy and the preacher, was a Puritan. As an independent student of the Scriptures, Christopher knew less than Stephens about theology but he surpassed the pastor in intensity and fervor. That the warden

listened was a tribute to Stephens' preaching power. Draytonites had not always been so docile. When, soon after his
accession to the pastorate, a promotion that came within his
first six months at Drayton, Nathaniel Stephens dug into
parish history, he learned that just about the time he was
born, Draytonites, rebelling at High Church innovations, had
refused to kneel at their Communion services. The rector at
the time, a pliable man more endowed with humor than with
principle, yielded with the quip that Drayton was both
stiff-necked and stiff-kneed.

The parishioners had an equal sense of humor. Long,
tangled sermons, knotty with dogma and, if they were
Stephens' sermons, couched in the long, pedantic words that
the Reverend Nathaniel Stephens never quite outgrew, bored
them to renewed rebellion. When rebuked by their pastor,
they proposed a fair solution. Each Sunday they would bring
a pole, set it on its base and, when it was steady and erect,
they would, at a given signal, all step back suddenly. If the
pole then fell toward the church they would, at this sign from
Heaven, file dutifully into their pews; if, perchance, the pole
fell toward the Royal Red Gate Inn, they must follow its
divine direction. Somehow, the legend slyly adds, the pole
almost never pointed toward the pulpit.[1]

Why should the scholarly Stephens have moved to Drayton?
The living paid well, to be sure, but it is doubtful that he
came for money only; the ascetic parson lived abstemiously.
Parish chores were light, but no one ever thought that

---

[1] The legend may be, and doubtless is, apocryphal, as is the story that,
for half a century, Drayton was a Gretna Green for Midland elopers. One
may be skeptical, as well, about the rumor that Dick Turpin, the highway-
man, had, to quote a later rector, "his place of business" not too far from
St. Michael's lovely churchyard. But, true or false, Dick Turpin was not
typical of Drayton; a much more accurate impression of the people arises
from the one-time constable who, having served a year, resigned his office
because he had no work to do.

Stephens was a lazy man. The heavy gaiety of Drayton would never have amused him; Stephens would have endorsed the pole gamble only if he were allowed to give that pole a hefty push. One cannot know his reasons, but it is likely that he came for freedom, for power and for opportunity to think out a course of action. As curate of his father's parish, he was still subordinate, a boy; by a move to Drayton, he would be the intellectual leader of his own community. He would teach the people to thirst after righteousness; he could instil his firm conviction that divine grace could be immediately felt within one's soul and that Christian practice must be stripped of human symbols.

Yet Drayton must have disappointed him. Stephens loved the byroads of theology, but there were none at Drayton with whom to argue subtleties. The scholar who pored over the Revelation of St. John the Divine cast his wisdom before an unresponsive congregation that must often have thought wistfully about that pole. Brother preachers lived nearby—eight of them within an easy ride—but these were parlous times; what with intervening marshes and roads infested by highwaymen, meetings were infrequent. Discussion, moreover, might be dangerous; too free exchange of views on politics or on religion—often the two were inseparable— could lead to treason charges. Books would have been a refuge, but, outside the mansion of the squire, there were few books in Drayton; Purefoy himself may not have owned more than one or two.

The good parson, therefore, buried himself in his study, frequently for sixteen hours a day. Seclusion was no hardship; Stephens wanted time to think. Unlike the predecessor who crumpled weakly when his people would not kneel, Stephens would not compromise with principle; but, unfortunately and uncharacteristically, he was not now wholly certain what principles he held. Observation, reading and deep thought were guiding him toward Presbyterianism; he must decide whether, in good conscience, he should support those Scottish Covenanters who were threatening to come to England to overthrow the King.[2] During these trials the weaver's cottage offered some relief. The churchwarden may have been a testy man, but he was well versed in the Bible and he respected an Oxford education. Where other women would have sat smilingly silent while the men were talking, Mary Fox chimed in with her fair share of intelligent contribution. Stephens enjoyed his calls; he dropped in often.

Neither Christopher nor Mary believed that children should be seen but never heard. Whenever George had holiday, he shared in the discussions, raising simple questions which, at first, Stephens answered brilliantly, but, as the boy matured, with increasing difficulty. He admired the lad's agility of mind, commending him to Purefoy. Young George, he said, was most exceptional; never before, he told the squire, "has such a plant been bred in England." It was a pity that such a mind should be wasted on business; how much better would it have been had young George taken holy orders.

With the passage of the years, however, Stephens grew concerned. George was outgrowing the stage of simple questions and of interpretation of Bible passages; he was finding answers for himself. More frequently, and more indignantly, he was noticing great gaps between precept and practice, between strict rules and loose observance. With the intolerance of youth, he was criticising the failings of his elders. Of course, he irritated them; no one cares to be incessantly reminded of his faults, certainly not by a whippersnapper. Youngsters should show deference to age, regardless of whether that defer-

---

[2] Looking backward, his decision seems foreordained; for Stephens the solution was not so easy. His thoughts were sometimes so intense, his friends reported, that "often he would strangely forget himself."

ence is warranted; they should be humble before authority. But George treated everyone, rich or poor, high or low, of any age or station, as though everyone were equal. Worse, he had the presumption that he was equal, too. In Drayton's eyes he had no manners.

Take, for instance, his annoying use of "thee" and "thou." These were perfectly proper words, but not for indiscriminate use. Friends might exchange them freely, but not acquaintences; parents used them to their children and superiors toward servants, but it was a one-way usage only. Underlings must say "you" to everyone; to do otherwise would be insulting.[3] The reasoning was clearer to George Fox than to those who thought themselves his betters. All men, he argued, are equal before the Lord, therefore, one man is equal to another. Special rank or status, special privilege, is thus a sin, a crime against God's teaching. To say "you" to one man but "thou" to another implies that one is greater than another; it flouts the Word of Scripture.

But what of etiquette and what of common courtesy? "Hypocrisy," said Fox, "and lies." Actions, like words, must be entirely truthful. To bow and say, "Your servant, sir," is false; for if men be equal before the Lord, none is a servant save unto the Lord. To doff one's hat, save in the presence of God, violates divine injunction; one must not say "Good morrow" or "Good evening."

Since George held such extreme opinions it was not surprising that he rebelled against the teaching that a favored few were specially elected to enter into glory while all others

[3] Fox later learned that English, unlike at least thirty-five other languages, was losing richness by failure to distinguish between singular and plural in its second person pronoun, but his custom was not due to scholarship considerations. He had a simpler, and to him, far more convincing reason: God would not permit him to say "you" to any individual.

suffered through eternity. He could not follow Stephens in the pastor's progress toward the Scottish Calvinism that was taking hold of England.

George failed to make it very clear just how he happened to arrive at his conclusions; he talked of "openings," of revelations "too great to be spoken," which doubtless were his reflections upon ideas he heard from others but which he believed were strict and binding heavenly commands. He also tested current customs by the acid of the Scriptures and, if the custom failed to meet the test, he challenged it. Where, for instance, was there Biblical precedent for marriage by a clergyman? Oxford had armed her students against errors in ritual or dogma, but Stephens had no defense for such a question. He tried to overwhelm George by the heavy weight of university scholarship, but, in the absence of a Scriptural citation dealing directly with the issue, George Fox was unconvinced.

Worse followed. The King, said Fox, demanded oaths of loyalty and courts required that witnesses be sworn, but did not the Apostles specifically forbid Christians to take any form of oath? To this, Stephens cited Scripture. Abraham swore, he pointed out and Isaac and Jacob, too; so did the priests and prophets, and, as a clincher, the Angel of the Lord. Could anyone then doubt that taking oaths was proper?

"Yes," retorted Fox. "All this is true. I see it in the Scriptures. But, once more I ask, did not Christ himself forbid his followers to swear? Did not he say: 'Swear not at all'?"

The reasoning was typical. George Fox accepted unquestioningly the letter of the Word whenever that letter was construed in the spirit of those who had written it. Stephens may have been nettled by his young opponent, but apparently he abandoned the argument. A later adversary, faced by the same retort, pursued the matter. "It is written," he pointed out triumphantly, "You shall swear in truth and righteousness!"

George was never at a loss. "Ah, yes," he admitted. "You are right. I commend you for your knowledge of the Scriptures though I do believe I can remember as many instances, or more. Here is the question that I ask you now : Was it you Jews or you Gentiles that were commanded? Where did God ever command Gentiles to swear? Was this *you* to you Jews or you Christians after Christ came?"

Though he was to suffer for it grievously, George Fox never took an oath. As he replied to a judge who demanded that he swear allegiance to the King : "Christ commands me not to swear at all, as does the Apostle James. I am neither Turk nor heathen but a Christian who must show forth Christianity. Do you not know that the Christians in primitive times refused to swear in the days of the persecutions and some of the martyrs in Queen Mary's days refused to swear because Christ and the Apostles had forbidden it? Whether I am to obey God or man I leave to thee to judge."

Relationship between the precocious boy and his pastor steadily deteriorated. In the beginning, the pastor, proud of his protégé's ability, could pass off minor setbacks. When difficulties rose, he evaded or ignored them; there had been occasions when his simple assertion, his office or his diplomas were enough to settle arguments. But soon, as George grew older, his calm self-assurance, his certainty of the spirit of Jesus as a final argument, and his tireless persistence cancelled out Stephens' twenty years of seniority.

Fox was no logician. In disputes that swirled about details of doctrine, he ignored those subtleties of argument in which the scholastic minded Stephens so excelled. Scarcely listening to elaborate hairsplittings, he used his Bible as a bludgeon to beat down the pastor. Night after night, poor bewildered

Stephens plodded homeward, dismayed rather than defeated. The Oxford graduate could not have relished these continued contradictions by an unschooled junior. In the quiet of his study, Stephens thought up telling replies, too late to use upon his youthful tormenter but useful for the coming Sunday's sermon. This practice irritated Fox, who charged, unjustly, that his parson took for himself the thoughts that Fox had voiced.

But Stephens had more worries than those centering about George Fox. In 1641, when Fox was seventeen, the Civil War was coming to a head. The qualms of conscience that bedevilled Stephens were driving him into alliance with the rebels. Leicestershire, however, was for the moment Royalist; and so for safety and for peace of mind, Nathaniel Stephens left his pulpit to take up what he hoped would be a temporary post, at Coventry. Here he was safe; a Purefoy kinsman was member of Parliament for Coventry; more important, perhaps, he was raising a dragoon regiment for Cromwell's army. George easily survived the loss of a spiritual advisor from whom he had been drifting. Armed with the Bible and secure in the cocksureness of a brash teen-ager, he was certain that he knew the truth. Moreover, he had work to do; at Atherstone, the fair was opening and Gee had goods for him to market.

George brought his Christian principles into the fairs. Early in life he had resolved—had it been anyone else one would say he swore a vow—to say precisely what he meant and to say it briefly. Had not the Bible enjoined the faithful to let their speech be "yea, yea and nay, nay" in everything? He did not, to be sure, hold fast to the decision, "let my words be few," for he always piled his arguments as high as possible; but his words were always "savory, seasoned with grace."

For Fox, whose words gushed forth like torrents, the injunction to be brief applied to the endless haggling of the market place. Wool merchants and drovers, the tanners from whom he bought the leather for George Gee's shoemaking, these men and nearly every other trader loved to bargain; it was their spice that seasoned trade. Many a dealer would have preferred to pay more or to sell for less rather than forego the pleasures of chaffering. Fox refused to bargain; it was, he said, dishonest and un-Christian. "How can it be right," he asked, "to tell a man that this is my highest bid when actually I expect, as he knows well, to pay a larger sum? How can I trust a man who offers me a price which he says is his best when he and I both know that he will lower it? These practices are lies. Everyone should tell the truth."

He prided himself on the finalities of his yea or nay, but if he wished to lay a little extra stress, he would add "verily." "If George says 'verily,' there is no changing him," his friends would say. Probably, George Fox lost many bargains, especially with strangers, by his stubbornness in holding to his first and only bids, but he built a reputation for himself and for the goods he sold.

He took as strong a stand against deception. The words of other dealers were neither savory, nor filled with grace; Fox called them deceitful. They sold adulterated goods, pretended that their shoddy wares were of good quality and cheated shamefully. Honesty was the secret of his success in trade, the reason that George Gee was blessed as long as George Fox was his manager.

Sometimes his sense of the proprieties led him to condemn conduct which others considered entirely innocent. At Atherstone fair, for instance, when he was nineteen, he broke with a cousin who invited him to drink a mug of beer. Fox willingly accepted thinking that each would pay his share, but the cousin also asked a friend and then suggested gaily that he who drank the least should pay for all. George had never taken part in such a party; he recoiled in grieved surprise. The cousin was a church member, a man who "had a sense of good." Fox invariably referred to such men as "professors"; that such a man should act so wantonly astonished young George Fox. He drank his beer, drew from his pocket a coin to pay for it, then, rising, calmly said, "If that's your plan, then I must leave."

He broke not only with his cousin, who thereafter does not reappear in history, but also with the rest of his acquaintances. After leaving his friends, who must have been stunned with wonderment, not knowing what they had done to cause the outburst, Fox finished his business at the fair and went home mournfully. That night he could not sleep but walked about all night, praying and "crying to the Lord," until, near dawn, the Lord revealed that, since young men were vain and old men earthy, he, George Fox, must go forth to lead a lonely life.

3

Disillusion

APPARENTLY WITHOUT OBJECTION FROM HIS FAMILY, OR concern for it, young Fox set forth in September, 1643, to live thereafter "as a stranger unto all."

Probably he left too early; for all his business successes, George Fox was still immature in many ways. Possibly, had Stephens still retained his Drayton pulpit, George would not have left so suddenly. Though Fox had lost much confidence in Stephens' ability and though that Oxford degree now cast little glamor, the parson still was influential. As the most intellectual, and by far the best educated, man whom George had yet encountered or whom he was to meet for several years to come, he was a man to whom the youth could still defer— as much, that is, as Fox deferred to anyone. But Stephens was not available; his exile left the teen-ager free from human intellectual guidance.

With the Lord God as personal advisor Fox needed none.

Whether unconsciously or by design, George avoided the one good road that led from Drayton. Close by, to the north, was Lichfield, where, in Mary Tudor's reign, his ancestor had been burned; to the south was Coventry, where Stephens lived in exile. The same straight highway would have taken him to Oxford, but Fox had no love for universities. Instead

he took bypaths or cut cross-country and so came to Lutterworth, a crossroads town in the Coventry–Rugby–Leicester
triangle. He thus found himself in a region from which some
of Christopher's people had come and where relatives may
still have lived. It was a settlement, moreover, far more
important than its size would warrant, for it was here, two
centuries and a half earlier, that John Wycliffe had preached
primitive Christianity and that his followers, the Lollards,
spread what the Church called heresy.

Much of the Wycliffe influence still survived. Fox found
himself wholly unprepared for the blazing religious agitation
which he met. Sparks, to be sure, had blown across the
marshes twenty miles to Drayton, enough of them to dislodge
Stephens; but probably only the parson realized how serious
was the fire. Other Draytonites, including Fox, would have
explained that the unrest was due to quarrels between King
and Parliament, between High Churchmen and Puritans or
between Cromwell and his Ironsides against Cavaliers; but the
origin of Lutterworth's religious unrest lay deep in the past.

Nor was the challenge to ecclesiastical authority a purely
local feeling. Wycliffe had kindled it at Lutterworth, as far as
England was concerned, but movements, similar in purpose
and often of more intensity, had burst out upon the Continent,
as well. Even isolated Drayton must have heard of the great
religious wars raging then in Europe and of bloody massacres
in Ireland, all scarred by atrocities committed by sincere and
righteous people contending for what they considered their one
true faith.

Chaos imperilled church and state. Rulers by divine right
feared for their thrones. Frightened clerics battled heresies that
invited disaster for everyone. But bishops and kings were not
the only persecutors of the unconventional. Many self-styled
prophets, certain that they alone received true revelation, con-

demned all rivals more vindictively and with more vituperation than they showered on royal officers or on clergy of the orthodox faiths.

As in Wycliffe's day, men craved peace. They yearned for unity, not only with their neighbors but with the nation, the world, and with creation as a whole. They wanted to identify themselves with the eternal truth. They sought a personal approach to God. To satisfy their needs, mystics, visionaries, ecstatics and prophets sprang up in profusion. Some were charlatans who preyed upon the gullible and some were crackpots whose cryptic messages no one could understand. Here and there an unbalanced raver claimed to be the reincarnation of the Lord, if not, indeed, the deity Himself.

But as many Englishmen when Fox was young lived not for the present world but for the world to come, sincere reformers were also to be heard. For centuries, squalor, oppression and distress had been the common lot. Certain scholars pointed to Bible passages to prove that this was foreordained and unavoidable unless men purified their hearts, cleansed their lives and freed their minds of error. So Fox thought in early youth. In his boyhood he supposed that the distant steeples pointed the escape route from the swamps of sin surrounding Drayton. They symbolized the way toward harmony of God and man. But then he found a bewildering confusion. All the steeples aimed toward heaven, but the preachers differed widely in their doctrines. Which of these many guides which promised the path to heaven really told the truth?

Sermons were of little help. Pastors often talked three hours on some minor matter of Biblical interpretation, or argued endlessly a knotty problem of theology. Congregations listened patiently, but to most of them, unskilled in dialectics, the weary words must have seemed like Drayton's marshes—a false step off the twisted path of truth and one was lost in error.

Long before George Fox was fully grown he realized that Nathaniel Stephens preached sterile sermons full of dreary logic that inspired no warmth, no sympathy, no heartfelt emotion. He was too young to know that once-dynamic Puritanism was becoming old and that conformity to formula was replacing true devotion. While accepting the sacredness of Scripture he was unready to receive it as the only divine revelation nor as the sole guide for human conduct. To do so in the changed conditions of a modern world would mean the placing of a professional mediator between man and God, whereas religion should be personal and private.

The boy could not yet express his thoughts with clarity and precision, but he believed that God was omnipresent, revealed, as some people were saying, by the eternal light of Christ which shines within everyone, showing them what thoughts and deeds are evil. If one, guided by this light, observes the Ten Commandments, fears God and loves his neighbor, he will live in perfect harmony with all creation. Anyone moved by the power of God to walk in this light shares the spirit of Moses and the Prophets, of the Apostles and of Christ; he is as sinless as was Adam before the Fall. True religious guidance is not, George thought, to be discovered only in a priestly hierarchy, as the Papists taught, nor in a strict construction of the Scriptures, as rigid Puritans believed, but in the Divine Word illuminated within a man's own soul.

The ideas were neither peculiar nor new. Mystics everywhere who read their Bibles carefully received similar inspiration. Their interpretations varied widely, from those who identified the eternal light with human reason to those who held that each man was himself a god entitled to do whatever pleased him; there were some who thought that God was nothing more than light or fire or possibly the sun. Fox could not have escaped hearing of the new sects rising out of these ideas. It was, to say the least, doubtful whether he read their books and pamphlets, for Drayton was unliterary. But wandering evangelists roamed everywhere. Unconsciously he absorbed a certain measure of their teaching; he repeated their words, but without borrowing their thoughts. His ideas, whether rejection of magic, sacerdotalism and ceremony, or acceptance of an inner light, were entirely his own.

High among these precursers was a Dutch mystic whom the English called Henry Nicholas. Born a century and a quarter before George Fox, Nicholas, too, had been a brooding boy who questioned what the preachers taught. The Lord had shown him visions of splendor and glory. As the "Third Prophet of the Lord," the long-bearded Hollander, clad in crimson satin and carrying a huge magic mirror wherein to view the reflection of his soul, demanded perfect obedience to the Light Within. His ideal was lofty and the name he chose, the Family of Love, was beautiful; it well described a sect pledged to nonviolence, purity and love for all mankind. Inevitably, however, the name, together with excesses by a few irresponsible elements, led scoffers to accuse the Familists of open immorality.

Nevertheless, though enemies called his principles the "drowsie dreams of a doting Dutchman," Nicholas won followers. Fox found many of them in the Lutterworth area. He could not agree with their stress upon love as an all-important factor and he thought of the light as emanating from God rather than as a subjective phenomenon, but he had more sympathy for Familists than for most of the native British sects.

Disciples of another Continental mystic, Jacob Boehme, were also numerous in eastern England. Boehme, a German who died in the year that Fox was born, was himself an apprentice shoemaker given to lonely wanderings; he, too, like Fox and Nicholas, received divine revelation that caused him to reject conventional beliefs in favor of a return to primitive Christianity. He, too, found guidance in an Inner Light.[1]

Yet much that he heard at Lutterworth, whether from professed Familists or from those who unknowingly echoed Boehme's teachings, fitted George Fox's philosophy. Members of the Family of Love, Boehme's followers and many others who had been bored by interminable Puritan sermons thought taciturnity in others a great virtue; consider long before you speak, they said, and then answer only yes or no or verily. Bear no weapons, they advised, against your neighbors, although, if so be you are attacked you may resist by clubs or staves. Keep silent in your worship, they recommended, until the spirit moves you to speak. And, since you and we walk in the light of the Lord, we only are the living; those who do not hold with us and those especially who once were with us but now have fallen into darkness, all such are dead.

Certainly George Fox would not have stamped complete approval on each and every doctrine of this type; but, breathing in such atmosphere, he unconsciously absorbed much and accepted much of what he heard. Rejecting what he considered dross or airy notions, he hungered for more truth; and so, when he exhausted Lutterworth he tramped across the fields

---

[1] Certainly George Fox read nothing of Boehme's writings at this time; they did not appear in English translation until after George left Drayton. But Boehme's vividness of preaching and the vigor of his style so impressed his hearers that many of his turns of speech were already current, taking hold so tenaciously that Englishmen innocently adopted them as their own. Fox, however, was less hospitable to Boehme than to Nicholas, for George was shocked at Boehme's suggestion that God created evil as well as good. In reminiscing about this period of his life, George Fox never mentioned Boehme, though he reported arguing with some who held similar ideas; on only one occasion did he refer to Familists as a cult.

to various other small settlements, staying in none for more than a few weeks. His goal was London, the capital and center of religious ferment.

Wherever he went, he argued. Never a man to listen passively to anything he disapproved, he disputed with extremists of all kinds. In more sedate times it is difficult to realize how the seventeenth century so tightly intertwined the supernatural with the mundane that virtually all conversation carried religious overtones; more polite and doubtless less intense people cannot but be shocked at the rude, intolerant and insulting language commonly employed.

However reticent before the Lord, George Fox impatiently condemned the advocates of error. He antagonized many; his impatience and his angry overstatements brought misunderstandings. But he also gathered sympathizers—people who, like himself, awaited an imminent Second Coming, who believed that the Word must be interpreted by the Spirit which inspired it, who wondered whether professional preachers were not sometimes agents of the Devil. He heard much talk of abolishing Oxford and Cambridge because they taught improper religion. Reformers hoped for a new and better ministry that would proclaim a pure religion, a ministry that would manifest itself by miracles. Because they searched for a new dispensation that called themselves the Seekers.[2]

Fox gleaned scattered crumbs of satisfaction from many of these sects, but none convinced him; from some, such as the astrologers, the pantheists and those who he thought preached that they might sinlessly do whatever pleased them most, he

[2] If the Seekers followed any one leader, which is doubtful, it would have been Bartholomew Legate, who preached a quarter-century before Fox was born. A textile merchant of Essex, a Family of Love stronghold, Legate predicted a miraculous revelation by a new Messiah yet to be revealed. This forecast was not in itself unorthodox, but when he questioned the divinity of Christ his enemies charged heresy and so, in 1612, Legate was burned. He was the last heretic to be burned in Britain.

recoiled in horror. He had, of course, long since lost faith in the old Established Church. Obviously, so it would seem to him, the rural folk were ignorant of eternal Truth, but London, center of all English wisdom, should be helpful.

By the summer of 1644, he arrived at the metropolis. Innumerable spires advertised its spiritual aspiration. Virtually every block of houses in the crowded city of 200,000 people had its church; some had two or three, with new ones, mostly nonconformist, rising everywhere. Fox was well aware that steeples were no guarantee that pure religion lay below, that often the spires were false guides built by the Devil to mislead; yet he still hoped that, as he would put it, London would answer to his condition.

He had at London a relative by marriage, Uncle Pickering, a Baptist, whom George did not identify more clearly but who seems to have been Edward Pickering, a merchant who some years before had helped finance the emigration of English nonconformists to America; he also helped Dutch religious congregations. Fox hoped to gain much spiritual consolation through his uncle, but was disappointed. Like other church members, vehement in prayer, he fobbed his nephew off with meaningless words. For all those churches, George found Lonron as sterile as the countryside.

"All was dark," said George, "and under the chain of darkness."

This was a double disappointment. George Fox had counted heavily on the Baptists. From all that he had heard, Baptists opposed the professional priesthood and though they believed in the regenerative power of the written word, held that the interpretation of Scripture was more important than the wording. With all this George felt in perfect accord; and so, with Uncle Pickering's assistance, he hoped to find fellow spirits. But, to his regret, he learned that most Baptists subordinated personal revelation to Scriptural authority. This denial of the light within was what he meant by darkness.[3]

London had plenty of other dissenters, among whom George hoped to hear the true religion, but these failed him more completely than did the Baptists. Many of the nonconformists were merchants or manufacturers, small businessmen who, confusing worldly success with spiritual salvation, denied the equality of man before God; only the elect, they argued, could hope for passports to Heaven. Rejecting Fox's revelation that because the light shines within everyone, all righteous people might receive direct inspiration, they insisted that only by informed study of the Bible might man know God.

To Fox this argument implied that only university graduates were to set forth truth; it further meant, though George did not express the idea in so many words, that only the rich or the learned were the elite. If this were true, then England had made but little gain. An Established Church had merely been replaced by an infallible Bible interpreted by university-trained leaders.

There were other disappointments in the capital, some of them, no doubt, due to Fox himself. Scores of Londoners were arguing vehemently on all sorts of questions—political, social, economic, scientific and, most especially, religious. Had George been more open-minded, more patient and more suave, he would have better understood his fellows, would have learned much more and would have had opportunity to teach much more. But Uncle Pickering had no means of introducing his nephew to the social and intellectual maelstrom of mid-seventeenth-century London, nor, apparently, much sympathy with half-baked youthful notions. He may have been one of

[3] There were, to be sure, among the Baptists a few who, like George Fox, felt discontented at the minor role given to the light; it was among these, the Seekers, both in London and the provinces, that he would later find support.

the narrow-minded men of property who feared that unconventional religious ideas undermined social and economic stability. George said merely, "I could not impart my mind to him," which might well mean that Uncle Pickering would not let the young man talk.

The lonely country boy again resorted to his night walks in the fields, where he might commune with the Lord God. He was unhappy, convinced that he had failed to keep some sacred trust committed to him. How or why he fell short he did not know; but he, who led a godly life, who never harmed a living soul, was sunk in sorrow.

Had he done wrong by leaving Drayton? Was he causing worry to his elders? Would he find peace by going home?

4

Young Rebel

His return to Drayton brought no consolation. In their concern for his happiness, his parents wholly failed to fathom his problem; had they not been so well intentioned their counsel would have been ridiculous. George was restless and dissatisfied, but they assumed that this was but a phase of youthful skepticism, a mental rebellion common to most adolescents. He should get married, settle down and raise a family.

Happily, George knew better. Had he wed it must have been to one of the frivolous milkmaids who giggled at his awkwardness. Mary Fox must have known, if Christopher did·not, that in all his Drayton life George Fox had never given any girl a passing glance. Once a woman came from behind and kissed him lightly on the top of his head before he knew that she was there; nothing further happened, but this was his wildest adventure into sex. On another occasion, a grateful woman volunteered to go with him anywhere; he had no thought of any implications.

Christopher was quite as blind as Mary. He should have been aware, if she were not, that George was ill prepared for family life. How was he to earn his living? Should he resume the management of George Gee's hit-or-miss affairs? Did

Drayton's twenty houses, plus the suburbs on the swamps, buy
shoes enough to warrant setting up as Gee's rival in that
business?

If the parental advice were no better than these alternatives,
it is difficult to understand why people thought the elder Foxes
more intelligent than other Drayton residents, except for that
someone, perhaps, who, mindful of the Civil War, suggested
that George become a soldier. "I was grieved," said George in
surprised understatement, "that they proffered such things
to me."

The questions, to be sure, were not new ones; they had arisen
when George first left home. How had he supported himself
while on his Midland wanderings? Christopher could not have
sent him much, for, though the weaver was rather better off
than his neighbors, there were four other children, younger
and still dependent, to support. As Gee's business agent, Fox
may have saved a bit but no large amount, nor could he have
made enough in private trade to keep himself fed and housed
and clothed for almost a full year. Perhaps, as in London, he
lived with relatives.[1]

From Stephens he expected little help, but he received even
less than he anticipated. Now that the political complexion had
been changed by Cromwell victories, the parson had returned
to Drayton and, of course, the arguments had been resumed.
Fox was not mature and, though less rich in book information
than was Stephens, had a fund of knowledge based on what
he had seen and heard. He no longer bewildered the Oxford
graduate nor did he batter him with the Bible, but, if only by
vehemence and by persistence, was defeating him in their

[1] In later years, George Fox would be cared for by devoted followers,
but as yet there were none. He himself said nothing on the subject, but,
in all probability, he worked as a migrant harvester, with here and there
a bit of leather working. Neither would have yielded much money, but
George required little. If there were a wife and family, he would have
needed to make much more.

debates. True, up to this time, Fox gives no indication that he had ever read a book, other than his ever present Scriptures, and in conversation he talked far more than he listened; but he absorbed ideas quickly and he made full use of everything he knew.

He drained Nathaniel Stephens dry. In doing so, he supposed he was opposing the pastor on almost every point; in fact Stephens was giving Fox a firm theological foundation for a better faith.

George, therefore, sought elsewhere for advice. As usual, he failed to find it. Gee's vicar gave sage counsel much like that which George had heard at home. An old man, reputed to be wise, he had counselled many who had come to him with doubts about those mysteries which are to be believed on faith alone. Well aware of the yearnings of a bachelor with all the luscious milkmaids roundabout, he smiled gently when George spoke of temptations. Depression and despair were common among post-adolescents—passing moods curable by that sense of security and well-being that comes when one is well adjusted to the world.

"Smoke," he answered wisely. "Smoke a pipe and sing a psalm."

For most of his parishioners the counsel would have been therapeutic. The leisureliness and good fellowship of taking tobacco at the Royal Red Gate Inn would have calmed nerves and brought relaxation. Had George's ills been as the vicar diagnosed them, the cure would have been effective. Had the old man thought to add one line to his prescription, he might have soothed George Fox, too, though the cure would not have lasted long. The pastor should have cited Scripture : "Make a joyful noise unto the Lord." Had he done so, George would have trudged home happy. As it was he stormed out, thinking the man a "miserable comforter."

Others were no better. George walked seven miles across the

swamps to see a man who proved "nothing but an empty hollow cask." He went down to Coventry to call upon a minister who showed more interest in his flower garden than in the torments of George Fox's soul and who, when George stepped inadvertently upon some plants, flew into "such a rage as if his house had been on fire." Still another thought that what Fox needed was a dose of salts.

Such experiences soured Fox. The priests—of whatever denomination the clergy might be, Fox always called them priests—the priests did not have the Inner Light, nor did they admit that others might possess it. When he naïvely spoke of sinless life, in which he and the Family of Love believed, the priests in their blindness denied that pure perfection was attainable on earth. It proved to Fox, whose logic was not impeccable, that priests not only condoned sin but actually pleaded for it. These agents of the Devil, he concluded, mouthed nothing but deceitfulness and lies.

With Fox in such a mood, priests found his challenge impossible to meet effectively. Stephens, for one, concerned lest his rebellious protégé fall into the snares of the sects or, worse, into complete religious anarchy. tried hard to save him. By admitting what was obviously true, by inducing George to abandon what might be palpably false, Stephens planned to compromise upon a middle ground.

But to argue thus with George Fox was to commit debater's suicide. Fox would accept surrender, though none too graciously; but he would yield absolutely nothing. How could he do so? On anything affecting Truth, open-mindedness or compromise was vicious. He knew the Truth. It was revealed, once and for all, to those who, like himself, were one with Christ and the Apostles. The Spirit of the Lord, the Divine Inner Light, was offered those ready to receive it. The Word thus given was final and unalterable. How, then, could opinion possibly differ? Dared anyone tolerate the least breach of the

Divine Will? Nothing revealed could possibly be false; nothing could be compromised. How might one compromise with evil? And how dared mortal man declare that this or that was unimportant? Who was man to give grades to the Word of God? To do so invited the powers of darkness to destroy creation.

But, even should one compromise, an error no righteous man would commit, just where would compromise end? To grant the smallest point opened the way to further yielding, and this, in turn, to yet more. Where would one draw the line and say "thus far and no farther"? Would not a slow eroding of conscience end by giving way on matters of the utmost importance?

No. Faith flowed from the heart. To entertain a wrong opinion, one hostile to Scripture, betrayed an evil heart. Stephens might call this compromise, a word which sounded fair; but in matters of worship the word was treacherous.

Not that compromise would bother priests, any more than it bothered Stephens. Too many priests, if not all, Fox thought, were parasites or worse. Though Scripture clearly showed that Jesus told his disciples to preach the truth as freely as He taught it, priests demanded pay and, "like dumb dogs that could never have enough," were ever greedy. Nowhere in Scripture could Fox find warrant for extras, such as Easter reckonings, Midsummer dues or "augmentations." What was more, they insisted upon tithes, a tax of 10 per cent on incomes of parishioners.

Stephens, to be sure, asked none; in lieu of tithes he had recently been granted some two hundred acres of good glebe land. But he defended tithing rights. Could George deny that tithes had Biblical authority, dating back to Abraham? Were they not approved by long existant English law?

Fox denied the Scriptural authority for tithing. Christ's coming, he retorted, cancelled tithes forever. As for English law, men who flouted the commands of Christ might say that tithes were legal, but priests, who professed the higher law of God, had no moral right to take them.

For that matter, the priests themselves were counterfeit. Christ's coming not only ended tithes but the Levitical priesthood as well. These lollers in pulpits were imposters, vile hirelings who preyed upon the poor and fatherless. Once, in delirium, he saw all religions, all church members and all priests as "a company of maneaters of cruel visage who ate up the people like bread, gnawing the flesh from their bones."

This might be discounted as the fevered raving of a good man warring in his dreams with evil spirits, under sufferings "beyond words to declare," had not Fox set it down in calmness as an authentic vision. Nor was it his first, or only, revelation that priests were scoundrels.[2]

George also protested vehemently against the way priests spoke of the Church. To them, it meant an earthly building, of wood or stone, of brick and mortar, wherein God dwelt on earth. Fox spurned the notion. He would not use the good word "church" for such a structure; invariably he called them "steeple-houses." The true Church, he insisted, was the pillar and ground of Truth, composed of living members, a spiritual household. God, he thundered again and again, dwells not in temples made by human hands but in the hearts of men.

Stephens tried to please everyone, but no one, however gentle, could endure a steady diet of pure vitriol. In genuine

[2] Clergymen necessarily insisted upon their tithing rights; they depended upon tithes for their support. Even if, like Stephens, they had other resources, they dared not waive their claims lest their successors suffer. In George's younger days ecclesiastical courts defended a priest's right to tithe, even to the point of clearing one who simply seized upon the property of a delinquent. Later, when civil courts took over jurisdiction, priests discovered that legal expenses were greater than the triple damages they would recover, and so they increased their seizures. The followers of George Fox suffered more from tithing troubles than from any other cause except their refusal to take oaths.

concern, he talked with Christopher and Mary, probably also with Colonel Purefoy, to probe the sources of the young man's discontent. He himself suspected that, because of envy and adolescent conceit, George was trying to undermine his leadership. "Neighbors," said he, "George is come to the light of the sun and now he thinks to put out my starlight."

Fox did not share the preacher's modesty. Tacitly admitting that he stood in the sun, he took his elder by the hand and, calling him by his first name—a liberty which George meant in friendliness but which Stephens may have thought presumption—assured Stephens that he, George Fox, had no intention of outshining him, if, he added rather patronizingly, "it be true starlight." What Nathaniel Stephens should do to demonstrate his virtue was to refuse to preach for hire. Stephens angrily pulled his hand away.

What, actually, was happening to young George Fox? Did he resent Stephens' superior education or, as a psychologist implied, the parson's too frequent visits to the straw-thatched cottage in the Dog Yard? Neither seems likely; it is more credible that Fox, in his close communion with the Lord, opposed anyone who, without such special ties, ventured to tell him how to worship. George had no respect for calf-house priests who preached for hire.

There were complicating factors. Fox told little of his personal affairs, but he dropped hints that all was not well at home. He was a grown man now, in his early twenties; he should have been well settled, but as yet, he was at best no more than a struggling shoemaker in a tiny village. He was strong minded and, while far from being selfish, was self willed; yet he remained subject to a father who professed fixed views at opposition to those of his son. Both men were inflexible and they were at odds; it is more than probable that they argued day and night.

George put the best face possible on his position. Completely

opposing his religious leader, he made a practice at Christmas-
tide, while Stephens preached and the Fox family feasted,
of seeking out the poor, particularly the widows and the
orphaned, to give them money to buy food. Disapproving of
marriages by priests, he refused invitations to marriages, but,
if the bride and groom were not well off, he would wait a day
or two and then take them little presents. His charities could
not have been extensive, for Fox had little money and his
neighborhood was thinly peopled; but his actions were gestures
of hostility to organized religion and its distasteful practices.

For George was certain that Puritans and Presbyterians,
Anglicans and all the rest were far from living, as Christ commanded, in the power of God; he saw the sects and creeds as
deferring to human reason and depending upon transmitted
knowledge about God and Christ rather than upon direct
revelation within the soul. Religious institutions and all who
professed them were out of harmony and out of the world of
light and life; they were corrupt, sunk deep in the dark world
of sin and death.

Feeling as he did, he could not bring himself to sit, literally
at Nathaniel Stephens' feet, in St. Michael's steeple-house.
There, standing high in his pulpit, virtually on top of his little
congregation—the most distant seat was less than twenty feet
away!—the pastor thundered that all but the elect were
doomed. George Fox could not bear to hear that men were
merely puppets incapable of walking in the light through their
free choice.

When Christopher and Mary chided him for not attending
service, he showed them Scripture saying that true believers
had no need for human teachers and that conscience showed
the right to those who wished to see it. He should, they
answered, at least hear what the Reverend Stephens had to
say; but George, indignant that the pastor, as he alleged, not
only stole the sermons from what George told him but took

pay for the pilfering, refused to budge. Nathaniel Stephens, he insisted, was a hypocrite, a covetous hireling whose only interest was his belly. So, he added bitterly, were almost all the congregation, including Christopher, Mary, his brother John and his three sisters. They may, he granted, have thought themselves true believers, but personally he doubted it; true believers walked in the spirit of the Lord and they, for all their pretensions, did not so walk.

The tension underneath that grass-thatched roof must have been extremely high; that his family endured the castigations spoke volumes for their understanding of young George's troubled heart.

Similarly, Stephens, for all his dictatorial ways, maintained friendship with the family, including the rebellious George, that uncompromising slanderer whom Stephens still hoped to bring within the fold. George, however, spurned all overtures; he warned his family against entering the man-made building whose steeple pointed falsely toward heaven. To attend the steeple-house was dangerous; the deceitful words showered upon them there would push them down into the abyss.

None of his close relatives were in the least convinced. The short-tempered churchwarden had no sympathy for half-baked ideas stemming from the Familists or Seekers. Failing to notice that George said nothing about common ownership of goods nor about all things being ruled by nature, as did the social and religious radicals, Christopher hastily assumed that his son was just another dupe of the crazy sects.

Though the rebellious boy was, in time, to bring the word of God to countless thousands, many of whom would suffer for their faith, not one member of his Drayton household is listed in the early records of Quakerism, and few, if any, in his home town. There was, to be sure, at Wymeswold, beyond Leicester, twenty-five miles away, a Quaker family named Fox who seem to have been Christopher's relatives; but, with this exception, none of his close kin by blood accepted Quakerism. If ever a prophet was without honor in his own community, George Fox was one.

The division within the family was very obvious. On Sunday mornings, the children, all but George, sat primly in their pews, their necks craned upward to the pulpit. George, who railed against the very word Sunday as homage to a heathen god, wandered in his spiritual wilderness.

He was alone, with no blood relatives whom he was willing to acknowledge. "My only kindred," he once said, "are they that stand in the power and life of God." But, though alone, he was no longer lonely; he walked the wilderness in the company of the Lord.

5

Search for Truth

THE LORD IN WHOM HE TRUSTED CAME TO HIS SUPPORT. ONE spring First Day morning, while Fox prayerfully waited, a thought flashed suddenly; though people had believed that only university-trained men could serve Christ as ministers, a diploma was unnecessary. Anyone, male or female, who had the spirit of the Lord within him, and every worthy one might have it if he willed, might bear true witness to the spirit.

George Fox, arrogant toward pretenders, was humble before God. Never did he hold himself to be the author of a word nor the originator of a deed; all credit and all glory was the Lord's. The great thought of individual ministry, this "opening," was not his personal discovery; it was a living truth revealed to him directly from on high. It was God's holy word, a revelation above all criticism by any mortal being.

For George Fox, by perfect faith, by contemplation of his soul, by close communion with the Lord, was now in harmony with the Holy Spirit, or, as he would put it, in unity with the creation. He was conscious that the Lord possessed him and that, if he but waited patiently and silently, the Lord would lead him into perfect truth.

This opening of the uselessness of college carried important corollaries. The universities bred priests, but a righteous heart raised ministers. Oxford and Cambridge trained false prophets, anti-Christs, deceivers and vain priests of the old dispensation which Christ had ended. Fox said he smiled as he saw how the revelation struck at Stephen's pretensions; none such as he could be a minister of God's pure gospel.

It was the only time George Fox admitted smiling.

Nor did mortals need professional intermediaries, interpreters or intercessors, with the Lord; each pure Christian, of whatever race, color or condition, was his own effective minister. Nathaniel Stephens and his ilk were quite unnecessary.

Unlike many mystics, who experience revelations when they are in spiritual distress, Fox, fully conscious of his sinlessness, stood at no crossroads; he needed no conversion. In all humility he deemed himself unworthy to be chosen as spokesman for the Lord, but he was not awed by it; such was the normal expectation of one who feared the Lord. As he attained security and peace, openings were less frequent, but always in his times of need the Lord sent guidance.

Often the revelation was a stimulus to action. George Fox was vigorous and restless. He found passivity distasteful. Had he not been filled with high ideals of service to both God and man he might have wandered through life aimlessly, but his openings gave him purpose and direction. A more self-centered man might have used the revelations as a means for personal aggrandizement, but Fox was more concerned with the salvation of his countrymen than with his own. His motives were social and not selfish. Even his indignations evidenced his objectivity. His fiery temper flared frequently and fiercely, but his anger poured forth against those who offended God or harmed the common good, and never against those who injured only him.

Others learned from human counsel, Fox learned by revelation. The Lord sent brilliant light that clearly showed the character of men and, what was more, the lasting truths of life.

Fox's senses were, to be sure, so acute that sometimes he saw or smelled or heard or touched natures that were hid from normal men, but, usually, the light within him illuminated truth.

George's trust in revelation developed self-assurance and self-confidence. After his initial openings, Fox was never undecided, never at a loss, about a course of action. Had he not been innately sweet and gentle—except against scoffers against truth!—grave danger might have lurked in this. One who understood all things by private revelation could have been a tyrant demanding absolute obedience. To tell the truth, there were in fact, in later years, those who suspected George of such autocracy. But Fox, for all his constant sense of power, was essentially a modest man. Only his closest intimates realized that a stern inflexibility masked inner sensitivity. No despot would have been so eager to teach others how to share the cosmic secrets of his power.

Though the openings concerning Stephens and his Oxford degree somewhat soothed the tortured, maladjusted man, George Fox had not yet wholly solved his problems. To understand the spirit of the prophets and apostles, and so to interpret Scripture rightly, he must search further for the truth. This he must do alone, independently of men or of their writings; and so, sometime, in 1647, he set forth again upon his wanderings. He was not to return for seven years.

In almost pathologic fear of being soiled by sinners, he evaded company, especially evil companions—as though, save for that cousin with his mug of beer, he had ever associated with any. He moved about the Midlands, none too happily, tarrying at one obscure village after another, moving on whenever he attracted notice anywhere.

Isolation did not distress him; he communed with God. He was not social; his friendships were with saints of Bible times. He had no need for works of man. He enjoyed no picture, no

work of art. Since the Puritans had closed the theaters he never saw a play, nor would he have entered one of those iniquitous dens had they been open. He had no ear for music nor appreciation of it; on one occasion when the power of the Lord moved him to sing, his voice was so raucous and so far off key that, as he confessed, the fiddler sighed and went away. Probably he read as yet no books.

Yet his senses were extraordinarily acute. Others responded to outward beauty; George Fox responded to the inward spirit. Others enjoyed form and color; he found harmony and grace. Their pleasure was fugitive, but his was everlasting. Not everyone liked George Fox, but no one deemed him stodgy. Wherever he passed, eyes followed him, not so much because of his powerful, stocky frame as for his personality, his spirit, his vitality. Actually, people sensed George Fox instead of seeing him; his appearance stirred them much more deeply than did any individual feature. Those who described him failed to comment on his height, his complexion or, in his youth at least, his size, other than to call him a big-boned man; but they never ceased to marvel at his magnetism. Neither friend nor foe pictured George Fox other than by comment on his wealth of curly hair or on the leather breeches that he customarily wore, yet they were always conscious of him.[1]

His eyes—most Leicestershire folk inherited the blue-grayness of the Danes and Angles—literally flashed; their brilliance startled everyone. Over and over again people, especially those with troubled consciences, cried out, as if in pain, "Don't pierce me so with your eyes! Turn your eyes away." A student crowd at Cambridge, no followers of Fox, shouted in astonishment, "Look! Look! He shines! He glistens."

A youth so striking in appearance, so radiant with spiritual

[1] There are no authentic portraits of George Fox. Two supposed pictures, one at Swarthmore College allegedly painted by Sir Peter Lely, have been discredited.

fire and yet so obviously distraught, could not avoid attention. Psychologists suggest that Fox's sparkle revealed "an inner stimulation rising from a virile blood supply and native glandular secretion," but Fox preferred to think it was the power of the Lord that shone.

As in his youth at Drayton, George avoided friendships. Those attracted to him he dismissed as frivolous, if not, indeed, as hardened hypocrites who served the Devil. For Fox demanded in others the absolute perfection he sought for himself. Man could be sinless; the Bible said so. He who lived by the Spirit of Christ, by the Divine Light given freely to all, walked the road that lead unerringly to Truth. All else was anathema.

So many were straying into error. Some, like the Family of Love, were, Fox thought, sincere but misguided. So were the Seekers, now firmly established near Lancaster and in Bristol, the second largest city in England. Many good people, also, were reading about Jacob Boehme—they called him Behmem— both in translation and in a seven-page biographical sketch that was circulating. Most of these people were high minded, and there was hope for them, but, as in every new movement, a lunatic fringe was putting forth outlandishly distorted doctrine.

One recently risen group, whom their enemies called Ranters, was particularly bothersome. Like the Seekers, they looked to no one leader, but an outstanding figure was a London goldsmith, Thomas Tany.

Tany's teachings, shouted in stuttering harangues through the London streets, were basically defensible; he said that God was everywhere and that everyone might know Him. He also said that the divine law took precedence over any mortal law.

Fox would not have doubted any of this. Nor would he have been disturbed by the goldsmith's discovery, while in an epileptic fit, that he, Thomas Tany, was really a Jew, of the tribe of Reuben, destined to become high priest of a restored Temple of Jerusalem. If Thomas Tany, who now styled himself Theaurau John, John the Evangelist, had such ambitions, it was none of Fox's concern. Fox did object, emphatically, to distorters who declared that if God were in everything, He was, therefore, in them, so that they, the elect, were privileged. They were, they argued, free from either law or gospel. No matter what they might do, however gross or immoral in ordinary eyes, they could not sin.

Extremists went even further. If God were in everything, then the only God was nature. And if everything were nature, then one might attain wisdom by studying the laws of nature. The stars, for instance. So said a certain apostate curate who, though he held no medical degree, called himself a physician. This quack, John Pordage, proclaimed astrology as the queen of sciences.

The self-styled doctor persuaded many crackpots, among them Thomas Tany; a combination of star reading and private revelation convinced the impressionable goldsmith that, instead of being a future high priest at Jerusalem, he was Earl of Essex and heir to the English throne. If, however, he was to ascend that shaky eminence, he would reap little material reward, for no worldly riches attended the crown. Everything in nature, Pordage proved, was to be held in common.

This type of primitive communism was growing, especially among poor townsfolk and some few peasants; it frightened Tany's right-thinking contemporaries, who thought it subversive of both government and religion. Army leaders, conscious that their unpaid soldiers were complaining against both Charles I and Cromwell, feared mutiny. A well-known agitator, John Lilburne, was actively demanding that no man be ruled by another against his will; terming his partisans Levellers, he called for absolute social and political equality.

The fact that rumors of these movements passed, in the absence of newspapers, only by word of mouth and were gravely distorted in the passage, limited the appeal that George Fox might have had in these early days; too many unthinking people carelessly identified him with political or economic revolutionaries. The unfair association would, in time, lead to persecution and imprisonment for suspected disloyalties of which he was wholly innocent; meetings which he held would be construed as disturbance of the peace.

Far from supporting Tany's communism or Lilburne's levelling. Fox recoiled from them. On first hearing Ranter theories he was, for one of the few times in his life, shocked into temporary speechlessness. But not for long; a heavenly voice reassured him :

"There is a living God who made all things."

His feeling of relief was so great that he became light hearted. On next meeting Ranters who boasted themselves so free of sin that they themselves were gods he asked them gaily if it would rain next day. They brushed his question aside as frivolous; how, they answered, should they know?

"Well, if you were gods, you'd know," said Fox.

So few had found the Inner Light that when George met a kindred soul, he was tempted, out of loneliness, to linger. In Nottinghamshire, for instance, in the rising country west of Mansfield, he met a woman who understood his concerns and, more than this, shared his anxieties.

This was Elizabeth Hooten, who, with her husband Oliver and their four early-teen-aged children, was living at Skegby. For some years she had been searching among the nonconformists for the truth, but the more she sought the more convinced she grew that they "were doing the Lord's work negligently."

Apparently the Hootens, like the Fox family, were disunited

in their religious activity. Oliver followed the priests, and so disapproved of his wife's drifting from conventional religion. When, then, in 1647, Elizabeth heard Fox's ideas and came to think that she at last had found the teachings that she sought, Oliver objected vigorously. He even considered leaving her, but luckily he did not do so.

There was in this no jealousy, no slightest sign of sentiment, for she was forty-four, twenty years older than George Fox, in an era when old age began much earlier than it does today. Doubtless, she displayed a certain amount of maternal solicitude and so may have aroused in Fox a feeling of gratitude; but since he sternly repressed all human sentiment, avoiding all expression of emotion toward anyone except the Lord, this must remain conjecture. We do know that this devoted woman who would become his first female disciple failed to banish those worries which he called temptations. He went through more travail; he was, he says, a man of sorrows.

To find solace, he fled with his Bible into solitude. He fasted much, for he believed that when his soul was sorely tried fasting was purification. Again and again, he called upon the Lord for help.

He was never disappointed when he did so.

Though everything conspired to sadden him, his revelations saved him from becoming morbid. For all his passionate denunciations of evil, he remained essentially cheerful, confident that in God's good time, when others saw the shallowness and falsity of their leaders, they, too, would choose the light. He was modest, too; though, like many other spiritual leaders, he claimed personal, divine inspiration, he asked no glory for himself. Whatever he said or did was dictated to him by the will of God.

Thus in 1647 he was moved to enter a Mansfield steeple-house to tell priest and people that their teacher, the spirit and the light of Jesus, lay within them; at Nottingham he clarified the difference between man's outward law and the inward law of God. By now, he was becoming known in the community. His example, his constant speaking and the enthusiastic support of Elizabeth Hooten had won a small following, people whom he described as "convinced" of the Truth.

That Truth, to one filled, as was Fox, with a pure fire, was now supremely simple : the pure and perfect love of God, which is over the flesh, can be understood only by the spirit of God. Knowledge of that Truth, however, was very far from simple. The Devil set endless snares, deluding all the senses and poisoning the mind. The flesh, Fox found, was weak indeed. False prophets and lying teachers lurked everywhere, luring mankind to destruction. Far too many priests and church members were counterfeits, pretending to teach the Word but, in reality, pleading for sin and imperfection.

But the pure in heart, the steadfast, will prevail. For George Fox the door of light and life opened. He found the path that led from worldly pleasure and carnal corruption into the state of fellowship with Christ. All dependence upon outward, human help ended; pure faith came upon him. He heard a Voice :

"There is one, even Christ Jesus, that can speak to thy condition."

Christ comforted the suffering George Fox. He, Jesus, had also been tempted by that same Devil who badgered all men, but, by the flaming sword which kept the tree of life, the Word of God had bruised the Serpent's head. The pure fire which burned within George Fox would overcome temptation.

Discernment descended upon him. He saw his earthly groans and sighs and sorrows to be confusions sent by the Serpent to quench the spirit. The prayers that sprang from them were but the same false prayers one heard in steeple-houses whose priests served sin. The true groaning of the spirit was for redemption of the body, of mankind and of the whole creation. Visions came. He saw the mountains burning and the rough and crooked ways made smooth and straight that the Lord might enter His tabernacle in men's hearts. He saw the wicked, hurtful things that creep within the hearts of evil men. He saw that wicked people were not images of God, but dogs and swine and snakes in human form. The visions were too painful to be borne. "Why," he cried to the Lord, "must I be thus afflicted? I have never done such wrongs!"

The Lord answered: "Thou must know of all conditions, that thou mayst speak of them." Thus Fox saw the infinite love of God. He also saw an ocean of darkness and of death; but, by that same infinite love of God, there was an ocean of light and love that overwhelmed the sea of darkness.[2]

Throngs of people, even a few priests, flocked to hear of these great openings. A certain Prophet Brown called from his deathbed for George to carry on his work. Whoever Prophet Brown may have been, his verbal legacy threw George into a two weeks' trance during which divine favor transported him across the sea of darkness into the ocean of light and love. He saw spiritual Babylon and Sodom, ancient Egypt and what lay beyond the grave. He gained a superknowledge of all creation. When he awoke, his face and person were so changed as to seem remolded.

[2] Fox's visions often paralleled those of earlier mystics. In reporting them he used expressions similar to those used by Jacob Boehme, by Seekers and by members of the Family of Love. Such phrases as the dark power, the Light of Christ, the Spirit of the Scriptures, the Serpent, the key that opens, were all in common currency. Sensitive people of similar background, with similar experience, steeped in Biblical lore, expressed themselves in similar fashion. In relating his visions, especially in the *Journal,* forty years after their occurrence, Fox was innocent of conscious plagiarism. Certainly none of his contemporaries thought him guilty of it.

Recast now into the image of God, brought to the bliss which Adam knew before the Fall, Fox soared high above the world's corruption. All things became bright and clean and fresh, emitting a fragrance indescribable. The Lord freed him from everything but purity, innocence and righteousness. Having seen that which was without and things unutterable, the infinitude of the love of God inexpressible by man, George Fox was at peace.

6

Healer and Prophet

THE HAPPINESS WHICH FLOWED FROM THE WONDROUS GIFTS
of insight and understanding thus bestowed entailed heavy
responsibilities. Joy and peace were not for him alone. He
must lead others from the darkness, as he had himself been
led. He must guide others to the spirit that gave forth the
Scriptures.

But how was he to serve the Lord? Not as a physician, for
though he now understood the properties of all things in creation, the Lord revealed that physicians were outside the Word
of wisdom. Not as a lawyer; no lawyer knew pure justice nor
the perfect law of God. Surely not as priest, for, with God
reigning in each person's heart, there was no need of priests.
The problem deeply worried Fox. His response to Prophet
Brown's legacy should be clear. Was not his hesitancy some
subtle temptation sent by the Serpent? Was he, in his uncer-
tainty, committing some vague sin against the Holy Ghost?

Characteristically, he solved his problem quickly. He was to
bring them all into the Truth. Reform the priests by revealing
the nature of wild Ishmael within them. Reform lawyers by
teaching them to love their neighbors as themselves. Reform
physicians by sharing with them the wisdom of the Lord. It
was a stupendous task. He must abolish all established religions

61

—all were vain; he must wipe away every empty ceremony, tradition, myth and fable. He must promote peace and charity, kindness, love, gentleness and pity.

A vision proved it could be done. He saw a great crack open in the earth, a thick and heavy smoke emerging and an earthquake following. It was the earth in human hearts, shaken that the Seed of God might grow.

Once George Fox received his revelation, conflict with other spiritual leaders was unavoidable. Inspired by the fervor of the Old Testament prophets he dedicated himself to unremitting war against false teachings.

In point of fact, his basic principles were not dissimilar to those against which he contended. He hated pride, laxity and selfishness, as did the Puritans; he, as well as they, demanded that all men fear God and keep his holy Word. He and his Puritan opponents despised a priestly hierarchy; they all might have fought shoulder to shoulder against worldly pleasures and fleshy joys.

They differed, however, on one fundamental issue. By Puritan theology, God had made known His Word and Will once and for all, ages ago, through divinely inspired prophets; having issued His commands, He closed the era of revelation and no more had been nor would be added. Fox, however, while obediently and gratefully accepting what God had proclaimed, insisted that revelation was continuous, that man remained in close personal communion with the Lord. All who denied his openings, his Inner Light, were enemies of truth.

Prophetically, in view of his life-long insistence upon equality, his ministry began when he broke up a steeple-house service to demand that a woman who wished to ask a question be given the opportunity. She wished to know what St. Peter meant by speaking of rebirth "of incorruptible seed by the

Word of God." This was in 1648, at Leicester, some fifteen miles from Drayton.

His interruption brought no solution to the question. Somehow, George Fox, the clergyman and members of the congregations became entangled in debate as to whether the word "church" meant a building or the faithful who worshipped in it. The question was forgotten, and the lady was never heard of more; but the semantic quarrel, starting in the steeplehouse, was transferred to an inn, where argument continued on and on and on, until all but George Fox "gave out and fled away."

It was not the first time that he drowned dispute. Few competed successfully with his deep, loud, never tiring voice. His verbal artillery thundered endlessly when he defended truth.

This was, however, not his lucky day. By shifting from his advocacy of equal rights for women to semantics, he argued against St. Paul, who, in the same Epistle to the Corinthians which told women to keep silent, used the word "church" as if he meant the edifice in which Christians met. Fox was, however, undisturbed. The actual words set down by the Apostle were not the only guide to proper thinking; one must consider also the spirit in which the words were given. Surely St. Paul would not regard a man-made building as a church when Scripture said that God dwelt in the human heart.

Undeniably his methods angered many. By countering hostile argument by special revelation (for every word Fox spoke was given from on high) he seemed to claim authority above that of ordinary men. No one dared oppose a divine message. When others objected, Fox asked them bluntly if what they said was their word or the Word of God. When, as modest men, they confessed their words were mortal, Fox insisted that their human words give way before his own, the Voice of God.

It is no wonder that on half a hundred occasions priests incontinently fled rather than argue with him. Once, a timorous priest, hearing that George was drawing near, hid under a hedge until Fox had gone.

Again, at Mansfield in 1648, he showed his concern for social justice. The so-called hiring fair was being held, that autumn festival when those seeking work stood in line, straws in their mouths if they were farmhands, bits of cow tail if herdsmen, whipcord if carters. Prospective employers walked along the line, inspecting men as though appraising livestock, choosing the likeliest among them. Wages, never more than a few pence a day, were set by local justices sitting for the purpose. Anyone who gave more than the maximum, or who received more, went to jail. It was blameless to settle for less.

The system, all too favorable for employers, angered Fox, for, in all probability, he had stood in just such lines. He felt called upon to intervene, to go before the justices to ask that they be merciful. When, however, he reached the Bowl-in-Hand, the inn where they were sitting, he heard fiddlers playing and, judging the moment inopportune, postponed his call till morning. Next morning, all the justices had gone. The disappointment shocked Fox deeply. He felt that he had failed in doing the duty that the Lord had put upon him. The recognition of his guilt was so severe that, Fox says, he was stricken blind.

Nevertheless, he persevered. Somehow groping his way to the landlord, he asked where the justices were holding sessions, and was told that they were eight miles distant. His blindness notwithstanding, Fox resolved to start off to find them. The decision partially restored his sight; he went off on the run and gradually his sight returned.

The justices received him kindly; no one could fail to be impressed by his obvious sincerity in coming before them in the flushed, dishevelled condition that would follow a cross-country run. They listened politely as he urged them to set the wage scales fairly; doubtless they considered they were already doing so. They heard, probably with greater approval, his appeal to workmen to give a fair day's service and to give it honestly. Whether the justices raised the wages or whether the farm boys and girls worked harder is unrecorded.

He could not resist an opportunity to attempt reform. After lecturing the priests, as well as the justices, for what Fox judged their oppressions, among which was the imposition of oaths, he met "one of the wickedest men in the country," a drunkard, a libertine, and, what was worse, a rhymester.

"I reproved him in the dread of mighty God," said Fox.

The wicked sinner saw the light, repented of his sins and thereafter lived an honest, sober life.

One lecherous drunkard set upon the proper road whetted George's appetite for saving mankind. He himself knew peace, but it must not be a selfish peace. He was happy in his closeness, his kinship, his veritable identity with the Lord, but, in his great love for his fellows, he could not be truly happy if others did not share his joy. His neighbors, which to George meant everyone, must know his happiness and know his peace. They, too, must come into the fellowship of God. The Lord God was a jealous God, incredibly, impossibly difficult to please.

George Fox, his agent upon earth, warred implacably against social ills. Seeing too many topers like the Mansfield poet, he invaded taverns to warn the owners not to sell their patrons more liquor than was good for them. With a fine sense of impartiality he denounced Church of Englanders and Puritans, Presbyterians and Baptists, Catholics and Jews, nonconformists, Separatists and Independents for frequenting steeple-houses on what they called their Sundays. If, on the other hand, they stayed away, feasting, dancing round a Maypole, getting too gay at wakes, and especially if they chose First Days as their time to thus dishonor God, he blasted them as evil. Athletes and actors, musicians and mountebanks were repugnant in God's eyes. Even those who stayed at home and read their Bible were imperilled if they did not read it in the spirit of the saints who wrote the Scriptures.

Few escaped the lash. At fairs and markets, he denounced merchants who cheated customers; if they persisted in their wickedness and lies, he warned, the Lord's Day of Vengeance would be great and terrible. Teachers must instil sobriety lest children be brought up to be light, vain and wanton. Parents must train their households in the fear of the Lord and must themselves be patterns of virtue. As for interpreters of dreams, stargazers and those who taught that women had no more souls than geese ———!

Worse than all these were priests; their black, earthly spirit struck him to the heart. To him, their steeple bells were brazen calls to come hear the priest set forth his wares for sale.

When, therefore, on a First Day morning in 1649, he spied from a hilltop the spire of St. Mary's Church, the Lord commanded him to go cry out against that monstrous idol. He entered St. Mary's, when the vicar, Nicholas Folkingham, was standing in his elevated pulpit, but Fox saw no human beings, only a great lump of earth towering above a fallow field, his congregation. Folkingham was preaching that the Scriptures were the touchstone by which to end all argument and whereby to test all doctrines, religions and ideas. At this, the Lord's power welled so strongly that Fox cried out that it was not the Scriptures but the Holy Spirit that gives knowledge of all truth. The Jews had Scripture, he said, but they rejected

Christ. They who tried doctrines by the Scripture but without
the Holy Ghost did not interpret them aright.

He would have gone on, in that deep, resonant voice, to
say much more, but officers came and threw him into prison,
a pitiful place whose stench stayed in his nostrils many days.

Mayor William Nix summoned his aldermen and his two
sheriffs to examine Fox, but the conference failed to agree on
what to do with him. Sheriff John Reckless thought Fox
justified; he unlocked George from the jail and brought him
home. Reckless was so moved that, of his own volition, he
restored to a woman some money that he and his partner, the
other sheriff, had exacted from her, though neither the woman
nor the partner realized that she had in any way been
wronged.

Moreover, a week later, Reckless suddenly dashed forth
into the market place, still wearing his house slippers, to
preach repentance to the people. Many, Fox says, were convinced; but the magistrates, angered at his removing Fox from
jail, ordered George back into the stinking prison.

Others came to Fox's support, among them a young man
who pleaded for the chance to take George's punishment upon
himself, to be jailed in Fox's stead or, if needs be, to give his
life.

How, or when, Fox went free does not appear. It was
custom then, when sermons reached their long-delayed end,
for members of the congregation, if they wished, to add to, to
argue or refute what had been said. George's interruption may
have been so construed, or possibly his stay in prison awaiting
trial may have been regarded as sufficient punishment. There
was to have been a trial, but Reckless was so dilatory in bringing Fox before the court that the judges left before the
prisoner arrived. After all, the offenses had been a mere breach

of the peace, so probably no one took great interest in what happened to the prisoner.

One woman who visited George Fox in jail was, however, deeply concerned. She was in torment, possessed, physicians said, and though, for thirty-two years, the priests had prayed for her and ordered fasts, she still was suffering. Fox invited her to meetings, but when she came she groaned loudly and writhed upon the floor, embarrassing everyone with "the stink that came from her."

He worried much about it. Rumors were beginning to spread that he and his followers might be witches; her seizures might add fuel to that fire. He feared, moreover, that the spirits which possessed her might escape and enter into those who were now beginning to be called Friends. But, on the other hand, if she were made well, the world must admit that the Friends were people loved by God.

The service to be done the Lord was greater than the fear of evil. At his suggestion, Elizabeth Hooten invited her to the Hooten home at Skegby. As usual, there were roars from the poor sufferer and tumblings on the floor, with much bad odor; worse, the epileptic fit lasted two full days. Then, suddenly, she rose, not knowing where she was nor what had happened to her, and cried out, "Ten thousand praise the Lord." Fox rejoiced. The world no longer could justly call the Friends false prophets, witches or deceivers.

Similar good fortune met him at another place nearby. He saw a raving woman, held down by several people, struggling with a doctor who was trying to soothe her madness by bleeding her. Fox had them unbind her, then he spoke quietly to her, bidding her be calm and still. She trusted him and she was healed.

This was good psychiatry, the effect of a strong personality, a commanding presence, the piercing eyes and the absolute assurance which his voice gave that he was equal to the occasion. For victims such as she, the treatment by George Fox was equal to that of physicians with a thousand lancets. Neither Fox nor his contemporaries so regarded it. To them the explanation was supremely simple; to George it was the everlasting power of the Lord, but to others it was witchcraft.

The witchcraft charge was very rife at Drayton. George had left, his parents said, with much coin in his pockets. Apparently, they did not know its source, nor did they know just where he had gone. The rest of the village made wild guesses.

Nathaniel Stephens, never before credited with much imagination nor with an elfin sense of light and airy fantasy, concocted the most exciting explanation. George, he pointed out, had left home hastily and now was nowhere to be found. The reason was, said Stephens, that George Fox had been caught up by a whirlwind which whisked him up into the skies. There he had his pockets filled with gold and silver. Now he was off, the Lord—or the devils?—alone knew where, doing whose will no one dared guess.

Incredibly, the village swallowed the story. It spread throughout the county. In haste, the family, fearing no doubt that witchcraft charges would soon follow, wrote their son to hurry home to scotch the scandal. Instead, he sent a letter which Stephens, whose imagination now was working overtime, refused to credit. Anyone, he sneered, might write a letter and say it was from Fox; where was the man himself? Again the family wrote, in panic, urging George to show himself.

George Fox started back, but luck was not running in his favor. Instead of reaching Drayton, he landed in the Derby jail.

7

Derby Jail

It was bound to happen. Disaster was overdue. Sooner or later, George Fox's calm assumption of infallibility, his boasts of sinlessness, his personal relationships with the Almighty were certain to bring trouble. Already, angry individuals, irresponsible youths who suspected Fox of witchcraft, were disturbing meetings of his followers.

Fox, to be sure, was doing much the same thing. By prevailing custom, parishioners took the floor after service to comment on the Sunday sermon. Fox, who pointedly avoided Stephens' services, began to visit other steeple-houses, and, as in the case of the lady who wished to ask a question, to take advantage of the speaking opportunity.

On such occasions, he said that he was declaring Truth, but usually his talks bitterly attacked the minister's character. Over and over again, he denounced clerics for rapacity, deceitfulness and lack of personal integrity. Loudly and persistently, he predicted that the wrath of God would destroy both priest and people.

Whether cr not his accusations were well founded, human beings could stand just so much of this sort of thing. At Nottingham, he escaped with but a brief imprisonment for breach of the peace. Later in the year, at a country church near Mansfield, he was not so lucky. No one knows just what he said, but he must have been more irritating than usual, for the congregation rose against him.

It is impossible to know what happened. We have only the *Journal* as a source of information. While George Fox was thoroughly honest and without the faintest trace of any desire to mislead, his reporting, if only because of the lapse of time before he wrote about happenings, was not beyond criticism, nor, for the sake of emphasis, was he above unconsciously heightening his experiences.

According to the *Journal,* a riot ensued. Members of the congregation punched him and knocked him down. He managed to rise, but they jammed him against the wall and beat him. Somehow he was able to get away, but the people caught him in the churchyard where they knocked him down again, put him in the stocks and were on the point of whipping him, before cooler heads intervened. Then the mob threw so many stones that he was bruised all over.

Belatedly, the authorities rescued him. George lodged no charges--it is noteworthy that in all the many attacks upon him few, if any, of his persecutors were arrested, much less punished—nor, apparently, were charges pressed against him. Instead, his hearing became a forum where he preached a lengthy sermon before being turned loose, with the warning to leave town.

The mob disapproved. Men, now armed with clubs, rushed up to beat him once more, but the authorities, for once, held the attackers off. There were, however, shouts that if ever he returned, he would be shot dead.

Within a week, he was up and about, completely healed of the heavy bruises that had covered him from head to foot. In defiance of the warning, he went back to a steeple-house. This time, the priest took precautions; hearing that Fox was on the way. the priest locked the church door, excluding not only George Fox but some of the parishioners, and held a service in peace. After the sermon, when the doors were unlocked, Fox went in and spoke for a short while before being hustled out into the churchyard. Apparently, his enemies took no notice of him.

Next, Fox wandered close to Drayton. Before he reached his home, however, he heard a market bell. The sound "struck at his life"—an expression of which Fox was so fond that he used it repeatedly—and moved him to enter the Atherstone steeple-house.

Atherstone was deceptively peaceful. Its people "raged"— a very favorite Fox term meaning only unfriendliness—but they did nothing other than to warn Christopher and Mary to tie up their crazy son.

George may have feared this would be done; he veered away from home and went instead to a more distant town. At the steeple-house he met, of all people, Nathaniel Stephens, who also raged much. He, too, called George crazy. Nevertheless, he permitted Fox to speak in the steeple-house. When George left the building, hundreds of people surrounded him in the market place, beat him up and stoned him out of town.

To one obeying the Lord's commands, attacks were unimportant; but Fox was dismayed at the prevalence of death and darkness among the people. Obviously, a miracle was required.

Providentially, the miracle occurred. At Twycross in Leicestershire, a certain great man—for all his strong sense of equality Fox never failed to be impressed by rank—a certain great man lay ill. He had been sick a long time and physicians had despaired of his life. Fox prayed by his bedside and the man was cured.

For some reason—was it because the cure was laid to witchcraft?—the healing angered the great man's household. A servant came running with a drawn sword which he held at George's side. Fox looked him in the face and said calmly, "Alack for thee; it's no more to me than a straw." The servant went off in a rage, mumbling threats, and his master dismissed him.

The angry man who, after rushing furiously, merely held his sword and who, though raging, slunk harmlessly away, testified anew to George Fox's powerful personality. Fox, of course, would never have so explained the incident. The power of the Lord, as he said, had stayed the villain's hand, but that power worked through the steely glitter of George Fox's eyes.

The abortive attack, together with the beatings and stonings, also revealed the spread of serious hostility. Reports were current of miraculous cures, which Fox admitted were greater and more wonderful than could be generally understood. That fantastic story of the whirlwind that showered wealth upon him was being passed from mouth to mouth. Actually, the country folk understood all too well. It was an age of superstitious fear. From their avid reading of the Bible, people knew all about evil spirits, witches and the casting out of devils. Was not his mother's ancestor a witch? The more charitable called him mad, as Nathaniel Stephens had done; the rest were sure he was possessed.

The climax came at Derby. There was to be a gathering of army officers, priests and churchgoers to hear a certain Nathaniel Barton, a local dignitary who held three high positions, being simultaneously a colonel, a pastor and a justice of the peace. He was also, his enemies charged, a thief who had stolen a crimson satin tablecloth from Peterborough Cathedral.

Fox listened, but when the colonel-pastor-justice sat down Fox rose to teach the Truth and Light. Apparently he did not rail, for the audience was fairly quiet; but an officer came up, took Fox by the hand and led him to the magistrates' offices. When the inquisitors examined him, Fox delivered a sermon. When they questioned him, as he himself had questioned priests, he argued with them. Had priests acted so, when Fox invaded steeple-houses, he would have called it raging, especially when he committed the grave error of warning them not to dispute about God and Christ but to obey His Word.

This was unfortunate. At first, the magistrates considered him only an ecstatic, suffering from some form of emotional disturbance; but, after eight hours of heated argument, when they, too, were excited, they misconstrued his warning. George Fox, they now suspected, was claiming to be a reincarnation of Christ.

They were, in their way, considerate. Reluctant to charge blasphemy, a most serious offense, they pressed him further. They asked if he were sanctified, to which Fox replied that he was, for he was in the Paradise of God. He admitted being sinless and that Christ lived within him and within others, by the Spirit He had given all men; but he denied that either he or any of his associates ever claimed to be divine. He closed with the injunction, "Tremble before the Word of God."

Barton, who felt his dignity had been affronted, and hot-tempered Gervase Bennet, his fellow magistrate, being both biassed and illogical, construed the warning as yet another proof that Fox was claiming to be God, but they disregarded the monition.

"Ah," said Barton, "You are the Quaker, not I."[1]

[1] Fox believed that this was the first time the nickname was applied to his small group. Actually, Barton borrowed a jibe already launched against others, even against a couple of Moslem women who preached in London in 1647. George himself hinted at the word when, after praying powerfully at Mansfield, he reported that the house seemed to shake. The term was current, to describe other sects than Fox's followers, and therefore saddled Friends with complicity in excesses committed by fanatics with whom neither Fox nor any of his people were connected.

Fox did not relish the nickname, but he was proud that he, like Moses and David, trembled before the Lord. To be a Quaker had Biblical sanction. "Was not Ezekiel a Quaker?" he asked. "The Lord commanded him to eat his bread with quaking and to drink his water with trembling." Nevertheless, on October 20, 1650, the magistrates sentenced Fox and John Fretwell, a companion, to six months' imprisonment.

Regardless of the justice of the sentence, the two Quakers may have escaped lightly. Blasphemy was a major crime, punishable under the early Stuarts by burning at the stake. True, this dramatic fate may not then have been legal, since the ecclesiastical courts, Star Chamber and the Court of High Commission, which once had jurisdiction over blasphemy, no longer existed; but blasphemy was still a grievous offence, particularly in a Commonwealth which laid much stress upon the Scriptures.

No one quite knew who was supposed to try blasphemy cases nor, for that matter, what the penalty should be. The law specifically required death, yet a convicted person might go free on recantation. New ordinances, adopted only a few weeks before Fox came up for trial, offered an escape from the worst dilemma; under it, Barton and Bennet could impose six months' sentences. Fretwell did not stay in prison long. Pleading that his mother needed him, he recanted and, Fox heard, accused Fox of having bewitched him.

George stood firm, but, remembering Sheriff Reckless' kindliness, he asked furloughs from prison so that he might preach in the market place. Denied these temporary freedoms, he warned the warden that the iniquity of the people must lie upon the warden's conscience.

From current viewpoints, prison life in England's seventeenth century was extremely strange. The state provided no food, no heat, no bedding for its prisoners; it gave neither medical nor janitorial attention. Inmates without relatives or friends ate whatever wardens sold at whatever price the jailers asked; firewood, mattresses and all else came from the wardens' commissaries. Cooking, too, was something which the prisoner must provide, usually by hiring the warden's wife. All this was legitimate and, indeed, unavoidable business, for jailers received little pay, if any; their income came from the profits of their stores and from fees which convicts were supposed to pay.

Private supplies of necessities would be tolerated, especially if the warden were remembered by frequent tips. The rich who paid well received preferred treatment—often private rooms; but those like Fox, who neither bought supplies nor paid fees, might expect cold treatment.

Conditions varied with the personalities of jailers, but the average was low. When social service was an unknown concept, who but low-calibre people, ignorant, degraded, otherwise un-employable, would take the job? Who else would willingly associate, day and night, with drunkards, ruffians and criminals in an overcrowded Bedlam? Who else would subject wife and children to these seminaries of vice, crime and disease? Sanitary standards were low enough in the best palaces; prison dirt, filth and stench were intolerable for any but the callous.

From the wardens' point of view, jailers were extraordinarily lenient. Ignorant and superstitious, they feared witches and, like every patriot, they hated traitors. Learned leaders, such as ministers and judges, damned Quakers as sorcerers and enemies of peace; were prison guards to overrule the judgment of the wise? None of this in any way justified the holding of lighted candles under the noses of Quakers nor the cruel bridling of women convicted of being common scolds, but people of the class from which jailers were drawn could not be expected to hold higher standards than their betters.

Fox made no allowance for persecutors; angered at the brutalities of his captors, he condemned them all. He showered letters on the magistrates, the courts, the mayor, even on the church bell ringers. Visitors who came to talk with him—he said, to argue and dispute—he bluntly commanded to keep still; they were pleading, he said, for sin and imperfection.

Toward penitents he was merciful and loving. Outwardly his manners were atrocious, but he radiated friendliness. He would not compromise with sin nor condone it, and he was truculent toward those he considered advocates of darkness; but he never despaired of saving the sinner. He might be, and at times he was, overly harsh, but he was also unselfish, sincere and filled with genuine love for all mankind.

He captivated Warden Thomas Sharman as he had won Sheriff Reckless. When Fox asked furlough, Sharman denied it, as was his duty, but Fox's warning that the evils of the world lay upon him so worried the warden that he feared the day of judgment. He also feared George Fox, but he was sure that George would be merciful to sinners.

"I have been as a lion against you," he said, "but now I come like a lamb, and come trembling." He asked permission to stay with Fox. Fox, not always quick in sensing changes in the moods of others, replied, somewhat stiffly, that, as jailer, Sharman was in a position to do whatever he pleased.

"No, no," Sharman interrupted. "Please let me stay with you. I wish always to be with you, but not to have you as my prisoner."

Fox did not record the outcome of this appeal, or for that matter, what disposition Sharman intended to make of his wife had the offer been accepted; but next morning the warden told the justices that he was plagued for what was done to Fox. The justices admitted that they, too, were plagued.

Barton and Bennet then offered George Fox freedom to roam wherever he pleased within a mile radius from the prison. They hoped, the warden admitted, that their troublesome prisoner would take the opportunity to run away. To their astonishment Fox refused to do so.

By this time, news of the imprisonment had reached his parents. Shocked that any of the family should be in jail, they hurried to Derby to get him out under bond to keep the peace. George would have none of it. To be bound over implied to him an admission of guilt and he denied ill behavior. Nor would he promise to stop annoying the priests; all that he had done was to speak the Word of Light and Truth to them.

The two failures to get rid of Fox angered Bennet, particularly when, in the midst of an appeal to Fox to be reasonable, George dropped to his knees and began to pray openly for him. The justice doubled up his fists, jumped toward the kneeling man and punched him. Fox prayed the Lord to forgive him.

The situation had its comic aspects. Bennet would flare up, cast George back into jail and swear the man was mad. Then he would receive a hail of letters wherein Fox reiterated that a sinless man could accept freedom only from the Lord. These would act as challenges for Bennet to prove that he, a magistrate, could set jail inmates free; but just as he would be on the point of doing so, Fox would exasperate him with another shower of extremely critical letters. Bennet, and Barton, too, would then lose their tempers, and the circle would begin anew. This, said Fox, happened many times.

It is not wholly unlikely that George was enjoying himself. He would in his time be shut in many prisons, but this was one of the very few, if not the only one, against which he voiced no complaint of ill treatment. He baited priests and magistrates; he argued incessantly with advocates of strange, outlandish sects. Usually he emerged victorious, at least in his own estimation; but there were setbacks. A certain Rhys Jones, for instance, who used to spend his Sundays playing shuffleboard, was persuaded that the game was unseemly, and he and a body of his followers pledged their support to Fox. But then Jones came to think that Fox denied that Christ died at Jerusalem, a slander Fox found much difficulty in scotching.

Jail was not a pleasant lodging, but a place where he might come and go at will, with ample opportunity to preach and write and argue, was almost exactly what Fox wanted. Except that it was becoming crowded, not by prisoners but by recruits for the Commonwealth's army. Some of these were pressed to serve and some were volunteers, but all were so charmed by Fox that they demanded that he command them. They said they offered the captaincy in love and kindness, but Fox, who never graciously accepted compliments, rejected their offer. "If this be your love and kindness," he said, "I trample it under foot." For this refusal the authorities, thrust him back into the jail again, this time to the dungeon.

Thereafter, jail was not so pleasant. Fox lived with thirty felons, without a bed in "a lousy, stinking low place in the ground." Once in a while, they let him walk in the garden, but usually he was under close guard. Here he remained for half a year.

How, in this predicament, he was able to write letters is difficult to understand; yet he did so. He complained about the injustice of hanging convicts for minor offenses; indeed, he saved a young woman from the gallows by so doing. He demanded speedier trials, for long imprisonment meant only that prisoners, some of whom might be innocent, learned evil from one another. The justices were not his only target. Constantly he reproved his dungeon mates for their misdeeds; he kept insisting that they mend their language and their conduct.

By this time probably no one wanted Fox in jail. Bennet tried once more to set him free. If George would not volunteer for army duty, why not, he suggested, press him into service. This, perhaps, would have been going a bit too far, but possibly he might be bribed to serve. The constables offered him money if he would take up arms. Fox said, "I am dead to it"—mean-

ing, as he went on to say, that he had come into the covenant
of peace which preceded war and strife. The constables, who
knew nothing of such a covenant and who did not understand
his words, insisted that he was not dead but very much alive.
They tried again, twice more, to buy his consent. When he
refused the money, back he went to prison.

Derby folk were saying now that Fox would never quit the
jail. But the same back-and-forth routine which baffled Bennet
and Barton but which, before the dungeon, brought their
prisoner only a sight of the glory of God shining over all, at
long last affected Fox. He had a vision. A great judgment came
upon the town of Derby. As the waters ran from the dam when
the flood gates were lifted, so the power of God went away
from the hardened sinners. Fox gave forth a lamentation : "It
doth break my heart to see how God is dishonored in thee, O
Derby."

Nevertheless, the vision was a sign that his imprisonment
was drawing to an end. He was soon to be let forth as a lion
from a den, amidst the wild beasts of the forest.

And so he was. Derby magistrates were not at all agreed as
to whether he was a deceiver, a seducer, a blasphemer, or an
honest and virtuous man, but no one wanted him on their
hands. They talked of sending him down to London to be tried
before Parliament, or to Ireland. But, since Derby had no
power to do either, they opened the gates. On October 8,
1651, George Fox went free. Sentenced to six months for
something of which no one was very certain, he had been in
jail for just short of a year.

8

The Eccentrics

THOUGH FOX'S MIND HAD BEEN STEADIED BY HIS CALL TO THE ministry and by his conviction that in heckling false priests he was serving the Lord, the Derby experiences disturbed him deeply. Save for that Atherstone bell and for the great rift in the earth, neither of them violent excitements, he had been relatively calm, with no strikings at his heart, no openings, nor any visions other than of the shining glory of the Lord. But then the stinking dungeon upset his delicate adjustments.

George was never ill at ease nor unsure of himself, but, he started back toward Drayton under most unfavorable circumstances. How would the godly parents whose advice he had rejected receive a son whom neighbors thought a brawling jailbird? They had listened to that absurd Stephens story and really seemed to credit it. They may have thought George mad. Was his mother wondering if the blood of that Lichfield ancestor was rising in his veins? Intent as he was upon his mission, George could not have escaped flashes of concern about what his family and friends were thinking.

When, therefore, in this state of at least mild confusion, he reached Lichfield, memories of his mother's stories flooded over him. The steeple-house spires struck at his life, recalling, as they did, not only the false promises of Atherstone and London

steeples but also the legends of the thousand Christians martyred there and of his own martyred ancestor.[1] This Lichfield
seemed to Fox a city drenched in blood. On seeing it in his
unstable condition, he reacted as a schoolboy loosed from discipline. To him, those spires did not tower over a city but over
a vast pool of blood where there should have been a market
place, over streams of blood instead of streets. Through this
blood he must wade to raise the blood of long-dead martyrs.
He must walk barefoot and alone. The Lord commanded him
to pull off his shoes and to give them to the shepherds for safe-
keeping. Fox must make it clear to the shepherds that they must
not entrust those shoes to anyone except for pay.

The shepherds trembled and were mystified, as well they
might have been, when Fox relayed the message; but they took
the shoes. Fox then went barefoot into town, a mile away.
Since it was market day, he found the place thronged, but,
obedient to command, he charged up and down the streets—
he saw them as bloody channels—shouting, "Woe unto the
bloody city of Lichfield."

Ordinarily, a barefoot man, elbowing through crowds while
prophesying woe, would draw considerable attention; but no
one even laid a hand upon him, nor did anyone question what
was going on. A few friendly souls inquired curiously what had
happened to his shoes, but, otherwise, no one paid attention
to him.

When he had fulfilled the Lord's command and was again
at peace, he went back to the fields, tipped the shepherds and
reclaimed the shoes; but, having received no divine direction
to put them on again, he wandered off with them in his hand.

[1] Historically, the Lichfield legend learned by Fox had faulty foundations. His mother had taught him the generally current story of persecutions under Diocletian a thousand years before. In fact, if the atrocities
had actual historic basis, they referred to events about 286 A.D., in the
reign of Emperor Maximianus.

Eventually, he came to a ditch, washed his feet and then felt free to wear the shoes again.

When his people heard of all this, they were offended at him. The parents were, to say the least, embarrassed. No matter how devoted they may have been, nothing could conceal the fact that, as they knew, most of the Midlands considered Fox a nuisance. He was making a spectacle of himself. He was continuously engaged in brawls—that he was the victim was merely a technicality. Since leaving home with all that mysteriously acquired money, he had been twice in jail and was, in addition, accused of witchcraft and blasphemy, was suspected of sedition because he would not fight, was notorious for rioting in churches. That he had disturbed a dozen communities by shouting and preaching in the streets proved that he was mad. Drayton neighbors may have been too polite to talk about such things to Christopher and Mary, but it was too much to hope that they were ignorant of what everyone else knew.

Their burdens would have been easier had George been unique; his antics could have been excused because of special revelation. Unhappily, he was not unique. Scores of eccentrics were running up and down shouting similar, and even more spectacular, assertions of divine favor. Drayton could have swallowed one new prophet, but a swarm of self-styled messiahs dulled its appetite. They sprang from turmoil raging particularly in the south. While George was preaching in the north and during his imprisonment at Derby, crop failures, famine prices and rising unemployment were causing misery and suffering.

Amid the fears of rebellion against the official church and the established government, pretenders and prophets flourished. Among them was a Lancashire cowherd, Gerrard Winstanley, a Seeker, who heard a voice from the Throne of the Heavenly Almightiness summoning him to set up a democratic government based upon the Scriptures, where everyone should be equal under a Golden Rule of Equity. There would be no lords nor lawyers, no special privilege and, best of all, no tax of any kind. In this Utopia the land was free to all.

As usual in those days when the Bible was Britain's only book, Winstanley, like Fox, discarded all human authority; he made but little reference, nor did Fox, to classical or modern writers; he disregarded mundane law and history. Believing, as did so many contemporaries, that inner spiritual experience was possible for everyone, he, too, insisted that his ideas were heavenly inspired and not from any book or any other man.

Probably, though their ideas ran closely parallel in so many ways, including a belief in the Inner Light, Winstanley had never heard of Fox nor, except possibly in highly garbled version, had George Fox heard of him before Winstanley, in 1649, saw a vision of a white-clad host plowing up community land, that food might grow for everyone.

Winstanley acted on the vision. He led half a dozen poor men in digging up and planting a commons at St. George's Hill, Kingston-upon-Thames, about ten miles southwest of London. Despite the support of John Lilburne and his Levellers, and of other discontented groups, the effort failed, as could have been predicted; the 5,000 local residents, whom he expected as supporters, arrived as enemies who destroyed his planting and who burned his tools. Winstanley went to jail.

Much more was made of the attempt than circumstances warranted. In the feverish conditions of the time, Winstanley's gesture became a peril to the state, a communist assault upon social stability. Though George Fox had no connection whatever with either the theories or the practices of these Diggers at St. George's Hill, if only because he shunned legislative effort to cure social and economic problems, the unthinking lumped him with Lilburne, Winstanley and, indeed, with the Ranters of the lunatic fringe.

These were numerous. Some, to be sure, had run their course, but there were many who swung wildly to extremes. The Ranters, for example, jubilantly proclaimed themselves as above the law, free to act precisely as they pleased; what might be sin for unregenerates was for them no sin whatever. Fox described their meetings as no gatherings for worship but gay, sinful festivals where pipes and bowls were sacred vessels.

Ranterism, to be sure, was dying in England. Even Tany, former Lord High Priest of Jerusalem and then the heir to England's crown, was, from his cell in jail, planning to move to France to mount the Bourbon throne.

No lack of mystics clamored for attention. There was, for instance, Lodowicke Muggleton, a cockney-born tailor with bizarre pretensions. The tall, high-cheekboned Muggleton had been an apprentice pawnbroker until a cousin, John Reeve, convinced him that money lending was a sin. Rather than be contaminated by the evil of usury, Muggleton abandoned the business; to be doubly sure of safety, he jilted the master pawnbroker's daughter to whom he was engaged. She may have been fortunate; within three years Muggleton was twice a widower.

Almost immediately after the second death, Muggleton received inward illumination. Science, he was told, was a delusion. The sun went round the earth and Heaven was but six miles distant, presided over by a crystal transparent deity, six feet high, for whom he, Muggleton of the long flowing auburn hair, was vice-regent on earth. The revelation shocked Reeve. Immediately he, too, received a message from on high : "Meddle no more with religion, but get as good a livelihood as possible on earth and let God alone."

But so did Muggleton get messages. On three successive days, February 3, 4 and 5, 1651, he was ordered to cancel out what Reeve was told. The two men were, he heard, the Lord's last two witnesses and prophets, those who were foretold in the eleventh chapter of *Revelation*. For three years and a half. they should have power. As often as they willed, during that span, they could shut the doors of heaven, turn water into blood, smite the earth with plagues and forbid the rain to fall. If anyone should dare to interfere, fire would dart from their mouths and destroy him.

Reeve, among other people, took these revelations seriously. The Lord sent him revised instructions. Muggleton was appointed his mouthpiece. If he, Reeve, was too squeamish to "bless to eternity or to curse to eternity," let Lodowicke Muggleton speak for him. If not, the Lord would send down dire torments and afflictions.

Reeve thereafter sat back while Muggleton roamed the taverns and the alleys back of Old St. Paul's, delivering oracular speeches and searching for Satan, a very human figure who had first been incarnate in Cain but who had since been seen in many other persons' forms. Instead he met John Robins, who had once been Adam, and who had power to raise the dead. Now that Tany had abdicated as High Priest of Jerusalem, Robins took up the idea. He was raising an army of 144,000 people, male and female, to capture the Holy Land. He anticipated no difficulty feeding them; they would live on bread, raw vegetables and water. He could not, however, leave just yet; he and his wife, whom he named, alternately, as Mary or Joan, were expecting a baby, the Messiah.

Muggleton and Reeve made short work of Robins; they damned him to eternity and, with him, presumably the unborn Messiah, so that neither was heard of more. They also condemned Thomas Tany, but the avenging power was slow, for it was not until four years later that the goldsmith drowned. At that, Tany was doubtless himself at fault, for he had set out in a small boat to cross to Holland; but the Muggletonians were certain that it had been they who had sent him to his death.

As good church members, Christopher and Mary must have been pleased that George had no links with the pretenders, but they must have worried lest their neighbors misunderstood his eccentricity. The Lichfield outburst, the Stephens story, the steeple-house interruptions not only won few followers but, together with the imprisonment, may have lost him some of the Seekers he had already gained. All too few Midlanders stood firm in this adversity. Elizabeth Hooten and similar folk who called themselves the Children of Light stayed staunch, but most people, knowing Fox only by hearsay, considered him at least annoying, if not downright dangerous.

But the outlook was not hopeless. Outside the Midlands, where rumors of the gold and silver shower had not spread, or where Boehmenites, Seekers and the Family of Love were less credulous, a welcome was prepared. Such idealists, impressed by reports of how Fox helped the afflicted, wondered if he might be the miracle worker they awaited. A small group at Balby, in Yorkshire sixty miles from Lichfield, invited him to visit.

Yorkshiremen, especially the plainsmen living on the high road into Scotland, had a nonconformist history. Pilgrims had gone from there, first to Leyden in the Netherlands and then to Massachusetts; numbers of religious dissenters still remained. The Balby Seekers had been particularly vigorous, and some of them had exchanged correspondence with George Fox while he was still in jail.

If in 1651 the yearning Yorkshire Seekers recognized any leaders they would have been Richard Farnsworth, Thomas Aldam, William Dewsbury and James Nayler. Each of these was slightly older than the twenty-seven-year-old Fox but all had undergone similar experience. All had been, from boyhood, spiritually dissatisfied; unlike George Fox, each had shopped in vain for satisfaction in one or another of the various sects and each had been disappointed. Two of them, at least, Nayler and Dewsbury, had joined the Parliamentary army, thinking that it was fighting for the Gospel, but had again been disillusioned. All had studied their Bibles so zealously that they had memorized whole chapters; as preachers they were powerful. Fox was fortunate in finding such able supporters. All four were outstanding—Aldam for his pertinacity, Dewsbury for sweetness, Farnsworth for leadership, while probably the most brilliant of all was James Nayler, a man of charm and sympathy.

Nayler was exceptional. During his seven years in the army, he had been an excellent soldier. His courtesy and ready wit charmed individuals; as quartermaster, his efficiency in managing difficult problems of billeting and foraging endeared him to superiors. His preaching against sin was so effective that a brother officer confessed, "I was struck with more terror by Nayler's preaching than by the battle of Dunbar."

Unlike most Seekers, his interests were broad. Concerned with social and economic affairs as well as with religion, he was, to some degree, sympathetic with that strange Gerrard Winstanley who, two years before, had inspired his Diggers to plant carrots on a village green as a sign that land was common property. Nayler did not indorse Winstanley's communism, nor his plan to wipe out professional scholars, lawyers, courts, priests, patents, tolls and tariffs, but he did believe, with Winstanley, in the abolition of arbitrary rule and in the establishment of a Golden Rule of Equity.

For Nayler, a man more proud and more ambitious than he ever realized, rebelled against mundane authority. Like Fox, he depended wholly upon the guidance of the Lord, but, unlike George, he never dared channel the Lord's movings toward an inner purpose of his own. Nayler needed a leader, and he found one in George Fox; but, in his innocence and his credulity, he also found leaders in almost any other who professed to have received divine revelation. He lacked utterly George's keen ability to discern at once the honesty and integrity of others.

The winning of the Balby Seekers opened a series of successes. Nayler complemented George Fox perfectly. Fox was a commander, a father figure, not too approachable and not too sensitive to the feelings of others; Nayler a follower, everyone's considerate brother, a confidant. Fox was an Old Testament prophet, a man of might to be obeyed; Nayler a softer, much more lovable, more human individual filled with tenderness and understanding. The partnership seemed perfect, all the more so because they had the aid of self-sacrificing and devoted associates like Aldam, Dewsbury and Farnsworth. Fox and his companions scoured Yorkshire, holding meetings, visiting the homes of the great, speaking in the steeple-houses, and everywhere the converts flocked to Quakerism.

For the first time since his dispute with Stephens, Fox met men of equal ability and, perhaps, of education superior to his own. Justice Durant Hotham, for instance, a man five years his senior, was a particularly valuable acquaintance; for Hotham, the translator and biographer of Jacob Boehme, saw exciting parallels between the teachings of George Fox and of the German mystic. He would have introduced Fox to "some great high priests and other doctors," but Fox, whose scholarship was less authoritative, was hesitant about meeting them.

It was just as well, for, soon after visiting Hotham, Fox went alone to the steeple-house and, objecting to the sermon, shouted "Come down, thou deceiver and hireling." Had Hotham been present the matter would have been embarrassing, for Hotham and the minister were close associates. "What could I have done?" the justice asked, on hearing of the incident; "Ignore the insult or send George Fox to prison?"

Restless and unable to suffer success gladly, Fox left the
legion of well-wishers who would have said, as did Hotham,
"My house is your house," and wandered north. He underwent hardship, much of it self-imposed, as when he slept out
of doors because he could not bear to stay in a lodging house
where a woman had lied to him. Moved by a revelation that
he must speak in steeple-houses to gather followers from the
congregations, he went into them after the sermons were
finished; he would not, however, mount the pulpits, but stood
upon the pews.

Two days after Christmas, he entered York Cathedral,
where Dr. Edward Bowles was preaching. Bowles, an
extremely popular clergyman who was said to "rule all York,"
had a ready sense of humor; but his temper flared when Fox
rose and announced that the Lord God commanded him to
say something.

"Say it quickly," answered Bowles, "for it is very cold."[2]

Fox described Yorkshire as a spiritually barren desert, but
there were many there, Seekers and their allies, who thirsted
for the light. With Hotham lending powerful support and the
priests failing dismally in rebutting the eloquence of George
Fox's messages, the Friends, as the Children of Light were
now calling themselves, flourished.

Something, however—one knows not what—went wrong.
Fox suspected that the priests, angry because he opposed their
tithing, raging because he called them hirelings and false
prophets, were making ruffians drunk so that they would
attack him. Perhaps with good reason, Fox believed they

[2] In his *Journal* Fox noted only that he told the shivering congregation
that God demanded deeds, not words. He must, however, had said more
than this, for the people rushed him out of the building and threw him
down the steps into the street. Fox rose unhurt, though groaning with
the weight and oppression that was upon the spirit of God within him.
The groans, however, were efficacious; he convinced several of Bowles'
congregation before leaving the city.

wished to kill him; one woman said openly that she would like to see him hanged. A priest invited Fox to visit him; when George entered the house, he took a good look at his host and decided that this priest was no man at all but was a dog. Apparently the indignant host took the insult calmly; but after his guest had gone, he struck his cane upon the ground and   swore that he would kill George Fox or die in the attempt. He meant the threat, George thought, the proof being that, soon after, the dog-priest suggested that he and George take a walk along the top of a cliff. George accepted, but he took the precaution of asking a friend to go along lest the wicked priest try to push him over the cliff. The plot, if there was one, failed; whereupon the priest offered to bet his head that George would die within a month.

The anticipation of persecution—it is not impossible that George Fox courted it—prevented his enjoying the adulation he often received. No one can possibly question Fox's humility and modesty, but neither may one ignore his delight in having recognition from the upper classes. Doubtless, he sincerely thought, when the populace suddenly packed a steeple-house on hearing he was there, that they had come to hear the Word of God; but when he wrote of it he said the crowd had come because he was there. Regardless of their reason for coming, the event pleased him; but instead of thanking his visitors he usually took the opportunity to tell them they were doomed.

A Ranter revealed, for instance, that he had been ordered in a vision to doff and bow before George Fox. George, however, spurned the man; he accepted no homage from people whom he considered money grabbers and Sodomites and whose meetings seemed mere excuses for smoking and drinking parties. When, therefore, the Ranter volunteered to carry out the orders of the vision, George bluntly shouted, "Repent, thou beastly swine."

According to Fox, the Ranter, thus rebuffed, laid the words to jealousy.

9

Yorkshire

DURING THE LATE MONTHS OF 1651 ALL WENT WELL IN
Yorkshire. Surprisingly, in view of George's steeple-house
speeches, the priests displayed extraordinary tolerance. Perhaps
they shared Justice Hotham's opinion that George had saved
the nation from Ranterism. Whatever their reasons, they
flocked to visit Fox at his inns. One priest greeted him as
brother, another tried to pay his dinner bill, a third offered
to clean his boots. Several ministers invited him to occupy
their pulpits.

George, impatient with the amenities, refused all offers,
though less brusquely than he had rebuffed the Ranter. He
drew fine distinctions. The Lord repeatedly moved him to
enter steeple-houses to confound the priests but forbade him
to dignify those buildings by accepting clerical hospitality. To
preach in churchyards was permissable, indeed was manda-
tory; to preach in pulpits was entirely wrong.

His voice was loud enough and clear enough for him to
speak effectively in the open air; but even here, where he had
a mandate to speak, he was sometimes at a loss. Once, for
instance, when an eager crowd waited impatiently, he sat
silent on a haystack for several hours. One of the more
friendly priests, an old man, quieted the people by reminding

them that Christ, too, had kept the populace waiting; so they stayed, fixed by those piercing eyes or curious to know what revelation Fox was receiving, until at last he spoke. Then Fox preached, with such eloquence that he won "a general convincement."

But then, when after crossing the moors to his own church, the kindly old man opened the door to his pulpit stairs and invited Brother Fox to mount them, George refused. The church walls bore frescoes which were to Fox not works of art but, as he told his friend, turned the steeple-house into "the painted house of the painted beast." George Fox, never noted for tact, courtesy or consideration for the feelings of other people, warned the friendly clergyman that frescoes led straight to superstition; probably he also mentioned the dangers of idolatry.

By direct command from Heaven, he preferred in any case to speak in the open, where audiences were larger. Wherever he spoke he commanded attention. No one could possibly ignore the hulking man whose long locks flowed beneath the wide white hat down to his broad shoulders. His leather clothes, while not unusual among working people, added to his picturesqueness; the coarse, brown covering symbolized the stern inflexibility of the ancient doctrines which he preached.

For one whose oratory violated the usual arts of elocution, whose phrases, as one listener reported, "fell abruptly and brokenly" and whose sermons "had nothing of man's wit and wisdom to recommend them," Fox spoke with extraordinary power. The same critic who objected to his diction went on to say, "The most awful, living, reverend frame I ever felt or beheld was his in prayer."

Powerful as he was in addressing crowds, he perhaps won more individuals by his sweetness and charm in private conversation. In speaking to large groups, to which many came

merely to satisfy their curiosity, his steel-sharp verbal attacks
roused the mob spirit. Though some unquestionably were convinced by what he said, other ganged up against him. Doubtless, he dramatized the dangers which he ran, probably he
exaggerated his injuries; but certainly he suffered greatly at
the hand of angered hearers.

How could George Fox manage to be at once both sweet
and vituperative? By loving his neighbor while hating the
evils that might possess that neighbor. Fox warred incessantly
against the dark powers that obsessed those who did not follow
the light, but he battled no individual sinner. Repeatedly he
condemned the dogs and vipers whom he saw in human form;
he denounced the devilish servants of the beasts, the men of
rotten hearts, the foul-mouthed reprobates who uttered wicked
doctrine, the hypocrites, liars and deceivers whose god was
their bellies and who pleaded for sin. But always he held the
door of hope wide open for even the most outwardly depraved
to confess their sins and to acknowledge truth.

When alone with some misguided soul or in small gatherings, he could plead and pray and bring comfort to those
whom the devils had captured; at such times he was an
unequalled angel of light. In dealing with a crowd, however,
the powerful personality which he focussed with such force
upon an individual was scattered among many. Here he had
grandeur rather than warm, personal appeal. The Scriptural
simplicity of his speech radiated less of his deep humanity than
of a solemn warning to beware the wrath of God that would
wipe out the wicked.

Rural priests were often so outclassed in privately debating
George Fox that, recognizing his invincibility they evaded
meeting him. When, however, he spoke in general terms to
multitudes, his magnetism less concentrated, they were more
successful. Here the mob spirit aided them. Vituperation,

aimed at no one in particular but offending all, angered everyone. Rough persons, protected by the anonymity of crowds, hooted and catcalled; they threw stones or clods or sticks. Rioting followed.

Strange itinerants who roam the countryside, shouting to the people to repent, prophesying calamity and stirring up commotion, are unlikely to receive warm welcome. Nor did George Fox. Innkeepers were not anxious to welcome a trouble maker who almost certainly would disturb more quiet customers; private citizens were hesitant to house him overnight. It is not surprising that the more cautious told him that they had no room, so that sometimes (frequently he said) he had to lie all night in open fields. Those who had heard him speak and who had been moved by his message did their best to spare him, but they were a minority; most people thought him mad.

In early 1652 there was worse to come. In the custom of the time, Fox delivered long, elaborated sermons. He taught the Inner Light that makes all things visible, the Light whereby mortal man experiences the spirit of Christ, becomes one with the saints and the apostles, feels and sees and knows the glory of God. All this was very beautiful and ennobling, but it was also very easily misinterpreted. A philosopher, a mystic, a meditative man would recognize that Christ was always within him, but most of Fox's listeners were far from philosophic. Usually they were rustics, unsubtle and unused to speculative thinking. Many sensed no beauty, no spirituality in what George said. For them the sermons, however highly spiced by warnings, by promises and by attacks upon the wicked, were difficult to follow. Some took away only the vague impression that George Fox, a sinless man, was claiming to be Christ.

If Fox were not mad, this was blasphemy, the crime for

which he had been jailed in Derby. It was the most dangerous of all offenses, for it exposed not only the perpetrator but all who heard him to eternal torture. And so at Gainsborough, near Lincoln Cathedral, when many shallow listeners preferred the awful charge, a terrified audience rose up against George Fox.

Though George himself said little about the incident, he then achieved spectacular success. Mounting upon a table, he quieted the raging mob by the power of his piercing eyes. He said that Christ was not in him alone but in all those present, save, of course, the reprobates. It was true, he said, that he spoke with power of God and that it was the Christ within him who spoke to them; but they, too, if they but believed the truth and recognized the Light, had that same possibility within themselves.

So he called his chief accuser Judas, and "all were satisfied except himself—and his own false witnesses." Fox predicted that this latter-day Judas would suffer the same fate as the Judas who betrayed Christ. "And the Lord's power came over all and all the people parted in peace, but this Judas went away and hanged himself shortly after and a stake was driven into his grave."[1]

Returning to Yorkshire, Fox found the priests less cordial. Slow and irregular communications over the rutted roads carried word, violently distorting it enroute, of the blasphemy charges and of that supposed Quaker suicide; if anything were also said of George's spectacular victory it would have been explained as witchcraft. At any rate, when Fox and Thomas Aldam entered a steeple-house in a village near Doncaster they so flustered the priest, Thomas Rookby, that he babbled,

---

[1] It was typical of contemporary reporting that the story was wholly distorted in the telling. An anti-Quaker tract spread the news that in Lincolnshire a Quaker had hanged himself and that a stake had been driven through him.

"Why have you come? Why have you come? What have you to say? What have you to say?" He turned the pages of his Bible nervously, losing his place and being wholly bewildered as Fox stood silent. When Rookby regained a little control, George began to speak, telling the parishioners that their priest was leading them after false prophets. The people would not listen but pushed Fox out of the building. Ht waited in the churchyard until the service was finished and then attempted again to speak. Rookby took hold of him and shook him and the people battered him with sticks and stones, Fox all the while continuing to warn them of the coming of the Lord.

"I received not much hurt," he said, "for the power of the Lord was over all."

On two succeeding Sundays he entered other steeple-houses. Each time the congregation threw him out. In one village the mayor and the magistrates warned him, if he valued his life, never to return. George, never daunted by a dare, returned twice with no hurt on either occasion. Rookby was not so lenient. When Fox and Aldam came again to his village, he swore out a warrant against them for breach of the peace, or, as the Quakers put it, "for speaking in the steeple-house."

Shortly before the issuance of the warrant, Fox had a dream, a vision, in which he saw himself unharmed by a bear and two great mastiffs. The dream proved prophetic, for the constable and his aides who arrested Aldam refused to take Fox into custody. Despite this fulfillment of his vision, George was indignant. While the officers were riding twenty miles to take Aldam to York prison, Fox rode with them, insisting vehemently that they arrest him also. According to Fox, the constable, while willing to throw a neighbor Yorkshireman into jail, was unwilling to annoy a stranger.

He was, however, considerate. En route the cavalcade met

Nayler, Dewsbury, Farnsworth and Thomas Goodaire. The constable suspended the journey to the jail to let the Quakers hold "a great meeting of many considerable men." When this was finished, he resumed the march to prison.[2]

There he found plenty of company. Yorkshire had a theory that if the leaders were jailed, the Quaker movement would quickly halt. They spared Fox, not merely because he was a stranger but because, as the most conspicuous offender, he would become a martyr, but they imprisoned Elizabeth Hooten and eight other Quakers for "speaking to a priest." One of these was Goodaire, who had called a certain justice of the peace a profane liar, a charge which the Quakers described as "unmannerly though notorious truth-speaking." For this, Goodaire served ten months but Aldam was held for two years and a half.

Fox, frustrated in his attempt to enter jail, moved onward. At Wakefield, a town famous for its Flemish cloth weavers, he visited the Congregational church from which James Nayler had been recently expelled. There the clergyman, Christopher Marshall, a less genial individual than Oliver Goldsmith's vicar, berated both Fox and his former parishioner unmercifully.

Fox bore the brunt of Marshall's long-growing resentments. The cleric was a good, sound scholar and was highly capable, but no one termed him tolerant. A sincere and dedicated Puritan, a student of John Cotton in Massachusetts, he had

---

[2] Actually, the discrimination, instead of being a carrying out of prophesy, was due to Aldam's history. In the eyes of Yorkshire authorities, Aldam was a hardened criminal. He owed £11 of unpaid tithes for 1652. When, to cover this debt, the authorities seized goods worth five times that amount, Aldam complained bitterly. Worse, when his case came up for hearing he refused to doff his hat in court. For this the judge fined him an additional £40. In view of this background, Yorkshire took a more serious view of his breach of the peace than they did of George Fox's actions. The judge found him guilty and sentenced him to prison.

helped Cotton battle the unorthodoxy of Anne Hutchinson and Roger Williams. He returned to Yorkshire in 1642 with fixed phobias against religious radicals, only to contend with the fervid oratory of James Nayler and with a restless congregation. These combined to turn his disquieted mind toward melancholia.

Nayler he condemned for theological unsoundness and for immorality; he charged James with wife desertion and adultery. George Fox, in Marshall's opinion, was more dangerous. Because Fox carried off some of the parishioners, Christopher Marshall, a more imaginative man than Nathaniel Stephens of whirlwind fame, explained that Fox practiced witchcraft. George carried magic bottles, he warned—bottles filled with magic potions; from these he forced the unwary to drink, whereupon the victims were at once enslaved. Beware also, he added, of Fox's great black horse, an enchanted animal which galloped so fast that, an hour after Fox was seen in Yorkshire, it bore him sixty miles away into the next county.

George, it is true, owned horses, though none as staunch and speedy, but just at this time he was walking, having sold a horse a year before, just following the Lichfield incident. Nor, it may be unnecessary to add, was he carrying magic bottles in his leather breeches. The accusations, therefore, revealed more than the preacher's imagination or his bad temper; they showed that, despite those earnest studies at the university or under the Reverend John Cotton, Marshall still believed in witchcraft, sorcery and medieval superstition.

Instead of harming Fox, the wicked slanders, George believed, backfired upon the minister. By stretching the longbow just a bit too far, the imaginative priest lost not only Nayler but many others of his flock. As further retribution, the Lord "cut off" the liar in his wickedness.

The expression, a common usage by George Fox, cannot be

taken literally. To cut off a man would imply a sudden death; but since, despite Fox's statement that punishment occurred "not long after," Marshall lived another score of years, the interpretation must be more elastic. Moreover, there were instances, though the Marshall case was no example, where, Fox declared, the Lord cut off a sinner whose misdeeds fell very short of being capital offenses.

No one can possibly doubt the sincerity or the essential truthfulness of George Fox, but a purist may hesitate to take the words he used so loosely at their face value.

To deprive a minor offender of life, or exile him from the mercy and the grace of God, from the Holy Spirit, from the fellowship of saints or from all hope of Heaven, because of what were often very minor lapses would be intolerable for one who, like George Fox, professed charity, love and forgiveness toward all mankind; he could not have believed a God of kindliness and mercy would inflict such terrible punishments.

The truth was that George Fox, never a master of English, used words carelessly, with but the faintest idea of the emotions they conveyed. Not everyone beyond his immediate circle could possibly have been rude, envious or wicked; there must have been some few who did not rail, or rage, or bawl, and some whose arguments were better than mere jangling or jumbling. However much he may have disliked Anglican theology, or disapproved of Baptists, Presbyterians or Puritans, he must have realized that not all of them were desperate thieves and liars who mouthed filth when they preached. Yet, save for that old man in the painted house, he gave no credit to his rivals for sincerity or truthfulness.

His seventeenth-century inability to be tolerant drove him, as it drove his adversaries, into overstatement, into writing with far more vehemence than accuracy. Indignation, the contemporary disability to sympathize with other points of view, caused him, as it caused others of his time, to distort the character of his opponents and to magnify the injustice of his sufferings.

Fox, to be sure, did not hand down sentences but merely reported the judgments of the Lord; there were occasions when, urged to bring suit against oppressors, he declined to do so, preferring to leave retribution to Almighty God. Superficially, he appeared complacent, even smug, at the discomfiture of enemies; actually their fate disturbed him. He seemed thick-skinned, but he was at heart uncommonly sensitive. Quick though he was to warn sinners and outwardly callous to the horrors that awaited them, he worried constantly.

The Wakefield lies, relatively unimportant as they were, helped undermine his health; they were links in a long chain of slanders, misunderstandings and misrepresentation. Sturdy as he was, his griefs, his anxieties, the enmities against him, his hardships in tramping, often half hungry, in the service of the Lord were steadily wearing him down.

He became pessimistic, fearful. In constant expectation of the martyrdom he unconsciously was courting, he sensed conspiracies on every side.

10

The White-Clad Host

IT WAS NO ACCIDENT THAT, LATE IN MAY, FOX AND
Farnsworth entered that part of northern England where
Yorkshire, Westmorland and Lancashire meet. Fox, as always,
gave the general impression that he wandered more or less
aimlessly; but just as he had gone to Yorkshire by invitation
so, responding to calls from the west, he went to the Lake
Country as a fertile field for his evangelism.

All northern England at the time was in religious chaos.
Puritans had ejected royalist and Episcopalian ministers.
Congregationalists, Baptists, Presbyterians and Independents
vied for the vacant pulpits. A few leaders, aware that rivalries
would benefit only a lunatic fringe of irresponsibles, vainly
pleaded for harmony and co-operation.

Seekers were particularly numerous and, unlike their fellows
elsewhere, were fairly well organized. The region was hilly,
rugged and thinly settled, the roads few and poorly kept, but
enthusiastic Seekers managed to maintain fairly regular local
meetings. Once a month they held a larger, and very thriving,
meeting at Preston Patrick, near the head of Morecambe Bay.

The moving spirit here was Thomas Taylor, a Separatist
preacher, who, with John Audland, a textile merchant, and
Francis Howgill, a tailor, were North Country men of George

Fox's type. All of them began in their early teens to be concerned about their sinfulness; the three read widely, studied
much and, in Howgill's case at least, sampled one variety of
religious experience after another in the search for truth.

After graduation from Oxford in 1650, Taylor became
preacher at Preston Patrick; but then he heard of Jacob
Boehme whose "sweet unfolding of the mystery of life" swept
him into Seekerism. A highly conscientious man, strongly
opposed to infant baptism, and so hostile to the tithing system
that he refused to take the £50 yearly to which the Preston
Patrick pulpit entitled him, Taylor searched for unity to end
the seething confusion of North Country religion.

Whether it was he who, hearing of the great work done
across the hills in Yorkshire, summoned George Fox is not now
clear. Taylor was, at the time, no Quaker, but he was open-
minded and he realized that Fox was spreading much the same
truth that Familists and Boehme proclaimed. The glowing
reports of what was happening in Yorkshire promised that
George Fox might offer effective leadership toward that co-
operation for which the scattered sects were pleading.

Fox came with such high hopes that he saw visions. On his
crossing into Lancashire, the Pendle Hill which loomed before
him seemed a great rostrum from which to sound the praises
of the Lord. As a matter of cold statistics, the hill was not so
very lofty—George's travels had already taken him to at least
four taller peaks—but enthusiasm and imagination magnified
its size. Fox climbed with some difficulty, there being no paths
cut, and from the summit glimpsed the Irish Sea in the far
distance. In his excitement and in his anticipation of the great
work to be done he saw, as Gerrard Winstanley had seen some
years before, a white-clad multitude coming toward the Lord.
The host awaited him at Sedbergh.

It is not surprising that he had the vision; he already knew where there were people to be gathered; he also knew that in early June, at Whitsuntide, the town would be thronged with visitors coming to attend the fair. It is, however, odd that with so many well-wishers expecting his arrival he and Farnsworth were forced, en route, to spend one night at an alehouse and another in the open fields.

The hardship was not unusual but it was unexpected; the experience disturbed him. He marched onward, along the river Lune, bidding merchants to be honest and listeners to repent, but all the while he anticipated trouble. On one or two occasions he was obliged to talk people out of locking him up as a madman. A man with whom he refused to have a drink resented his admonition to take heed of sin and evil; Fox suspected that the fellow had a club and knives with which to harm him. A sympathizer offered money, but George waved it away; another gave him a night's lodging, but when his host locked the doors at night Fox conceived the idea that it was not to keep burglars out but to pen George Fox within.

Sedbergh restored his confidence. True, the town was not all he could have desired. Set in a valley surrounded by high open lands, the gray-stone village was attractive, but the people were no white-clad host; much less than a thousand in number, they were divided, so it was said, into at least forty squabbling sects. Moreover, those few hundred inhabitants supported fourteen alehouses. Yet, Fox was assured, for all the disadvantages, the host was ready for the harvest.

He took advantage of the hiring fair at Whitsuntide. A month before his twenty-eighth birthday, he mounted a bench in the central square beneath a giant yew, the square church towers at his back, the market cross before him. He was assured attention not only because of the natural curiosity of the restless crowd that had come into town but also because the local justice, Gervase Benson, Sedbergh's leading citizen, sponsored him.

The sturdy young man in leather breeches and hair falling to his shoulders required no introduction. He captured attention by telling his listeners, the workers seeking jobs, the numerous sect leaders, the lounging soldiers, the itinerant hawkers who followed fairs, the local worthies and all the rest, that each and every one might be himself God's temple.

The Lord, said Fox, was offended by the false teachings of those forty sects. He was at hand to teach them personally. Christ Jesus was come to free the people from their worldly ways and to lead them to salvation.

It was very dangerous teaching, open to easy misconstruction. Careless hearers in a milling crowd, rustics unaccustomed to close reasoning, their perceptions dulled by indulgence at one or another of those fourteen taverns, might readily assume that Fox was claiming to be Christ. In almost any other town, under similar conditions, some thoughtless zealot would have lodged complaint before the nearest magistrate.

Here in Sedbergh Fox was relatively safe. Justice Benson was his friend; only a day or two before he had opened his house for Fox to hold a meeting. Under these circumstances, not a voice was raised against George Fox.

No voice, that is, in protest. An army captain, thrilled by George's message, broke in to ask why Fox was speaking in the village square when close by was the church, the proper place to preach. George seized the opportunity to expound a favorite topic, calling St. Paul to witness that the church was not a man-made building but lived in God the Father and in the Lord Jesus Christ. A small discussion started, but Howgill, who had heard of Fox but who was hearing him for the first time, stilled it by shouting for silence. "This man," he said, "speaks with authority."

Fox continued at his best. He spoke for hours. At one point, a clergyman tried to counteract the spell by telling the people that George was mad, but the people did not heed. Fox won numbers of influential followers.

On the next First Day, these new Friends took him to a great Seekers' meeting at Firbank Chapel, five miles away across the Lune in Westmorland. Here, tucked away among the hills in some of the wildest and most majestic scenery of the county, Howgill and Audland were to speak. These were neither hirelings nor false teachers, but George would not enter the chapel until their service was complete. So, after letting it be known that he would speak in the open that afternoon, he went off by himself to sit, as Christ had sat, upon a rocky hilltop. It was a most appropriate rostrum, a rugged pulpit, a thousand feet above the sea, commanding a magnificent view of hills and fells.

Close to a thousand Seekers struggled over the one rough, hilly path to hear Howgill and Audland preach at Firbank. Their religious fever burned so high that after the long morning service, the Seekers ate picnic lunches in the untilled fields and then, with long distances to be travelled on the journey home, they listened three hours more to what Fox had to say. He spoke so well that all the leaders and most of the rank and file became his followers.

Just as Benson and Howgill had cared for Fox at Sedbergh so, after Firbank, Audland took him home to Crosslands. A day or so later, the pink-cheeked Audland and his bride of but a few weeks introduced George to the Seekers' monthly meeting at Preston Patrick, twenty miles southwest of Sedbergh.

The country here was somewhat better tilled, the lower lands at least, but the higher ground was yet unfenced, yielding little but a small amount of wheat. Few roads existed, only ill-marked tracks along which sturdy ponies carried goods and people, there being no wheeled vehicles. Houses were but few, and those comfortless, where farm folk ate their coarse, monotonous fare—pickled or dried meat, tough and unpalatable.

Yet, down the one good road that led from Kendal in Westmorland to Lancashire or over the rude trail from Yorkshire, hundreds of devoted Seekers came monthly to worship together. This June meeting in 1652 was no exception; the little structure where they met was crowded. Audland and Howgill would have had George sit with them in their preachers' pew, but he declined the honor. He let the leaders go forward, while he sat modestly in a rear bench with twelve-year-old Tommy Camm, son of a Westmorland leader who was so effective that he brought every member of his household into vigorous participation in the Seeker, and later in the Quaker, movement.

Apparently the meeting was unusually tense, the Seekers, having heard so much of Fox's ministry, being keyed up and expectant. For half an hour, all sat silent, waiting for the Lord. Howgill, especially, seemed ill at ease. Several times he opened his Bible and half rose to his feet, only to sink down and close the Book. "A dread and fear was upon him," young Tommy reported. "He durst not begin to preach." Then George Fox arose. He talked with such authority that nearly all the several hundreds present "were effectively reached to the heart and convinced of the truth that very day."

It was, indeed, a momentous meeting, one of the most important in Quaker annals. At this and other successful gatherings in the neighborhood, Fox gained a large and extraordinarily capable group of earnest converts, men and women who, with the Yorkshiremen, heralded other Quaker "convincements," a term commonly used by Fox.

They came from every possible source, these evangelists who would be known as Publishers of Truth. Most of them, of course, were farmers—owners, tenants or laborers, with their wives and families—but a full quarter of them were merchants or professional men. Over half, it was reported, were of good material position, some with superior education and of influential standing. The judgment might be challenged as subjective and the words are quite elastic, but certainly the range of quality was wide. Benson, the mayor and justice of the peace, a colonel and former high lay officer of the official church, topped a social scale balanced by laborers and serving maids. Youngsters such as Tommy Camm and nineteen-year-old Edward Burrough, "Son of Consolation and Thunder," vied with their elders.

Burrough was an especially interesting acquisition. He, too, had been a sober lad, so remarkable for gravity that, as Howgill said, "Gray hairs were upon him when he was but a youth; he was clothed with wisdom from infancy." Determined to become a minister, he, too, had cast about among the sects for truth. Fox, at first, confused him, for Burrough did not grasp the Quaker message; but he understood enough to wish to know much more.

As happened so often to young Quakers, to Howgill and to Fox himself, parental objection met his announcement that he wished to join the Friends. Burrough's parents disowned him; they refused his offer to stay with them as a paid servant.

George Fox's power of convincement showed its strength not only in his wrenching people from their family ties to follow him but also in his ability to imbue them with his own peculiarities. He taught no new beliefs; he but revived the teachings of the Scriptures. He did, however, type them with his special tricks of speech, his personal prejudices and his emphases upon matters that the world deemed frivolous. To others than Quakers, the use of the singular second person pronoun, the denial of what Publishers of the Truth called hat honors or of other ceremonial observances may not rank as matters worth risking jail sentences for, but to George Fox, and consequently to his disciples, they were all-important. That trivia, or quasi-superstition, could be hardened into dogma that must not be altered is astonishing testimony to Fox's personality.

Every loyal Publisher, of whatever degree, patterned himself upon the model of George Fox. Revelation that stressed freedom of conscience, independent interpretation and private illumination developed, through the power of George Fox's character, a group of devotees not merely willing but anxious to be persecuted for what most people thought insignificant details.

The small things were, however, symbols of matters of great magnitude. Quakers stood for principles such as the equality of all men and consequent denial of special honor to anyone but God. If magistrates and others in authority believed that speaking to them familiarly was an insult, were they not guilty of that pettiness for which they punished Quakers?

Fired by Fox's precept and example, the Publishers certainly thought so. They were, all of them, so thoroughly convinced that they were ready, in their own way, to fight for what was right. The list included army officers, justices, clergymen, schoolmasters and yeomen, scholars and adults who could scarcely read nor write. A few backslid or showed themselves unworthy, but many others demonstrated that they possessed the martyr spirit.

Though they represented men and women of all ages and conditions, most of them were young enthusiasts who knew their Bibles well and who were strong enough to stand the rigors of the evangelistic life. They came forward also at a psychologic moment, when religious fever flamed, when spiritual and social unrest was in the air, when British people, most particularly in this northwest corner of the kingdom, were most ready to receive their teachings. Nowhere else in England, a chronicler reports, was the proportion of nonconformists so great as in Lancashire, Westmorland, Cumberland and Yorkshire. In Fox's mind these comprised the white-clad host which he foresaw at Pendle Hill; these were harbingers of Quaker victory.

Not all the people of that thinly settled region were, however, as responsive as the Publishers of Truth. Some were Ranters, amiable folks who offered him tobacco, saying, "Come, all is ours in common." George brushed such shallow people aside, but, for a change, politely. Others seemed hardhearted because they gave no money to travellers in need; in his compassion, Fox ran after the strangers to give them a few coins. For his reward, the uncharitable accused him of witchcraft, for only a winged witch could run as fast as he.

There could not have been, at that time, any accusation more serious. Not many years had passed since witches dwelt in the nearby valleys in startling number. Informers overran the county, creatures who, for trifling rewards, forged utterly incredible evidence upon which so many unfortunates were sent to death. The courts required but little proof; the bare statement of the accuser was sufficient. If, under torture, the accused confessed, he was an acknowledged witch to be hanged at once; if he refused to confess sins he had not committed, he was declared an obstinate offender and was hanged as such. The man or woman against whom the charge was brought had not a shred of hope.

George gave no hint that he realized his luck in evading the notorious Lancashire witch hunters, but his escape was far too narrow for comfort, nor were all dangers yet completely over. After a successful meeting at Cartmel, whose magnificent church across Morecambe Bay was decidedly the most beautiful for miles about, he penetrated upper Lancashire. Here, in a bleak, ill-cultivated region, seldom visited by outsiders, he met Gabriel Camelford, long-time curate of a minor chapel.

Acquaintances regarded Camelford as a godly man but thought him "painful in his calling"—by which they meant that he expected everyone to carry Puritan asceticism to extremes. He would have had no quarrel with George Fox on such a score, but he did object to Quakerism. As the village intellectual, he also was a man of pride, so vain that he had a youth, John Braithwaite, take down every word of his sermons in shorthand. When, therefore, after an especially eloquent address, Fox rose to contradict him and to expound "the word of life," Camelford lost his temper.

Taken aback by the interruption, the eighteen-year-old Braithwaite did not copy down what Fox declared; but, apparently, the witchcraft imputations so disturbed George that he reverted to the irritating denunciations he had voiced at earlier steeple-house gatherings. The sharp criticisms angered Lancashire as they angered Leicestershire and Yorkshire. Camelford's congregations punched Fox and pushed him from the building; in the graveyard the churchwarden, John Knipe, threw him headlong over a stone wall.

George rose unhurt and, learning that many of the congregation had gone to the ale house to eat and drink before the afternoon service began, won over to Quakerism many of Camelford's people, including young Braithwaite. He had the satisfaction, later, of learning that the Lord, incensed at what Knipe had done, punished the churchwarden by cutting him off.

Then George Fox came to Ulverston.

11

Swarthmoor

ULVERSTON, A FREE BOROUGH SINCE 1196, WAS A MARKET town. It lay in Furness, an isolated, hilly peninsula, hemmed in on three sides by the sea and cut off on the north by the waters and mountains of the lovely Lake District. Today the region prospers by its manufacturing, but, when Fox came in late June, 1652, only a few shepherds and small farmers wrested a poor living from the reddish iron- and copper-impregnated soil.

These Furness folk were staunchly individual. For centuries they were restive under the rule of Furness Abbey, a rich and often turbulent establishment; after Henry VIII suppressed the monastery they resented the manor lords set over them. Independent in religion, they opposed the Stuarts and sometimes Cromwell, also. They disliked control by those whom they called "outcomes," officers from any other part of Britain.

Their detachment helped them maintain their free ways. Access was difficult. Early visitors came by sea, as many Scandinavian place names attested, but a rugged coast, perilous because of rocks and shoals and poorly charted, discouraged sailors. Land travel involved crossing Morecambe Bay, a shallow ever changing estuary which, at full tide, was treacherous enough but which at ebb-tide was a wide expanse of quicksand. Before the railway and the modern motor road speeded traffic, communication with the rest of Lancashire was perilous, for fogs were frequent, and strong southwest winds, springing up suddenly, drove in the tides so fast that many travellers were drowned while crossing.

Late in June, Fox crossed the sands to Ulverston. He was about to visit a family named Fell, whose members, nominally Puritan, were deeply interested in Seekerism and who, he was told, welcomed all evangelists. The Fells were prosperous country gentry, who, in Elizabethan times, acquired former abbey lands. Their ancestor, George Fell, settled here early in the century, taking up a stretch of fertile lowlands three miles in length and correspondingly broad. About midway in this estate, a mile south of Ulverston, he built a mansion which he named Swarthmoor but which loose tongues, clipping the last syllable, pronounced Swarthmore.

Swarthmoor, a fine three-story pebble-dashed stone building with mullioned bay windows was in the best tradition of English manor houses. Situated on the edge of the shrub-covered heath from which its name derived, it commanded an impressive view of mountains, woods and water. To the left were barns and stables, to the right, lawns, gardens and a large walled orchard. Within thirty yards a brook flowed quietly.

Early in 1599, George Fell's son Thomas was born. Brought up to the law, a barrister of Gray's Inn, London, he married, when he was thirty-two, a neighbor, eighteen-year-old Margaret Askew of Marsh Grange, just across the Furness Hills. Thomas Fell inherited money, but Margaret brought at least £3,000 more, in an era when purchasing power was eight or ten times as great as today. She was a serious girl, well educated, who, like Mary Fox, may have been of martyr stock. Family tradition insisted, though proof was lacking, that an Askew relative, perhaps her great-grandmother, was burned for heresy. Whether the legend were true, there was no doubt of her religious bent. She was a Seeker who, though attending the 500-year-old St. Mary's Church in Ulverston, was not content with the Puritanism she heard there.

Thomas, her husband, a nominal Puritan, paid more attention to law and to administration than to religion. Under Charles I, he was justice of the peace for Lancaster, but when the Civil War broke out Thomas sided with the Parliament. He went down to London as a legislator, but, having reservations about Oliver Cromwell's increasing assumption of authority, he was so irregular in attending Parliament that he was fined £20 for being absent without cause. Nevertheless, through Cromwell's favor, he was made vice-chancellor of Lancashire and attorney-general both for the county and for northern Wales. Soon afterward, he was promoted to be judge of assizes for the same area.

Judge Fell knew of Fox. Yorkshire acquaintances, among them a parishioner of the clergyman who offered to clean Fox's boots, had spoken so enthusiastically of the evangelist that when the judge repeated the report to Margaret she dreamed of a white-hatted man who would come to confound the priests. George had lost that hat in one of the attacks upon him in Yorkshire, but had not lost his power to confound his adversaries. That the Fells specifically invited Fox to come to Swarthmoor is unlikely, but their hospitality was so well known that when he crossed into Furness he went through the fields and walked up to the mansion.

Unfortunately, neither of the adults was at home. The judge was in Wales on circuit, while Margaret, for some reason, was absent for the day. In their stead, their son, thirteen-year-old George, and six daughters welcomed their visitor. The three oldest daughters, Margaret, aged nineteen, Bridget and Isabel, played hostesses and led him into the Great Hall. It was a pleasant room, bright with its eight recessed windows. cheerful with its panelled walls and with the huge fireplace, which in winter kept it as warm as seventeenth-century rooms could ever be. Two comfortable chairs, set in the bay-window alcove, invited occupants to look out upon the garden and the orchard.

Quite probably, those chairs were filled at the moment by William Caton, a sixteen-year-old companion of young George Fell and by the Reverend William Lampitt, for the past two years the pastor of St. Mary's. They were interesting people. Caton, a Lancashire lad and kinsman both to Margaret Fell and to Lampitt, came originally to Swarthmoor to study under the latter, but was soon sent, with young George, to Hawkshead School, a few miles to the north. Neither was doing too well there, George because he would not study and Caton because, he said, the place was renowned for temptation, folly and wantonness. Ot the time of Fox's visit both boys were on vacation from school and Caton had no wish to return.

Lampitt, the family tutor and, with Judge Fell's approval, the parish pastor, was a frequent Swarthmoor guest. He was a colorful individual whom followers praised as warm and lively, a man of strong convictions and of resolute purpose. But numerous enemies condemned him as an opinionated extrovert who clung to Ranterism. An Oxford graduate with a background of thirty years as minister and governor of an isolated Devon island, he was twice ejected from pulpits during the Civil War before Fell found a place for him at Ulverston.[1]

Much as both men would have resented the comparison, Lampitt and Fox had similar personalities. Each was frank and outspoken, given to exaggeration and not always careful about bruising the feelings of others. Fox, perhaps, was more cocksure and more intolerant and Lampitt more open to compromise; but, at the same time, the pastor was quite as sure as Fox that he alone possessed the truth.

[1] The Fells liked him personally, though Margaret, a distant relative, was at times disturbed by his tendency to gossip freely about his brother clerics. In criticizing them, he alleged that all too many were drunken and licentious; with more vividness than clarity he spoke of one offender as "a Scot who has an adulterous bastard."

The Ulverston pastor greeted Fox cheerfully and, apparently unmoved by the clouds of rumor concerning Fox's witchcraft, blasphemy and treason, would have accepted him. George refused any co-operation. After only a brief conversation, Fox found him "full of filth," not because of Lampitt's slanderings but because he echoed Ranterism. They argued all day long, each man probably thoroughly enjoying their verbal battle. How much of their loud discussion the children understood is problematic. Caton himself, who hungered after wisdom, confessed himself intrigued by George Fox's nonconformity of fashion, customs and salutations, and the others must have been fascinated by them; but the three smallest girls, Sarah, Mary and Susannah, may have been frightened at hearing the two grown men trying to shout each other down. Margaret did not return until after Lampitt had left and was much dismayed at hearing of the quarrel.

George spent the evening expounding the truth.

Next morning the two men resumed debate. Neither was very generous toward his rival. As she listened, Margaret's feelings were divided. Lampitt was a family protégé and friend; she knew nothing of the "dirty actions" which George alleged the minister had committed and of which, incidentally, Fox, as an "outcome" had only hearsay evidence. Though strongly influenced by the man in the white hat of whom she had dreamed, she withheld judgment both on Fox's accusations and on the charges Lampitt made against her guest.

These charges were, in the main, the gist of the indictment drawn by conventional north country clergymen against Quakerism. Convinced though they were that the fittest opponent for a Quaker was "a scold with a stentorian voice," they would not have picked Lampitt, the scandalmonger, as official spokesman to accuse George Fox of "strange, unchristian railing, reviling, censuring and lying." Nevertheless, wholly unintentionally, Lampitt voiced their general abhorrence of

Quakerism. Fervently and lengthily, Lampitt set forth their argument.

Quakers set up their conceits and experiences as equal to the Scriptures; they say that Scripture does not bind them unless their hearts approve it. They follow the light within, denying past interpretation of the Scriptures. They say that interpretation of the Scriptures is wrong when done by others but not when done by themselves. They subvert the nature of Christ. They neglect observance of the Lord's Day and they deny baptism and the Lord's Supper. They plead the necessity of being saved by absolute perfection. They base religion on such trivial things as plain speech and keeping on their hats, but neglect the more important need for communion with God. They hold "ignorant and sottish conceits" about the illegality of using words such as Trinity and Sacrament, which are not used in Scripture.

No record exists whether George interrupted these Lampitt accusations, though certainly he must have done so with heat and forcefulness, nor of what he answered in rebuttal. Margaret was deeply moved in Fox's favor though not entirely convinced. George stayed on at Swarthmoor, doubtless continuing his arguments. A day or two later, she invited him to go with her to service at St. Mary's, but Fox, hearing no call from the Lord, preferred to walk by himself in the fields. Before the service ended, however, while Lampitt and the congregation were singing a hymn, he entered.

Just how the hymn revealed that Lampitt's "spirit and his stuff were foul" is not entirely clear; but George was, as usual, moved to speak. He attacked the churches and their modes of worship so bitterly and at such length that Justice John Sawrey lost his patience and ordered officers to put Fox out of the building. Margaret, however, promptly rushed to his defense.

"Let him alone," she cried. "Others speak. Let him speak also." Lampitt also protested Sawrey's order; he may have been acting from a sense of fair play or from a desire to stand in well with the mistress of Swarthmoor, but Fox had a much simpler explanation—Lampitt's action was deceitful. In any case, George resumed his declarations; he spoke so long that Sawrey once more ordered his ejection, this time, apparently, without protest.

On subsequent Sundays, Fox talked in other Furness steeple-houses. He also retraced his steps to revisit the Sedbergh area again. He was, in large degree, marking time. Though he was winning important converts, his chief interest was apparently in the convincing of Margaret Fell. But she, though moving steadily toward accepting Quakerism, hesitated to accept it openly until she had consulted with her husband.

Lampitt's supporters were not so sure she hesitated. Early in July, when news arrived that Judge Fell was returning home, she sent word to Fox, and he, with Farnsworth and Nayler to help him, was rushing back toward Swarthmoor. The Lampitt group, magistrates and gentry of the neighbor-hood, took horse hastily and galloped off. Intercepting the judge on the offshore sands, they told him excitedly that Margaret and most of the Swarthmoor household had been bewitched by a travelling preacher and that even ten-year-old Sarah was under a spell.

The news, distorted as it was, must have given Thomas Fell a stunning shock, particularly when, on arriving at his home, he found two Quakers, Nayler and Farnsworth, staying there. With great tact, the latter suggested that they leave, but, ever hospitable, the Fells urged them to stay. The judge, however, was worried. Margaret reported that the situation was very tense.

"And then was he pretty moderate and quiet; and his dinner being ready, he went to it; and I went in and sat me down by him. And whilst I was sitting the power of the Lord seized upon me; and he was struck with amazement, and knew not what to think; but was quiet and still. And the children were all quiet and still, and grown sober, and could not play on their music that they were learning; and all these things made him quiet and still."

Margaret herself was very ill at ease. She was by this time thoroughly convinced that Quakerism was right, but she had no idea how Thomas Fell would feel about the matter. She feared that he, a closer friend than she of William Lampitt, would be angry. "Any may think," she said, "what a condition I was like to be in, that either I must displease my husband or offend God."

After the extremely quiet meal was finished and the judge was sitting in his parlor, George Fox came to the outer door. Margaret met him there, and asked him to wait a moment while, in what must have been a rather trying situation, she went to ask her husband if George might enter. Judge Fell, of course, consented; whereupon George Fox strode in, without apologies or greetings, and started in to speak. Margaret said that he spoke well, so well that had all England been present no one could have denied the truth of what he said. Judge Fell listened but made no comment; he went to bed without a word.

Such was Margaret's version of the meeting; Fox had a somewhat different recollection. After identifying himself as the man of whom the judge had heard from his Yorkshire acquaintance, he answered all Fell's questions and objections so completely, and with such Scriptural citation, that the judge was satisfied. Fox said that it was years thereafter before Fell went again to hear the priests. Margaret, however, remembered that he talked long and earnestly next day with Lampitt, but she also said that Lampitt made but slight impression on him.

Lampitt's laymen fared no better. Though they tried with all their zeal to blacken Fox in Judge Fell's eyes, Fell remained the impartial judge. He raised no objection to Margaret's accepting Quakerism nor to the conversion of virtually his entire household staff, but he himself remained aloof. Swarthmoor became a Quaker rendezvous. To accommodate the stream of visitors who came from all parts of the north country to confer with Nayler, Fox and Farnsworth, the judge threw open the large open-beamed attic as a dormitory. Probably the number of Friends sleeping here at any one time never equalled the sixty Roundhead soldiers billeted in the attic during one period of the Civil War, but the transients were always numerous.

Much of the time the judge was absent on official business, but when he was at home his Quaker guests must have caused considerable inconvenience. Food had to be prepared, water brought from the brook, household chores cared for. The confusion caused by housing and feeding so many people, the endless traffic on the single oak staircase and the noise and bustle unavoidable even among the quiet Friends must have seriously interfered with Judge Fell's work. He never, however, voiced complaint.

On First Days, when Fox was not preaching from the balcony outside the judge's second-floor bedroom, the Great Hall was a Quaker meetinghouse. George and Margaret usually occupied the two alcove chairs, but the judge did not attend. He sat, always with the door open, in his adjoining study. Quakers thought that this practice implied at least a partial acceptance of their preaching, but Fell's action may have been, at least in part, a monitoring device. Fox's enemies were accusing George of various illegal words and deeds, charges which Fell, because of his unseen presence, would be able to dismiss as false. Judge Thomas Fell was never an enrolled Friend, but he was, at least, a most benevolent neutral.

12

Riot and Retribution

ALTHOUGH EVERYTHING WAS GOING SO WELL, CONSTANT opposition, ineffective as it was, goaded George again into spraying his foes with acid words. Again, the consequences were unpleasant. Furness folk were no different from those of Yorkshire or the Midlands; while they themselves were prone to criticize their neighbors, they resented Fox's calling their ministers foul, their magistrates rotten hearted, their gentry wicked hypocrites. Above all, they objected to what they considered his inference that non-Quakers were dogs and swine of briery, thistly, thorny nature.

The sweeping condemnations united Fox's foes. Most of the Furness clergy disliked each other's theology and they protested Lampitt's gossiping tongue, but they joined the Ulverston minister in combatting Fox. Apparently not realizing how grievously his vituperation wounded listeners, Fox lumped all priests who would not own the Inner Light as false prophets, belly worshippers and anti-Christs. On hearing that some of them looked on Quakerism as a passing fad that would die down within a month, he suspected plots to murder him.

On Quaker evidence alone, it seems that even those opposed to Fox made honest efforts to meet the difficult situation. Lampitt invited him to St. Mary's and Sawrey arranged to have him speak; but Fox said something that led Sawrey to think he intended to loose a verbal blast against the minister, and so the invitation was withdrawn. At one or two meetings, moreover, fair-minded listeners, some of them converts, came to Fox's aid when trouble loomed. A few preachers, such as Thomas Taylor, the Yorkshire patron of Audland and Howgill, may not have approved George's assumption that he alone had heard the voice of God, but they accepted his general principles. Fox was especially delighted that Taylor, that "ancient priest," who actually was only seven years his elder, became a close associate.

The laity were far less pleasant. Hypocritical Sawrey, the rotten, deceitful, envious magistrate, seeing Fox manhandled by an angered mob, intervened to save him, but did so by ordering him whipped out of town. Four officers spared the whip but pushed and pulled George through mire and water, knocking down all bystanders who were in their way. When thirteen-year-old George Fell ran up to see what was happening, they tossed him into a ditch and threatened to knock out his teeth. Eventually the officers did as Sawrey had bid, whipping Fox with willow sticks; but when they reached the swamp at Ulverston town limits the constables turned back and then a mob beat George unconscious. Recovering his senses, George stood up, stretched out his arms and cried, "Strike again." A mason did so, hitting Fox so hard with a metal rod that, for a few minutes, George thought his arm was paralyzed. But he recovered and began again to preach.

The mob refused to listen. Angered anew because Fox called them heathens, they shouted that if ever he returned to Ulverston they would murder him. They did not know George Fox. He would not take a dare. Promptly, he turned about, strode straight through the mob and went to the market place, not a single person daring to touch him. Instead, a soldier approached.

"Sir," the soldier said, "you are a man. I am ashamed to see you treated like this." He drew his sword and faced the mob. Fox, disapproving of violence even for his own protection, left the market place and withdrew from Ulverston. The soldier's reward, he later learned, was that seven men fell upon him and beat him up. It was the custom in Furness, said Fox, for twenty or forty people to attack one man.

Fox's body turned yellow, black and blue from the blows and bruises.

He was scarcely recovered before he met new dangers. Late in October, 1652, he and Nayler went down from Swarthmoor toward Walney island. At the tip of Furness, a man who had sworn to kill Fox snapped a pistol at him; luckily it misfired. He made a new friend, James Lancaster, whose wife was so convinced that Fox had bewitched her husband that she collected a forty-man gang, "rude fellows, fishermen and the like," who also vowed to murder George. They lay in ambush until Fox arrived to call on his new convert, then clubbed him into unconsciousness and tried to drown him. Lancaster rescued him and, to protect him from the mob and from the stones that Mrs. Lancaster was hurling, threw his body over Fox's shoulders.

Suddenly the mob noticed that Naylor was escaping; they ran after him shouting, "Kill him." Lancaster rushed back to help Nayler and the scene of battle shifted from Fox, but only temporarily. A new crowd appeared before him, armed with sticks and pitchforks, crying, "Kill him! Hit him in the head! Take him to the grave-yard." For some reason, however, they failed to carry out their threats, contenting themselves with escorting Fox beyond the town limits. Fox walked three miles to a friend's house, had a man go with a spare horse to fetch James Nayler, and went to bed so sore that he could not move a muscle. Next day Margaret sent a horse to bring him to

Swarthmoor, but, as Fox was riding back, the horse stumbled, paining him worse than all the blows he had received.

On hearing of these persecutions, Judge Fell urged George to lodge charges against the members of the mob, but Fox refused. Fell commended George for his forgiving spirit, but, in November, 1652, he issued a warrant on his own initiative. Nothing apparently came of it, since the rioters were not readily identified, but Fox was certain that many persecutors fled from Furness and that others had destruction come upon them.

All these troubles should have been sufficient, but they were not. Fox crossed the treacherous sands again to hold another meeting. A priest approached, cupping something in his hands as though he were lighting a pipe. A maid saw that he was holding a pistol, and she told her master, who barred the way. So the Lord prevented the bloody design.

Sawrey then embarrassed Judge Fell by threatening to swear out a warrant against George Fox for blasphemy. Had he done so, the case would have been tried before a three-man court over which Judge Fell customarily presided but from which judicial ethics would have required him to withdraw if his guest were to be tried. Sawrey, however, delayed so long in carrying out his threat that Fell was in some doubt whether to go to court or not. He told Fox of his dilemma.

Fox, as usual, had not the faintest doubt concerning what to do. He insisted on appearing before the court even though he was not yet arrested nor, for that matter, informed officially of any charges against him. George invited himself to ride with Fell to Lancaster and argued with the judge throughout the journey.

At Lancaster, he found that, though Sawrey had failed to swear out a warrant, several schoolmasters and priests had already alleged eight counts of blasphemy against Fox's teachings. Fox, they said, affirmed himself essentially divine. He claimed equality with God, said that he was as upright as

Christ and that he, George Fox, was judge of all the world. Nor was this all; the prosecutors alleged that Fox declared that God taught deceitfulness. George moreover, they declared, dissuaded people from reading the Scriptures, said that the Bible was anti-Christian, and that both baptism and the Lord's Supper were illegal.

The hearing was chaotic. Forty priests all insisted that Fox was guilty, but nearly all their evidence was hearsay and none of it was true; they flatly contradicted each other. Fox had no difficulty in pointing out that they quoted his statements inexactly and that they misunderstood his meaning. The proceedings ended in triumph. Fox was not only cleared but was invited to deliver a sermon before the court.

It was a glorious day. Fox celebrated by ending the fast he had kept throughout the trial.

The forty priests, however, met more reverses. Raging because at least one of the judges rebuked them for trying to jail George when they could not kill him, they rushed out of court. Fox implied, though he did not specifically assert, that they incited a lunatic to attack him and ruffians to toss him over a bridge and to thrash him. None of the plot succeeded.

Their luck was poor. After drafting an appeal they failed to raise enough money to present the petition to Parliament. They induced a friendly judge to issue a new warrant only to have Colonel William West, the clerk of assizes, refuse to write it. When the judge insisted, West coolly told him, "Do it yourself." Rather than have Fox penalized, West said, he would forfeit his own estate and go to jail in George's stead. The clerk's defiance, and still more his offer of personal sacrifice, so took the judge aback that he dropped the whole idea.

His action may have been wise. To cross George Fox was becoming most unsafe. The churchwarden who had hurled him over the wall at Gabriel Camelford's steeple-house had been cut off. One of his judges in this very blasphemy case dropped dead upon the bench. Sawrey drowned. True, no ill had come as yet to foul-mouthed Lampitt or to Nathaniel Stephens, but retribution, though it might be slow, was very certain. George Fox had every confidence that they would get their proper due.

He needed confidence. All around him he was sensing swords and pistols lurking close. He went to a meeting and left in peace, but no sooner had he gone than a gang of masked men rushed in. Failing to find Fox they slashed about with swords and put out all the candles. They were Frenchmen, servants, the type of people who tied men to trees and whipped them to death. There was a servant, at another time, who threatened Fox by poking a naked sword through the window; what he would have done no one knows for a fellow—no Friend—knocked him over with a cudgel. A priest came with some followers, intending to disturb a meeting, but suddenly he ran away, crying that the Devil frightened him. That, said Fox, was a lie, but it provided material for the priest to write a book about.

It also piled up fuel for Fox's enemies. These were more numerous than were his friends, for while his charity and charm and sweetness were winning converts singly, his sweeping condemnations were enraging scores. At Ulverston he had captured all the Swarthmoor household, except the judge himself; but then Fox wrote a letter to Lampitt's parishioners branding the parish as a nest of liars, drunkards, whoremongers, thieves and followers of filthy pleasures. Assuredly he did not mean that everyone fell into one or another of those categories, but parish resentment was predictable.

The more scathing his attacks, the worse were the counter-charges. Instead of soothing angers, Fox fanned the flames. The more he travelled, the more he talked, the more he wrote epistles, the worse were the rumors raised against him. He was a master of witchcraft, his enemies alleged, whom water would not drown and who, like every witch, did not bleed when hurt. These were silly statements, but Fox himself encouraged them. As early as his return from London, years before, he announced that physicians could not draw a single drop of blood from him, "my body being, as it were, dried up with sorrows, grief and troubles." Beaten though he was by clubs and stones, he bled but little. Fox explained the phenomenon as due to divine protection, but all knowledgeable people of his day were certain it proved witchcraft.

Only witchcraft, moreover, explained his amazing luck in avoiding snares set for him. Time and time again, pursuers came too late to find him, looked in wrong places, picketed wrong roads or failed to recognize him when he passed. George understood the special favors showered on him in such matters, but those who would not admit his close communion with the Lord saw nothing but the Devil's aid. The more Fox boasted of escapes the more they feared his witchcraft. What else but witchcraft were these retributions of which Fox was making public advertisement? And had he not proclaimed the visions which he saw from Pendle Hill? From Pendle Hill, which everyone in Lancashire knew was the most notorious haunt of witches!

A hostile tide was setting in. Only a handful of seventeenth-century Englishmen doubted the existence of witches. George himself did not stand in awe of them, but he did not question that they had the evil eye; he prided himself on his ability to discern a witch at sight. Unhappily, others claimed similar powers, and they saw the telltale signs in Fox.

Unfortunately, he played into their hands by proving, to their satisfaction at least, the suspicions that they held against him. His powerful sermons induced hysterical excitement among his more susceptible listeners, producing tremblings so powerful, said Fox, that whole buildings seemed to shake. Quakers knew this phenomenon to be the workings of the power of the Lord but non-Quakers had other explanation. They, too, believed, as Christopher Marshall alleged in Yorkshire, that George carried magic potions to bewitch the innocent. When these were drunk the poor unfortunates became Quaker puppets; their trembling was dancing to the Devil's piping.

No longer was Fox announcing "openings" or seeing the shining heavens gleam. Instead he was proclaiming his ability to discern conditions and of being moved to word or deed. Loyal followers were well aware that he was possessed by the spirit of the Lord, but skeptics frowned on such ideas. George Fox must be possessed, they agreed, but by the Devil; did he not dream of dogs and boars and were not these animals familiars of the Prince of Darkness?

Then, too, he was asserting that, through the everlasting power of the Lord, he was witnessing strange happenings which might indeed be miracles. Richard Myers, a convert, had an injured arm. Fox looked at him and ordered him, Prophet Myers, to stand up. At once the arm was cured. Spectators were astonished. Not even Myers' parents would believe their eyes until their son stripped off his doublet to show an arm completely healed.

The "cure," one of about 170 attributed to George Fox, differed from his soothing of the distracted. Some forms of mental disturbance responded to psychotherapy; though Fox did not know the name, he anticipated its methods, calming some patients by suggestion or persuasion, by the authority of his powerful personality or by awakening interests more absorbing than any others that had engrossed them. Though he enjoyed no formal training, he evidently knew at least a smattering of folk medicine. After his vision following Prophet Brown's death, he claimed to know the properties of all things in creation, which certainly implied an elementary knowledge of the curative value of plants and herbs, and to this knowledge. Thomas Lawson, a recent recruit, a former priest and a well-known botanist, almost certainly contributed.[1]

Lack of full data marred an understanding of George Fox's 170 "cures." Occasionally he gave names and dates and places, and sometimes he set down the symptoms that he saw; but, as his critics complained, the story usually was vague and uncorroborated; in forty-five cases the patient was "sick" and in almost all the others they were weak, unwell or dying.

Want of scientific evidence did not deter followers, who saw many parallels between the life of George Fox and that of Jesus Christ. Receipt of visions, private inner revelations, a universal understanding, together with such parallels as wandering in the wilderness, preaching from high places, gathering of disciples, teaching in the temples and steeple-houses, attacks upon the Pharisees and now the inexplicable cures, convinced many loyal followers that miracles were no more than was to be expected.

George Fox, to be sure, laid no claim to working miracles, nor did his closest associates; but neither did the Lord Jesus Christ. Such cures as Fox accomplished were accomplished, he insisted, only through the power of the Lord.

For at least a century, Seekers and other nonconformists had been awaiting miracles; they would be a sign that a new Messiah was at hand. Such incidents, and others, which Fox said were "too large to utter," played important parts in bringing Seekers into Quakerism. Thoughtful listeners would have noticed that in telling of these events Fox made no claim to supernatural power; but neither those who craved miracles nor

[1] The Myers case may well have been a faith cure, rising out of an expectant mental state, and a firm confidence that Fox could call upon the power of the Lord to cure. Such phenomena are not uncommon, especially among those emotionally conditioned to expect them. Unfortunately for scientific judgment, no further evidence remains to indicate whether the recovery was complete or but a brief flash, followed by a permanent relapse.

those who scented witchcraft analyzed coolly and without prejudice just what it was that Fox said. Just as the forty priests distorted what Fox preached about the Inner Light so the witch hunters and the snuffers-out of blasphemy believed that Fox was claiming to be Christ.

Again, unwittingly, Fox helped them. He predicted that within two weeks Cromwell would dissolve the Parliament, and Cromwell fulfilled the prophesy. The accuracy of the forecast might have been divine inspiration or shrewd interpretation of the information contained in the news books that came to Swarthmoor; but ill wishers preferred to think it divination, soothsaying or some other traffic with the Devil.

Treatment of two defecting Quakers did not ease the situation. James Milner, a tailor so devoted that he referred to Fox as Zebedee, the father of St. James, wandered from the paths Fox charted. Suffering from the shock of a two weeks' fast, Milner set a specific, and very imminent, date for the Day of Judgment. Fox, on hearing the prediction, at once denounced it as completely false. Milner, he said, had, out of pride, gone out into imaginations; the tailor had committed folly. The rebuke was, of course, of no concern to anti-Quakers, but they pointed to it as a proof that George Fox had become "the pope of northern England."

Fox coupled the case, probably anachronistically, with that of Richard Myers, the man whose arm was healed. The Lord moved Fox to send Myers as a messenger to York, but Myers refused to go. The refusal was fatal. For the disobedience, the Lord struck him anew. Within nine months, Myers was dead.[2] No one could possibly allege witchcraft in the Milner case, whatever they might think of Fox's explanation of it, but how else might one explain Myer's sudden death?

[2] The mutiny must have been, however, at a much later time, for Myers, after having been fined for refusing to pay tithes, served two and a half years in Lancaster Castle before he died.

13

Strange Judgment

TROUBLES WERE MOUNTING IN THE NORTH COUNTRY. INDIGnant at Judge Fell's toleration of Quaker evils that could lead only to disaster, a group of ministers and laymen petitioned the Council of State in London to intervene. Unless something were done at once, they warned, there might be revolution.

Fox and Nayler, they alleged, were dangerous, both men being disaffected to religion and hostile to the wholesome laws of the land. Quakers were inciting wives to disobey their husbands, children their parents, servants their masters, congregations their ministers, and people their God. They implied that Quakers were possessed by evil spirits. How else might one explain the foamings at the mouth, the roaring, the swellings of the bellies, the strange actions one saw at Quaker meetings? Some Quakers, (neither Fox nor Nayler was specifically named) affirmed themselves equal to God! Finally, as though these accusations were not enough, the complaint alleged "many other dangerous and damnable heresies." Please, the petitioners implored, do something quickly to stop all this.

Fox replied by a pamphlet, "Saul's Errand to Damascus." He admitted holding meetings where quiet, honest, peaceful, pious men glorified God. These were needed, he declared, because the regular churches—Fox called them parochial assemblies—have no proper Christian teaching. His accusers, men puffed up by luxury and pride, broke in with swords and pistols, but, Fox asked the Council to notice, none of those accusers had ever swung a sword to help the Commonwealth. For once in his life, he ventured a little flattery. How could anyone dare, as these accusers dared, to annoy the Council of State with imaginations and lies while it was so busy managing mighty and glorious improvements for the infant Commonwealth? He was certain that so wise a body would never permit "that monster, prejudice" again to enter the precincts of Whitehall. Secure in the conviction that each side was loyal and that each eyed the other to detect subversion, the Council did nothing.

Meanwhile, farther north in Cumberland, the forces of darkness were persecuting Nayler and Howgill. Following his mauling at the tip of Furness, Nayler continued to predict woes for the wicked. To shut him up, his enemies threatened to push him off a bridge and to beat out his brains. They did neither, but they did stone him out of town. They also swore out a warrant for his arrest, but Judge Fell and Justice Gervase Benson dismissed it as illegal.

Failing a regular trial, Nayler's opponents haled him before an open-air kangaroo court. After knocking off his hat with a pitchfork and vainly trying to trap him into blasphemy, a justice of the peace clapped him into prison as a vagabond. No one, the justice said, knew who this fellow was. Nayler indignantly protested.

"You know me," he cried. "I was with you in the army for eight years."

"That makes no difference," the justice replied. "This isn't the army."

At about the same time the authorities picked up Howgill, who, like Fox, had been calling hireling priests anti-Christs and liars. Such epithets, the arresting officers declared, were criminal. Since ministers received state maintenance, to call them anti-Christs was more than slander—it was close to treason.

After twenty months' imprisonment, Nayler and Howgill came up for trial, not for vagabondage nor for slander but for blasphemy. No one thought Justice Anthony Pearson impartial for he admitted looking on Quakerism as the product of giddy minds and he thought James Nayler, at least, a dangerous fanatic. Nevertheless, whether because of Judge Fell's interest or because Margaret Fell had sent Nayler £2 for expenses— Nayler kept only five shillings—both men were cleared of blasphemy charges.

On hearing of the acquittals, Fox saw the sparks of life arise in Cumberland and so rode northward. As usual, he challenged priests in their steeple-houses and, as usual, met rough treatment. A heavy blow almost broke his hand to pieces, yet "I felt no harm." A knife slashed his coat, a little boy came toward him with a sword, and there were witches all about.

Cumberland, obviously, tried hard to be peaceful. A youthful minister asked George mildly, "Sir, why do you judge so? You must not judge." But Fox rebuked him for a false prophet and a covetous hireling, so the fellow slunk away. Later he returned, to tell Fox that if George wished to preach he, the minister, would not interfere by word or thought; Fox answered that the minister, being foolish, irrational and hypocritical, might do exactly as he pleased. Another clergyman, surely an optimist, undertook to outtalk Fox; George accepted the challenge, tired the man out and weaned away his congregation. At a fishing village, the great men of the town, anxious to avoid argument, confessed that they had no learned men to argue with him; but George, undeterred, preached anyway, declaring "largely the way of salvation."

After a series of three-hour sermons and the discovery of witches and harlots, George came to Carlisle. His fame preceded him. In no mood to welcome him, the magistrates warned that he would be arrested and their ladies promised to pull out his long hair. Nevertheless, Fox came and, standing on top of the market cross, condemned the town's deceitful ways. So many people crowded around that neither the officers nor their ladies could get near him. On First Day, when he went to the steeple-house, the magistrates again warned him not to speak, but George paid no heed. There might have been a riot but soldiers protected him. Taking him by the hand, they led him through the streets under a hail of stones, until the governor arrived to calm the mob.

The governor's protecting arm did not, however, ward off the arrest against which George Fox had been twice warned. Two magistrates, one of them, ironically, the same turncoat who ejected Lampitt from his pre-Ulverston pulpit, brought Fox up for an examination.

Though his report of the hearing was somewhat vague, merely that many rude people swore strange things against him—"one sware one thing and one sware another thing"— George, in reality, convicted himself. He was, he professed, the son of God; he himself had looked upon God's face. As not even the Apostles upon earth had ever seen God's face the magistrates, not being psychiatrists and having no skill in the interpretation of poetic symbols, could only conclude that Fox was claiming to be Christ. Probably most contemporary Englishmen would have agreed with them. Few, if any, outside the Fox coterie—his cubs, as a later justice of the peace described them— would have cleared George Fox.[1]

---

[1] Fox invariably insisted that rude and wicked enemies persecuted him. Actually, he was lucky in his prosecutors. Thus far, at least, nearly all of them, whether through stupidity or charity, failed to press their accusations thoroughly; almost always they charged him with relatively

After a long hearing, the magistrates sent him to prison "as a blasphemer, a heretic and a seducer," although, George protested, "they could not justly charge any such thing against me."

Carlisle was not as pleasant a prison as Derby. The warden offered Fox any comfort he desired, but at a price. George sat up all night, hungry, rather than pay a penny for his dinner or a bed. The warden allowed Friends to bring in food, but he set three musketeers on guard lest Fox escape. In the morning, as though he were a wild animal exhibitor, he let in the county gentry, great ladies and countesses, to see the man who was to die; in the evening he admitted droves of rude, devilish priests to disturb the prisoner. Other visitors, however, he refused, barring such dignitaries as Justice Gervase Benson and Anthony Pearson, the prejudiced justice who committed Nayler.

As a judicial officer, Pearson was particularly indignant at being denied admision. In protesting, he cited other violations of the law. Fox, he pointed out, was unfairly tried, was not fully informed of the charges against him, was not faced by his accusers and received no chance to defend himself. Moreover, the hearing was before city magistrates, without competency in blasphemy cases, and not before the proper court.

Pearson's complaints were absolutely correct, but the judges, instead of taking action, left town. The warden, despairing of

minor offenses; his judges imposed lighter sentences than could have been inflicted. Had the tormenters been clever, had they collected evidence from other parts of Britain, had they badgered George by intense cross-examination, they could certainly have proved him guilty of asserting divinity, of challenging orthodox belief concerning the revealed Word, of opposing the national religion, of scurrility toward priests—in short, of false doctrine, heresy and schism. What could not a vindictive prosecutor have done with Fox's warnings "not to dispute with God but to obey him"? After all, the old law *de hæretico comburenda,* the burning of heretics, was still upon the statute books.

getting any money out of Fox, threw him into a dungeon, amid a miscellaneous batch of bandits, men and women. The place was so filthy that, Fox reported, one woman was almost bitten to death by lice. Dorothy Benson, wife of the justice, came regularly with food, which she passed through the dungeon bars, but when other visitors came the warden beat them off with clubs.

After George spent seven weeks in jail, the governor appeared, at Pearson's insistence and, after seeing the conditions, set Fox free. What was more, he threw the jailer into the dungeon which Fox left. This was retribution, but not the only instance. The Lord cut off two of the magistrates who committed Fox and drove the third out of town.

The release came just in time to ward off a Parliamentary investigation. The idea of appealing to London, first voiced by the forty priests at Lancaster and taken up by other northerners, was being adopted by Fox's followers. Gervase Benson, Margaret Fell and William West, among others, complained to Parliament about the illegality of the imprisonment; Pearson, too, was calling for redress. The legislators, then in session as the ultrareformist Barebones Parliament, had not a shred of sympathy for Quakerism but were concerned for justice. They started an inquiry, but, before anything could be accomplished, Fox had been released and, what is more, its sessions ended.

Strengthened, rather than weakened, by the Carlisle difficulties, Quakerism bounded forward in the northern counties. Seekers, now convinced that George Fox was the man they awaited, joined in large numbers. Despite hostile crowds that in some localities kept Quaker leaders out of town by pitchforks, Fox and his Friends preached often and effectively. They proclaimed the truth from hilltops with such success, as Fox declared, "The plants of God grew and flourished by Heavenly rain and God's glory shined."

The priests protested, but they dared not face him in debate. They ceased now to predict that Quakerism would die out within a month; instead they prophesied that because the evangelists were being housed and fed by sympathizers the Friends would soon eat each other out of house and home. Actually, Fox reported, the Lord blessed Friends and furthered their prosperity. Quaker merchants, once boycotted by the general public, were being patronized because all knew that they were honest and that their wares were good.

"If we let these people alone," their competitors were saying, "they will take the trading of the nation out of our hands."

Everything was going well, perhaps going much too smoothly. Fox witnessed cures galore, spiritual healings such as that of Richard Myers. The Lord frustrated plots. A Welsh mystic sent a lieutenant to see if the Quakers could be annexed, only to have the emissary join George Fox.

Unfortunately, less stable souls also joined, among them certain half-cracked enthusiasts who, after being swept into Quakerism by hysterical impulse, backslid when they found they had to live in purity and poverty.

One such was John Gilpin, who, at the time of his convincement, howled and cried and trembled all night long, precisely as the witch hunters charged that Quakers always did. But this was not all; Gilpin had hallucinations. Two swallows flew down his chimney; he knew them to be angels. A dove penetrated his body. By no volition of his own, he ran down the street, entered a fiddler's house, seized a bass viol and began to play and sing. Never having done anything of the sort before, he wondered why he acted thus, but an inner voice told him, "This is not because I love music, for I hate it, but it is to show the joy in heaven at thy conversion." He ran home, shouting as he went, "I am the resurrection and the life," but he stayed in the house only long enough to strip off his clothes. He went back into the street, clad only in a nightshirt, caught a butterfly and swallowed it.

All this he published in a book, whose truth was attested by the schoolmaster, the mayor and the vicar, among others. It received wide publicity, especially as Gilpin pleaded that the Quakers had deluded him and that, on recantation, he saw them in their proper light as witches.

For their part, the Quakers branded the whole story as lies and nonsense. In their opinion, Gilpin was a fellow given to riotous excess, a drunkard, a brawler, a gambler and one unworthy to receive the Gospel.

Though Gilpin's ravings were accepted by some who disliked Quakerism, other critics had less success. Rhys Jones, for instance, the shuffleboard player who had slandered Fox in Derby jail, reappeared, this time to prophesy that Quakerism had reached its peak and now was certain to collapse; but it was Jones and his crew who fell to pieces.

"Many such false prophets have risen against me," said Fox, "but the Lord has blasted them and will blast all who rise against the blessed Seed and me in it."

As, for instance, the butchers who swore to kill George Fox. One of them had already killed a man and a woman; but, while getting ready to kill George, he committed another murder and was sent to jail for it. An accomplice volunteered to kill Fox in his stead. This was a fellow who used to stick out his tongue at Friends as they passed by, but suddenly his tongue swelled so large he could not get it back into his mouth, and so he died.

"Several strange and sudden judgments came upon many

of these conspirators against me which would be too large to declare."

Friends were not always fortunate. During 1654, except for the eloquent and patient Farnsworth, every important Quaker leader went to jail. Usually the charge was speaking to a priest, vagabondage or showing disrespect by keeping on a hat; but Aldam and one or two others were imprisoned for nothing more than returning to the jail after their release to visit cell mates. These, being the causes cited by the Friends, may have been partisan and softened versions of the actual charges, for Quakers did not elaborate on what had been said in speaking to the priests or what was done while visiting the jail. Doubtless, their persecutors were cruel and vindictive; but neither can there be doubt that Quakers could be extremely provocative; what they said and did was often less objectionable than was their attitude or their behavior.

Certainly William Simpson's actions were not to be condoned. One of the Fell neighbors, he felt called upon to demonstrate that hireling priests and corrupt officials must be stripped of power. To symbolize this stripping, he took off all his clothes and ran stark naked through the war-ravaged streets of Skipton. The magistrates, for some reason, spared him—they may have read the symbol aright—and so did the authorities at Leeds when he repeated the symbolic offense. Spectators were less lenient; in Skipton they slashed Simpson, beat him and then trampled on him, while at Leeds, although they let him escape, they pummeled the man who carried his clothes.

Persecution, public and private, mounted in intensity; but, surprisingly, the higher the official the greater the clemency extended. Top magistrates and justices were often understanding and, at times, were sympathetic, but local law enforcers, whether through ignorance or in fear of being thought traitorous to either church or state, insisted on the letter of the law. Even the lowest in rank, however, were, as a rule, more generous than Quakers were willing to admit. Flagrant flouting of the rules requiring church attendance, tithes and decorous behavior must necessarily result in court proceedings against offenders, but even when offense was evident accused Friends were frequently acquitted.

Quakers were jailed, to be sure, and often for lengthy periods while awaiting trial; but their hardships and the indignities heaped upon them sprang less from the wickedness of jailers than from primitive seventeenth-century penology. Exoneration did not necessarily mean that prisoners went free, for wardens had the legal right to detain them until they paid for their board and keep. As Quakers, in all innocence, maintained that they owed nothing, this detention might be indefinite. James Lancaster, for one, languished in prison until his jailer died.

14

Margaret Fell

ONLY BY REMEMBERING GEORGE FOX'S FIRM CONVICTION THAT the Lord dictated his every act is it possible to understand how he managed what, by New Year's, 1655, had become a thriving movement.

Quakerism had won much of northern England. Between the Scottish border and Nottingham and Derby at least a hundred groups were meeting regularly. Not all these circles were of considerable size, some were of tenuous allegiance and few had regular meeting houses; but strong, populous centers at Mansfield and Skegby, at Balby, Preston Patrick and Swarthmoor balanced the weaker bands.

While Fox stressed the individual rather than the circle to which he belonged, some sort of general direction was essential. He frowned on hierarchies and, even more, on ministers who preached for hire; yet, if each Quaker were not to go his independent way, leaders were essential and those leaders must be fed and clothed and housed. Evangelism was imperative, for the Word must be carried to every nook and corner, but the sixty or seventy earnest missionaries anxious to take the field must not, if conflict and duplication were to be avoided, roam wherever fancy lured them. The Inner Light might shine in all, but there were times when, as Gilpin's error showed, the Devil lit false beacons; Quakerism could have no dogma and no creed, but somehow truth must be kept clear of error.

Such tasks required a steady guiding hand. Surprisingly, to those who did not know how, as a stripling, Fox managed George Gee's business, George Fox supplied the need. Though in ten or a dozen years of evangelism he displayed more mysticism, more emotionalism and more impracticality than firm, constructive ability, he now revealed latent executive skills.

True, he built upon a firm foundation. The Preston Patrick Seekers held well-run monthly meetings. Farnsworth and Dewsbury organized orderly and efficient religious groups. Certain separatist sects, affiliated in the north, provided models which George Fox improved

But organizational machinery, while of utmost importance, was not the only need. Inspiration was essential, and this Fox radiated. But, unless the movement was to fly into a thousand pieces, both inspiration and revelation must be carefully examined to protect it from error. To guarantee a harmony of doctrine and practice, Fox asked, in 1652, that all Quaker writings be funnelled through him prior to publication. Had anyone else assumed the task, a way might have been opened to censorship; but everyone trusted Fox.

For, though a blunt manner and an edged tongue misled many into thinking Fox conceited and imperious, Friends knew him as inwardly a modest man. Apparently an unbearable egotist when echoing what the Lord commanded him to say, he invariably minimized all personal contributions. Though, in roving from town to town, he seemed rudderless and without a chart, he mapped his moves well in advance.

Now that Quakerism was taking root, he ceased the earlier, more spectacular practices. By the middle of the 1650 decade, he was no longer wandering disconsolately in the woods and fields, he was having fewer openings, no visions and virtually no doubts or temptations. He was not fasting as much nor sleeping in haystacks; he was slackening his invasions of the steeple-houses and was less virulent in attacking priests. He had seen his last witch; fewer things struck his life. His calming saved him from the roughings-up and beatings which had been his lot. None of this meant that George Fox was modifying his convictions—he was as adamant as ever against false teachings and forced tithing, for examples—but he was increasingly directing the activities of others.

To do this was perhaps an error. Quakerism needed skilled administration, but even more it needed enterprise, initiative and ideas. Fox's management was skilful, for he showed the same acumen he had used in George Gee's interest, but administrative work limited his range of action, weakened his effectiveness and drained even his almost limitless energy. Others less well endowed could do these routine chores as well. Fox should be free for more important duties.

Margaret Fell was among the first to recognize that Fox, the gadfly, was in danger of becoming office-bound, as Fox the business manager. With all those children to be cared for, she herself was tied to Swarthmoor and the Ulverston area, but in such sparse moments as she possessed she could lift a burden from his shoulders.

Her voluntary activity brought a change in Fox's outward personality. Those who had judged him an irresponsible and sensational herald of gloom saw, to their astonishment, that he had become a thoughtful and dynamic leader. Inwardly, of course, there was no change whatever but merely a revealing of another facet of Fox's many-sided character.

Fox had already written numerous epistles to various meetings and to individuals, mostly expository or hortatory letters;

he now increased the number and used them to express general principles applicable to all areas. As early as his boyhood arguments with Stephens, George denied any Scriptural authority for either marriage or burial by priests; he questioned the theory of infant baptism. During those Stephens' debates, he was content with destroying the practices. But now that Quakerism thrived, he saw a practical, if not a sacramental, need for them. Without some such official record, how might the Friends record who was, or who could be considered, a birthright member? He proposed that every meeting maintain a register.

Fox had no necessity to initiate leadership; the papacy of the north inevitably devolved upon him. Other leaders were winning converts and some of them were men and women of great sweetness, but none commanded George Fox's tremendous influence. Incredible as it seems to those knowing only his scathing denunciation of hypocrites and plunderers, George exuded a charm that fascinated his followers. Just as the conscripts in the Derby jail had clamored that they would have no other as their captain, so the Friends accepted no other as their leader.

Their admiration was unbounded. Men and women alike wrote to him as though to a beloved. Audland called him "thou fairest of the sons of men" and Burrough addressed him as "my dearest and eternal brother with whom and in whom my life dwells." Margaret Fell, her two eldest daughters and four others of the Swarthmoor household wrote a letter to "our dear father in the Lord," crying out, "our souls doth thirst and languish after thee." To them, George Fox was "thou bread of life, without which bread our souls will starve."

George accepted the adulation not as a tribute to himself but to the spirit of the Lord that lay within him. For all his modesty, however, some of the fulsome praise was accepted.

Fox noted approvingly that at one town old people and work-men looked at him and said, "He is such a man as never was; he knows people's thoughts," and that another women, coming from a glorious Quaker meeting, commented enthusiastically, "This man is a pearl."

Fox would have been more than human had he remained unmoved by floods of flattery showered on him by sincere and dedicated followers. At no time whatever did he think himself divine nor confuse his mortal mind and voice with those of the supernatural beings who spoke through him, but sometimes critics suspected him of doing so. Never a master of the English language, too prone to give forth as the Lord's word his own ideas, convinced that, because he acted by divine command, his sayings were beyond criticism, he laid himself wide open to misinterpretation. A pure soul, inspired from on high, he seemed less George Fox speaking the words of the Lord God than George Fox laying down the law. Especially when he closed his message, even one to Oliver Cromwell, with the line, "This is the word of the Lord God to thee."

Quakerism was blessed with courageous men and women; there were many who fought with as steel-hard earnestness, but few possessed George Fox's calm conviction of infallibility. He alone possessed the rocklike certainty that whatever he might say or do was modern gospel. However democratic the Friends might be in principle, no one doubted that George Fox was leader.

Inevitably Fox developed autocratic tendencies. Never a humble man nor one to disparage himself, he would have sincerely rejected homage to George Fox the human being, but he dared not discourage deference to the Word of God which he expressed. Increasingly, therefore, he resented the sporadic minor criticisms sometimes raised against his policies and methods. If challenged, however gently, he felt, and showed himself, aggrieved. Nor, in countering minute objection, did he vary his defense but always wheeled up the heavy ordnance of damnation against any who opposed him. Worse, he seemed to delight in the discomfiture of critics.

Steeped as they were in the Old Testament tradition of love and submission to the omnipotent, most of his followers bowed dutifully. But there were some, James Nayler for example, who were oversensitive. If, as everyone believed, the Inner Light shone equally in all, why was one man's revelation overriding? Why should anyone suppose that the Lord God played favorites?

The doubts appeared so slowly that, at first, not even Nayler recognized that rebellion might be rising. Dazzled by his swift rise to acceptance as second in command, basking in the warmth of his reception first in Yorkshire and then in London, Nayler, too, was being molded to a different pattern. He, too, was unconscious of the change, but, just as Fox was growing dictatorial so Nayler was becoming more and more reluctant to being subject. It would be too much to suggest that he was disillusioned, or disappointed, in George Fox's leadership, but, increasingly, James Nayler was uneasy.

Neither Fox nor Nayler were aware of what was happening. Quakerism was prospering; its field of action was ever widening as missioners fanned out over Britain, not only in areas where the message was well known but also to new quarters yet to be exploited.

In the name of the Lord, Fox counselled his missionaries, the Publishers of Truth whom he dispatched to dark areas he planned to enlighten. In what must surely have been most unnecessary advice, he urged them to be orderly, peaceful, wise and gracious; he warned against strife, bitterness, self-will or boastfulness.

Neither Fox nor the Publishers wandered haphazardly.

They went where they were moved to go, bound by no time schedule but after considerable scouting and reconnaissance of needs and possibilities and under careful co-ordination and direction. Fox inspired their work and laid down policy, with Margaret Fell as unofficial executive secretary.

She was also a treasurer. Generally speaking, the Publishers lived, as Fox lived, on the bounty of fellow Friends. They travelled, as George travelled, by horse or foot, preaching to pack-train carters flogging weary horses through the mud, to scoffing gentry in bone-racking carriages, and to their jeering outriders on horseback, to yeomen and laborers tilling crops or resting at their noonday meals. They paused in tiny settlements to speak in market places, on village greens or in the steeple-houses. Often they lacked money to buy lodging, but they missed no chance to exhort patrons in the taverns; when there were no fellow Friends to feed and shelter them, they slept, hungry, in the open.

Spartan as was their existence, they still needed money, for food, for clothing, for unavoidable necessities—at times, alas, for medical expenses brought on by hardship or attack. To pay these costs, various Friends, at Margaret's instigation, set up a central fund at Kendal. Margaret, in all likelihood the mainstay of this Kendal Fund, was certainly its staunchest advocate. She wrote to various meetings, pointing out modestly that "Our Friends in Westmorland hath borne the heat of the day" but that others might now wish to help "in unity and fellowship."

To some degree, this canvassing for funds opened Quakerism to thoughtless criticism. Fox had campaigned earnestly against hirelings who exacted money for their services; he called it fleecing the lambs. But now, his enemies averred, Quaker Publishers and George himself, were asking pay.

They omitted the vital differences. Ministers of established faiths accepted tithes wrung from the people under penalty of fines; Quakers received only voluntary offerings. Ministers recognized by government enjoyed state maintenance denied to Quakers, with the result that Friends supported their own people as well as contributing to those of whom they disapproved.

Quakerism, at this point, faced serious danger. Thus far, it had weathered both political and clerical opposition; it had thrived on persecution. Despite Yorkshire theorists, jailing the leaders had been an ineffective deterrent. Quakerism was, however, imperilled by its own success. Numbers of adherents, each of them encouraged to follow an inward light, might all too readily wander off into hundreds of individual wildernesses. Some central control was essential, but central control was precisely what Fox and his followers detested most.

For one assured that his every thought and word came straight from Heaven, the temptation to assume infallibility was almost irresistible. George's indignation against Milner and Gilpin, his pronouncement that the Lord would blast dissenters from orthodox Quakerism, his conviction that death followed Myers' disobedience of orders, all indicated stiffness toward nonconformists. It would have been an easy step to excommunicate those who differed with him, those who, in his words, ran out of the truth. Somehow Fox resisted the temptation. He never welcomed difference, nor was he patient with it. For all his insistence upon charity and love, when faced by opposition he was usually rude and angry, often unfair. Deviators were vain, scheming, dirty people who must wither like the grass until such time as they were blasted; if, to avoid their fate, they recanted, he forgave them slowly.

It is not unthinkable that Margaret Fell moderated his indignation; as liaison officer she was in a position to filter reports coming from the Publishers and, if needs be, to soften

George Fox's replies. Armed with greater tact and more social grace than Fox, she was an understanding diplomat. Not that her intercession was essential when George dealt with his missionaries, for each was wholly devoted to his leader; but if misunderstanding rose, Margaret, ever loyal, smoothed the difficulties.

Her household was equally effective. Under their mother's enthusiastic encouragement, and with their father's benevolent neutrality, every daughter became an energetic Quaker worker. Margaret, the eldest, born in 1633, and Bridget, two years her junior, were, in Caton's company, visiting Friends in prison as early as 1654. Only a year later, Mary, the eight-year-old, received a message from the Lord to pass on to her pastor. Addressing him simply as "Lampitt," without either a title or a Christian name, she called down "the plaiges of god" upon him, promising that "the seven viols shall bee powered upon thee and the milstone shall fall upon thee and crush thee as dust under the Lord's feete." As a conclusion she inquired, "How canst thou escape the damnation of Hell?"

Religious fever must have been running extraordinarily high at Swarthmoor Hall for an eight-year-old to write such a letter to her parson and her tutor. Two younger sisters, Susannah and Rachel, did not then subscribe to Quaker doctrines, but the one was but two years old and the other newly born.

The son, George, he whose teeth had been menaced, was less amenable. For some eight years after Fox appeared at Swarthmoor, young Fell was in London. Presumably he was studying law, as his father had done, but gossip reported him as running more after worldly pleasures than after religion. Unlike Caton, he had not escaped the Hawkshead blight.

But Caton had outgrown worldly delights. Captivated, like the rest of the household, by the Fox charm, Caton had found Hawkshead unendurable. No longer able to write the themes nor the Latin verses Hawkshead asked, and unwilling to pay his headmaster the trivial compliment of doffing his hat, he persuaded Margaret to let him come back to Swarthmoor as tutor to the girls. Later he became her secretary and, within a few months, before his nineteenth birthday, a Publisher of Truth. Three family employees also spread the truth. Thomas Salthouse, Judge Fell's estate manager, Mary Askew, a retainer who may have been a relative of Margaret Fox, and Ann Clayton were all convinced of Quakerism. All three became missionaries and all suffered for their faith.

Swarthmoor presented a sharp contrast to Fenny Drayton, where not one member of George's family helped the Quaker movement.

There was, of course, a ready explanation. The Fells, even the judge, were Seekers, looking for the truth and ready to receive it; most of them were susceptible to Quakerism even before meeting Fox. The churchwarden's family, on the other hand, were content with Puritanism and with Presbyterianism. The difference was also due, at least in part, to their spiritual advisors. Stephens, an intelligent man, and to some degree a questioner, was a satisfying preacher in whom parishioners had confidence. Lampitt evoked no such loyalty; the looseness of his tongue, the gossiping which, for once, gave color to Fox's accusations, did not endear him to thoughtful listeners.

While George Fox in the eyes of both his family and their neighbors, remained a bumptious boy, too big for his leather breeches and without respect for elders, Swarthmoor saw him as a spiritual adult whose ideas, however unconventional, were Scriptural, exciting and attractive.

15

Thresh the Heathen

QUAKERISM WAS BY NO MEANS THE MOST POPULAR nonconformist sect, but it attracted more attention than did others; certainly it was the most spectacular in leadership and vigor.

Yet, thus far, Quakerism remained a parochial group concentrated in the northern counties. Its membership was limited culturally as well as geographically. Some college graduates belonged, for the most part discontented separatist preachers and a sprinkling of other intellectuals, but the largest number of adherents were rural folk and villagers, semieducated at best.

At this stage, it was just as well that Quakers kept away from sophisticated centers and that they did not argue with scholars, except for Stephens, especially with those possessing more ammunition than the Bible. Fox, to be sure, unquestionably accepted the Holy Scriptures as divinely inspired and, if construed in the spirit of the Prophets and Apostles, as infallible; but, unlike the more rigid theologians, he accepted modern revelation. To him, belief in the Inner Light meant a sharing in the spirit of Christ; those who disagreed with him, he charged, labored to darken the minds of men. When arguing with small-town clergymen he could silence them with ease, for knowing quite as much as they did, and probably much more, about the Holy Bible, he was lightning quick in citing Scriptural passages, and his deep, loud voice blanketed whatever they might say.

Surprisingly, the village parsons played into his hands. He claimed firsthand revelation by the Inner Light, a claim no one, in the north at least, as yet seemed to challenge. He said that anyone might find that same light shining within himself, so that each man, if he were saintly, might have revelations, also. This was spiritual individualism carried to extremes, but no hostile country parson used the weapon against Fox. Had he done so, of course, the result would have been an exchange of accusations that the other man was speaking not the voice of God but the dictates of the Devil. This would have led to unseemly squabbling, to be sure, but, by their modesty, the clergymen seemed, through their restraint, to be admitting Fox's claims.

More learned divines would not have been stampeded; they would have been more critical of Fox's arguments and more adept at finding loopholes in them. They would have noted inconsistencies in Fox's acceptance of the letter of the Scriptures when the Bible favored him and in his insertion of special revelation when editing was needed. They would have pounced upon George Fox's use of the Apocrypha and of other sources not approved by Protestants. Fox was not a scholar; he would have come off poorly in such argument. Probably he would have lost his temper, blasted his opponent with vituperation and so lost his cause. He wisely avoided arguments with the intelligentsia to whom Justice Hotham would have introduced him; only very seldom during the remainder of his life did he argue with well-educated adversaries.

With his burning passion to spread the truth, George Fox

was well aware, however, that Quakerism must be spread more widely. Beyond the north counties, England lay in darkness. The mission of bringing light would certainly be difficult. He knew, if only by experience with his own family and neighbors, that the Midlands would resist convincement and that the south, where Seekerism was weak, would be unpromising; but, despite what he had seen at Uncle Pickering's, London seemed inviting.

Possibly the capital offered more abundant fruit than either Lancashire or Yorkshire. Quakerism prospered by capturing Seekers and nonconformists, and of these London had many. Only a few years before an unhappy cleric noted 176 different heresies in the metropolis. Now that Puritanism was somewhat subsided and that Presbyterianism was failing to absorb the Church of Englanders left adrift by disestablishment, the number was probably increased. George Fox was not obliged to scale another Pendle Hill to find a great host awaiting Quakerism. Justice Gervase Benson had already told him as much. In a letter sent jointly to Fox and Nayler, Benson reported that the Lord was raising a light in London.

As usual, Fox planned carefully. Publishers of Truth must not go forth at random into the "unbroken places." To "thresh the heathen nature," by which he meant to win the unconvinced, they should set out two by two, carrying a standard authorized message. Officially, Quakerism had no supreme executive, no inviolate dogma, no required ritual—there being no common bond save love of man and fear of the Lord—but, nevertheless, it was well that Quaker practice should be uniform and Quaker teaching free of human fallibility.

For this, and for the necessary financing, a central clearing house was needed. Margaret Fell was serving well in this capacity; she should continue the work on a larger scale. To her should flow all reports from workers in the field; through her should go George Fox's counsel, admonitions and advice.

The Apostles set a precedent. St. Paul's epistles refreshed and guided struggling Christian groups; he and other saints united and inspired the Christian movement. George Fox adopted their ideas.

Burrough and Howgill, the best evangels, set out for London, to be reinforced, if needed, by Aldam, Camm and Richard Hubberthorne. Nayler, who, as might have been expected, had private revelations on this, as on everything, also went into the city.

While on their way to London, all the Publishers met trouble. Hubberthorne, going by way of Cambridge to visit an imprisoned Friend, was himself thrown into jail for disobeying the mayor's order to leave town.

Cambridge was one of the more intolerant centers because, George suspected, its university prepared scholars for the priesthood. During the year just passed, at least a dozen Quakers were jailed. Seven of them were women, among them 21-year-old Mary Fisher, who had already served a total of two years in prison for steeple-house offenses. For women missionaries, jail sentences were not enough; Cambridge lashed them heavily because they might be prostitutes.

Students, whose high standards of conduct the local magistrates were protecting, behaved as disgracefully as did the officials. When Publishers hired a hall to hold a meeting, the boys threw down their books and hurried to the building. There they distinguished themselves by flinging stones and filth through the windows, shooting bullets into the air and threatening to burn the building over the Quakers' heads. Friends asked them to quiet down and to behave more soberly; the rowdies answered that they intended to get drunk. They invaded the meeting, ran noisily up and down the aisles, shouting and beating drums. They broke up furniture, hurled garbage at the speakers and ripped off the women's clothes. The college proctors stood idly by; they could not keep the students quiet, they explained, nor would they if they could.

Oxford was no better. Elizabeth Leavens and Elizabeth Fletcher visited that seat of scholarship only to be held under the St. Johns College pump until they almost drowned; they were then bound together and dragged up and down the college grounds. This was not enough; they were arrested for disturbing the peace.

To be sure, Elizabeth Fletcher had certainly done so. A young lady of sixteen, hitherto "very modest and grave," she was driven "against her own will or inclination, in obedience to the Lord," to go half-naked through the streets "as a sign against hypocritical profession of which the Lord would strip them."

The students failed to read the sign aright; they thought she was a prostitute.

The mayor considered that, while a good case might be made out against Elizabeth Fletcher, there was no excuse for trying her companion; he defended both women. If the town were lenient, the gown was not. The vice-chancellor of the university, the Reverend Dr. John Owen, hastened to guard his young men. He was a versatile individual, this Dr. Owen —an intellectual, an athlete, a flute player and a dandy who knew everything about everything except human beings. Supposedly, he was an Independent, but he did not stomach nonconformity in others, especially not in women At his insistance the two ladies were whipped out of town.

Under such guidance, Oxford outdid its Cambridge rival. When the women returned to hold a meeting, the college hoodlums, theological students though they were, jumped upon the backs of men and women and rode them like horses. They yelled for beer, and when somehow they got it they poured it over the Quaker's heads. They, too, tore off the women's clothes.

"I am weary of transcribing these abominations," the chronicler reported. "I shall cease with the remark that had these scholars been professedly educated there for ministers of the Devil they could not have given more certain proof of their proficiency."[1]

Male Publishers were also suffering. John Stubbs and Lancaster each went twice to prison. Richard Hubberthorne and sixteen other men were pulled out of a peaceful meeting, bound hand and foot and left in the open through a wintry night. Authorities in five different counties sent Quakers to jail for no apparent offense save refusal to lift their hats. Aldam was six times beaten and several times imprisoned. At one of his hearings a lawyer snatched away his hat and Aldam demanded that he be censored for it. The judge ordered the hat returned, but Aldam refused to take it without an apology to him and a rebuke to the offender. Failing to receive either, he went bareheaded for seven months. The Lord told him to do this as a symbol that many were covered but not with justice.

Despite their difficulties, the Publishers, by July, 1654, reached their London goal. Hubberthorne was still in Cambridge jail, but Howgill and his 21-year-old companion, Edward Burrough, promptly set up a London meeting. Anthony Pearson, the once-prejudiced justice, set out at once to call on Cromwell.

---

[1] Eastern and southern England seemed bent on persecuting women. Mary Fisher went to jail three times within a couple of years, as did Jane Waugh, John Camm's serving maid; Jane's sister Dorothy, Elizabeth Hooten, the first woman convert, and Elizabeth Leavens were twice imprisoned during the same time, the usual charge being speaking to a priest which, being translated, meant asking embarrassing questions. Elizabeth Fletcher escaped, but only after the playful Oxford boys had thrown her so heavily against a tombstone that she was maimed for life. There were numbers of other instances, one poor woman being beaten so severely that as Fox was told, she was "carried away in a basket."

The Protector, who seems to have been extraordinarily accessible, received him graciously, but Pearson failed to make a good impression. He did not offend Cromwell by failure to remove his hat, but he did worse; in recounting at great length the wondrous things done by the Lord in the North and soon to be done in all England, in fact in all the world, he bored the Protector. Moreover, he fell into a trance and delivered an impassioned harangue which Cromwell neither understood nor cared to hear. Howgill and Camm were no more effective. Oliver agreed that all men should have liberty to worship, provided only that there was no trespass upon the rights of others, but Howgill and Camm doubted his sincerity; suspecting him of being blind to truth and anxious only to curry favor, they thought him condescending. They, too, bored the Protector; he suggested that, as he had work to do, they leave him.

Cromwell, having heard the message, thought the Inner Light an unsafe guide that might lead men into all kinds of excesses.

Cromwell's toleration offset his indifference as far as London was concerned. While Fox continued in the north, directing operations through a constant stream of messages, the Publishers won over large numbers of spiritually drifting Londoners. The work progressed so well that, in conformity with George's suggestions, the Publishers split their forces. Howgill and Burrough remained in the capital, with an independent Nayler preaching fervently to increasingly large numbers of enraptured females, while other ministers spread out in pairs over the as yet untested southern counties.

Camm and Audland started off for Bristol. Here, also, as at Preston Patrick and at London, were large communities of Seekers to be harvested, and Camm and Audland were so welcomed that, in October, Howgill and Burrough also went down to preach to those whom Camm and Audland had attracted. Influential people joined the cause, men like Captain

Edward Pyott, who knew the entire western country, Dennis Hollister, a landed member of Parliament and owner of a large suburban orchard which he threw open for Quaker meetings, and Josiah Coale, who would become a pioneer in carrying the truth to America.

Many of those convinced were Baptists, whose pastor, understandably enraged at losing one-fourth of his congregation, joined with his Presbyterian colleague to halt the raid upon their membership. The Presbyterian, the Reverend Ralph Farmer, was, as it happened, extremely skilful with a poisoned pen; he wrote to London complaining that the Publishers, whom he described as "morris-dancers" and "northern locusts," had come under the pretense of Cromwell's favor to "exercise some spiritual cheats." Referring perhaps to Pyott, he protested against petty captains who dallied with the law and who rode away from their obedience.

Whether the clergymen were directly responsible is not quite clear, but somehow word got about Bristol that grave danger was imminent. Fox and Nayler, it was said, were on their way to join the missionaries already in the city. Nor was theirs an ordinary visit. These men claimed to be British, the rumors said, but their claims were false; actually they were foreigners —Italians, Franciscans in disguise—coming straight from Rome to bring back Popery. The mayor vouched for the truth of these reports, as did seven of his aldermen; one of the latter was so nervously alarmed that he signed the warning twice.

Yet, such was the influence of Pyott the soldier and Hollister the politician, that when the supposed Franciscans, all but Fox and Nayler, held meetings in the Hollister orchard, the magistrates did nothing more than ask them to stay out of the city. The Friends refused to give a promise; they answered, with what they called their Christian courage. "We came not in the will of man nor stand in the will of man, but when He moves us to depart who moved us hither, we shall obey. Your will we cannot obey, for your will is no law."

This reply to an unexpectedly considerate suggestion is open to some criticism as unnecessarily rude, but the magistrates meekly accepted the rebuff. The populace did not. Some fifteen hundred persons lingered all day to kill the disguised Romans, but the authorities sent out a guard to lead the Quakers to a safer place. The Friends were duly grateful to be thus preserved from persecution, but they laid their luck not to the magistrates but to the providence of God.

The escape was another evidence that the Lord smiled on Quakers. When earlier, Cromwell, who like Fox was convinced that Heaven heeded prayer, asked a national fast for rain, George pointed out a more effective way. In a letter entitled in part "A Warning from the Lord to all such as hang down the head for a day . . . ," he showed that dryness was a sign of spiritual barrenness; those who owned God's truth should have rain aplenty. To Fox the facts were crystal clear. North England was accepting Quakerism—in George's phraseology it was tender and loving—and it had no drought. The South was persecuting and it was athirst.

What stronger evidence was needed?

16

Cromwell

EARLY IN 1655 WILDLY EXAGGERATED REPORTS OF QUAKER excesses were reaching Cromwell's ears, fantastic yarns about Papist rioters and rebels, sorcerers, scorners of religion, self-styled messiahs threatening everyone with everlasting torment.

The Protector, being an intelligent man with a sense of proportion and, indeed, a little sense of humor, put slight faith in any such nonsense; but, at the same time, he dared not ignore the rumors that George Fox, ringleader of the fanatics, was calling a mass meeting of Quaker leaders to consider, it was said, an uprising against the Commonwealth.

He had, of course, met Quakers—Howgill, Camm and Pearson—and he had received letters from George Fox counselling peacefulness and obedience to the laws of God, and so he knew that Friends would not resort to arms. Yet only recently Thomas Aldam had come before him, wearing a linen cap which he refused to lift but which, after "clearing his conscience" by revealing the truth to Cromwell, he suddenly snatched from his head and ripped apart as a sign that all Cromwell's counsels and coverings would be rent asunder. Aldam reported to Fox that the Protector's heart was so hardened that he did not heed the sign and, in all probability, Oliver failed to understand the symbolism; but the action strengthened his impression that Quakerism was the product of a giddy mind.

Reports from the North radiated great heat against Quaker practices but shed little light on what the Quakers taught. Cromwell's agents, his eyes and ears in every town, were so intent on guarding against insurrection that, like spies in every country and in every age, they suspected plots in every unconventionality. Still trembling at the possibility that Winstanley's pathetic Diggers or Lilburne's Levellers might miraculously upset the government, they branded every restive person as a fearsome rebel. Puritans and Presbyterians, worried lest the ejected Anglicans return or the diabolically clever Jesuits carry out successful plots, magnified innocent Quaker meetings into full-scale revolutionary efforts.

London, also, chattered endlessly about the Friends. Local justices who attended Parliament traded anecdotes about the Quakers, each story unfavorable to George Fox and his cubs. Law officials recounted charges brought against the Friends and what procedures were most effective against them. Now, with Publishers of Truth established at the capital, close to Whitehall and to Parliament, the timorous anticipated riots in the streets and meeting houses.

Cromwell, whom Fox called Oliver Protector, was himself a man of intense religious conviction, but he was a man who, unlike most others of his time, respected the sincerely held beliefs of others even though they differed from his own. His restless curiosity could not fail to be aroused by such hysterical reports as those, for instance, recently arrived from Bristol. His sense of fair play, however undeveloped, must have been outraged by the evident injustice inflicted upon the innocent.

Nothing he had thus far seen or heard, certainly nothing in the attitude or words of any of his Quaker callers, would have led him to believe that Quakers were magicians, blasphemers or traitors—he was fully aware and well convinced that under no circumstances would Friends resort to carnal weapons, but, if only for the sake of keeping up morale among his spy corpsmen, he felt obliged to give some heed to their fevered warnings.[1]

The truth was that the authorities were terrified. Astonishing rumors were afloat that Quakers, Royalists and Catholics, who certainly agreed on nothing, were united in plots against the Commonwealth. Doubtless, Cromwell the realist was not himself alarmed, but local officers lost their heads.

They kept careful watch on George Fox's movements; anyone who would not swear allegiance to the Commonwealth must be a traitor. When, in January 1655, Fox summoned two hundred Quakers to a meeting, they scented rebellion.

Disturbance occurred, but not by Quaker instigation. Ranters, intent on breaking up the meeting, sang and danced and whistled, but Fox spoke to them so convincingly that many "are come to be a pretty people and live and walk soberly in the Truth of Christ."

Then he went home, for the first time since 1647. He argued, for the last time, with Stephens and enjoyed the satisfaction of hearing his father, a Stephens parishioner, admit, while thwacking his cane upon the ground, "He that will but stand to the truth, it will carry him out." It may have been the last time he ever saw his father, for George never mentioned him again.

No matter what the Quakers thought of Cromwell, they were peaceable enough. They may have been too quiet. Nervous officials such as Colonel Francis Hacker may have felt uneasy; he sent seventeen troopers to seize George Fox. He was a Commonwealth soldier whose own loyalty soared high

---

[1] The Protector may have heard of Dewsbury, currently in trouble in three different counties on charges of blasphemy and sedition. Though nothing was proved against him, in fact he was not actually tried on anv of these charges, he spent months in jail without being officially informed of his alleged offenses.

above suspicion. Twice captured by the Cavaliers during the Civil War, he spurned Charles I's offer of a regiment if he would change sides; instead he signed the king's death warrant and supervised the execution. He would not tolerate disloyalty, least of all in Leicestershire, his birthplace.

In taking Fox into custody, Hacker presented no charges. He would have much preferred to stay clear of the whole situation. Actually, he faced a dilemma. George had done no wrong. If he jailed an innocent man, he would be a tyrant; if he ignored Fox and something happened, he might be accused of neglect of duty. Moreover, if he were too hard on Fox, he would offend his wife and also his chief advisor, both of whom were sympathetic to Fox (they later became Quakers); if he were too easy, he would offend Oliver Cromwell, who was known to dislike "rude and un-Christian disturbances of ministers by Quakers and Ranters."

Hacker did not share London's fear that serious insurrection was afoot. A conference of Friends from several counties might mean that some concerted action was being planned but Hacker suspected no sedition; had he done so he would have apprehended every one of them instead of only Fox. He was, however, unwilling to take chances.

But by taking up Fox he raised yet another problem. Some-one, whether Cromwell or an aide, had evidently suggested that the next time Fox got into difficulty, he should be sent down to London, so that the Protector might see and hear the troublemaker. Here was an opportunity to please Oliver Cromwell, but Cromwell would not be happy at the forced deportation of an innocent man.

Hacker, therefore, held an inquiry, rather than a hearing or a trial. In arguing theology and religion with George Fox, the army officers were at serious disadvantage. One captain, at least, lost his temper and cried out, "This man hath reigned too long; it's time to cut him off." Hacker, himself, may have

tried to trick George into saying something blasphemous. He
questioned whether it were not the Inner Light that led Judas
into betrayal and then to hang himself, but George answered
that it was not the Inner Light but the spirit of darkness.

Unable to find any guilt, Hacker offered to release Fox if
the latter would agree to attend no more meetings. George
refused. To accept, he said, would be to confess that he was
guilty of something. The colonel repeated the offer and Fox
again refused. He must, he said, go to meetings when the Lord
commanded him to go.

"Well, then," said Hacker, "I will send you tomorrow by
six o'clock to my Lord Protector."

Fox spent the night in prison, this time as a guest rather
than as a captive; in the morning he made ready for his trip
to London. Hacker made a last effort to persuade him to accept
a conditional freedom, but Fox, dropping to his knees, prayed
the Lord to forgive this Pilate. He told Hacker to remember,
when retribution should befall, that he had been forewarned.[2]

Captain Drury did not enjoy the assignment of escorting
Fox. At every stop George preached; while on the road, he
shouted warnings and exhortations. Just as the Derby authorities vainly suggested that Fox escape from jail, so Drury,
apparently under orders, did his best to have George go home
on parole. He gave Fox every opportunity to slip away, but
George, although going off alone to visit Dewsbury and other
Friends in prison, declined parole and would not accept freedom. Arriving at London, Drury lodged his guest at the Mermaid Inn and left him there, unguarded, while he himself
reported to Cromwell. On his return, Fox was still at the
Mermaid exhorting everyone within earshot to fear God and
flee from hireling priests.

Because Cromwell was too busy to see George Fox—though
not too busy to issue a proclamation of religious liberty—the

[2] Five years later, at the Restoration, Colonel Hacker was hanged.

evangelism continued. For three weeks the bored captain stood around while Fox argued and sermonized. To shorten the waiting time, George, in March, 1655, wrote a letter, "in the presence of the Lord God," denying any intention of drawing a carnal sword against Cromwell or against any other man. He signed it, "One who is of the world called George Fox whom a new name hath which the world knows not."[3]

Cromwell's comment was as cryptic as George's signature. "I have never before seen such a paper," he remarked; but next day he received George Fox. George entered the room, crying, "Peace be on this house," and promptly launched into a loud appeal to the Protector to hold fast in the fear of God. Cromwell interrupted to ask why Fox quarrelled with the clergy, but George denied all responsibility; it was not he who quarrelled but the false teachers, the hirelings, the dumb dogs, who quarrelled with him. He renewed the sermonizing stream. Cromwell, who could not have been listening very attentively, nodded now and then and murmured approval, but failed to stop the torrent.

Crowds of people poured into the room to hear the hatted man in leather breeches lecture the Protector. The press was so heavy that somehow Fox was pushed away. Cromwell, who, Fox reported, behaved very modestly throughout, caught him by the hand and, with tears in his eyes, begged George to come again.

"If thou and I were but an hour together each day we should be better friends. I wish you no more ill than I do to my own soul."

"Thou wrongest thy soul," George answered. "Hearken to God's voice."

[3] What this new name might be, George did not reveal. Some commentators believe, though without much convincing evidence, that the signature betrays Gnostic influence. Henry Cadbury traces the secret name to Revelation 2 : 17, etc.

Drury lingered a few moments in the room. He came out probably relieved. "The Lord Protector says," he told Fox, "that you are free. Go where you will. My Lord also says you are no fool."

To be rid of the guardianship must have been a pleasure, but Drury still had troubles. He led George to a dining room filled with people. Cromwell, he announced, was inviting them to stay to dinner. Fox would have none of it.

"Let Oliver Protector know," said he, "that I shall not eat a bit of his bread nor drink a sup of his drink."

He returned, a free man, to the Mermaid, confident that Cromwell would know that, unlike all others of this world, Quakers were not to be bribed by honors, offices or gifts. To his dismay he found that, instead of being Cromwell's guest, he was supposed to be the Ranters' host. Loyal to their theory that "all is ours," they had been ordering up drinks and tobacco, probably food as well, and charging it on the bill. When George complained, a peevish fellow rebuked him, saying everything was quite all right.

"How is all well," Fox replied, "when thou are so peevish and envious and crabbed?" He then "spake to their condition," which means he told them what he thought of them, and bade them clear out and do their carousing elsewhere.

"They looked at one another wondering."

Not even yet was Drury safe. Although he had committed no sin save refusing to become a Friend, and though some of Fox's party considered him "very loving" and a man who would not rob George of any freedom, Fox thought him a scoffer of the truth. It was, therefore, only a fitting punishment that the Captain, after taking an afternoon's nap, wakened very ill, shaking so badly that his knees knocked together and his body trembled; he could not rise from bed.

The judgment brought Drury to his senses. Tumbling from

his bed to the floor, he promised the Lord that never again would he utter a single word against the Quakers.[4]

All this afforded interesting gossip which editors ate up eagerly and printed, with ample embellishment, in what Fox called their "news-books." One editor, a minister for whom reporting was a side line, questioned George during a sermon and drew from him a public rebuke as an envious priest. When the story appeared in the newsbook's next issue, Fox called him a liar. The editor retaliated by digging up the old canard that Fox bewitched people by hanging ribbons on their arms; he also said that the Quaker wore silver buttons. George resented both items; he never used ribbons in his life, he protested, and, as for those buttons, they were brass.

Other Friends took up the criticisms. They called upon the ministerial editor and demanded that he reveal his source; he said it was a woman. They asked her name and he replied it was a man. Again they asked the name; the editor dodged by saying that if Fox would write out a denial, he would print it. Fox wrote the statement, but the news-book man failed to publish it.

George had no better luck at Whitehall. On returning to pay the visit Cromwell had suggested, he was denied admission. Worse, the soldiers and the household attendants mauled him; they jeered at his leather breeches.

They pierced a weak spot in his armor. George Fox, whose bludgeon-like retorts were almost always devastating and whose Biblical citations invariably discomfited rivals, was defenseless against ridicule. Critics who giggled at his brass buttons or his stoutness disconcerted him. Few comments stirred his anger more quickly than those making fun of his curly hair or sneering at his leather clothes. The solders' mock-

[4] Since he thereafter was unmentioned in Fox's *Journal,* it is unknown whether he kept his vow.

ing seemed, moreover, somewhat disloyal to the Protector's rough and inexpensive coat and to all those Roundheads who made such a point of simplicity in dress.

Fox retorted by a tirade addressed "to those as follow after the fashions of the world," a scathing denunciation of gold ornaments, gay apparel, powdered and perfumed hair styling, and the flaunting of parti-colored ribbons, laces and beauty patches. "Do not these encumber God's work?" he demanded.

He almost spluttered in his sarcasm. "To get a pair of breeches like a coat and hang them with points and almost up to the middle, and a pair of double cuffs upon the hands and a feather in his cap, here's a gentleman, put off your hats, bow, get a company of fiddlers, a set of music and dance . . ."[5]

Nevertheless Fox never again mentioned his leather suit. Thereafter, he wore drab textiles, dove-colored or gray. The change, to be sure, may well have been due to changed circumstances, for he was not now sleeping in fields, lying in ditches or travelling by horse or foot, and so stood in no need of the most durable clothing. But, whatever the reason, he was no longer to be identified as the man in leather.

While in his letter-writing mood, he wrote to all heads of state, rulers, kings and nobles, bidding them cease the persecution of the innocent lambs of God. He also told the Pope to be godly.

For this outburst, Oliver Cromwell was, in large degree, responsible. Almost immediately after seeing Fox, the Protector issued an order which, in effect, broke his promise of free worship. His action was an outgrowth of the morbid fear of

[5] Priscilla Barclay recalled that, when Fox was walking in Cheapside, a coach drew up and out stepped a little woman, perhaps the widow Mary James, in very gay apparel. George immediately laid a hand upon her, warning her to "mind the Light within thee." The injunction proved effective; "she was effectually convinced," married a Friend and "became a respectable member of our Society."

Jesuit plotting which obsessed the Commonwealth, and later the Restoration as well; for the order, signed in April, required all persons suspected of Catholicism to forswear the Pope under pain of imprisonment and forfeiture of estate.

Local justices, the real villains in the persecution of Quakers, used the decree as a weapon against Friends, whom, of course, the magistrates believed allied with Catholic agents. On raiding Quaker meetings, officials dragged Friends into court, put to them this Oath of Abjuration and, knowing well that Quakers would not swear, fined and imprisoned them forthwith. When Cromwell failed to intervene, Howgill, Camm and Pearson, all of whom had warned George Fox that the Protector was insincere, believed their premonitions justified.

George Fox, as well, believed Cromwell a master hypocrite, not only for this breach of faith but because the Protector proposed that England fast as protest against anti-Protestantism on the Continent. Fox demanded, very properly, to know why, if Oliver was so sensitive because of injustices abroad, he condoned the same intolerance at home. Cromwell's call for a national fast, said Fox, reminded him of Jezebel; to issue such a proclamation merely meant that mischief was afoot.

17

Premature Missions

HOWEVER RESTRAINED CROMWELL'S ENTHUSIASMS MAY HAVE been, his courtesy toward Fox and other Quakers clothed the Friends with a certain measure of respectability. Nonconformists flocked to join the movement; more traditional worshippers, mindless of Bristol's extravagant slanders and free of fear of witchcraft, took occasion to see and hear the Quaker preachers. To attend a Quaker meeting became, in certain circles, a sort of fad. The Friends attained such popularity that they acquired a headquarters, known as the Bull and Mouth because of its location in Aldersgate adjacent to an inn that bore that sign.

The Bull and Mouth housed approximately a thousand people willing to stand through lengthy Quaker meetings; the crush was so great that after Fox met Cromwell seven or eight meetings were being held each First Day. Not all of these were large; the Fox injunction still held that dedicated Friends should meet in small, private groups, while Publishers, by twos or threes, threshed the multitudes to separate the good grain from the chaff.

Quakerism's brief popularity as a fashionable spectacle did not mislead George Fox; he realized that the crowds who thronged Bull and Mouth were yielding fewer conversions than he could have wished. That same faddish craze, however, may have been protection, for in London persecution was far less severe than elsewhere in the Commonwealth. There was some, to be sure; Ann Downer, a clergyman's daughter from Oxfordshire, was arrested for annoying a priest and, while in jail, was whipped by a knotted rope for refusing to work. Within the same month two other Friends were imprisoned for bothering the same priest. These were, however, isolated cases. London, and, for that matter, Middlesex, with a larger population than other English centers, had as yet few Quaker martyrs.

Tolerance and popularity encouraged Friends to dream of wider evangelism. George Fox, of course, always proclaimed that Quakerism was universal—by this time he had read enough, or heard enough, to trace its roots far back in Christian times—and Margaret Fell was confident that it would rule the world. But Fox, for all his enthusiasms, was a practical leader who realized that the spiritual conquest of Britain must precede an overseas expansion.

Suddenly, however, in late spring of 1655, someone touched off a premature outburst of missionary energy. Who it was, or why it was done, remains unknown, but, from all indications, some powerful speaker or some electrifying personality was moved unexpectedly to urge that Quakers take the truth to foreign lands.

Absolute identification is impossible. Only the most tenuous guesses can be made. If, as seems most probable, it were not George Fox, who certainly would have mentioned any opening or vision, it may have been that other inspiring leader, James Nayler, a co-worker to whom George Fox did not invariably accord due credit. As a London leader, Nayler was winning great success, but, by Fox's direction, he was sharing leadership with Burrough and Howgill. The ambitious Nayler may well have meditated striking out in new directions.

Might one of his disciples have sparked the interest? Nayler's passionate evangelism was infectious; he was surrounded by a hysterical coterie of feminine admirers whom he inspired to preach. Ann Gargill, whom jealous rivals called an unruly, froward spirit, cherished the ambition to bring the King of Portugal into the Quaker fold. Frowned upon by Howgill and Burrough for talking too freely in the Quaker meetings, and, to her disappointment, refused support by Nayler, she may have kindled a missionary flame.

That fire flamed early among the women who surrounded Nayler, but there were also men who were warmed by it. William Caton, then in his first flush as a missionary, was moved toward foreign service, and so was John Stubbs, the former soldier. Stubbs, quite possibly a relative of the Dutch wife of Edward Pickering, felt drawn toward Holland, where Pickering had extensive business and personal relationships. The interest in Dutch affairs was understandable; at least half the foreigners in London were Hollanders, many of the Kentish folk were of Dutch descent and there were many Yorkshire Puritans and Seekers in the Netherlands. Under such circumstances, it was not strange that Friends saw a harvest to be reaped. The idea was not new; George Fox had seen bright prospects as early as 1651, but the time was not then ripe for action there. Four years later, Stubbs was anxious to convince the tolerant Dutch Protestants.

Whoever proposed expansion, a rash of revelations followed. Miraculously, in a week or two, pairs of young evangelists were moved to take the Quaker message into Scotland and Ireland, both foreign nations at the time, as well as into Europe and overseas to the Americas; it would not be long before intrepid souls yearned for the Orient and the fabled land of Prester John. Enthusiastic spirits visioned quick conversion of the Turkish Sultan and the Pope.

Fox braked the rush as best he could. Realizing that, before the world was won, a broader, firmer foundation must be laid in Britain, he recommended more intensive efforts in the southeast and the west. Then, fortified by this experience, the Publishers would go abroad with better preparation. Thus, he sent Stubbs and Caton into Kent, Howgill and Burrough on exploratory missions into Ireland, and others toward Scotland, while he himself planned work in Devonshire and Cornwall.

The men, as a rule, accepted his suggestions, though the impatient Caton slipped over to Calais, where, since he spoke no French, he made no converts, but the women were harder to restrain. Ann Gargill reached Portugal, whence she was immediately deported for ignoring a royal order to be silent. Hester Biddle made a fruitless voyage to inhospitable Newfoundland. Elizabeth Harris, Mary Fisher and Ann Austin sailed for the rich sugar island of Barbados, Elizabeth intending to proceed to Maryland while the two others looked toward the Massachusetts Bay Plantation.

For the Friends, America was an obvious field for cultivation; George Fox did not hold as strong an aversion to its immediate invasion as he held for excursions on the Continent. The colonists were English, speaking the same tongue, having the same backgrounds, drawn from the same stock as Quakers; they shared similar spiritual aspirations. Maryland, to be sure, favored Roman Catholicism, but Lord Baltimore's tolerance had brought so large an influx that a considerable proportion, if not indeed a majority, of the inhabitants were Protestant. Fox, therefore, believed that Quakers would be welcomed; he did not fear that a law of 1649 denying equality to non-Trinitarians would be applied to Quakers. New England Puritanism was weakened; there were even a few Ranters and Seekers. Virginia, originally an Anglican monopoly, had lessened its restrictions under the Commonwealth; it, too, was, as Fox would say, more tender toward consciences. The American colonies, therefore, were undergoing the same spiritual ferment as was England; the same knots of dissatisfied souls thirsted for the light.

As for areas not yet organized as English colonies, they were peopled by Dutchmen—Calvinists who were not unfriendly— or awaited settlement; it would not be long before Quakers might seek shelter there.

But if the colonists thought and acted much as did their British relatives they also shared the same superstitions, fears and prejudices. Few Americans read widely, but when they read anything it was the anti-Quaker tracts that talked of Quaker folly. Well-educated people were not numerous, nor were all of these blessed with open minds; it was not surprising that those who had heard of Quakerism thought of the strange sect as seditious to the government and hostile to organized religion. News reports, in letters from the mother country, were extremely scarce and wholly unreliable; but when they came they told of riots in the steeple-houses and of unruly madmen who proclaimed the day of doom.

Elizabeth Harris did reasonably well in the region near what is now Annapolis, convincing a number of planters, including an assemblyman whom she believed to be the governor, but Mary Fisher and Ann Austin were far less fortunate. Upon their arrival at Boston, in July, 1656, they were arrested and held *incommunicado*. Deputy Governor Richard Bellingham, acting in the absence of his chief, John Endecott, decreed a £5 fine for anyone who spoke to them; to guard against the possibility that anyone would try to do so, he boarded up the windows of the jail.

Bellingham was an honest, sincere administrator who had himself been governor. He had a high respect for law, though he was not averse to bending it upon occasion, as when he performed a marriage ceremony for himself and then declined to stand trial for it on the ground that a governor, as he was then, had special privilege. He was a vigilant man, determined that no Quaker should defile the colony nor sell it to the devil.

These two women, he would have said had any Bostonian raised the question, seemed innocent enough, Mary being only twenty-two and Ann, a mother of five, being more "stricken in years"; but their appearance might well be a deceitful mask. The devil was quite capable of strategems. Quite probably these dangerous arrivals were witches; he ordered them stripped, so that their witches' tokens would be seen.

The fact that there were no tokens failed to convince the frightened deputy governor; he had a ready explanation. The witches knew that those marks would betray them; they banished them by magic spells in order to deceive the righteous. Bellingham kept the women five weeks in prison before expelling them to Barbados.

Though, in point of fact, Ann and Mary made few convincements they did report some hopeful signs in Massachusetts Bay Plantation. Seekers, they somehow learned, had an enthusiastic circle in nearby Salem. Sandwich, on Cape Cod, was ready for the truth and, in what is now Rhode Island, there was eagerness and toleration. One man, Nicholas Upshall, was so anxious for the truth that he volunteered to pay the £5 penalty for the privilege of talking to prisoners; what was more, he paid the costs of their food while they remained in jail.

If Bellingham expected praise for his defense of Boston against the wicked Quaker women, he was disappointed. When Governor Endecott returned, Bellingham was criticised because his punishments were too light. Endecott, an ardent advocate of the Puritans' right to worship freely, regretted that the women escaped whipping.

Boston was not yet clear of danger. Two days after Bellingham rejoiced at being rid of Mary Fisher and Ann Austin, eight other Quakers came. Once more, Bellingham, after seizing their "erroneous books and hellish pamphlets," threw the missionaries, four women and four men, into jail. This time, he committed a blunder more serious than withholding the lash; he allowed the Quakers opportunity, in open court, to preach the gospel. The prisoners, not allowed to enter meetinghouses, thus spread the very doctrines Bellingham was trying to suppress.

To add to his unhappiness, word arrived that Samuel Gorton was inviting the prisoners to settle in Rhode Island. Bellingham, and Endecott, also, knew Gorton well; for twenty years they had vainly battled the uncompromising religious rebel. They tried every weapon they possessed—whipping, imprisonment, banishment—and at one time they banished him, only to send a military force to invade Rhode Island and recover him by arms so that he might be exiled once again. But Gorton would not change his ways. To have both Gorton and the Quakers on the Massachusetts border was an appalling prospect.

It may have been more frightening that the Quakers answered politely that they would rather stay in Massachusetts.

To curb "the cursed sect of heretics," the Massachusetts General Court ordered a fine of £100 for any ship's captain who brought a Quaker to the colony, and set a £5 fine upon anyone who should import a Quaker book or keep one in his house. If, moreover, any Quaker came, he should be jailed at hard labor, whipped and banished. The first to suffer penalty by this new law was Nicholas Upshall, who was exiled from Boston to Sandwich in Plymouth colony and thence to Rhode Island.

The eight Quakers, not one of whom had committed any

act whatever contrary to the strict laws of the colony, except setting foot in Massachusetts, were hurried back to England.

Connecticut soil was quite as stony and its people more hypocritical. Panic-stricken by fear of religious rebels, the colony copied Massachusetts methods while pretending to more tolerance. Quakers might enter, but only on lawful business—whatever that might mean—but if they stayed longer than a fortnight they must pay £5 per week; those who could not or would not pay must work out their fines in jail.

How any business, lawful or otherwise, was to be transacted, when New Havenites were forbidden to speak to Quakers under similar penalties, the lawmakers did not explain, nor was entry easy, when anyone who helped them come was subject to a £50 fine. If, in spite of all the hurdles, Quakers entered and if they found New Havenites willing to listen, there was a further barrier; Quakers must not utter one word that could possibly be construed as preaching; wherever a Friend moved he had a Connecticut guard to censor him. As additional precaution, any owner of a Quaker book must pay ten shillings for the privilege.

It was too much to expect that the whip or the branding iron would be forgotten, nor, for that matter, the boring of the tongue by a hot wire. The penalties applied to men and women equally. The only ray of hope that Quakers could discern was that in Connecticut penalties were lighter than in Massachusetts.

Meanwhile, in total ignorance of what was happening in the American colonies, Fox was directing the activities of Stubbs and Caton in Kent. Here, too, the soil was infertile. Local officials fined those who housed the evangelists and then arrested the two Publishers as vagrants. Stubbs convinced the magistrates that he was solvent, and therefore not guilty of the charge; but Caton angered them by insisting that he had an occupation—"making known the everlasting truth, as he was moved of the Lord, turning people from darkness to the light."

As the ancient Vagrancy Act recognized no such occupation, the justices ordered Caton, and with him Stubbs, to work a full year for their board and lodging plus £4 yearly wages. The evangelists refused to serve, whereupon they were stripped, placed in the stocks, whipped, put into irons and sent back to work. Again they refused, and, as punishment, were supplied no food. Four days later, they were sent homeward under guard; but when, at the county line, their escort left them, the two Quakers turned about and resumed their preaching.

The authorities gave up. "God chained down the red dragon of persecution." The explanation, however, like that of the ending of persecution in Bristol, carried no gratitude to the human figures who assisted the Friends. In this instance, a Dover shoemaker, Luke Howard, shocked by seeing the two missionaries trying to live on bread and beer, sheltered and fed them; insisting on the right of an Englishman to privacy in his home, he refused admission to the justices. For this he went to jail, though his beneficiaries went free.

Through Howard's aid, Stubbs and Caton won a valued convert. John Lilburne, four or five times himself in prison for opposing each of England's successive governments, lay in Dover Castle. He was a cantankerous creature but a firm believer in democracy; some of his followers, the Levellers, who wore a sea-green ribbon as a badge, were with Gerrard Winstanley when the Diggers planted carrots on the commons. Lilburne was never active as a Friend, but his allegiance spurred reports that Quakers were communistically inclined and that, ambitious for a better social order, they were ripe for revolution.

The identification, tenuous as it was, with revolution was unfortunate; by linking Quaker humanitarianism with economic radicalism their opponents delayed needed reformation.

Though Fox was accused of otherworldliness, of living in the ancient atmosphere of Biblical Palestine, he was sensitive to the injustices that lay about him. Unlike many of his contemporaries, he could no more think that some were doomed to poverty and appression than he could accept the thought that some were saved while others were shut out from salvation. He pleaded for the poor, the handicapped, the unfortunate and the downtrodden. How, he demanded of rich London merchants, could they be happy in their luxury when so many begged for bread?

"Spare one of your dishes," he advised, "and let it be carried to the place for the poor and do not let them come begging for it neither."

Charity would cost them nothing; they had luxury to spare. The rich apparel trimmed with lace that neither kept them warm nor served a useful purpose would clothe the poor. Doubtless the appeal would not have moved vain and selfish hearts, in any event, for it was easy for the fortunate to identify misfortune with immorality and irreligion; but by lumping Quakerism with rebels, crackpots, Utopians and communists, the rich and privileged found excuse for ignoring the deserving poor. To them George Fox was just another mad, illiterate street-corner prophet shouting an impending doom. As a contemporary versifier wrote:

These kind of vermin swarm like caterpillars
And hold conventicles in barns and stables.
Some preach, or prate, in woods, in fields, in stables,
In hollow trees, in tubs, on tops of tables.

18

Dark Cornwall

WHETHER GEORGE FOX REALLY SENSED IMPENDING PERILS AS yet invisible to others or whether, reminiscing decades later in the dimmer light of afterthought, he remembered having been forewarned is, after all, comparatively unimportant. If, in actuality, he anticipated the troubles lurking just around the corner, his forebodings would have been completely justified.

They began when he went down to Kent to visit areas cultivated by John Stubbs and William Caton. He approved their work, established their meetings still more firmly and then, to their delight, permitted them to go to Holland.

Thus far, everything was well. But then he received bad news. A young Friend, James Parnell, an undersized seventeen-year-old, already imprisoned for urging the ejection of corrupt officials and for annoying priests, was again in trouble. He certainly had ample justification; a minister had devoted an entire sermon to attacking Quakers. Yet, curiously, the charge against the boy was neither breach of the peace nor speaking out of turn, but vagrancy.

His punishment was disproportionate to anything he did. Parnell was marched eighteen miles in a chain gang for his trial and then was taken handcuffed into court. He was, of course, convicted, and was sentenced to pay £40, as though any vagrant could command so huge a sum; he was to stay in solitary confinement until the fine was paid.

Fox found the boy half starved, the food sent to him by Friends having been stolen from him. The jailer ignored all protests; he knew nothing, he said, about the lost food and, as a matter of fact, was under orders to keep unbalanced people away.

Worse was to happen. High in the castle wall were vaulted niches, something like ovens but narrower, accessible only by rope and ladder and open to wind and rain. To one of these the boy was transferred. To get his food he had to slide down a rope to the ladder and then climb back with the basket which Friends brought him—if, that is, it were not stolen first. A simpler, and certainly far safer, method would have been to let down a basket by a cord; but this, for some reason, was forbidden. It was not surprising, therefore, that he missed his hold and fell to the rocks. Knocked unconscious, he was revived and sent back to another niche, this one provided with a door, which made it dark and gloomy. When he opened the door to get a little light he was punished by being locked out all night on the face of the cliff in bitter cold.

After two months of such treatment he fell sick and died. The jailer said he died of overeating.

It seems incredible that despite such ordeals Quakerism flourished, but it did so, and not as mere fashionable caprice. New techniques had to be adopted for its control, especially as arrests for breach of the peace dropped off after the passage of laws forbidding steeple-house interruptions. Blasphemy continued to be alleged, but arrests were rare because convictions were not easily won. Rebellion, too, was extraordinarily hard to prove against peaceful folk who would not take up arms. One point remained, however, on which Friends were vulnerable.

This was the refusal to swear oaths. To overzealous magistrates the refusal meant that Quakers were traitors, either real or potential; the unwillingness to take Cromwell's Oath of Abjuration confessed complicity in Jesuit plots to overturn the Commonwealth. No charge of crime, no suspicion of wrongdoing, no complaint, whether honest or perjured, need be made before casting Quakers into jail. To demand from them an oath, which, as everyone knew, they would not take, resulted in jail sentences. As innocent men, they refused to pay the fees due wardens; but, as the law provided that prisoners must stay in jail until the dues were paid, Friends might be imprisoned indefinitely.

Fox protested against what he called trampling on the royal law of Christ. He himself talked with Cromwell, he pointed out, and the Protector had been kind; he could not understand why Oliver, who raised no objection to wearing hats nor to refusals to take oaths, should suddenly harden his heart.

True to his nonviolent convictions, George suggested that Friends heap coals of fire upon the heads of enemies of God. Why not, he asked, shame the persecutors by volunteering to serve the prison terms of Friends in jail? Six years ago, in Nottingham, a youth, James Fenner, had offered to take Fox's punishment upon himself; the example was a noble instance of self-sacrifice. Several Friends immediately came forward to relieve the sufferings of imprisoned Publishers, but, there being no provision in the laws for substitutions, the authorities could not accept the offers.

To the credit of local officials, though George himself withheld acknowledgment, most justices ignored the deadly weapon of the oath. In certain places, as in Worcestershire, magistrates who used it too freely brought upon themselves the criticism of Cromwell's military officers. Quakers, one general said, were peaceful people who deserved protection rather than persecution, but, being a fair-minded man, he warned the Friends against disrupting religious services.

Though, on the whole, Fox's premonitions were well grounded, there were other signs of relaxation of the anti-Quaker campaign. Fox and his companions rode unmolested through several counties, including Colonel Hacker's territory and Fox's home town, Drayton. George noticed the freedom; he asked a relative why the priests raised no hand against him. The relative, apparently more favorably disposed toward George than was any other member of the family, explained that a priest had died, leaving a rich living open; the brethren of the cloth, he said, were in contention for it.

"They will let you alone now," he said, "for they are like a company of crows; when a rotten sheep is dead they all gather together to pluck out his puddings and so do the priests for a fallen benefice."

Forbearance was not general nor were successes unbroken. George Fox held glorious meetings, as he usually did, winning wide acclaim for seeming to restore two ailing women to full health, but other Quakers were unfortunate.

Two of the Swarthmoor group, plain-spoken Miles Halhead and Thomas Salthouse, the Fell estate manager, rode into Devon, where, against a sheriff's insistence upon their innocence, a magistrate jailed them as Cavalier conspirators. After ten days they were released, only to be deported from the county for failing to produce loyalty certificates signed by military authorities.

On their way homeward, they stopped at Plymouth, where they were arrested for disturbing the peace. The circumstances were, to say the least, peculiar. A ship's captain heard them and, breaking in upon the meeting as Friends had themselves spoken in steeple-houses, lauded them for speaking truth. Someone, neither Halhead nor Salthouse, challenged the captain's words, so angering him that he swore out a warrant against the Friends he had just praised.

Halhead and Salthouse lay in jail six weeks awaiting trial, not knowing that they were supposed to ask for it; when at last they petitioned, their plea was rejected because the request did not specify a wish to be tried "by God and my country," as was the usual formula. They remained seven months more in jail, the warden being under orders to arrest anyone who came to see them.

Meanwhile, Fox returned to London, where missionary agitation, though still rife, was less feverish. He found omens unfavorable. Nayler was still gaining converts, but something about the man's manner caused Fox to feel uneasy. He had twinges of fear, presentiments of trouble; he saw darkness looming.

He was about to enter Cornwall, the last dark corner of the Commonwealth, but in making this pilgrimage, his first invasion of unbroken territory since opening Yorkshire, he had scanty advance information. He knew that Cornwall, geographically isolated and speaking a dialect incomprehensible to other Englishmen, possessed a strong and fiercely independent spirit. Religious conflict raged, as elsewhere, but Cornwall was less divided; there were fewer Seekers here.

George Fox may not have been the ideal man to open Cornwall to the truth. Sincere and dedicated though he was, his appeal was to the spirit and the heart. Knowing but two types of man, the good and the depraved, he owned but little subtlety. He convinced by sweetness or by strength; if listeners were ready to receive his message, he won them by love, but if they resisted, he would warn and wait until the terror worked within their hearts to soften them.

Had Cornishmen been simpler folk, as were other Englishmen, George Fox would have handled them with ease. But Cornish people were complex and paradoxical. He found in

Cornwall a strange mixture of traditionalism and adventurousness, of lawlessness and addiction to petty litigation, of restlessness and conservatism. Royalists were stronger here than in any other part of England, yet Cornishmen prided themselves on independence. They were bold and brave, yet only half a dozen years before they hid in their harbors because, they said, Moorish pirates lurked just beyond the horizon line.

Fox, almost never able to adjust his methods to his audience, branded Cornishmen as rude and uncivil, raging, jangling and superstitious. On his journey toward Cornwall, he left his belt at an inn where he stayed one night; his host kept it, but, fearful that it was bewitched, burned it in self-protection. George also judged the people frivolous. He met a cavalry captain who invited him to stay, but Fox, repelled because the captain was the merriest, most cheerful—and also the fattest—man whom he had ever seen, refused the invitation. Instead, he lectured him into seriousness, so that, in the end, the captain died in the truth.

Some, being frivolous, refused to take Fox seriously. Even before he came to Cornwall, in Devon he found dark towns. George came to an inn which was raucous with laughter. He entered the taproom and tried to turn people to the light. The innkeeper, having a sense of humor as well as a sharp eye to business, snatched up a candle and handed it to Fox. "Here's your light," he cried; "now go to your room." George saw no humor in the uncivil gesture; he warned the innkeeper of the day of the Lord.[1]

Before entering Cornwall, Fox and two companions forwarded to the dark people a letter announcing that Christ was

---

[1] He may have pained the innkeeper worse by ignoring the local legend that the town's founder was a refugee Trojan, incredibly named Brutus, who landed here, set himself upon a stone and said, in perfect English,
Here I am and here I rest,
And this town shall be called Totnes.

coming and that those who would not listen would be cut off. The warning was forthright and explicit; believe or be damned.

As on so many occasions, Fox invited trouble. Although three times tried for blasphemy and twice convicted, he deliberately chose expressions which a non-Quaker, even if unprejudiced, could easily construe as a claim to personal divinity. Completely indifferent to worldly thought or prejudice, regardless of interpretations other people might give his words, he was reckless in his writing. He did not weigh his words. Convinced that he was carrying Christ's words, he gave no heed to the idea that some might think that he was claiming to be Christ.

Major Peter Ceely, justice of the peace, certainly thought so; he summoned the Quakers to appear before him at St. Ives. Fox came and, without waiting to learn what charge Ceely was about to lay, launched into an indignant lecture on the town's impoliteness. "I never saw ruder people. The Indians were more like Christians."

What George Fox meant by the comparison is difficult to determine. He had never seen an Indian, either of the Old World or the New; all that he knew of America, in fact, was that the Massachusetts colonists were savage, while the Indians were kind. At any rate the outburst angered Ceely who, Fox said, cursed and insulted him before demanding to know if Fox wrote the warning letter. When George admitted authorship, Ceely demanded that he take the oath of abjuration.

Instead, Fox handed the justices of the peace a copy of the paper given Oliver Cromwell "in the presence of the Lord God," the document of which the Protector remarked that he had never seen the like.

It may have been good enough for Cromwell, but for Peter Ceely it was not. On January 18, 1656, he sent George Fox and his two associates to Launceston jail. If, as George believed, Major Ceely was a persecutor, he followed a strange course; for, while he had perfectly valid reasons for committing Fox as a blasphemer, subject as a repeated offender, to exile or death, he charged him only as a traveller without a valid passport, a disturber of the peace and, which was much worse, a refuser of the oath, which meant, of course, a suspected rebel.

As happened so often when Fox travelled under guard, the march to Launceston was somewhat informal. His soldier escorts did not enjoy their assignment; they wished to finish it as rapidly as possible. George would not have it so. He insisted on preaching to people whom he met upon the roads and, surprisingly, the troops allowed him to speak. Fox, however, was not as considerate, although he professed concern for the soldiers' welfare. When Sunday came, for instance, the guard desired to push ahead, but George refused to travel; they should not work, he said, upon their Sabbath but should rest and listen to his sermon. The three Quakers talked in relays all day long.

When Monday dawned, the soldiers started off, but no sooner were they under way than George remembered that there was an old man some distance back to whom he wished to speak some more; abandoning the column, disregarding warnings that the guard would shoot, he strode back toward the village. Thus the jail-bound convoy turned about. George talked to his friend, delivered another sermon and then consented to start off again.

He showed no gratitude for the tolerance. A more vindictive guard, faced by a prisoner's refusal to obey orders, would have shot him and, though a court-martial would have followed, would have been acquitted for the deed. Fox's escort, comprised as it was of dark, worldly troops, humored their exasperating charge.

Fox, however, reproved them for their rudeness and violence. The Quaker behavior so displeased John Keate, commander of the military escort, that Fox suspected he would seek revenge. George foiled the design by bolting his door that night; but next day Keate billeted a rude, wicked fellow with the Friends. Fox, as usual, bid his roommate fear the Lord but the fellow punched him. Keate was standing guard outside the door.

"Keate," called Fox, "do you allow this?"

"Yes," Keate answered curtly.

"Is this manly, civil or Christian?" Fox persisted.

Keate gave no answer, so Fox sent for a constable. When the officer arrived, George had him look at the warrant of arrest commanding Keate to take the Quakers safe to jail. As Keate had disobeyed that order by approving the attack, Fox argued, the warrant was now void and so the Quakers must go free. The constable agreed and, as a one-man civilian police force, he overruled the military.

Fox was not content; he showed the soldiers the baseness of their attitude toward him; they wilted pitifully at the reproof. At last, they came to Fox and begged him to change his mind; they would be civil, they promised, if only he would go to jail.

George was agreeable, but the constable had reservations; he must, he said, consult the governor about the matter. Unfortunately, the governor was not at home; he had gone to meet the major general commanding the six southwestern counties. News of the general's proximity further disturbed the soldiers; again they pleaded with George Fox to be co-operative. On their promise to behave more civilly, Fox agreed to stay arrested.

Keate probably hoped to avoid meeting Major General John Desborough, his recently appointed commander in chief. Desborough, famous in the west for his suppression of royalist uprisings, had just arrived from London, where he had been a councillor of state and commissioner for both the navy and the treasury. He was rustic in origin, person and manner, but he was powerful, not only as an officer but because he happened to be Cromwell's brother-in-law. He was also a martinet who would have no patience with army personnel who knuckled down to constables.

Thanks to a Desborough captain who knew Fox and pleaded for him, the general, to everyone's surprise, ignored what Keate had done; probably no one told him of it. He saw Fox, but, on the plea that the weather was cold, begged off from speaking to him, much less hearing a sermon. Fox called him hardhearted, ignoring his offer of liberty for the Quakers if only they would go home and stay there, an invitation the Quakers predictably refused.

Keate, breathing more easily because the general had failed to reprimand him, tried again, Fox thought, to have the Quakers murdered. Fox found himself billeted with a swordcarrying man; when George complained, Keate bade him be quiet for the fellow was an uncontrollable lunatic. Fox then was assigned a room to himself, whence he emerged to lecture the hardened dark people at the inn. He made no converts and the soldiers, their mission virtually complete, broke their promises and bothered him all night with drunken shouts. Next day, Keate turned his prisoners over to the jailer and went his way.

For nine weeks the Friends lay in prison awaiting trial. Like previous wardens, the jailer began by being cruel and abusive, but, unlike Sharman of Derby or Sheriff Reckless of Nottingham, he did not soften—probably because none of the Quakers paid the fourteen shillings weekly he demanded from each for their food and lodging.

His anger did not prevent his allowing the usual stream of visitors to hear Fox preach the gospel. They also came, as at Derby, to see the men who were to die, for local priests, according to George Fox, assured parishioners that all three Quakers would be hanged.

Their confidence was difficult to fathom. Vagrancy, breach of the peace or refusal to give bond were certainly not capital offenses and, while refusal to take the Oath of Abjurgation involved suspicion of treason, the penalty was imprisonment and forfeiture of estate. Fox did not seem surprised at their prediction; he may have thought that blasphemy, though not yet charged against him, might be read into his warning that Christ was coming into Cornwall.

19

Doomsdale

THE TRIAL, IN MARCH, WAS SOMETHING OF A SOCIAL EVENT.
Swarms of curiosity seekers came through fertile fields and
well-watered valleys from Dartmoor on the east or over the
Cornish hills upon the west. They crossed the swift-flowing
Tamar river by Polsten bridge and climbed uphill to the dark
and lofty ancient castle. From every doorway and window of
the medieval town villagers watched Captain William Braddon, famous for his zeal seven years before in ejecting Church
of England ministers, patrol his cavalry along the narrow
streets.

George Fox and his Quaker colleagues were beyond surprise, else they would have wondered why Sir John Glynne,
Lord Chief Justice of England, presided over what was ostensibly a provincial trial for vagrancy, or why, in such a minor
case, he was so touchy about his dignity. The testy Welshman
twice demanded that his Quaker prisoners remove their hats;
twice the Friends, standing silently, failed to obey. He ordered
them a third time to comply, whereupon Fox inquired where
in the Bible, "from Moses to Daniel," or, for that matter, in
British law, were defendants commanded to remove their hats.

Glynne, a zealous Presbyterian, respected the Bible, but he
failed to see that Scripture justified Quaker rudeness. He sent

the prisoners back to jail to think their action over, but they had scarcely left the room when he had a sudden thought. Recalling the culprits, he asked triumphantly, "Come, where had they hats from Moses to Daniel?"

"In the third of Daniel," George shot back. "The three children were cast into the fiery furnace by Nebuchadnezzar with their cloaks, hose and hats on. And you may see that Nebuchadnezzar was not offended at their hats."

Unlike Nebuchadnezzar, Glynne was offended; he sent the Quakers back to jail among the thieves. Eventually, he summoned them again, this time complaining against a paper Fox had written against oath taking. Fox dared him to read the paper aloud so that the audience might judge if it were seditious, but Glynne dropped the matter. Instead, he again objected to the hats, so Fox asked, with maddening politeness, if he and his companions had lain nine weeks in jail for no reason other than their hats. Glynne launched into a tirade. He was, he pointed out, the personal representative of the Lord Protector; an insult to him was an insult to Cromwell. To insult Cromwell confessed one's self a royalist and royalists were traitors to the Commonwealth. As Cromwell's appointee as Lord Chief Justice he was entitled to courtesy.

"Well," interrupted Fox, "if you are Lord Chief Justice, give us justice for our false imprisonment."

The true cause of the long imprisonment and for the trial itself then came to light. Major Peter Ceely, who had sworn out the original warrant of arrest was sitting on the bench with the judges. Abandoning the charges upon which he had arrested Fox, he now testified under oath that George was a royalist rebel. Fox had attempted, Ceely swore, to recruit the major in a fantastic plot to raise thousands of men "in an hour's time," to restore King Charles.

Ceely, being, as he said, an honest and loyal servant of the

Commonwealth, rejected the devilish design. Instead, he did his best to hurry the wicked Fox out of Cornwall, but as George Fox would not go, he, Major Peter Ceely, had arrested him.

"And, if it please you, my Lord, I have a witness to swear it."

No witness was ever called, for the plain and simple reason that there was no witness to such a blatant lie. The outraged Fox filled the courtroom with shouts that the whole story was false. If, by any remote imagining, there might have been a grain of truth in it, which there was not, then he, George Fox, was not the guilty man but Peter Ceely was. Had not Ceely testified, and under oath, that he was willing to connive in letting a traitor flee?

In any event, George Fox informed the Lord Chief Justice of the nation, the whole trial was illegal; he was being tried for something not specified in the warrant. He demanded that the warrant be read aloud. The judge refused. Fox insisted, and the judge again denied him.

"Take him away," Glynne ordered the jailer. "I will see whether he or I shall be master."

He soon saw. Fox handed the warrant to a companion who read it aloud in a hushed court. Ceely was not yet silenced. Once more, from his seat upon the bench, he asked permission to be heard.

"My Lord," he said, "this man struck me and gave me such a blow as I never had in my life."

Fox flared again. "Where did I strike thee and who is thy witness?"

"In the Castle Green," said Ceely, "and Captain Braddon was standing by."

Braddon bowed his head and did not speak a word, though George pressed him to testify. As neither the judge nor anyone else believed the lying charges, Glynne dismissed the case; but he fined the Quakers about £15 each for not removing their hats and ordered them held in jail until they paid the fines. Braddon called that night to see Fox in prison and George asked him when he saw Ceely struck.

"Why," he explained, "when Major Ceely and I came by you when you were walking in the Castle Green, he doffed his hat to you and said, 'How do you, Mr. Fox? Your servant, Sir.' Then you said, 'Major Ceely, take heed of hypocrisy and a rotten heart, for when came I to be thy master and thee my servant?'"

Such was the great blow of which Ceely complained. His perjuries failed to weaken his standing in the community; in subsequent elections they chose him as a member of Parliament.

Launceston prison may not have been the worst in England, as Fox considered it, but, if his description is correct, it was a strong contender for the title.

At all events, it was a most unhappy and unfortunate place. All natural advantages were its own. Lying on the Devon-Cornwall border where the London-Exeter-Land's End road crossed the road from Biddeford to Plymouth, set high upon Windmill Hill, the hub of every major street of the thriving market town, it commanded a magnificent view. With but a little labor the slopes were steepened and the top flattened to form a castle mound of typical Norman pattern, its strength increased by earthworks, palisades and walls. Yet, from the beginning, the place was badly built and more badly kept; its double concentric walls falling into decay, its moat so poor that, as early as the fourteenth century, complaints were heard that town swine had trampled down the embankment. Nor, Fox judged, had it been repaired or even cleaned for several centuries.

Even had it been immaculate, the prison would have been unbearable. Colonel Robert Bennett, member of Parliament and Baptist preacher, who owned the jail—he also owned Tintagel, of King Arthur fame—chose ex-convicts as its wardens. The chief jailer, his underkeeper, and their wives all bore the brands of thieves upon their hands; they had been branded also on their shoulders. Fox found them devilish and wicked, vindictive toward Quakers who would not pay the prison fees, sadists and vicious torturers.

The Quakers, officially committed for nothing but refusal to pay fines, were clapped into a small room off the North Gate beneath the chamber where the warden slept with a few of the more favored convicts. Originally this Quaker room possessed two doors, one leading into the gate vestibule and the other into the courtyard; but before Fox arrived the latter had been blocked up so that, except for the one door, kept locked, the only ventilation was through the ladder way into the room above. There was, to be sure, also a small inch-wide slit some seven feet above the floor through which a little air might have come from the gateway, but since Fox did not mention this opening it may, in his time, also have been blocked up.

In this small room, no more than twelve feet by twenty, the three Quakers were confined. It was a stinking hole, indescribably filthy, customarily used for two purposes—to house witches, of whom Cornwall had plenty, and as a death house for murderers awaiting execution. Because no one, as Fox was assured, escaped alive, the place was known as Doomsdale; if inmates were not hanged, killed by fellow prisoners or sickened unto death, the hordes of evil spirits infesting the air drove them to suicide.[1]

---

[1].Even so, Doomsdale, contrary to Fox's assertion, may have been an improvement on other prisons. The death house at Cheshire, for example, crawled with snakes; there was also a niche, a foot and a half wide, about

Quite possibly, George Fox drew a blacker picture than was justified. He complained that there was insufficient ventilation, yet he told of townsfolk passing food and various supplies through the bars; he spoke of isolation, yet he recorded that visitors came by night with no apparent interference from the guards.

Worse than the brutality of the keepers was the filth of Doomsdale, the sludge and slime of centuries. Fox pleaded for permission to clean up the rotting muck, but the warden refused him. George then asked for bedding, a load or two of straw to raise the prisoners above the mess; this, too, was denied, as was a request to have the door opened once in a while to clear the fetid air. Somehow, nevertheless, Fox received a little straw, though not from the warden, and a candle for light; but, seemingly, someone knocked the lighted candle over and the straw caught fire.

The reek of the sodden straw added to the smell. It choked the Quakers. Rising through the ladder opening, it also choked the warden. He and his convict cronies pounded on the floor above; they yelled to those tney called "hatchet-faced dogs" to quench the fire; the warden followed this by pouring the contents of his waste bucket upon the Quakers below.

"We had the stink under our feet before," Fox complained. "Now we had it on our backs; we could not touch ourselves or one another. In this manner we stood all night, for we could not sit down, the place being so foul."

Yet, under all these difficulties, George managed, as at Derby, to draft a petition for relief and, what is more, to send

as deep and only five feet high, on the face of its wall, where prisoners stood, precariously balanced, half-crouched, for hours.

Doomsdale was probably no worse than the Essex prison where James Parnell tumbled to his death, but it was bad enough. Nor were its evil wardens worse than prison keepers elsewhere; to change the personnel by bringing in the staff of any other jail would not have eased the situation.

copies not only to the court but also to Oliver Cromwell. The petition brought quick action; the justices ordered Doomsdale cleaned, the door opened and the Quakers given permission to buy food in the town.

The improvements coincided with the arrival at Launceston of Ann Downer, the thirty-year-old Friend who had been the first woman to preach in the metropolis. Knowing from her own experience how grievously the prisoners needed help, she had walked two hundred miles to be their cook and secretary.

Ann Downer was not the only Samaritan. From every shire in England, Friends and sympathizers flocked to Launceston, if, that is, they escaped Cornish constables, who arrested twenty-six Quaker travellers as vagabonds. By argument, persuasion, above all by the force of his example, Fox sufficiently overcame Cornish conservatism as to convince important people, including a baronet's daughter and two justices of the peace.

The winning of one of these, Colonel Anthony Rous, member of half a hundred Parliamentary committees, almost dumbfounded the colonel's friends. A rich tin magnate, proud of being affluent enough to have paid a fine of £700, he was an inveterate talker. Fox said of him, and surely George Fox of all people was an authority upon the subject, that Rous was "as full of words and talk as ever I heard a man in my life."

Rous opened the floodgates upon George Fox. He would not be interrupted. Fox disliked the medicine he himself usually administered. In vain, he tried several times to get in a word. Rous would not yield the floor. At last, Fox tried shock treatment.

"Wast thou ever in school?" he asked suddenly.

Rous, taken by surprise, stopped short. "At school? Certainly."

"At school?" cried the soldiers. "Why the colonel's a scholar!"

"Knowest thou about questions and answers?"

"Why, of course."

"Then keep quiet, if thou canst, whilst thou hearest some answers."

George then unloosed his own torrent of words, telling Rous in a loud voice exactly what he thought of the colonel's sinful life and how he might either accept the truth or be condemned. "Now," he concluded, "if thou hast anything to say, thou mayest."

Colonel Rous, justice of the peace, member of Parliament, business executive and a leading citizen of Cornwall, behaved exactly like a schoolboy lectured by his principal. "He was stricken dumb and his mouth was shut, and he cast his head up and down and his face swelled, and he could not speak for a good space. His face was red as a turkey. His lips rent and he mumbled and the people thought he would have fallen down." George started over to comfort him, while Rous muttered, "I was never like this before."

"Forever after the man was very loving to Friends and never so full of airy words after to me."

All was not as easy as the Rous conversion. Fox sensed snares; he saw drawn knives threatening. He heard a conjurer threaten to cut his chops. The warden got drunk and abused the Friends; he and the mayor stole a cheese from the prisoner on the pretense that it hid treasonable letters and, when they found no such letters, refused to give it back.

The mayor, a very wicked man, professed himself watchful about seditious correspondence. He stopped perfectly respectable women and ran his hands under their clothes to see if they had letters about them.

George baited a trap for the prying official. Writing a scathing letter about such indignities, he sealed it and then sent it out of town to be brought back by a Quaker visitor. The mayor, as anticipated, halted the courier, made his search and, pouncing upon the decoy letter, opened it in gleeful expectation. Instead of finding treason he read his own misdeeds.

"From that time he meddled little more with the servants of the Lord."

By this time, the Quaker protests had reached Oliver Cromwell. Though the news-book *Mercurius Politicus* was complaining that Cromwell's punishments were entirely too light for giddy people like the Friends, Cromwell thought differently. His chaplain assured him that no greater service could be rendered Quakerism than to keep George Fox in jail. He was deeply impressed, moreover, by two requests he had received, one from Humphrey Norton, himself just out of Durham jail, and the other from Joseph Nicholson, to serve out Fox's sentence themselves.

"Which of you," he asked his embarrassed Council, "would do the same for me if I was in the same condition?"

The Protector ordered an investigation. He may, at the same time, have hinted to his brother-in-law, General Desborough, that burdens upon the Quakers be reduced, but perhaps Desborough, in gratitude for Ann Downer's nursing his sick wife, needed no such hint. Whatever the motivating cause, Fox and his Friends now wandered freely in Launceston, but the jailer was beaten, put into irons and cast into Doomsdale, where he begged of the Friends.

Fox gave Cromwell little credit and Desborough none. "I saw it was the Lord alone that did preserve me out of and over their bloody hands, for the Devil had a great enmity to me and stirred up his instruments to seek my hurt."[2]

[2] The Devil's instruments were ill rewarded. The jailer "grew to be very poor and died in prison and his wife and family came to misery." Desborough, whom Fox saw bowling merrily upon the Green, went to jail himself. Ceely lost his high position and Lord Chief Justice Glynne died. Some of these retributions fell four years later, when the Restoration punished Cromwell's aides, and Glynne's death occurred ten years after Fox left jail. But George was positive that all had suffered for the wrongs inflicted on the Friends.

Full release arrived in September, 1656, five months after the Quakers had been sent to Doomsdale. Colonel Bennet made a last despairing try to collect the warden's fees—the persecutors never learned!—"but at last the power of the Lord came over him so that he set us free at liberty."

As the Quakers were riding out of town, a constable came running with the cheese. The mayor, the constable declared, was tormented by it. The Friends, experiencing no desire to lighten his worries, refused to accept it.

20

London Uprising

JAMES NAYLER "RAN OUT INTO IMAGINATION AND A COMPANY with him and they raised up a great darkness in the nation. And he came to Bristol and raised a disturbance."

He did, indeed. George Fox's brief account is Quakerism's greatest understatement. Nayler's imagination and George's resentment of it seriously undermined the Quaker movement. Both men were at fault. Each fell victim of the excessive adulation which hysterical admirers thrust upon them. There was, however, a great difference. Fox, as managing director of Quakerism, was steadily attracting greater power and was increasingly accepting flattery as his due; the jeering title "Pope of the North," while certainly an exaggeration, was not entirely misapplied. Though he now received no visions and though openings had ceased, he was so certain that the Lord inspired his every thought and action that his *Journal* less frequently carried proper credit to his source of inspiration. At times, he showed signs of being miffed if doubt appeared as to his right to lay down Quaker policy or to arrange Quaker affairs; occasionally he acted as though jealous of another's pretension. Nevertheless, he kept a level head, nor did he, at any time, presume upon his privilege.

Nayler, on the other hand, was highly susceptible. More

spectacular than Fox, though less intense and less convincing, powerful in preaching where Fox was powerful in prayer, Nayler gained a personal popularity that spared him great suffering. He was imprisoned, to be sure, and sometimes beaten, but, for four years after his Furness experience, he was not seriously bothered. Then, in July, 1656, he and twenty-one companions were arrested in Devonshire merely for trying to visit Fox in Launceston. Among those companions were nine women.

For Nayler especially attracted women. They liked him and he reciprocated their attentions. Upon his call to military service for the Commonwealth in 1642, he left his wife and family and never returned to them, but other women flocked about him. Necessarily, there were rumors, many of them maliciously false, growing out of the fact that Quaker women idolized him and that, when they told him that he looked like Jesus Christ, he carefully trimmed his reddish-brown hair and his short, forked beard to further the illusion.

Looking back upon events, Fox recalled that, on at least two occasions, he had felt uneasy about James Nayler; he did not pinpoint the cause, but possibly he noticed that, when Friends gathered, men circled about him while women fluttered about Nayler. Had he asked some of the more sedate ladies, he would have been told that Nayler was being bewitched, that the emotional and unpredictable Martha Simonds was casting spells upon him.[1]

Howgill and Burrough, sensing her instability, strongly discouraged her ambitions. Nayler, who at first agreed with his associates, softened when she applied her flattery, her witchcraft. He listened when she implied that though George Fox

[1] Martha knew from experience the horrors of imprisonment, but neither she, her husband nor, for that matter, anyone else at the time, realized how deeply her four months in Norfolk prison had deranged her. She emerged convinced that she must be a minister and that she must follow in the footsteps of her spiritual master, Nayler.

spoke the word of the Lord, others, meaning of course James
Nayler, might be equally inspired by revelations. In fact, she
more than implied, that one who spoke by the power of the
Lord, and one whose features so resembled those of Jesus
Christ, might himself actually be . . .

There was no need to complete the sentence. Nayler anticipated her meaning. Nor was Martha Simonds alone in her
wonderment. Neither her husband, himself just out of prison,
nor her brother, Giles Calvert the Quaker publisher, saw anything amiss in her unspoken blasphemy. Nayler himself was
too flattered to protest; if he raised the least objection it was
very weak. Who was he to question what the Lord moved her
to speak?

To put the matter plainly, he, too, was probably not mentally responsible. Filled by the Inner Light, moved by the spirit
of Christ and the Apostles, he, like George Fox himself, found
it difficult to differentiate between what he said as the voice of
God and what he said as mortal man. Those who did not own
the Inner Light would certainly misunderstand, but if the Lord
God chose an agent upon earth what human being could refuse
the role?

When George Fox heard all this he protested vehemently.
As source and guardian of truth, jealous of the purity of
Quaker principles, he recoiled in horror. As director of Quaker
activities, he rightly judged that Nayler's pretensions, whether
his own or imputed to him, would retard Quaker progress for
many, many years; it would lead to severe persecutions.

Nayler himself had qualms. This was the motive for his
hastening to Launceston to explain himself to Fox at the time
when he and his retinue were arrested. Instead of his calling
upon Fox at Doomsdale, Fox, just released from prison, visited
the jailed Nayler.

Reports vary concerning what occurred when the two men
met. Some said that Martha angered George by presenting

Nayler as his superior; others reported that Nayler, weak and nervous as the result of a long fast, pleaded almost pathetically for forgiveness. In either event, Fox had little talent in dealing with emotional women or with infatuated men. He treated Martha and Nayler as though they were normal, which they certainly were not; when they failed to respond as he thought they should, he accused them of wickedness of heart.

What Nayler really needed was freedom from the worshipping women and a great deal of sympathetic understanding. Fox achieved the first, but in a manner which wrought quite as much harm as good; he angrily accused Nayler of being their puppet, an accusation with which no man with delusions of grandeur could possibly agree. Instead of mollifying Naylar, Fox made him more sullen and resentful. As for sympathetic understanding, there was none. Nayler was not too far gone from reality to respond to tender, loving care, but George, who expected others to show kindness, sympathy and tolerance, was not the man to give such things to those who ran out from his truth.

He held a meeting in the prison, not to persuade Nayler but to bludgeon him. Nayler came, still fuming and resentful, still convinced that George was trying to play the overlord. For some inexplicable reason, his disordered mind conceived the thought that, as Quakers wore their hats in the presence of mortal men, he should also wear his hat before George Fox. Thus, while George spoke at the meeting, Nayler wore his hat; he failed to remove it when George began to pray.

Fox reacted precisely as judges reacted when hats were worn in court; he considered the matter a deliberate affront to God and to himself.

"So, after I had been warring with the world, now there was a wicked spirit risen up amongst Friends to war against."

Probably, there was no such thing; more likely, Nayler's failure to remove his hat was nothing but a temporary aberration of one not yet in full possession of his faculties. At the beginning of the prayer, he may have been unconscious of his hat, he may, indeed, have been absorbed by other thoughts; when, afterward, he realized that all others but himself were uncovered, his pride or his indignation may have induced a childish stubbornness. Certainly, it could not have been a declaration of war against George Fox.

Fox thought it was. Indignantly, he went back next day to the prison. He found James Nayler weeping, pathetically anxious to be friendly. As was then the fashion among intimates, he would have kissed George Fox, but George drew back.

"The Lord God moved me to slight him and to set the power of God over him."

Instead of taking a kiss upon the cheek or mouth, or even on his hand, Fox thrust forth his foot for Nayler's kiss. It was an unnecessarily rude gesture, which, like Nayler's retention of the hat, was the instinctive act of a resentful individual. Instead of helping to close the breach, the insult widened it. Nayler, who even yet might have been won back to friendship, lost what little repentance he had felt; he hardened against Fox.

Quickly, other Quakers chose sides. By far the larger faction supported Fox. Margaret Fell, in a letter intended for James Nayler, wrote: "Since I have heard that thou would not be subject to him to whom all nations shall bow, it hath grieved my spirit. . . . Oh, dear heart, mind while it is still called today what thou art doing, lest thou walk naked and be a stumbling block to the simple—return to thy first husband, my dear brother—I warn thee from the Lord God that thou beware of siding with unclean spirits lest thou be cut off for ever."

The letter is important, not only because it reveals the place of George Fox in contemporary Quakerism but for the language it employs. Expressions such as "dear heart" or "thy

first husband" are not to be taken literally; the one was a conventional phrase, the common greeting of one Friend, male or
female, to another, the other a synonym for spiritual leader.

It was this sort of language that induced non-Quakers, "the
world," to misinterpret the Quaker message, to scent blasphemy where no such offense was intended. Margaret Fell
could have had no thought that Fox should rule the world; it
is improbable that she threatened eternal damnation because
a man kept on his hat. Friends understood their own peculiar
language, the jargon of an uneducated people using Biblical
words and imagery without reflecting critically upon their
meaning; but outsiders did not realize the innocence with
which the words were used.

Nor, for that matter, did the Fox faction properly interpret
the tributes paid to Nayler by the latter's friends. Hannah
Stranger called him "the fairest of ten thousand," the "only
begotten Son of God"; her husband, surely a man without a
shred of jealousy, added a prediction, "Thy name shall be no
more James Nayler but Jesus."

Hannah's letter, with its addition, overwhelmed the praise-
hungry Nayler. Had he been wise or foresighted he would have
torn it up, but his vanity was stronger than his prudence and
so he pocketed the paper. Later, he would bitterly regret having saved that letter; it would be dangerous evidence when
found upon him.

He also kept a message from George Fox, blaming him for
allowing Martha and Hannah to act so foolishly. Their behavior, Fox complained, divided Quakerism; their impudence
defiled the truth. This letter also, intended only for James
Nayler, should have been destroyed, but it was not; it, too,
was evidence against the man. At the same time, it cleared
George Fox of any complicity in Nayler's extravagant pretensions.

Finding Nayler immovable, Fox opened a month-long evangelistic campaign which brought him to Bristol, his first visit to that seaport. A morning rally went off well and an afternoon open-air meeting was announced; but, when a notorious town rowdy named Paul Gwin boasted that he would make trouble, Friends suggested that George stay away. Gwin, they said, was the mayor's protege; if a disturbance occurred it would not be Gwin who would be jailed for it but Fox, the peaceful victim. George, never one to dodge danger, insisted on attending.

Thousands of expectant people waited for the promised excitement. Gwin, well fortified by a dinner supplied him by the mayor, swaggered up close to the great rock which was to be the rostrum. The crowd hushed as Fox appeared; it opened a way for him to reach the rock. The people waited tensely for Gwin to interrupt.

George played on Gwin's impatience. He stood silent on the rock, took off his broad-rimmed hat and let the wind blow through his long, curly hair. Those sharp eyes slowly surveyed the audience, resting with a special intensity upon Paul Gwin, but Fox said nothing. Accomplished heckler though he was, Gwin had nothing to brawl about. In a weak attempt to anger Fox, he jeered at George's hair, but George took no notice; the childish insult faded out.

It was excellent psychology; the bully had no notion what to do. He, too, stood silent for a while, then he burst out in complaint, not against George Fox but against his fellow townsmen. Why, he demanded, were so many intelligent people standing around to hear a man say something that he could not prove.

Fox had not yet said a single syllable, but now he asked what kind of fellow this was who said things like that about a man he had never heard, nor even seen, before. There was no answer, but George supplied one for them. A lying, envious, malicious spirit spoke in Gwin, said Fox, a spirit of the Devil. Then, focussing those piercing eyes on Gwin, he charged, "In the dread and power of the Lord, be silent."

The meeting thereafter was glorious and peaceable. Fox spoke for many hours, declaring virtually the whole body of Quaker doctrine and ending with one of his thundering, over-powering prayers. The Lord's power, he said, came over all. Gwin slunk away, so discredited among his associates, Fox implied, that he left town and emigrated to Barbados. Fox would meet him later in that overseas colony, but there was no further trouble in Bristol, or, for that matter, in the surrounding areas.

After some further meetings, Fox went down to London. Purely by chance, as he was riding into the city, he met Oliver Cromwell seated in a coach surrounded by a bodyguard. George, recalling the Protector's invitation to become better acquainted, rode toward him, but the guards blocked the way. Oliver, however, recognized Fox and told the guards to let him pass. They proceeded together from Hyde Park to White-hall, Fox shouting all the way exactly what the Lord thought of Cromwell for permitting an unchristian persecution of the Quakers. Cromwell took it very patiently and, when they reached his palace gate, again asked Fox to come see him sometime.

George did so, taking Edward Pyott, his Bristol companion, with him. Unlike his last, unsuccessful visit, when the guards barred his entrance, he was admitted. The Protector had another visitor, John Owen, the vice-chancellor of Oxford. What Fox actually said to this woman whipper is unrecorded except for the obvious understatement, "He spoke of the suffer-ings of Friends"; but we do know that George ordered Oliver to "lay down his crown at the feet of Jesus."

Cromwell, who apparently held no grudge because George

refused his dinner invitation or because of that loud and long-continued public lecture on the road, kept his temper at his command. Moreover, whether because of Fox's order or because he did not wish to be enthroned, he waved aside the crown.

Indeed, Oliver seemed to enjoy George Fox's outburst and his company. When he returned to Whitehall following the lecture, he went out of his way to tell a Quaker serving maid that he had good news for her, that George Fox was in town; he gave her time off to call on him. While at the audience, Fox, tilting his head up toward the taller Protector, was delivering a lengthy sermon, Cromwell moved over toward him and sat upon a table top so that, as he said, he might be on George's level. He chaffed Fox somewhat—George called it "speaking against the light of Christ Jesus"—until, tiring of the game, he went off chuckling.

Fox may have misinterpreted the subdued merriment; he reported that the Lord's power came over the Protector, but he failed to specify in what respect. He may have referred to Cromwell's willingness to listen and to credit what Fox said about reliance upon spiritual weapons only.

Yet, if Cromwell were content, others were not so sure. A growing band of religious enthusiasts, many of them Baptists, had been very vocal in predicting, on mystic grounds, that in this year 1656 a new era would begin, a millenium, when Christ would return to earth and, with his saints, rule a thousand years. This was foretold in Daniel and, with the passing of four great kingdoms, Assyrian, Persian, Greek and Roman, the time was ripe for this Fifth Monarchy. It would begin by the coming of the Messiah and by the overthrow of Oliver Cromwell.

There were not many of these Fifth Monarchists nor were they very dangerous; but, in a fearful Commonwealth which suspected revolution whenever half a dozen people gathered in a corner, no chances could be taken. The Quakers were suspicious people and they voiced seditious doctrine; were they not incessantly proclaiming that the Day of the Lord was close at hand and were there not those who hailed George Fox as a Messiah?

Or, if not Fox, James Nayler or, for that matter, any of the Quakers who professed to have an Inner Light that shone direct from Heaven.

If revolution came, worried officials felt, Cromwell would have only himself to blame. He tolerated Quakers. Moreover, earlier in the year, he allowed immigrant Jews to settle in England, though, save for a few temporarily resident foreign merchants, Jews had been absent for almost four hundred years. Jews were as dangerous as Jesuits, and, now that Oliver was coddling Fox, all might very possibly unite with the Fifth Monarchists. Cromwell was courting his own destruction.

Fear of such a coalition inspired much of the persecution Quakers underwent. As a group, the Friends took absolutely no part in any plot, nor was any responsible leader in any way involved in a conspiracy, but ultrafearful law-enforcing agents misconstrued what Quakers said, especially when Friends talked loosely. All too often, both army officers and local authorities accused Quakers of plots of which the Friends had never heard.

21

James Nayler

MEANWHILE, JAMES NAYLER, FREED FROM PRISON, WAS setting out through Devon and Somersetshire as the central figure of a fantastic cavalcade. He was a victim of his faith. Completely certain that, like George Fox and probably in greater measure, he walked in the Light and spoke the word of God, he knew himself to be a favored man, one high above his fellows.

Others shared his belief. Half a dozen enraptured women, and some men, caught up in exaltation, bowed low to James Nayler and to the Light within him; one or two of the more hysterically devout worshipped him as the Messiah come to earth.

Nayler, thoroughly befuddled to begin with, unconsciously accepted adulation as his due, though continuing, in complete sincerity, to disclaim his merit as a man. The fervor of each disciple so fanned the flames of all the others that emotion mounted high.

Even the locale enhanced excitement. Somerset was the mystic shire where Dunstan, the saintly hermit, uprooted heathenism and where Arthur's knights aspired to the Holy Grail. The legends would have left George Fox unmoved, but

Nayler's more poetic mind responded eagerly; the stories seemed appropriate to his condition.

Certainly, Glastonbury must have kindled his imagination. Local lore, which church authorities only very gently deprecate, insist that it was here that Joseph of Arimathea, the secret disciple who lent his own tomb to bury Jesus, founded the first Christian church in Britain. Near the rude shed of boughs and branches he set a thorn tree which, to this day, according to the faithful, blossoms every Christmas.[1]

If Nayler was thrilled by these stories, his susceptible attendants, Martha Simonds and Hannah Stranger, were electrified. As he rode through this Round Table country, Martha on one side of him and Hannah on the other sang his ecstatic praises; they spread their garments and late-autumn flowers over the narrow, muddy cart tracks where he rode. Whenever the procession stopped, they knelt before him, their heads lowered toward the earth.

Thus they came, in mid-afternoon of October 24th, to densely crowded Bristol. As though James Nayler were Jesus returned to earth, they led him through the ill-kept lanes toward St. Mary Redcliffe church. As the silent Nayler sat mounted, his hands clasped in prayer, his entourage waved boughs and chanted, "Holy, holy, holy, Lord God of Sabaoth."

Great crowds braved the rain to see the travesty, but the magistrates, shocked by what they thought blasphemy, arrested all of Nayler's people, including Dorcas Erbury, who was proclaiming that when she had fainted James had raised her from the dead.

---

[1] This, too, is secret; the flowering is visible only to those whose faith is boundless. Glastonbury and, for that matter, its neighbor, Street Friends Meeting, claim that a meetinghouse was set up in the abbot's kitchen, an octagonal room seventy-two feet high, as early as 1656. Euston House, however, has no record of it.

Nayler did not deny the miracle; he gave the credit to the Lord. He was not divine, he said, though, like all who lived by the Light, he was the child of God. When asked why he allowed the girls to sing his praises, he replied that the ladies sang only what the Lord moved them to sing.

These were standard answers, clear enough to Quakers but also clear, in quite a different sense, to worldly law enforcers. Friends understood the workings of the Inner Light and of the spirit of Christ within a true believer, and they knew that Nayler spoke with innocence; but non-Quakers—and, in this case, George Fox as well—saw nothing but the blackest guilt.

For Fox was angry because Nayler's pretensions perilled Quakerism. Never able to see more than his own side of any controversy, having not the faintest sympathy for any idea different from his own revealed Truth, he saw in James Nayler an enemy as black as any hireling priest.

There were personal differences, as well. Some supposed the men were jealous of each other's influence, but, though a good case might be made for this, it is more likely that their opposition sprang from their unlike temperaments. Fox was a domineering man, direct in method, unyielding in his principles; he knew as little about deviousness as of compromise. Nayler was a weaker individual, a follower rather than a leader, a nervous man who practiced the tenderness that George Fox preached. But, like so many people born to yield, he resented being driven; he could be managed easily if the reins were not drawn taut.

Though both were spiritually minded men and each was equally sincere, they saw things very differently. Fox's eyes were on the heavens; he lived for the future, knowing well that the road to Heaven lay along the routes plotted by the Hebrew Prophets and Apostles. Nayler, quite as devout, paid more attention to the economic problems of the current world; he sympathized with such reformers as the Diggers and the Levellers whom Fox ignored. Fox believed that labor problems would be solved when men feared God. Nayler wanted humane laws as well as softer hearts.

Nayler was a proud man, too, a man of sensitivity. Where Fox was shocked by rudeness to the Inner Light or to the word of God which he expressed, Nayler was hurt by discourtesy to a human being.

As neither the authoritarian classicist nor the liberal modernist really ever understood each other, they worked in harmony only when Fox's crudity was invisible and Nayler's charm was hidden or when George led unobtrusively while Nayler followed willingly; in short, to be blunt about it, when Fox and Nayler were apart. When George was in the North and James shining in London all went well, but when they neared each other there were sparks.

Because the magician of words spoke softly, smoothly and with lucidity, James Nayler admirably weathered most of the Bristol questioning. Little, in point of fact, was chargeable against him; actually he did nothing more upon his ride than sit a horse while others sang and genuflected. Whatever blasphemy was committed was not by him but by his hysterical companions. He might, to be sure, have restrained them, but he did not, nor would George Fox have done so; but neither failure to prevent blasphemy nor being a passive recipient of adulation was actionable under any existing law.

To the amazement of many Quakers, nothing was charged against Nayler's emotional companions; they were released, so that Nayler bore the entire burden of blame for that ride that mocked the uphill ride from the Garden of Gethsemane to the high walls of Jerusalem. Thomas Simonds, husband of the chanting Martha, was surprised; expecting that his wife would be tried for blasphemy, he wrote her to ask sadly why she had not held her tongue while others cried Hosannah.

It was well that she was not charged; she and Hannah Stranger, too, would have burst out emotionally had they been on trial, and would have ruined the case of all the Quaker defendants. Nayler, on the other hand, conducted himself admirably. Only once did he lose composure. A justice, reading the confiscated letter from George Fox, asked in curiosity why George said that Nayler called Martha his mother when, in fact, she was eight years his junior. Apparently, the question touched a nerve for Nayler answered angrily, "George Fox is a liar and a firebrand of hell, for neither I, nor any with me, called her so."

That the outburst was far more heated than the query warranted revealed the tumult boiling within James Nayler, partly because of the foot-kissing episode and partly because he knew that Fox had virtually disowned him.

Bristol magistrates washed their hands of the whole affair; they passed the matter on to London. Their avoidance may have been an accident, coming about because, when they inquired of their city clerk what should be done, he, a member of Parliament, brought the incident before the House of Commons. A huge committee, fifty-five members in all, took up the case, summoning Nayler and most of his entourage to London for a hearing.

The curious company weakened its cause. Nayler's party came, not as suspects, for as yet they were not formally charged with an offense, but as triumphant martyrs; they sang songs of praise as they marched along the roads. The tribute to Nayler was touching but the actions evidenced no repentence.

Nayler made a surprisingly good impression on the examining committee. Free now of the adoring women, he recovered much of his composure. He spoke convincingly and the committee members, while by no means scholars, were better able than provincial magistrates to appreciate the semantics and the subtleties of Quaker argument. They approved Nayler's summary :

"I do abhor that any of that honor which is due to God should be given to me as I am a creature. But it pleased the Lord to set me up as a sign of the coming of the righteous One and what hath been done in my passing through the towns, I was commanded by the power of the Lord to suffer such things to be done—as a sign. I abhor any honor as a creature."

Nevertheless, for political reasons, the committee reported, unfairly, that Nayler "assumed the gesture, words, honor, worship and miracles of our blessed Savior and His names."

Again Nayler denied the charges, this time before the full House. Long and often acrimonious debate ensued, not so much on the question of his guilt, for to defend Nayler would seem to be participation in his blasphemy, as on that of whether he or his companions were more at fault. He was judged guilty, but, the questions rose, how was he to be punished and who should inflict the punishment.

Precisely the same questions arose when Fox was tried at Derby, but the answers were much different. Nayler barely escaped death; a shift of but eight votes would have sent him to the block or to the pyre. Convicted on December 17, 1656, without the right of appeal, his punishment was to begin next day, a punishment which no civilized nation should have tolerated, much less described, as the Speaker described it, as merciful.

It was to be a four-part penalty, each section of which would seem more than adequate for his offense. After being pilloried two hours, half naked, on an icy day, he was roped to a cart, dragged through the streets and given more than three hundred lashes with a seven-cord knotted whip. When the ordeal was finished, every square inch of his body down to his waist was a mass of bloody cuts.

The "mercy" continued. Several ministers, including the chaplain of Cromwell's New Model Army, petitioned Parliament to remit the balance of the sentence, but the House, after consenting by a one-vote margin to receive the petition, rejected the idea. Sir George Downing, recently returned from protesting in France against the massacre of Huguenots, piously explained, "We are God's executioners and ought to be tender of His honor."

Cromwell himself asked why Parliament was acting as it did. He seemed to have been doubtful of its authority, but, if so, he failed to intervene. A week after the whipping, Nayler stood again for two hours in the pillory, Martha, Hannah and Dorcas beside him, while a placard, placed above his head by a fellow Quaker, read, "This is the King of the Jews." Taken from the pillory, Nayler was then branded on the forehead with a B for blasphemy, and a red-hot wire bored a hole through his tongue.

Robert Rich, a patriarchial gentleman who stalked through Quaker meetings with long, white beard and black-velvet coat half covered by a loose white duster, did little to ease poor Nayler's sufferings. It was he who, desisting for a time his constant chant, "Amen, amen, amen," fastened the King of the Jews sign over Nayler's head and so, however innocently, rekindled the charge of blasphemy. When the branding was done, Rich licked the wounds. "I am the dog," he boasted, "that licked Lazarus's sores."

Part three of the punishment took place in January at Bristol, the scene of the offense for which Nayler was being punished. Mounted backward on a horse, he was led along the same route he had taken before, Rich re-enacting the role that Hannah and Martha had played by singing "Holy, holy, holy" as they passed. Just what this was supposed to represent, no one quite knew, but certainly Rich was no help whatever.

When the ride was finished, a whipping followed; this time the strokes were more symbolic than painful. Act four took place in London again, when Nayler was jailed, *incommuncado,* at hard labor, until such time as Parliament should choose to release him. He remained there for almost three years.

Thus was Parliament tender of the honor of the Lord.

It would be easy at this point to criticise George Fox, to charge him with callous indifference toward an ailing mind, desertion of a colleague, jealous revenge against a rival who had been a loyal friend, passive acceptance of another's persecution. These would be harsh charges, but they could be brought and they could be supported by clear, cold evidence.

Nayler posed a challenge to his leadership, but Fox was not so petty as to use that challenge as excuse for throwing Nayler to the wolves. The self-deluded pretender to the throne, egged on by hysterical worshippers, proclaimed that he had the spirit of the Lord within him, but so did every other Quaker minister. If this assertion convicted Nayler of blasphemy, why, many others asked, was not George Fox equally at fault? Had he not confessed himself a son of God? Had he not professed to have seen God's very face? Had he not spoken as the mouthpiece of the Lord? And had George Fox not been glorified, if not idolized, less dramatically, perhaps, but quite as effusively as had James Nayler?

Other Friends, men as close to Fox as Hubberthorne, George Whitehead and Alexander Parker, pleaded Nayler's cause. None defended his hosannah processions, but they realized that he was suffering for what the women folk had done. Fox lent no aid nor comfort; his concern was not for Nayler, the man, individuals being unimportant in the cosmic scene, but for the future of the Quaker movement. The Friends were seriously split; the Nayler precedent might blight a thriving growth.

The defection was all the more serious because it was

220 VOICEVOICE OF THE LORD

of a different type from earlier deviations. Gilpin and Milner
set forth outlandish doctrines, but those dictations of the
Devil could be disowned by Quakerism's high command; Nayler, however unwittingly, was encouraging a faction that
threatened the leadership. His example could lead to further
splintering and so eventually kill Quakerism. Furthermore,
however humble James Nayler might be at heart, his giddy
chorus might shift their worship from the Lord God in Heaven
to James Nayler upon earth.

With catastrophe threatening the Friends and, more than
that, the acceptance of eternal Truth, Fox dared not fritter
away time or energy. To counteract Naylerism and thus protect
the larger good of all mankind, he hastened to rally his forces.
Unlike the impetuous Nayler, he planned carefully, mapping a
triangular itinerary that, by touching London, Yorkshire and
Bristol, would cover most of England and all the disaffected
centers. His presence at innumerable places, his preaching and
his counsel at hurriedly called conferences would heal the hurts
that Nayler had inflicted.

At the same time he became enthusiastic about sending
missionaries overseas. Nothing, except possibly Elizabeth Harris' Maryland visit, had gone well upon the North American
continent, but Halhead and Lancaster, Burrough and Howgill
had not done too badly in Ireland and there were hopes in
Scotland. During his stay at Launceston, Fox had changed his
mind; he now envisioned an ambitious program embracing
not only the British Isles but the Western European nations
and, in God's good time, the world.

"Let all nations hear the word by word or writing," Fox
announced. "Spare no place, spare not tongue or pen . . . be
valiant for the truth upon earth; tread and trample all that is
contrary under. . . . Bring all to the worship of God; plough
up the fallow ground. . . . Be patterns, be examples, in all
countries, places, islands, nations. . . ."

22

Mending the Breach

EVERYTHING WENT WELL UPON THE TOUR. FOX REPORTED THAT
the Truth was finely planted and that many thousands were
turning toward the Lord.

Quaker ideas were certainly acceptable. Every moral person
hated vice, dishonesty, wickedness and sin. Many already held
the concept of the Inner Light, though not invariably as
Quakers preached it. Thousands who questioned traditional
religious practices were already meditating silently, and some
were receiving revelations. The time was very ripe for Fox's
preaching.

He and the other dedicated men and women who illumined
spiritual darkness were tireless and self-sacrificing; many were
true saints. Their appeal was powerful, yet, for all the emotion
which surrounded them, their message was more to the brain
than to the heart; the term Fox used, convincement, expressed
precisely their method of conversion.

Would the Quaker movement have grown as fast without
the dramatics which Fox and his Publishers employed? The
staid Family of Love lagged behind the Ranters, and the more
sensational sects rushed beyond the quietists. Quakerism was
cerebral and would have gained its followers in any case, but
steeple-house interruptions, half-naked marches, George Fox's

invasion of bloody Lichfield and the floods of violent vituperation all advertised the movement to those who never would have heard the arguments.

Doubtless the excesses alienated many potential members and probably the queer ways and discourtesies of many Quakers annoyed others; nevertheless, large numbers of Britain's sturdy middle class accepted their ideas. Even their enemies acknowledged Quaker sincerity. The rudeness could be overlooked.

Actually, in most cases they were minimized, if not condoned. The impressive list of Quaker sufferings, many of them serious and uncalled-for, concealed the fact that, though ten or a dozen laws prohibited Quaker practices, the vast majority of Friends escaped punishment. Quakers could be, and many of them were, fined or imprisoned for violating the Blasphemy Act, for refusing oaths of allegiance, for breaking the Abjuration Act, for travelling on Sunday, for disturbing services, for not attending church, for alleged complicity in plots or for other reasons. However unwise, unfair, unreasonable or unconstitutional these various laws may have been, they were enactments which good citizens were bound to obey and Friends were liable under them. That during the ten years of the Commonwealth only about a thousand punishments were inflicted, many of them minor, and some of these deliberately invited, was evidence that only a fraction of the professing Quaker membership was penalised.

Nevertheless, the impact of persecution bore most heavily upon the leaders. Quakerism needed more fervent, emotional, colorful ministers to inspire its rank and file. Again, as always when Friends required a skilful manager, George Fox supplied the need. To those who had seen or heard him preach, his words conveyed a power that the printed message cannot possibly suggest.

"To the elect seed of God called Quakers," he wrote, "where

the death is brought unto the death, and the elder is servant to the younger, and the elect is known, which cannot be deceived, but obtains victory. This is the word of the Lord God to you all. Go not forth to the aggravating part, to strive with it out of the power of God, lest you hurt yourselves, and run into the same nature, out of the life. For patience must get the victory and answer that of God in every one, must bring everyone to it, and bring them from the contrary."

The words are, for the most part, sharp, brief, rugged, monosyllabic Anglo-Saxon, but the meaning is anything but clear. No English teacher would give the composition a passing grade. Yet, somehow, Fox injected into this jumble a glowing personality that captured and held listeners and readers, so holding them captive that, long after he was gone, his words, though meaningless, continued to exert their magic.

The North, scene of his first triumphs, remained his staunchest stronghold. Here Naylerism was weakest. The solid foundations of Preston Patrick and Margaret's work at the thriving Swarthmoor center were effective; new meetings, both quarterly and monthly, were operating smoothly.

Neither the efficient organizational machinery nor the vigorous leadership, however, safeguarded Quakerism against a serious inherent danger. The concept of private revelation by the Inner Light was beautiful and must, at all costs, be preserved; but, as Nayler's example showed, there was no guarantee that private revelations were authentic. Just as the Inner Light showed the godly how and where to walk, so there were other beacons, false guides set by the powers of darkness to lead the unwary into error. How was one to know what was right and what was wrong? If each individual followed the guidance within himself, Quakerism would disintegrate into a thousand factions, many of them, quite likely nearly all of them, directed by the Devil.

In the absence of an all-powerful central agency empowered

to sift the heretical from the orthodox, the problem of determining the truth was difficult to solve. Quakerism disapproved of hierarchies; they were hostile to the theory of spiritual democracy. Nor did Friends desire to discourage or to condemn the idea of continued revelation. Yet, as everyone was quite aware, not every person possessed equal ability to discern the truth.

To escape as best he could from the dilemma, Fox early in the Quaker movement appointed a group of the better endowed—he called them elders—to sift truth from error and so to keep faith pure. These individuals, easily recognized as favored by the Lord, received special treatment; often the Kendal Fund, or some private philanthropy, subsidized them, so that, as itinerant ministers, they might spread the truth throughout the elaborate network of meetings.

Great care was necessary lest the system degenerate into a type of paid priesthood similar to that to which Quakers so strenuously objected; detractors charged that, by assessing themselves to maintain the Kendal Fund, Friends were themselves resorting to tithing. There was, of course, a vital difference; ministers were not appointed to their livings by any group of clerics nor by a government, and their support was voluntary instead of forced by law. Quakers, moreover, liked to think that their evangelists qualified for their work by spiritual excellence rather than by proficiency in university studies.

Skilful deployment of these ministers by George Fox or, in his stead, the Fell group at Swarthmoor Hall, bound scattered Friends into a firm brotherhood cherishing a common belief and following similar practices. The itinerant ministers accustomed them to nation-wide joint action for constructive social ends.

For, unlike many mystics, Fox applied religion to immediate worldly needs. He stressed equality and justice, called for simplicity and peace, for humane labor relations and honesty in business, for prison reform and poor relief. As early as 1657, far in advance of his time, he pleaded for improvement of conditions among slaves; Negroes and Indians, he insisted, were as much children of God as were their masters. When people feared God and loved their fellow men all these reforms would come to pass.

The ideals of social betterment, spread by George Fox in his epistles and by the itinerant ministers, welded Quakers into an influential national society. Even yet the membership was but a small percentage of the English people, but because Quakerism was one of the first well disciplined, nation-wide propaganda agencies, Friends wielded an influence far greater than their numbers warranted.

Much of their impact was due to their publicity methods. In the absence of mass-circulation newspapers—the news-books had only limited distribution—Englishmen knew little of what was said and done beyond their immediate neighbor-hoods. Itinerant ministers, visiting every meeting in the country, guaranteed that Friends throughout the nation worked harmoniously and consistently toward common goals.

Early in the organizational period, Fox saw the value of published propaganda. He himself, in 1653, published a paper, the first of a lengthy series, with a long but catchy title beginning "To all who would know the way to the kingdom. . . ." His companions were equally prolific with their pens, there being, at the time of Nayler's extravagance, well over a hundred productions, varying in size from simple broadsides to thousand-page volumes. Probably he did not foresee that within the next five years the number of publications would quadruple, but he did sense that supervision was imperative.

Use the general meetings, Fox suggested, as a testing ground to prove which revelations were acceptable and, for further guarantee, let no doctrine be spread until endorsed by competent authority.

This constituted a form of censorship, a practice wholly out of keeping with professed Quaker principles yet an unavoidable method employed almost from the beginning. As early as 1653 there was an understanding that no Quaker writing should be printed without a Farnsworth, Nayler or Fox imprimatur, nor, for that matter, except by a certain approved Yorkshire publisher. Later this injunction was relaxed, with manuscripts being sent to London prior to publication. But because both Simonds and Calvert published on their own responsibility, the system did not work out too well.

Prepublication scrutiny not only unified Quaker doctrine; it also standardized Quaker speech and writing. Intense preoccupation with the King James version of the Bible by both writers and censors saved Quaker papers from either the involved rhetoric or the sesquipedalian verbiage that later became fashionable. The simple prose of common English speech so reached the hearts of humble people that approved writings were as readily received as was the Bible itself.

Acceptance was easier because the weeding process favored autobiography—not the recounting of family history, education or, for the most part, current events, but the narration of spiritual experience leading to convincement. Such journals, of which no less than sixteen were published prior to the Restoration, bound the group together; their self-examination, their revelations of the workings of the spirit within the writers helped others who thus saw that their spiritual unrest was not unique and that the outcome would be peace.

Fox sensed great propaganda value in the publishing of "sufferings," the injustices inflicted upon martyrs who lost property, freedom, health or life, and in making known the infractions against the rights either of individuals or of the Society of Friends. The recitals might have been vigorous complaints, but more often the testimony took the form of a memoir. In this, Fox was very wise for the bare narration was, in itself, a powerful protest against abuses.[1]

Once the message received approval, it usually came out in printings of a thousand copies, all of them paid for and half of them distributed at first by energetic Northern meetings. Here, too, Fox's executive ability was evident. Each local meeting might have as many copies as it desired, but Fox saw to it that rulers of all ranks, kings, Parliaments, mayors, justices and others in authority, received the Quaker message. He understood the uses of publicity.

With organization perfected, leadership established, censorship set up and heresy controlled, George Fox felt ready to embark on more campaigning.

He met, as might have been expected, considerable difficulty. Nayler's excited associates reawakened prejudice against the Friends, as did the outpouring of Quaker books and tracts. Conservatives objected not only to the Salvation Army tactics used by Quaker missioners but also to the principles of free speech, free press, free religion and, above all, the fraternity and equality which Friends advertised.

Though Friends, incessantly preoccupied by their soul searching, seldom spoke of or seemed to care about worldly politics—Fox's *Journal* virtually ignored the English Civil War —orthodox observers considered them revolutionists bent upon destruction of the state. Hidebound clerics, whether Anglican or Presbyterian, Baptist or Independent, thundered from their

[1] Surprisingly, the Friends published few sermons. To some extent, the Quaker epistle, of which George Fox wrote more than four hundred, served the purpose, for, as a rule, the epistle carried little news but much exhortation toward a godly life. The sermon, it has been suggested, was minimized as being a speech prepared well in advance and thus less dependent upon extemporaneous outpouring of the spirit; for this reason, Quakers frowned upon it. To take it down in shorthand or to reconstruct it from memory might tempt a speaker to rely upon a printed aid. No such prudence, however, applied to an epistle.

pulpits, assailing not only Quaker views but Quaker propaganda practices. No less a person than John Bunyan criticized
the Friends; incidentally, he not only thoroughly misunderstood what Quakers taught but also thought them witches.

In counteracting these misconceptions, Fox again met the
usual adversities. At Farnham, some forty miles from London,
he issued a general invitation to "all that feared God" to come
to his inn. A throng appeared, among them many of the town
notables, and, under the impression that George was giving a
party, called for food and drink, leaving Fox to pay the bill.

A few days later he came to Basingstoke, "a very rude
place," so called because in the preceding summer the authorities had not only arrested Quakers for holding a meeting but
stole their Bibles. Here Fox told the innkeeper of the Farnham
incident, whereupon the fellow called for beer and faggots—
today we would call them hamburgers—and, after drinking a
quart of beer, invited half a dozen others to join him, all
apparently to be at George's expense. When Fox objected, the
innkeeper became angry as well as drunk, and Fox had to lock
himself all night in his room.

There were, however, Fox reported, various "heavenly"
meetings and a couple of narrow escapes from officers of the
law. Fox also happened upon a group of itinerant quacks,
whom he confounded by inquiring whether Adam and Eve
were ever ill before their fall. He posed the question : "Whether
any knew the virtue of all the creatures in the creation, whose
virtue and nature was according to its first name, except they
were in the wisdom of God."

When they could not answer, which is scarcely surprising,
Fox had the question stuck up on the market cross. By this
action, he said, some were turned by the light and spirit of
Christ to His free teaching.

By this time it was March, 1657, and there was talk in

Parliament of inviting Cromwell to assume the Crown. Whether for this reason or, as is more likely, to protest once more against the continued maltreatment of Friends, Fox broke off his tour to rush up to London. Again, he met the Protector in the Park; this time, he warned Oliver against becoming king.

"They who would put thee on an earthly crown," George predicted, "will take away thy life. The only true crown is immortal."

Cromwell thanked him and, a few days later, rejected the kingship.

It was about this time that George Fox preached so effectively that Isaac Penington the Younger was convinced. The conversion was extraordinarily important. Penington was the eldest son of a former Lord Mayor of London; though not a profound intellectual, he was an able writer. His convincement marked a turning point in Quaker progress. Hitherto, members had been, for the most part, bourgeois; from now on they enlisted members of the upper classes. Quaker thinking, and more especially their writing, had been diffuse and disorganized; henceforth, ideas would be expressed more logically, more clearly and in better literary style. And, though proof is lacking, Penington's convincement in these last months of the Protector's life may have moved Oliver Cromwell toward a kindlier, more tolerant view of Quakerism.

Penington's accession cheered George Fox. Though Naylerism was by no means dead, he considered Friends relatively safe against disruption. Only one important pocket of discontent remained—in Wales, where Fox had not yet gone. He determined to attack the last dark region. To give misguided Naylerites ample opportunity to mend their ways, he sent word that "the day of their visitation was over."

The warning caused some to see their errors and repent. Those who did not, said Fox, "did not prosper noways."

The statement, a subjective judgment without statistical proof, may not have been entirely accurate, but the fact remained that Naylerism withered. A more trustworthy explanation for its collapse was his removal from the spotlight.

For, beyond a shadow of doubt, Nayler's appearance attracted the hysterical. If Martha Simonds and Hannah Stranger knelt before him, drying his wet feet with their hair and kissing them, so also men revered him. Martha's husband was not alone in admiration; another devoted man called Nayler "Son of Zion, whose mother is a Virgin and whose birth is immortal." Even after his downfall, with the exception of George Fox, every Quaker leader who saw James Nayler pleaded for his reinstatement.

Shut up in his cell, however, no longer able to cast spells by his personality, Nayler's appeal faded. While other Quaker deviations managed to persist with more or less intensity, the Nayler cult declined. Though apologists to this day, moved by the magic of his written word, excuse his weakness and denounce those who led him into error, there are no Naylor followers.

23

Wales and Scotland

WALES WELCOMED QUAKER TEACHINGS. AS IN ENGLAND, church organization lay in ruins. Welshmen disliked established religion because they thought it cold, routine and formal. The ejection of their Anglican rectors delighted them, but the colorless, barren Puritanism which followed held no appeal and unseemly squabbling over vacant benefices shocked them. Their enthusiastic Celtic temperaments approved of Quakerism not only because it was a return to primitive Christianity but because it encouraged individuality.

Actually, Wales invited Quakerism. In the summer of 1653, just before Fox was jailed at Carlisle, Morgan Llwyd, a Wrexham pastor, sent a two-man mission to Swarthmoor to investigate the glowing reports he was hearing of Fox's work. The envoys were so impressed that they returned to Wales convinced that Quakerism was the true faith; one missioner, John ap John, became the Quaker pioneer of Wales.

Their conversion was not difficult. Llwyd was already preaching doctrines similar to those of Fox. George's opposition to infant baptism was not strange to them, nor was his insistance that the church was not a man-made structure; Llwyd had taught them that a barn might be as holy as a great cathedral. Disdaining contemporary schooling, Llwyd asserted,

231

as did Fox, that learning was not necessary for a proper understanding of the Scriptures and that anyone whom the spirit
moved, be he a cobbler or a tinker, might preach the word
of God.

The similarity of ideas, if not Morgan Llwyd's anticipation
of Fox's thought, should have endeared the spiritual Welshman to George; but Fox harbored suspicions of the man.
Instead of being flattered by the mission to Swarthmoor, Fox
regarded the envoys as spies. He doubted, at first, ap John's
good faith. As soon as Carlisle freed him, therefore, Fox sent
two trustworthy Friends, Hubberthorne and John Lawson, to
hear Llwyd preach at Wrexham.

They found him in what was, for Llwyd, a most unusual
state of mind; he was wholeheartedly approving a religious
movement. Hitherto, he was uncertain just where he belonged,
for no sect suited him. In early manhood an Anglican, entitled
to take tithes, he resigned a living rather than accept the
money. Baptists claimed him, but he rejected their doctrines,
as well as those of the Puritans; he also quarrelled with the
Presbyterians. In desperation, he founded his own Independent
church, but this, too, was unsatisfactory; he felt uncomfortable
in isolation. But, on hearing ap John's report, he broke out,
excitedly,

"The dawn hath broken. The Sun hath risen. Awake, O
Welshmen, awake."

Lawson and Hubberthorne were not impressed; they may
have thought him too volatile. Though they approved his
stand on tithes, on church dues and on the equality of all men,
they were dissatisfied. That "great idol," the Wrexham church,
denied the power of God, they said—which meant that Llwyd
denied the pre-eminence of George Fox. They also charged
that Llwyd lived in pride, envy and covetousness, but they cited
no evidence.

The unfavorable report was prompted by Llwyd's sturdy independence; it also reflected his previous connections with so many sects which accused Quakers of blasphemy and witchcraft. Llwyd himself was wholly innocent of any such slanders, but Hubberthorne and Lawson lumped him with the covetous hirelings who mouthed hypocrisy.

Persecution befel both Hubberthorne and Lawson. As soon as the latter left Wales, the mayor of Chester jailed him, for no other cause, the Quakers said, than sitting quietly, but with his hat on, in a steeple-house. If this were indeed the only cause, the punishment was certainly excessive, for the botanist, one of the unluckiest of men, remained in prison half a year.

When Hubberthorne asked to visit his companion, the mayor, with sardonic humor, clapped him also into prison, though only for a week. Elizabeth Leavens and Jane Waugh, those inveterate martyrs, met the same fate; they, too, asked permission to see the Friends, and so, as they walked quietly along a street, they, too, were taken up and sent to jail.

None of these mishaps interrupted the evangelistic campaign in Wales. As soon as she was freed, Elizabeth Leavens, pausing only long enough to marry Thomas Holme, a Kendal weaver, brought her bridegroom, together with Elizabeth Fletcher, her fellow sufferer at Oxford, and the unconquerable Jane, back to Wales. This time they avoided Chester, entering Wales from the south.

They saw bright prospects. While Lawson, Hubberthorne and the women were being persecuted, ap John was spreading the Quaker message. The Welsh were welcoming the word; they admired the Quaker stress on simplicity, equal rights, private revelation and freedom of the individual.

There was, however, one great flaw in Wales, a weakness so serious that Holme, abandoning his honeymoon, hurried to disclose it to George Fox. Wales was being won for Quakerism, he reported, but not for the pure doctrine of George Fox.

The emotional Welsh were still infatuated by the glamor of James Nayler.

Holme held poor, vacillating Morgan Llwyd responsible. Two converging influences were corrupting him. A fellow Independent, William Erbury, a notorious religious malcontent, had long been singing Nayler's praises, and, though Erbury was now dead and gone, his daughter Dorcas, she whom Nayler raised from the dead, was continuing the propaganda. Nor was this all: Llwyd's London friends were none other than Giles Calvert, the publisher, and his sister Martha Simonds, the evil genius of the Nayler blasphemy.

Llwyd was also infected by Fifth Monarchism. He may have seen Quakerism as a vehicle for bringing in the millenium, but he rejected George Fox as its Messiah. None of these connections endeared him to Fox, who found Llwyd's parishioners rude, wild and airy, with little sense of truth.

In Wales, George faced a triple problem: he must dislodge the popular Llwyd, counteract Naylerism and campaign in what was virtually a foreign land whose people spoke an alien tongue.

To some degree he came prepared. Though the Welsh were as strange as were the words they spoke, psychologically they were akin to the Cornishmen, and, for that matter, to James Nayler. They, too, were paradoxical, emotional conservatives, practical mystics, disciplined folk who valued individuality. They, too, were hypersensitive, but they were quick to respond to Fox's magnetism, to the power of those piercing eyes and to the fire and eloquence of his matchless voice. Often, they must have missed much of what he said, for, at its best, George Fox's syntax was never clear, simple and direct; but they could not mistake his fervor. For those who needed words, John ap John interpreted the speeches into Welsh.

It cannot be said that Fox was enthusiastic over Wales. The people lied and, to quote ap John, were spiritually asleep.

Twice they stole oats—and they were very poor oats—from under his horse's nose. The inns were bad and ill supplied. Three times the law-enforcers jailed ap John overnight, twice for speaking in the streets, though Fox did so with impunity, and once for keeping on his hat in a steeple-house.

Hundreds were convinced, but, as happens so frequently with emotional conversion, sometimes the impact was short-lived. Men and women who were enthusiastic at afternoon meetings turned hostile in the evening. Fox suspected mysterious influences at work upon them. Though he had no specific evidence for his fears, he sensed murder plots against him.

Nevertheless, Fox conquered. He climbed a mountain which he said was two miles high—the loftiest British peak is less than one third that height—and from that eminence sounded the day of the Lord, just as he had sounded it from Pendle Hill. Again, as at Pendle Hill, he pointed out localities where God would raise a mighty host.

While Fox, the prophetic tongue of Pentecost, remained in Wales, the missionary campaign flourished, but factors other than bloody plots or language barriers worked against a permanent success. One shrewd observer regretted the silence of Quaker meetings and the lack of singing; the quiet, he said, did not suit the fervent Welsh temperament.

The psychologic gap widened as Quakerism moderated its force. When Fox and other Friends attacked aggressively, they won converts; admiring Welshmen called George "a cunning fox." But calm appeals to reason lost effectiveness. Fox might awe them, as he did twice by standing silent upon a chair and glaring at them for three hours at a time, but no one else possessed this strength.

Everyone saw and recognized that power. As Fox was leaving Wales, he heard people declare that if he should come again he would convince half the nation. They could not foresee that within a few years the opening of Quaker settlements overseas would drain from Wales many hundreds of zealous, energetic youths who would take the message abroad, while leaving Wales to the older, stodgier and more religiously conservative.

Before Fox rode out of Wales a well-cherished legend was born, a legend that still persists in both Britain and America, half as humor, half as solemn fact.

It always rains, the legend runs, at times of Quaker meetings.[1]

The story rose because, in 1657, when Wales and western England were undergoing such severe drought that much of the area was dust, Fox opened a meeting in Warrington in Cheshire and, coincidentally, rain came down in torrents at that place, while all the surrounding lands stayed dry. Grateful farmers marvelled at the miracle, but George Fox had a ready explanation.

Drought, he said, was God's sign to men of their barrenness of the water of life; they who receive the truth and become fruitful unto God shall receive from Him their fruitful seasons also.

After visiting every county in Wales, George Fox returned to Swarthmoor, the one place he now called home. Here he took a needed rest from travel, though he filled his days and nights by endless conferences and by catching up on the voluminous correspondence Margaret Fell was conducting; it is to be hoped he also read the two pamphlets she had written, the first of her long series of writings. Then, in September, he rushed off again, this time northward.

He was being drawn toward Scotland, where Nayler had preached to his troops as early as 1651, and where at least fifty

---

[1] True or false, the legend is impregnable, if only because reinforced by a myth running parallel, for Quaker meetings often coincide with equinoxes, which, as everybody knows, are also rainy periods.

Publishers, many of them women, had also preached. In co-operation with native Scottish Friends they had set up meet-ings, but, as Scotland was firmly Presbyterian, they attracted opposition, especially after William Caton, attempting to speak in St. Giles' at Edinburgh, had to be led to safety by soldiers with drawn swords. Caton's report that ruin and destruction threatened the Quaker effort in "dark and untoward" Scotland spurred Fox to hurry to the rescue.

He was, of course, well aware that Scotland would be hostile; on two occasions he dreamed that enemies—he saw them as raging dogs, bears or wild horses—would attack him; but he was confident that God would give him victory. As he rode northward, his horse's hoofs struck sparks, "the Seed of God sparkling," about him. However thick the clods of Scottish hypocrisy, however briery and brambly their false religion, God's spiritual plough would clear the earth, the Word would burn the brambles.

The portents were truthful. An Edinburgh Friend, a lieutenant colonel, came down to meet him at the border as a guide, bearing word that the governor of Glasgow, whose wife was a Friend, would extend such protection as he could. An earl welcomed him. Fox found the people puffed up with black, airy notions, an "abundance of chaff, dross and dung." These were the doctrines of infant baptism, predestination, "election, reprobation and limited atonement," against which he had rebelled at Fenny Drayton and which he now attacked throughout the Clydesdale area.

The Scots fought back. Alarmed because "the people were opened to me and a spring of life riz up among them," the Presbyterian Synod drafted a series of maledictions :

Cursed be he who says an Inner Light leads him to
    salvation.
Cursed be he who says that faith is sinless.
Cursed be he who defiles the Sabbath.

George pounced upon the third curse. "They make the people curse themselves," he said; "for upon the sabbath day, which is the seventh day of the week, which the Jews keep, which was the command of God, they kept markets and fairs and so brought the curse upon their own heads."

In point of fact, the Scottish ministers boycotted Friends; Fox called it excommunication. They forbade the Scots to buy from Quakers or to sell to them; if anyone broke the ban, the priests loaded him with so many curses that the offender rushed away to cancel the sale. No Scot was to eat or drink with Friends.[2]

Such convincement as was won was chiefly among occupation troops. It was, moreover, far more short-lived than it had been in Wales. General George Monk, a pliable gentleman who sometimes played both sides of the political street, may have been open to persuasion on some questions but never on matters of military discipline. A Quaker soldier may well have been, as Fox insisted, having known Dewsbury and Nayler, the equal of seven ordinary men, but Monk wanted no Quakers under his command. What good was a soldier too democratic to salute, too individualistic to obey without questioning, too Biblical to swear allegiance, too merciful to kill an enemy? Less than a month after George's horse struck sparks on entering Scotland, Monk cashiered every Quaker officer and purged the rank and file.

One might have thought that Fox would have approved the action, but he did not. Himself a dedicated pacifist who, in

[2] Not even a divine portent halted clerical opposition. Standing in his pulpit, a priest, echoing the Synod's malediction against the Inner Light, fell senseless. His people carried him into the open, laid him upon a gravestone and poured liquor into him until he revived. Thereupon, feeling, according to Fox, rather mopish, the priest put on a kilt, fled into the countryside and, for two weeks, drank nothing but buttermilk. He returned to his pulpit sober, but, as Fox heard the story, he never regained his senses. The lesson was lost as far as other Scottish priests were concerned.

Derby jail, would not become a soldier nor, as he assured
Cromwell and Drury, take up the sword for any cause whatever, he had not as yet imposed nonviolence as obligatory upon
Friends. The sword was not for him, nor for any man with
conscientious scruples against war; but, in protesting to Monk
against the purge, he apparently recognized the right of others
to make war if only they fought in a just cause. The need of
war would be removed if love were universal, but it might
sometime be necessary. What other means would bring justice
in Spain, in Rome, or in the Turkish realm?

Fox matched the Scots in intensity of feeling. While they
were obsessed by hatred of British occupation troops and of
foreign military government, as well as by religious feeling,
he was equally single-minded in opposing Calvinist ecclesi-
asticism. He was so absorbed that when, in entering Edinburgh,
he saw thousands of people gathered, with many priests, preparing to burn a witch, he took the opportunity to declare the
day of the Lord to them but went away without paying the
slightest attention to the unfortunate victim.

The dark, carnal Scots continued to resist the truth, although
with less roughness than had the English. True, on one occasion, some "devilish clansmen" ran with pitchforks toward the
Quakers and their horses but did no harm; the threat may have
been no more than a practical joke by rough farm hands. A
projected meeting at Glasgow under the auspices of the friendly
governor proved a far worse blow, for not a single Scotsman
came.

On October 8th, the ruling Council, seven Englishmen and
two Scots, summoned George Fox to appear before them.
Showing more sagacity than most judicial or governmental
bodies in dealing with George Fox, they refused to enter into
arguments, and, by adroitly asking what was his outward
business in Scotland rather than giving him an opportunity to
talk about his spiritual mission, they effectively prevented him

from preaching. George asked an opportunity to speak and they refused permission; when, in spite of this, Fox protested that, as the heathen Pharoah heard Moses and Herod heard John the Baptist, the Scottish Council should hear him, they ordered him removed from the room.

The upshot was an order that George Fox leave Scotland within seven days. Fox paid no attention to the order, but continued preaching. His opportunities, however, were somewhat limited. At Stirling he announced a meeting, but the place was so "closed up in darkness" that, as at Glasgow, no one came to it; George learned that most of the people were planning to see a man run a race against a horse, and so he went to the course and had "a brave opportunity to declare the day of the Lord." On another occasion, soldiers escorted the Quakers out of town; the Friends went singing and shouting the Gospel. Fox stood at market crosses and spoke in crowded streets.

All this could have been stopped in a hurry had the Council so desired; but, having issued their order for Fox to quit Scotland within a week, the Council apparently lost interest in enforcing it. Warrants against him were issued, but, when George waived them aside with the remark that he would pay no attention to a wagonload of warrants, nothing more was done. His week's permissable stay lengthened into more than three months.

In the end, he was helpless, however, and he left for England. He had failed to achieve outstanding success.

24

For Unity and Truth

Fox returned to England downcast and disappointed. A rousing welcome would have melted the gloom, but, instead, he met cold criticism. Five envious Newcastle priests, writers of pamphlets against the Friends, scoffed at Quakers. Fox's followers, they sneered, were flighty folk who might do well enough with country bumpkins but who dared not pit themselves against clerics of the cultured cities.[1]

Quakers, in short, were butterflies.

The nickname was harmless and certainly a less severe attack than anything yet launched against the movement, but George was touchy; he took exception to it. Storming into Gateshead, across the Tyne from Newcastle, he dared the priests to bring their books and argue with him. When they ignored the challenge, he threw the insult back upon them.

"Who," he asked, "are the butterflies now?"

To add to his troubles, he ran across a gentleman sent to Durham to set up a divinity school. The government, which fifteen years before seriously debated abolishing Oxford and Cambridge, now considered widening its educational program.

[1] It was fitting retribution that six years after the appearance of those wicked works King Charles II ejected all five envious priests from their pulpits.

241

Recalling his early openings against colleges and righteously indignant at the prospect of more seminaries that might maltreat his Publishers, George protested the establishment.

His argument was somewhat peculiar. Babel proved, he said, that teaching foreign language and the seven arts was no way to educate a ministry. Why teach Greek when the Greeks thought Christ a fool? Why Hebrew when the Jews found Him a stumbling block? The Romans knew both Latin and Italian, yet they persecuted Jesus. Pilate crucified Him under a trilingual placard. He might have added: why speak English in view of all the persecutions undergone by Quakers?[2]

It would be wholly unjust to think that Fox's Durham comments reflected fairly his ideas on education. He was not himself a learned man. He knew the King James Bible so perfectly that, as one man said, were it to be lost he could restore it from his memory. Seemingly he knew a little Hebrew, a few words of Welsh and, in later life, a small amount of Dutch; but in none of these was he even haltingly fluent. Of science, literature, philosophy and non-Biblical history he was completely unaware. At times he carried books in his saddlebags, but it is difficult to read attentively while riding and, on dismounting, he began at once incessant speaking.

A companion of this period reported: "He spoke of the glory of the first body and of the Egyptian learning and of the language of the birds and of what was wonderful to me to hear, so that I believed he was of a deep and wonderful understanding in natural, but especially in spiritual, things." The Swarthmoor circle testified that, though "of no great literature, nor seeming much learned as to the outward, yet he had the tongue of the learned."

[2] Whether or not George Fox's arguments seemed valid, Durham College was not founded until more than a century and a half later. Fox himself was certain that his protests made the man so loving and tender that the idea was abandoned.

George Fox's scholarship was neither broad nor deep, but his mystic allusions—the glory of the first body, the Egyptian learning, the language of the birds—lent mystery to his words. The Swarthmoor circle and the Bristol physician who was his companion were not alone in thinking him profoundly wise. In his calling upon Cabalistic lore, however, he was not attempting consciously to impress his listeners; he was genuinely yearning for Adam's Paradise, the Utopia lost when fallible man yielded to the Serpent's lure.

He recognized the need for schooling. Only a few years after condemning the Durham project, he urged Friends to establish elementary boarding schools to teach "whatsoever things are civil and useful" and also a higher school for botany, home medicine and, of all things, the languages against which he had protested.

Friends must, however, be careful about the calibre of teachers. They must not, he warned as he had warned a dozen years before, train children to be light or vain or wanton; rather they must educate them in the law of life, the law of the spirit and the law of love and faith. Only thus might Friends be free of the evil law of sin and death.

He showed clear examples of what he meant. "God was the first teacher, in Paradise, and whilst man kept under His teaching he was happy. The serpent was the second, and when man followed his teachings, he came into misery. Christ Jesus was the third."

The period following Fox's return was studded by still further dispute. Having turned the butterfly taunt into a boomerang against the Newcastle priests and having crushed the college project, he took up a matter which, arising during his absence in Scotland, was imperilling a basic Quaker principle.

Two men, the Quaker Anthony Pearson and Sir Henry Vane, the latter of whom had been governor of Massachusetts when only twenty-three, had caused a serious jumble. Vane, only a year out of a Cromwell prison, was urging a nonconformist coalition to ensure civilian control over the military; critics who heard him talk of government by "pious and holy persons," nicknamed him "King of the Fifth Monarchy Men." Pearson, who certainly understood that Friends sedulously refrained from meddling in political affairs, was sympathetic to the plan. He saw no conflict with established Quaker policy; at the most recent parliamentary election at York, those two staunch Friends, Thomas Aldam and Gervase Benson, had invited Quaker electors to vote as a bloc.

The call caused some stir and doubtless was much discussed when Fox was in Yorkshire, but a general meeting of elders voiced no criticism; indeed, there was a feeling that all servants of the Commonwealth should discharge their duties cheerfully and faithfully. This, by inference if not by specific word, implied permission for Quakers to vote and to hold public office.

The meeting in no way overruled George Fox, nor did he disapprove its action, but he was not particularly happy at the decision. Seeking no king but Christ, he was probably more strongly antimonarchial than was Henry Vane; no one could be more eager for a government by saints. Convinced that the day of the Lord was imminent, he thought the time was ripe for the elect to rule. He lacked faith, however, in Sir Henry Vane; disliking the carnal element in politics as much as he disliked the carnal sword in war, he did not feel that Vane was spiritually sound.

Vane would have been wiser had he not insisted upon meeting George Fox at just this time. Fox had no wish to see him, but, at Pearson's urging, he did so. Both men, apparently, were tense; the situation was not eased by the presence of a New England magistrate. Oddly enough, though at least half a year had elapsed since Boston had whipped and exiled Quaker women, no mention seems to have been made of that outrage. Instead, Fox lashed out so vehemently against Vane's lack of spiritual truth that Sir Henry lost his temper and called Fox a madman.

"And I did see that he was vain and high and proud and conceited and that the Lord would blast him."

The two men parted angrily, but both Vane and Parker continued agitating for a political coalition.

Next on the calling list was Rhys Jones, the shuffleboard player who drew away some Quaker sympathizers. They, too, were frivolous, vainer than the rest of the world. Outsiders called them Proud Quakers, as well they may have been, since, to Fox's disgust, they included football stars and wrestling champions.

George deemed them hostile, yet, for all their lightheartedness, they could not have been too bad. When Fox asked Rhys Jones to call a meeting of his Proud Quakers to hear a message from the Lord, some eighty followers gathered. Fox lectured them for two hours, so impressing them that no one even opened his mouth in opposition. Then, with victory within reach, George turned toward Jones, called him a vain man deluded by the serpent and denounced his followers as simpletons. Thus, he lost some whom he had all but salvaged from backsliding.[3]

Though Proud Quakerism never really threatened Quaker unity, it was typical of other splinter movements. From the beginning, seeds of disruption lay inherent among Friends. Since the Inner Light might reveal itself to anyone and since the Lord might move anyone to speech or action, individuality ran rampant. Thus, as the serpent often clothed himself in false garb, the Devil found opportunity to delude the credulous.

---

[3] Retribution was inevitable. As punishment for his pride, and for his worse sin in swearing to an oath, Jones fell into evil ways. He opened a tavern and saw his chief lieutenant become a miserable drunkard.

For all that Fox could do to check deviation and deceit, the forces of darkness won at least a few successes.

Why else would people like Rhys Jones and James Nayler run out from the Truth?

At the 1658 Yearly Meeting, George Fox bore testimony to the danger. There was, he warned, but one Seed, one Truth; let all be watchful lest, by reckless, hasty action, they destroy the good.

By hasty action he may have meant the premature expansion overseas. Excited evangelists had gone abroad before proper preparation was made. Some, of course, went with George's full approval but brought back meager harvest. Others, such as Ann Gargill, venturing upon their own responsibility, wasted time and energy. European missionary work, thus far, was relatively unproductive. In America, results were little better. Ann Austin and Mary Fisher, the latter a lady prone to persecution, failed in Boston. Certainly Fox suffered in spirit with his Friends, their misfortune causing him physical and mental anguish, but it was noteworthy that he failed to plead their case before Sir Henry Vane and the New England magistrate, and that in his *Journal* he completely ignored what happened to unauthorized missionaries.

"Preach to all nations and to every creature," he urged the Yearly Meeting, but he cautioned against foreign travel not moved by the Lord—or, in more understandable terms, not under official sponsorship.

He added three further injunctions. Be frugal of words in speech or publication, a counsel he would himself have done well to heed. Live the way you preach, as certainly he did. And, most important in those days when all in worldly authority scented plots on every side, "Meddle not with the powers of the earth."

He now opened a short, and somewhat inconclusive, attack

upon the Roman Catholics. Thus far he had spared both Jews and Papists—as he almost always called them—doubtless because there were so few in Britain and those few as unhappy as were Quakers. The omission had not gone unnoticed; it had invited suspicion that the Friends might well be Jesuits disguised. One reason, bigots in some areas suspected, why Quakers were so reluctant to remove their hats was that the covering concealed a shaven pate!

The attack was not by Fox's instigation; a Jesuit attendant of the Spanish Embassy insisted on debate. At least, he did at the beginning; he repented his rash invitation almost as soon as he extended it. His courage oozed away. After inviting "all the Quakers" to argue with him, he cut the number to "twelve of the wisest learned men," then to six and finally to three. Fox sent but two, commissioning them to inquire whether the Church of Rome had degenerated from the church of primitive days. When this had been discussed, both lengthily and fruitlessly, Fox himself arrived with a demand for precise Scriptural authority for cloisters and monasteries, rosaries and fast days, and for putting heretics to death. He posed the question he had put to Stephens—where in the Bible was there sanction for marriage by a priest?

Fox also challenged transubstantiation, not by argument nor by Scripture but, for once in his life, by scientific experiment. Take, he suggested, any bottle of wine and any loaf of bread. Divide the food and drink into halves, let the Jesuit choose either portion and let him consecrate it. Then, said Fox, set both halves in a cellar, under heavy guard, with seven locks upon the doors, and see what happens.

He offered a wager. If the consecrated half stayed fresh, George Fox would turn Roman Catholic; but if the bread were mouldy and the wine sour, the Jesuit must join the Quakers.

The bet was not accepted. "So we parted and his subtlety

was comprehended by simplicity." George was so pleased with his own cleverness that, ten years later when he was in Ireland, he repeated his willingness to stake his religion against Catholicism on the same terms. The victory—for so Fox rated it—put him for a time into a more chipper mood. As confidently as ever in the past, he undertook the bringing of the truth to Cromwell.

The Friends always found the Protector difficult to understand. He would greet them cheerfully and, when they complained that innocent men and women were in jail, would set them free, almost without investigation. He promised toleration. Apparently he liked George Fox. But, somehow, those pleasant interviews seemed always to be followed by more persecution and by the imposition of new oaths. Howgill did not trust Cromwell; he warned Margaret Fell that Oliver was hardening his heart and that he was full of subtlety, deceit and secrecy. Hubberthorne told Fox that, while Cromwell professed tolerance, he privately assured his officers that he would stand by them if they strictly enforced the laws against the Quaker vagrants.

Armed with his renewed confidence, George Fox cherished hopes. Everyone knew that Lady Elizabeth Claypoole, the Protector's 29-year-old daughter, lay critically ill. She had been a Seeker and had leaned toward Quakerism; recently she was troubled mentally. George wrote her a cheering letter, advising her to be still and cool in her own mind and spirit; this, he said, as he had written to her father, "is the word of the Lord God unto thee." It was a long letter, some of it tortuously worded.

"When thou art in the transgression of the life of God in the particular, the mind flies up into the air, and the creature is led into the night, and nature goes out of its course, and an old garment goes on, and an uppermost clothing, and nature leads out of its course, and so it comes to be all of a fire, in the transgression; and that defeateth the glory of the first body. . . ."

The Lady Elizabeth, grasping the spirit rather than the wording of the message, understood that those who cease to fear God fall into sin and so are denied the joys of Paradise. Fox's letter "settled and stayed her mind for the present." Friends made copies of the epistle, sent them to numbers of distracted people and found that the message soothed their minds, also. "They did great service with it."

Unfortunately, Lady Elizabeth died soon after. If Cromwell did not soften out of gratitude for the soothing of the last hours of his favorite daughter, he might be moved by prophecy.

While Fox was walking in the Strand, a women stopped him to relate a revelation. She was Hester Biddle, a steeple-house interrupter who had made a fleeting, but unproductive, trip to Newfoundland. She had received a dream that told her that Charles Stuart was about to be restored; she suggested that she spread the news abroad.

Fox advised against it. To tell the story publicly, he said, would be a clear infraction of his warning against meddling with the powers of the earth; she might be tried for treason. Hester, however, persisted. She must, she said, tell Charles of this and, what was more, she must bring him to England.

Fox himself had anticipated the coming restoration and he discerned her revelation to be true. Cromwell's days were numbered. The Protector was, of course, aware that Charles was ready with an army to return to England, but perhaps Oliver did not know that God was with the Royalists. Somehow persuading Hester to withhold her revelations for the moment, he went off at once to warn Cromwell to fear God and so protect the Commonwealth.[4]

[4] Hester Biddle resumed her remarkable missionary journeys, intending to convert the Pope, Louis XIV and the Grand Turk.

Late in August, 1658, Fox sought out the Protector. Again he met Oliver riding in the park, this time at the head of his life guards. The sight shocked him. The powers in possession of authority had grown too high and haughty; a great stroke must fall upon them. As the procession came closer he was more deeply moved.

"I saw and felt a waft of death." Cromwell looked like a dead man.

George spoke to him of the persecutions being suffered by the Quakers and also of the prophecies; he warned Oliver of what lay in store. Cromwell, always gracious to George Fox, invited him to come to the palace where they might talk still further. But, next day when George arrived, the Protector was too ill to see him.

"I never saw him more."

He did, however, see the many effigies of Oliver Cromwell, lying in state about the capital, with honor guards about and trumpets sounding. He did not approve. "The Lord, I found, was highly offended."

A month later a more serious personal blow brought sorrow to George Fox. Judge Thomas Fell, his close associate, the master of Swarthmoor Hall, passed away.

25

Boston Hunts Witches

BY THIS TIME, A SURPRISING NUMBER OF EVANGELISTS WERE experiencing strong calls to foreign service. In various meetings throughout Britain they confessed their need to spread the word abroad.

Fox, convinced at Launceston that the Lord God willed missionary work overseas, devised two methods. Among English-speaking peoples, in the American colonies, for example, Seekers must be harvested. Using the same techniques as in England, the ministers must publish truth in public gatherings, though not now in the steeple-houses, since such interruptions were declared illegal. In alien lands, no such appeals were possible, since the common people knew little, if any, English and since convincement through interpreters was difficult. Here the appeal must be to the highly placed. If, he reasoned, the Pope were won, all Catholics would come within the fold. Once the Sultan was persuaded, every Moslem would become a Quaker.

For these ambitious campaigns, a precedent was already set. Every ruler in the civilized world and many of the leading officials of every country had received, and it was hoped had read, at least one of George Fox's epistles. Neither their failure to reply nor Ann Gargill's failure to win the King of Portugal's adherence weakened Fox's enthusiasm.

Virtually all transatlantic colonies persecuted Quakers. Rhode Island, of course, was an exception; but even here the people did not spread wide their arms in welcome. Save for Gorton, they merely tolerated refugees professing religions other than the official creed. Neighbor settlements strongly disapproved the live-and-let-live philosophy; a bitter commentator wrote, with more forcefulness than generosity, that Rhode Island was "the receptacle for all sorts of riff-raff people and is nothing else than the sewer of New England."

Mary Fisher visited Barbados and, aided by John Rous, nephew of the justice whom Fox had silenced at Launceston, set up "a nursery of truth" from which missionaries went forth to evangelize the mainland. But Quakers, with their insistence upon the equality of man, met much resistance among slave-holding sugar planters. Persecution ensued upon the island, no less than 260 Quakers suffering for their faith.

Virginia set up barriers against the Friends. For half a century the colony had been an Anglican monopoly and, though the Commonwealth tore away some discriminations, laws continued to fine and exile those who would not swear allegiance to the government.

Fox, nevertheless, approved efforts to open the colony. Thomas Thurston, one of Bellingham's deportees, received the assignment, together with Josiah Coale, only twenty-five years old but already well seasoned by being half drowned at Bristol, beaten in Somerset and jailed in Dorsetshire. Upon their arrival at Jamestown, in 1658, they were imprisoned for disturbing the peace and then ordered to leave Virginia. They found refuge in the more sparsely settled eastern shore of the Chesapeake, which was legally Virginia territory but which was less strictly ruled. Here they found a Friend, William Robinson, who, when he was not in prison, was busily erecting a meeting in a ten-foot-square cabin. Judging that all was going well, Coale and Thurston moved onward into Maryland.

Much the same conditions existed here as in Virginia. Maryland prided itself on tolerance, but its hospitality toward Protestants was accompanied by hostility toward conscientious objectors and toward those who would not swear allegiance. Thurston and Coale were both arrested for what the authorities considered refusal to register their presence, thus making their offense a political rather than a religious matter. Within a few months, about thirty others, probably every Quaker in the province, was fined, either for pacifism or for harboring those who refused military service.

Upon their release, Coale and Thurston embarked upon explorations. Induced by what may very well have been suggestion from George Fox's London headquarters, they canoed up the Chesapeake to the mouth of the Susquehanna River. Thus far, it was a routine journey, accomplished by a number of Marylanders since Captain John Smith's initial visit in the early years of the century, but Coale and Thurston went farther. Gathering a number of Indian guides, they mounted the river into the interior.

That they were able to do so was the fruit of an alliance between Lord Baltimore and the Susquehannocks. Maryland lay open to Indian attack from the north, where the warlike Iroquois lived; only the Susquehannocks and a related tribe, the Andastes, lay between them. The Susquehannocks, however, were a small tribe, with no more than three hundred braves, many of them boys in their middle-teens nor were the Andastes, though more numerous, a much stronger protection. Lord Baltimore, therefore, gave the Susquehannocks guns and ammunition, even a few small cannon, to protect their log-palisaded hamlets, and they, in return, brought in venison, fish and crabs, trapped mink and beaver and, now and then, performed small chores.

Susquehannock guides, therefore, led Coale and Thurston upstream toward the border of New Netherland, where the Andastes took over as guides. The two Quakers were delighted at their treatment. Indians housed and fed them; probably they also clothed the venturers in the bearskin robes and turkey-feathered frocks that Indians found better fitted for woodland travel. In this travel through lands where Coale and Thurston believed no white man had ever preceded them (they were not correct in their assumption), the heathen, Coale reported, were more hospitable than Englishmen.

The basin of the Susquehanna River, stretching north and south for at least 120 miles and draining a wooded mountain area whose width nobody knew, would make, Coale believed, a magnificent area where Quakers might someday worship peaceably. No Europeans then held it as a colony, though the British and the Dutch, and, for that matter, the French, laid shadowy claim to it on very thin authority; it seemed to Coale to be available to anyone who settled there. Just as the Pilgrims, forty years before, set up a special colony, why should not the Quakers possess a haven in America? Obviously the Indians would be friendly. Coale and Thurston quoted their guides as saying, "Quakers are honest men who do no harm."

Unfortunately, neither Quaker possessed the authority, nor probably enough resources, to buy Indian permission to bring in colonists. Indeed, it was doubtless better in the long run that they did not buy. Susquehannocks, like most other Indians, had only a hazy idea what Europeans meant by ownership of land. Westerners believed it meant exclusive right to live thereon, to till the soil and hunt the game to be found there, but Indians, without the sense of personal proprietorship, thought only of a sort of club membership in the use of common property. Had Coale, by the presentation of knives and guns and gaily colored jackets, "bought" this Susquehannock land from guides who had no right to sell, considerable trouble might have followed.

If the Susquehannocks thought that Friends were honest, harmless people. Massachusetts heartily disagreed. Governor Endecott continued his defense of his colony against the dangerous sect, especially against their unarmed women.

In March, 1657, Ann Burden, a widow who formerly lived in Massachusetts, returned to collect some money due her. She was a Quaker, though not a minister; but with her was another woman, Mary Dyer, who did evangelize and who, moreover, had a history of troublemaking as an associate of Anne Hutchinson.

Endecott took no chances. He locked up Ann Burden for three months before deporting her to Barbados. In all that time, she managed to collect but six shillings of the money due her and was not able to salvage even this pittance, for Endecott approved a charge of seven shillings to ferry her to her ship. Everything that she possessed then went to pay her passage.

For the moment, Mary, the Quaker preacher, escaped more lightly. Her husband, a non-Quaker, hastened from Rhode Island to post bond that, if she were released, she would neither linger anywhere in Massachusetts nor let anyone speak with her. Mary was indignant; neither she nor any other Quaker would have agreed to any such bargain, but there was nothing she could do but fulfil the agreement. She left Boston, but, immediately upon setting foot on Rhode Island soil, she turned about and hurried back toward Boston. For several months thereafter her story was a monotonous repetition of trudgings into Massachusetts, whippings, imprisonments, deportations and more returnings to what Fox used to call "the dragon's mouth."

Endecott and the other lawmakers, incensed against "the

cursed sect of Quakers," issued new decrees imposing a fine of
£100 upon any shipmaster or other person bringing a Quaker
to Massachusetts, and fining anyone 40 shillings for harboring
a Friend. Any man who returned after being exiled would lose
an ear, a second return would cost the other ear, and a third
would bring Nayler's penalty of a bored tongue.

The governor had not lost his love for the lash. Women who
offended would, by this law of September, 1657, be whipped;
if there were a third offense Endecott would bore their
tongues. These were laws that New Haven also passed.

The reign of terror only intensified Quaker efforts. The
eight Friends deported from Boston reported their treatment to
George Fox and were at once inspired to try again. Robert
Fowler, of Yorkshire, was no deep-sea navigator, but he felt
called upon to build a small fishing smack, the *Woodhouse,*
and to sail it, regardless of the fines awaiting him, into the
forbidden waters of the colony. Though seasoned sailors refused to travel in the ship, "not even if he gave it to me,"
Fowler could not be dissuaded. Eleven Quakers went with
him, among them Humphrey Norton, who had volunteered to
take Fox's place in Launceston and who had since been doing
missionary work in Ireland.

Not one of the passengers, nor the skipper, nor the two
men and three boys who comprised the crew, knew anything
of ocean sailing, not even how to calculate positions at sea.
They sailed by inspiration. Each night a Quaker meeting sat
in silence, awaiting the Lord's command concerning what to
do or what course to follow. They did not wait in vain. Sometimes the messages were clear, as when Norton predicted that
next day they would sight a hostile fleet but that the Lord
would wrap the ship in fog; sure enough, the enemy appeared
and the mist came down, so that the *Woodhouse* escaped capture. There were, however, times when messages were mystic,

as when a Quaker foretold, in midocean, that they would come upon a lion and another visioned anchors floating on the sea; such messages were interpreted symbolically, as persecutions to be met but security eventually assured.

Under the Lord's guidance, "as a man leads a horse by the head," the little fishing smack threaded Hell Gate and sailed into the haven of New Amsterdam. It was a Dutch colony and the Friends, accustomed to the tolerance of the Netherlands, anticipated a pleasant welcome. They reckoned without Peter Stuyvesant, who, in defiance of his employers, the Dutch West India Company, had, just about a year before, procured a local law barring all religions but his own. He had already banished nine Friends from New Amsterdam, and when Dorothy Waugh went ashore, with another girl, to preach the Truth, he shut them in a miry, vermin-infested jail. Eight days later he expelled the *Woodhouse* venturers.

New Haven, the nearest English settlement, was even less hospitable. Norton landed and was immediately jailed. To prevent his speaking, the authorities jammed a huge iron key into his mouth, as Dorothy Waugh was once gagged by a horse's bridle bit. They then gave him thirty-six lashes, branded him, fined him £30 and exiled him.

Norton and the rest went on to Newport, where the people were less cruel. Roger Williams was no great admirer of the Quakers, but he was tolerant. Rhode Island became a Quaker foothold on the American continent; the Friends used it as a base for their invasions of more-northern districts.

None of the Massachusetts settlements wanted them. Anti-Quaker regulations, and even more the vigor of enforcement, varied in the several towns, but all agreed that Quakers should be whipped, kept in jail until they earned sufficient at hard labor to pay the fines imposed upon them, and then be hurried from the colony. There was much talk of lopping off ears and of boring the tongues of obstinate offenders.[1]

Nevertheless, Quakers, accustomed to persecution, persisted in their efforts. From their Rhode Island sanctuary, they walked up to Massachusetts, to the Seekers awaiting them at Sandwich on Cape Cod, at Salem or in unpropitious Boston.

For there were signs that even in Endecott's own town not everyone rejected truth. On several occasions, private citizens collected funds to pay fines which dedicated Quaker missionaries would not pay. Nathaniel Sylvester, who had troubles of his own, in Barbados, Connecticut and Massachusetts, used an island which he owned in Oyster Bay, Long Island, just east of the New Netherlands frontier, as a sanctuary for the persecuted—he called it Shelter Island. Persecution, however, continued. By a one-vote majority, the General Court banished all Friends, under penalty of death.

Mary Dyer, William Robinson and Marmaduke Stephenson, well aware of what would happen to them, deliberately disregarded all warnings by returning to Boston after exile. There was no question that, under Massachusetts law, they were guilty, nor any doubt what their punishment must be. The law was barbaric, but it was legal. Whatever justices might privately have thought of it, they had no choice but to impose the penalty. Endecott would have said that his victims courted death, that in reality they committed suicide.

But Quakers had a higher duty than obedience to mortal law; they had clear calls to perform the will of God. All these three, and others who followed, hearkened to the voice of the Lord. Robinson stated the situation clearly; on October 8, 1659, in the afternoon, the Lord commanded him to go to Boston to lay down his life. "I was a child and obedience was demanded of me." Doubtless, none of the three had ever heard

---

[1] Norton retaliated by calling down a "curse" upon Governor Endecott.

of Martin Luther's famous "Here I stand. God help me, I can do no other"; but they would have shouted the same words with pride.

They flaunted their transgression. A group of sixteen Friends marched triumphantly from Salem, carrying shrouds for those who were to die. One Friend, supposedly a Cromwell protégé, escaped the death sentence, but, on October 27th, three expectant martyrs mounted the scaffold. Mary Dyer watched her two companions hanged; she felt the halter tightened round her neck.

Why, at the last moment, she received reprieve was not clear to the watching crowds; they did not know that two governors, of Connecticut and of Acadia, had pleaded for her life, nor that, a week before, the General Court had reduced her sentence to exile—provided that she be subjected to the ordeal of the scaffold before she was banished. It may have been Endecott's notion of a proper punishment, but neither chivalry nor humanity could be expected among those who whipped women and, a few years later, hanged witches.

Mary learned no lesson; six months later she was back in Boston, and this time she was hanged.[2]

Meanwhile, other overseas adventurers were also faring ill. Sporadic attempts to enter the Holy Land failed, but Quakers, in 1657, collected £177, which they thought sufficient to send a mission of three men and three women, including Mary Fisher, to the East. None of the group knew a word of Arabic or Turkish and all their knowledge of the region came from the Bible; but what they lacked in preparation they made up by enthusiasm. John Perrott, an ambitious, energetic Irishman, certain that his spiritual powers surpassed those of George Fox

[2] A fourth victim would be executed in a year or so. It is an interesting commentary that New England was the only British territory where Quakers were officially put to death by a Puritan Commonwealth for religious nonconformity.

himself, had not the faintest doubt of his ability to convert both Pope and Sultan. John Luffe was equally sure that he could show the Pope by Bible texts that he, the Pope, was anti-Christ.

Few welcomed the evangelists, least of all the British consuls, some of them businessmen who feared that madmen would destroy the trade relations. At Smyrna, the consul was polite enough, but he was also insistent that the party go home; in what amounted to deportation, he turned the missionaries back toward Venice.

En route, Mary Fisher and two others slipped away and saw the Sultan. Mohammed IV, a lad of seventeen, listened courteously, said that he understood her words and acknowledged that she spoke the truth. Disarmed by this polite reception, so different from her previous experience, she carefully avoided assailing either his religion or his Prophet, and so received an invitation to remain. Having satisfied her call, she declined the invitation, and also an honor-guard escort, and returned to England. She had not experienced "the least hurt or scoff."

Why could not Christians be as kind? When Perrott and Luffe went down to Rome, they were clapped into jail as madmen, but not until after Luffe managed an audience with the Pope. It is surprising how readily Quakers, and, for that matter, others, were enabled freely to meet with those in high places and to speak their minds without restriction; it is also interesting to notice how little preparation the interviewers thought necessary. Luffe, for instance, could not have had the faintest idea what kind of man he was to see, else he never would have used the approach he did:

"Thou pretendest to sit in Peter's chair. Now, know that Peter had no chair but a boat. Peter was a fisherman; thou art a prince. Peter fasted and prayed; but thou farest deliciously and sleepest softly. He was mean in attire; thou art set in ornament."

Nothing could have been less adroit. Alexander VII was a scholar of sorts and far from luxurious; he was, indeed, ascetic. Luffe had no chance in the world of convincing him, but the Pope, though not prejudiced in favor of Quakerism, was ready to hear any doctrine, especially from those who, like himself, had trouble with the Portuguese. A little common courtesy would not have been amiss, but this was not forthcoming from John Luffe. Instead, he told the Pope, who held himself God's regent on earth, that he, the Pope, was no disciple of the Lord but anti-Christ.

Probably the Vatican interpreter greatly softened Luffe's address, though the hostile manner could not be concealed, but Alexander was not persuaded. Luffe returned to prison, where they hanged him; "not that they had anything against him," Fox reported, "but that they said he was a dangerous person who might harm their religion."

Perrott, whose fate in this affair Fox failed to mention, escaped the gallows, but remained three years in the madhouse.

26

Readjustment

LUCKILY, GEORGE FOX DID NOT AT THE TIME KNOW OF ALL THE tragedies in foreign parts. English misfortunes pressed heavily enough upon him. Suspicious politicians, jealous priests and a general misunderstanding of Quaker purposes plagued the innocent and peaceful Quakers.

Fox traced much of the trouble to hypocritical noncon-formists. At first, when they were underdogs, they seemed sympathetic toward "tender" consciences. They cried out loudly against forced tithes for the benefit of Anglicans. But then, after the Commonwealth placed them in high positions, these same objectors insisted that tithing was right and proper. They, too, demanded contributions; when Friends refused to pay, they, too, seized property and threw Quakers into jail.[1]

The prevalence of persecution reawakened Quaker interest in mass emigration as a means of establishing a government by

[1] No one really knew the extent of suffering, but Fox believed that, under the Commonwealth and the Protectorate, 3,000 were jailed and that, at Oliver's death, 700 still remained in prison. Joseph Besse, who carefully collated data from every shire, listed only about a third as many during the whole 1650 decade. A Friends' petition sent to Parliament early in 1659 reported only 144 Quakers then in jail.

Fox did not consciously exaggerate. Having neither time nor opportunity to investigate the excited rumors flooding into the Bull and Mouth, he accepted them uncritically. Whatever the figures may have been, the number was certainly too large, the sufferings too heavy and uncalled-for.

saints. Recalling Josiah Coale's descriptions of rich, vacant lands north of Maryland and the enthusiastic reports of Susquehannock hospitality, the thought recurred that, if England continued hostile, emigration might be necessary.

George Fox did not press the matter. Rather than accept an easy escape by flight, he preferred to spread the truth at home. Nevertheless, as a practical man, he kept the possibility alive. He urged Coale to explore the purchase of Susquehannock lands.

A further reason for delay was that some Quakers, perhaps for a time George Fox himself, anticipated political reform to end injustice. Anthony Pearson, not in the least depressed by Fox's unfavorable opinion of Sir Henry Vane, was again working with that gentleman for a republic of the pious and the holy; they had the support of Sir Arthur Heselrige, a rising councillor of state, and, quite possibly, of Fifth Monarchy Men.

Pearson was an excellent bridge between the Vane group and the Quakers. Formerly Heselrige's secretary, he took Fox as his spiritual and Sir Arthur as his temporal guide. There were some who suspected, without warrant, that he was ambitious for high place in any government; but, whatever his ultimate design, he was dedicated and incorruptible.

When, in May, 1659, Vane and Heselrige reconvened the old Rump Parliament, Pearson urged Fox to join the coalition. George, though still fuming over Vane's conceit and pride, and though indignant that Sir Henry demanded that Quakers lift their hats while speaking to him, considered the suggestion seriously. As a rule, Friends abstained from worldly politics, but the Rump, by freeing a number of Quaker prisoners and by hinting at its readiness to abolish tithes, seemed bent on friendship. It invited Friends to report the justices who had been persecutors and also asked nominations of men qualified by training and experience to be appointed justices. Several

Friends, including Pearson, were named commissioners of militia. The Rump was winning Quaker confidence.

Had not the coalition committed glaring blunders, Fox might himself have been won over. Acting on the rumor that tithes might be abolished, he encouraged the drafting of a monster petition against tithing; but when the paper, signed by seven thousand women, came before the House, Parliament rejected it. Word leaked out that while abolishing tithes might please the Quakers, it would alienate all the Presbyterian incumbent preachers. Worse, some one in authority had the stupidity to ask George Fox to raise a troop of cavalry which he might command, as colonel.

Not all Friends felt as Fox did about warfare. Some few— George called them foolish, rash spirits—helped quell a short-lived royalist uprising under a leader who would later be created Lord Delaware.

The political, and still more, the military activities disturbed Quaker leaders. Howgill, for one, confessed that he was avoiding Pearson for fear of being thought covetous of public office; Pearson, he said, was too deeply embroiled in worldliness. George Fox, quite literally, worried himself sick.

When George was younger, psychic disturbance revealed itself by the frequency of openings; physical and mental distress found relief through outbursts in the steeple-houses or through endurance of hardships—once by that extraordinary Lichfield explosion. But in his middle thirties, when by modern standards he would still be young, he had grown sedate, less given to exuberance. Deep affliction no longer drove him into spectacular exploits but made him physically ill.

He had much to burden him. Foolish rash spirits who went to war, the hypocrisy of Sir Henry Vane, the politics of Parliament were painful to him; these seemed to him like powers plucking themselves to pieces. The disappointments of those

missions to the East, the hanging of John Luffe, the cruel
sufferings inflicted by Americans tortured his spirit.

At Reading, in August, 1659, he fell grievously ill. For ten
weeks he lay unconscious, choking and in torment. His body
wasted away; his face grew drawn and thin. Ill-wishers—he
thought them unclean spirits—gloated; they declared the
plagues of God were on him, these same plagues of which little
Mary Fell warned her pastor, Lampitt.

Autumn brought better news and, with it, physical recovery.
The great Quaker rift was closing. After almost three years in
jail, James Nayler was repentent; one Quaker missioner after
another reported him as anxious to make peace. In September,
when Nayler was at last set free, his first important move was
to hurry to Reading. George was still too ill to see him, but
the knowledge that Nayler's heart was softened was good
medicine. The two men met in January and were reconciled,
but Nayler died within two months thereafter.

Fox's refusal to rely upon the carnal sword was also yielding
good results. The country was in turmoil, but Quakers, though
supporting the Commonwealth against the monarchy, refrained from taking office and from fighting, and so incurred
no strong antagonisms. When it became evident that the Protectorate would collapse, especially as Vane and Heselrige were
at odds, and that Charles II would return as King precisely as
Hester Biddle and George Fox prophesied, there would be no
reprisals against the harmless Quakers.

There was, in fact, a growing belief that the Friends had a
social message of value to mankind. If their religion was still
frowned upon, their charity was praised. Before becoming ill,
Fox wrote a plea for welfare efforts that, by caring for the
handicapped and for the poor, would, in the end, abolish beggary. The means which he proposed for financing aid to social
debtors—the confiscation of great mansions, of abbeys, palaces

and churches—reflected the radicalism of John Lilburne; this was disapproved, but the humanitarianism was applauded.

Fox recovered; his face and frame filled out. There was no pleasing the unclean spirits; they now complained he was too fat.

Signs of progress sprouted everywhere. Fox visioned a victorious Royalist army tearing down the London walls and burning the wicked city. A military order, issued by the Commonwealth forces in their last days of glory, forbade interference with "the peaceful meetings of the Quakers; they do nothing prejudicial." A month later, Charles Stuart, still waiting on the Continent, proclaimed at Breda full liberty to tender consciences. Henceforth, he promised, none should be disquieted for religious views that did not peril public peace.

Fox's sense of well-being, the comfortable assurance that, with both Parliament and King pledging toleration, Quakers would be unmolested, reflected innocent optimism. Fox should have known better than to trust either promise. A keener reading of the statements would have revealed weasel words about peacefulness and perils to the peace. Those words might be, and would be, so interpreted as to throw open wide the doors to persecution.

The truth was that, in such disturbed days, as in the past, few people, not even Quakers, fully believed in liberty of conscience for others than themselves. Those who knew the truth, particularly those whose inspiration came undiluted from the Lord, cherished no concept that error should be freely spread. Toleration was too much to be expected. When a nation boiled with intrigue, with every malcontent claiming that his goal was righteousness, none dared trust a rival to be just or even humane.

Fox did his utmost to escape becoming embroiled. Again and again, he counselled Friends, especially the younger and less experienced, to stay out of politics, to shun the sword and to keep away from plottings.

"This I charge you, which is the word of the Lord God unto you all, live in peace, in Christ, the way of peace, and therein seek the peace of all men and no man's hurt."

There could have been no clearer proof of Quakerism's dedication to the welfare of mankind. No thoughtful person could have misconstrued the message. But these were not normal times, and there were many nervous law enforcers. As usual, the local agents far outdid the higher executives in zeal. Charles may have been insincere, but, to his credit, neither he nor any of his top aides broke the Breda pledge. City and county officials, however, fearing that armed insurrection might arise within their jurisdictions, dared take no risks. Instead of lessening their persecutions, local leaders intensified them.

Fox, in his innocence, gave them what they considered an excuse. He wrote an epistle, breathing peace and love of God and man, but incautiously added :

"So know a kingdom which hath no end, and fight for that with spiritual weapons, which take away the occasion of the carnal, and there gather men to war, as many as you can and set up as many as you will with these weapons."

Once more he circled throughout England, calling Quaker meetings to spread love and peace. Every Quaker knew exactly what he meant, but not all listeners were spiritually minded nor did all interpret him aright. Some guardians of the law, paying no heed to what Fox actually said but looking only for what might be dangerous, caught the appeal to gather men for war and twisted that figure of speech into an incitement to violence !

Happily, through the power of the Lord, George Fox, while on this 1660 circuit, escaped arrest a dozen times. Warning omens did not deter those who bothered Quakers. An annoying practical joker frequented meetings in the West. His custom was to wrap himself in a bearskin and stand, tongue lolling from his mouth, in mockery of speakers. George called this low-grade moron a wicked man, but, whatever his condition, he paid a proper penalty. After having had what he supposed great sport, he watched a bull baiting, but he went too near the angry animal. The bull gored him, striking him so forcibly under the chin that the fellow died with his tongue sticking out, just as he had stuck it out in Quaker meetings.[2]

While on this third tour of the kingdom, Fox came again to Cornwall. This time he was safe against another term in Launceston. On the eve of royal restoration, Ceely dared not re-arrest one whom he had accused of plotting to bring back the king. Fox came full of indignation, not because of his sufferings in Cornwall but because he heard that Cornishmen were murderers and robbers. They were accustomed, he was told, to ride along the shore holding lanterns. Steersmen on dark nights would see the light and would suppose it carried by another ship sailing in deep water; they would be induced by that deceit to sail closer to the shore and so would dash their ships against the rocks. If no creature, man or beast, escaped alive to shore, the law gave half the value of the wreckage to the Crown, with the remainder going to the salvager. Under such provisions, there was every inducement to Cornishmen to make certain there were no survivors.

Similar charges were lodged against coastal peoples both in England and America; but, as indignant Cornishmen point out, there is no legal documentary proof that anything of the sort occurred. Nevertheless, George Fox believed the practice prevalent about Land's End. "It was the custom for rich and

[2] Whether the incident occurred in 1660, as George Fox recorded it, or three years previously and at a different place, as other historians relate, is unessential to the story; the moral still remains. Except for the presence of the bull, the story is also reminiscent of what had happened to the butcher in 1654.

poor to go out and get as much as they could of the wreck, not caring to spare the people's lives." Instead of preying on unfortunates, he said, consuming the spoil upon their lusts in alehouses and taverns, the goods should be returned. Were not the heathen of Malta courteous and kind to shipwrecked Paul?

Even Bristol, forgiving Friends for the Nayler episode, did no more than bar Fox from the Hollister orchard, though soldiers hinted darkly of what might happen if he ever came again. So far had the city relented that the mayor weighed a Quaker offer that if he would let Friends use the city hall as a meetinghouse they would contribute £20 yearly for poor relief. The deal, however, fell through; the city would not yield the municipal building and the Quakers would not accept a less convenient place.

Despite the ever recurrent rumors of Quaker plots, hostilities against Friends ceased almost everywhere; but sore spots still remained. Some of these Fox tried to heal as various unhealthy symptoms became visible; others were considered at special conferences or general meetings. At Skipton, for example, in 1660, social-service work at home and the state of foreign missions became major topics.

The inquiry into the condition of the poor was particularly timely and fruitful. As usual, a nation-wide gathering incited law-enforcement officers to suspect that mischief was afoot. They came to break up the dangerous meeting but found Friends discussing means for fighting poverty. Listening to reports of work in progress and to the careful financial statements, they realized that Quakers felt deep concern for the unfortunate.[3]

[3] A surprising, and most important, innovation was established. Army officers and local officials took part in what amounted to a conference on community affairs. A relief program developed, of a type which current social theory might not wholly approve but which was humanitarian in its time. The knowledge that Quakers were concerned with poverty led to an influx of two hundred beggars, each of whom received a loaf of bread each day.

One must not question the Almighty, but it seemed a pity that the Lord chose just this moment of Quaker respectability to move William Simpson to run once more half-naked through the streets. It was, Simpson explained, a testimony to all and sundry that, unless they saw the light, they, too, would all be stripped as naked as he was.

Not everyone understood the message. A certain justice of the peace, who may have been miffed by exclusion from the round-table conference, sent ruffians to break up the meeting. One man came with an axe, prepared to chop Friends down, but, finding the meeting adjourned, he threw down the axe and turned to grabbing at the women's clothes and trying to kiss the girls. To give the other ruffians their due, they pulled him away.

Completing his third swing about the nation, George Fox returned in May to Swarthmoor. He had been absent exactly two years. He expected to find changes. Judge Fell's death, a month after that of Oliver Protector, left Margaret and Justices Gervase Benson and Anthony Pearson as managers of the estate. Her situation was, to some degree, difficult, for the judge had bequeathed almost all his property to their seven daughters, all of them as yet unmarried, leaving the nineteen-year-old son nothing but law books and allowing Margaret but £50. She was, however, to have the use of Swarthmoor Hall, with fifty acres, for as long a time as she remained a widow.

The legacies to George Fell and to Margaret were small, but they implied no criticism either of the son or of the widow. Each was already amply provided for, George by ownership of two-thirds of Marsh Grange, his mother's birthplace, and Margaret by inheritance from her father.

There were, however, potential difficulties. Margaret's control over the property was weakened. Her livelihood was assured, and Benson and Pearson, both Quakers, were solicitous for her interest; but she was less secure. Those daughters, the eldest now twenty-five, probably would marry soon, and thus seriously entangle the joint ownership of the estate. The son, leading what Margaret believed a profane and dissolute life in London, was discontented; there were worries that he might try to break the will.

All this imperilled Quaker affairs. Thus far, as the older girls took over increasing shares of household responsibilities, Margaret Fell had been free to supervise the Kendal Fund, to maneuver missionaries, to advise the growing number of meetings, and to conduct the innumerable letter writings. But when the girls married and moved away she must give more time to the estate—if, that is, her dissatisfied son did not deprive her of it.

This development would, in turn, affect George Fox's activities. Hitherto, he had been constantly upon the road, organizing, visiting and inspiring meetings, unravelling problems, correcting deviations before they grew too serious; hereafter, he must lead a quieter, more sedentary life. To one as restless, as much in need of motion, constant office work might prove upsetting; his absence from struggling meetings which sorely needed personal attention might spell their death sentence.

Swarthmoor also needed him. Judge Fell had never officially accepted Quakerism, nor, except for his assistance to Friends unjustly arrested, had he taken overt action favoring Friends. But, unobtrusively, he had played important roles in furthering the Quaker movement. Despite his friendship for Priest Lampitt—a patronage that dwindled steadily—he fostered Friends, else he never would have let his house become a Quaker refuge and his great hall a meetinghouse. Doubtless, he counselled Margaret in business matters—it is impossible to think that husband and wife so devoted to each other would not discuss the problems that concerned them most. Fox's

Journal carried no mention of any activity by the judge after 1652, but Fell's interest in Quakerism remained strong and active, as his deathbed appointment of the two Quakers as estate trustees attests. Margaret needed someone like Fox as her business counsellor.

About a month after Fox returned to Swarthmoor he sensed a great darkness gathering, a premonition which, as with so many of his omens and forebodings, was followed by disaster.

27

The Kingly Word

MAJOR HENRY PORTER, CONSTABLE OF LANCASTER CASTLE, rode up with deputies to Swarthmoor Hall. Ostensibly they came to search the house for arms, a thin excuse they never would have ventured had Judge Fell been alive. Finding none, they took George Fox away. This, actually, was the purpose of their visit, but they were very loath to give a reason for arresting him. The fact was that no valid reason existed. For the past few weeks George had said little to which anyone could take exception, and he had done less, certainly nothing whatever in Lancashire.

Porter was trying to rehabilitate his reputation. Once a staunch Parliamentarian, he was now a fervent royalist. But his past haunted him; he must do something to demonstrate his loyalty to the restored King Charles. Fox and his Friends seemed to offer the opportunity. All these silent meetings up and down the country, did they not portend an armed rebellion? Would not a preventive arrest bring credit from the Crown? Would not this zeal balance a little looting of a royal residence committed while the King was travelling in Europe?

The major kept Fox overnight in Ulverston, surrounding him with a sixteen-man guard, some of them detailed to sit close by the fireplace lest George Fox fly up the chimney. Porter confiscated George's riding spurs, as possible lethal weapons; a guard took a pocketknife from the prisoner and sulked when Fox refused to let him have it as a present. When morning came, they sat Fox upon a horse, a poor horse, but they provided no bridle for fear Fox would kick the poor nag into galloping away. In the midst of an augmented guard—there were now thirty deputies and soldiers—a trooper led Fox's horse across the sands to Lancaster.

In some ways, the shabby column was reminiscent of the Nayler ride. No one sang hosannahs but a "wicked fellow" knelt, lifted up his arms and blessed God that Fox was taken; George answered by chanting praises to the Lord. When they came to the castle, the warden's wife greeted Fox with promises that his tongue would be cut out and that he would be hanged. George replied by warning of the impending day of doom.

"The Lord cut her off and she died in a miserable condition."

If George Fox did not, it is certain that others reminded worried Major Porter of the unhappy fate of those who persecuted Quakers without even bothering to cite a cause.

Major Porter did not let prisoners know why they were locked up in Lancaster Castle; presumably they had no right to know. He fined a jailer who gave a captive a copy of his *mittimus,* the warrant of commitment. But the warden, though a rude and wicked fellow, handed two Friends the *mittimus* on which George Fox had been arrested on condition that they read it in his office and return it.

The warrant specifically charged George Fox with plotting bloody insurrection against "His Majesty, our Lord the King." No evidence was shown, nor was any basis given, except that in the troubled times Fox was holding many meetings. To Porter, a man who fought for Parliament against the King and who threatened to lay the county waste unless the people provisioned Cromwell's garrison, those meetings seemed suspicious. Whenever security officers dropped in, the meetings were quiet enough, he admitted, but who knew what mischief was afoot when those Quakers were alone? Anyone such as George Fox, who travelled so extensively, who received so many unknown visitors and so many letters, some of them in code, must be extremely dangerous.

Porter overreached himself by the arrest. Fox, Margaret Fell and Ann Curtis each wrote protests to the king; the two women went down to London to press the case in person. Porter, too, rode there, but when he reached Whitehall so many people accused him of looting their houses while they, staunch royalists, were supporting the king, that he thought it wiser to go home.[1]

The women saw the king. Because rebels had hanged Ann Curtis' father, the Bristol sheriff, for supporting Charles I, the restored king promised to investigate her complaint against Porter.

Few things ever went smoothly where George Fox was concerned. Charles II set machinery in motion, but when he sent an order to have Fox brought to London, he addressed it wrongly, to the chancellor, the judiciary head, instead of to the sheriff. Both men stood firmly on their dignity and neither would accept the order; it had to go back to London for amendment. When it was again received, this time in proper form, they would do nothing until George Fox paid the costs. This, as usual, he would not do, so he remained all summer in the prison.

The Assizes came in late September, but the session brought Fox no relief. Because a writ existed freeing Fox from jail, the

---

[1] Fox added to his worries by suggesting that, if Porter were so anxious to curry royal favor, he might tell the King where Porter acquired the great buck horns in his house and whence came the panelling. This was the property that the major stole from the royal mansion, and so, in hopes, perhaps, that if he did nothing more Fox would refrain from telling the King about it, Porter withdrew from the case as best he could.

court had no authority to try him; since costs were payable before the writ was operative, he was not freed. Instead, he posted himself at one of the slit windows of the Castle and lectured loudly to the crowds gathered on the grassy slopes.

With customary tact, he sent another message to King Charles, not in complaint against imprisonment but because the Restoration had brought profanity and laxity. Though the king had been tolerant and considerate, George addressed him roughly:

"King Charles, thou came not into this nation by sword, and not by the victory of war, but by the power of the Lord. Now if thou do not live in it, thou wilt not prosper. . . ."

Though the king returned no direct answer, the sheriff, either by royal command or because he despaired of ever collecting his fees, proposed that Fox give bond for appearance before the King's Bench in London. As always, Fox refused; with mock solicitude for the welfare of the state, he suggested that, if he were guilty of the charges laid against him, it would be unsafe to let him go except under guard of a cavalry troop or two. The sheriff approved the idea—until, that is, he calculated the cost; then he reduced the proposed guard to a jailer and some bailiffs, only to change his mind again when he realized that it would be he who paid the bills. Finally, he asked Fox to travel alone, but under bail; George answered that he would go, if the Lord permitted it, but not under bail.

Released on his own responsibility, Fox went to Swarthmoor for a few days to catch up on Quaker business; he then returned to Lancaster and, taking the high road to London, travelled leisurely, holding meetings all the way. Though he rode through towns close to Drayton, he did not call upon his relatives.

At London, Fox stayed again at Charing Cross. He notified Whitehall of his arrival, adding graciously that while he was perfectly ready to visit the king, the monarch would be welcomed if he cared to call upon George Fox.

Few kings delight in being patronized by their subjects. Charles II, however chastened by his exile, was not one to obey a summons from an itinerant evangelist, especially not from one suspected of antimonarchial tendencies. He turned the matter over to his high judiciary. The judges, meeting Fox in their chambers, did not appear at first to take offense at his hat, but, on hearing the charge of plotting armed rebellion, Fox said, they turned hostile and demanded that he doff it. When Fox did not comply, they summoned a marshal.

If, indeed, the judges were angry, they acted strangely, for, when the marshal came, they bade him treat Fox kindly and to house him in a private room. Discovering then that no such room was available, they set George free without bail, on his promise to return next day for a hearing.

At the hearing, Fox made a telling speech. If he were not innocent and clean and pure, he asked, why was not Porter here to testify against him? Why had no accuser appeared? If he were so dangerous, why had Lancashire sent him down to London without a guard? Was not Henry Porter as guilty as Peter Ceely had been in conniving at the escape of a suspected plotter?

The judges would have freed Fox in any case, but there was additional weight in Fox's favor. Richard Marche, the king's chief usher—George invariably called him Esquire Marsh— announced the royal wish that Fox be released.

George waved aside suggestions that he prosecute Major Porter for false arrest and the twenty-weeks' detention; he left revenge, he said, to the Lord. The retribution he anticipated was not swift but it was terrible, and it was indiscriminate. Except for Esquire Marsh and Fox himself, the Lord cut off everyone connected with the case, even the lenient judges.

By this time it was very evident, to Friends at least, that to oppose George Fox was to invite disaster. Almost invariably persecutors were struck down, cut off or blasted. Their fates varied widely, enemies to truth having been stricken with palsy, drowned, or felled by heart disease; if they lived, they were driven mad, imprisoned or reduced to beggary. One man had been stabbed, another hanged; at this very moment, hundreds were awaiting punishment, for offenses against the crown, according to report, but really, Fox implied, for harming Quakers.

George was not vindictive nor did he delight in the downfall of his foes; but at times he was not above a little human gloating over their fate. On several occasions he taunted his fallen persecutors with the same epithets—butterflies, giddy-heads, house-creepers—that they had thrown at him.

George Fox's good fortune was not to last. Early on a January morning in 1661, the Fifth Monarchy Men rebelled in London. The rising was relatively unimportant, there being but thirty rebels, but the consequences were severe. Londoners, cowed by the tearing down of their walls and fearful of the expected royalist revenges, anticipated violence and bloodshed.

For at least five years individual Quakers had been popularly suspected as Fifth Monarchy plotters and, among the more gullible, the Friends were supposed to be implicated. The association was, of course, entirely groundless. No Quaker leader, with the doubtful exception of Anthony Pearson, was a Fifth Monarchist; certainly no Friend countenanced resort to arms. Nevertheless, because of Pearson's close connection with Vane and Heselrige and because Fox had conferred with them, the general public classed Quakers with the malcontents.

When, therefore, George Fox, roused at midnight by drum beats and calls to arms, hurried to Whitehall, people looked strangely at him. Some of the more excitable attacked Quakers and threatened to burn down Quaker houses. So general was the fear that in London, and in other counties to which the contagion spread, more that four thousand Friends were put in prison as conspirators.

Royal circles befriended Quaker leaders. James, Duke of York, personally intervened to save the life of one man. Esquire Marsh moved from the palace to stay with Fox, as a protection. It was a thoughful action, for soldiers came, arrested George and took him to Scotland Yard, where Marsh interceded for him.

But once more the Friends, by their impassioned longing to perform the will of God, made matters harder for themselves. A proclamation, issued to preserve the peace, forbade political meetings that masqueraded as religious, but Fox, whether ignorant of, or regardless of, the fact that Quaker services fell under the ban, encouraged Friends to continue their attendance. When he was arrested, he refused the oath, as everyone knew he would, but then he took the opportunity to preach, so angering his captors that they jailed him. Marsh managed to have him released, but then came the old problem of who should pay the prison fees.

George Fox flatly refused, but, in what was for him an unusual gesture, he offered the marshal twopence to buy drinks for the soldiers. They jeered at his generosity—probably the sum was insufficient—but, when George gave them the alternative of taking that amount or nothing, they let him go.

Fox and Hubberthorne, to clear the atmosphere once and for all, then drew up a declaration, signed by themselves and ten other leaders on behalf of "the harmless and innocent people of God, called Quakers." Pointing out that Friends already suffered more than any other people in the kingdom, they stated clearly and specifically that Quaker weapons were spiritual, not carnal, and that Friends would take part in no wars nor in any plot.

This Declaration of 1660 denied that Quakers ever wronged any man's person or possessions, ever used force or violence, ever engaged in plotting or sedition, ever resisted authority or, despite injuries inflicted upon them, ever sought vengeance.[2]

Though George Fox believed from the beginning that warfare was a devil's instrument, its outright rejection as Quaker policy developed late. He himself would not take up the carnal sword, but, until such time as the Society became unjustly accused of plotting and sedition, he did not condemn the place of warfare in a righteous cause. He enlisted soldiers among his Publishers without insisting that they give up their careers, and he could by no stretch of the imagination be considered as a nonresistant in any other sense than a personal unwillingness to employ physical force. His verbal assaults were anything but pacifistic.

Charles II fully trusted the Declaration. Encouraged by the earnest pleadings of Margaret Fell, he ordered the immediate release of all Quakers imprisoned for religious reasons; he said they must not be compelled to pay any costs whatever.

Charles more than fulfilled his Breda promises. Edward Burrough protested the New England atrocities, whereupon the king immediately called a secretary to draft an order forbidding further executions for religious differences. Since no ship was scheduled to sail for Boston in the immediate future, he gave Burrough permission to send the document, if he wished, in a private Quaker vessel. He also allowed Burrough to appoint a special King's Messenger to deliver the order to John Endecott.

Burrough, having a well-developed sense of the fitness of things, named Samuel Shattuck, a Salem merchant recently exiled for the crime of being a Quaker.

[2] The actual date, under the present calendar, was January 21, 1661, but as, under then existing custom, the new year did not begin until March, the Declaration was dated 1660.

Shattuck, under Massachusetts law, risked hanging if he returned, but he eagerly agreed to take the message. Fox and his Friends chartered a ship, paying £300 for it to sail for Boston, with cargo or in ballast, within ten days. Fair winds of almost gale force brought the ship, loaded with Quakers, into Boston harbor within six weeks.

The Quakers were not above playing with the port officers who came out to meet the vessel. The captain announced that, yes, he had letters for the governor, but, no, he would not deliver them today for it was Sunday and the Puritans kept that day sacred. Yes, he had passengers; they were Quakers. Yes, he knew this was illegal—for the moment—and that he was supposed to pay £100 fine for each of them; but, no, he would not prevent their landing just as soon as Sabbath ended. And, yes indeed, he brought Samuel Shattuck with him, too, though he and Shattuck both were well aware that Massachusetts was intent on executing any exile who returned. Why, then, was he so intent on risking fine for himself and death for Samuel Shattuck? Well, the governor would hear all about this in the morning.

Soon after daybreak, Shattuck landed, walked through the Boston streets to the governor's mansion and knocked on Endecott's door. A servant appeared, asked Shattuck's business and, when told there was a letter to be handed to the governor himself, ushered him into a waiting room. Endecott entered and saw Shattuck standing, wearing a hat. Whether he first demanded that the hat be removed or that Shattuck be arrested for returning is immaterial, for the king's letter told its own story. It commanded the release of all Quakers in New England and their dispatch, together with written details of all charges against them, for examination before the King's Court in England.

No one disagreed more fundamentally with Charles' toleration policy than did John Endecott, but the governor was a loyal Englishman. In deference to his king he removed his hat in the presence of the messenger, and at once declared, "We shall obey His Majesty's commands."

He was, in all probability, not too unhappy to be compelled to do so. The royal order ran counter to his deep convictions, but it allowed him to bow gracefully to rising popular demands. Massachusetts colonists had been increasingly protesting against harsh anti-Quaker laws; before Shattuck's arrival, the penalties of exile and death had been reduced to whipping and, as last resort, to branding.

Beyond the tight circle of the saintly rulers, there were many who insisted on further relaxation. The fate of poor Elizabeth Hooten, Fox's first woman convert, sickened large numbers of sensitive people. Elizabeth, then in her sixties, had been thrice whipped out of Boston, only to return with a royal license permitting her to live anywhere in New England. Nevertheless, she was twice jailed, abused by "a wicked crew" of Harvard students, and thrice more whipped through the Massachusetts settlements. Governor Endecott and his legislators would not yield to public clamor for more humane treatment, but the king's command allowed him to satisfy the public without loss of face.[3]

Insofar as the royal authority ran, Endecott complied with the instructions. He released all Quaker prisoners, but he failed to send them to the mother land for trial. The king, for his part, did not press the point. Realizing that the home government also had harsh laws affecting the unconventional, he insisted only on equality for peaceful, law-abiding Christians.

Charles let the matter drop and so, except for debate with Simon Bradstreet and John Winthrop, who happened to be in

[3] Yet, by striking down the anti-Quaker exclusion policy, Charles II imperilled the structure of colonial self-government. However justified on grounds of morality or justice, his interference infringed American charter rights and gave precedent for autocratic inroads upon freedom.

England, did George Fox; but the Lord did not desert the Friends. The judgments of God fell heavily upon New England, George noted, for two years later the Indians cut off many of the persecutors.

28

Darkness Gathers

DISSENSION ROSE AGAIN WITHIN THE QUAKER RANKS. JOHN Perrot, freed after three years in the Roman madhouse, reappeared in London and, in Fox's phrase, ran out from the truth.

George immediately prophesied that the Lord would blast him and all his followers; they would wither like the grass thatch of the housetops.

To outsiders, the whole affair seemed trivial. Apparently, Perrot's offense was that while he was in prison he heard the Lord God of Heaven order him to tell Quakers that they must wear their hats while they were praying. Non-Friends wondered why, after Friends had suffered torture for wearing hats, Perrot should be rebuked for telling them to keep them on.

More than hairsplitting was involved, however. To wear a hat before fellow mortals was to show the equality of man, but to wear a hat before the Lord was to deny His divinity. Perhaps, in drafty, unheated English churches it might be excusable to wear hats during large portions of the service— as so many Baptists, Puritans and Presbyterians did—but never when praying directly to the Lord, for that insulted God.

Perrot's innovation also carried overtones. He had no

slightest taint of Naylerism, but to prescribe wearing the hat while praying revived memories of Nayler's insubordination. That schism had been crushed; to accept Perrot's revelation as authentic might revive the heresy.

But Fox found further reason to oppose Perrot. To accept his conceit about the hat undermined the basic concept of Quaker thought. The Inner Light within a human soul reveals the will of God. That Inner Light, that divine Seed, the living presence of the Lord, brings mortal man into eternal harmony with God; it shows the path that he must walk if he would seek salvation. But suppose the Devil kindles a false light, a false light such as the insulting of God by wearing a hat while praying? Man is finite and fallible; he cannot always distinguish between the true Inner Light and the false light sent from Satan. Obviously, Perrot was deluded; his heresy must be halted.

The condemnation, however justified, inflamed the smouldering dispute concerning continued revelation. All Quakers agreed that inspiration flowed steadily from Heaven into the soul of man, and they recognized that some spirits were certainly more sensitive than others; but, though all revered George Fox, some hesitated to allow any one person the power to decide which revelations were divine and which were diabolic.

Perrot's hat heresy became a test case for Quaker discipline. If continued revelations were accepted uncritically, chaos might result. Forms of worship and systems of organization would be fluid and unstable, the uniformity of doctrine and the common practices that united and strengthened Quakerism throughout Britain, and eventually throughout the world, would be destroyed. To tolerate the hat heresy would encourage further deviation. Quakerism would be split into a thousand fragments.

George Fox recognized that to oppose Perrot was to risk the charge that he was claiming absolute authority and that he alone was able to decide which private inspirations were authentic. Even now his enemies were taunting him with being pope of the North; within the Quaker movement there would be some who would believe that he was usurping too great authority.

George dared take no risks with John Perrot, whom he, as the Romans, suspected to be mentally unstable as well as inordinately ambitious. Perrot had already accused him of usurping dictatorial powers and of crediting no revelations other than his own. Therefore, he attacked Perrot. But, Perrot nevertheless gained followers, some of them influential.

Largely because the hat heretic emigrated to Barbados, and later to Jamaica, where, clad in gaudy velvet and wearing a sword, he became a rich merchant and official, the worst furore subsided in England, though it did not end for many years. Eventually, however, retribution overtook John Perrot; he died heavily in debt.

As had the Nayler controversy, the Perrot hat-honor wrangle drove Fox into further dispute; he argued during 1661 with at least fifteen other sects and creeds.

"None of them would confess to the same power and spirit that the apostles had, and were in, and so the Lord's power gave us dominion over them all." They, like the Fifth Monarchy Men, "were all blown away with God's wind as the chaff on the summer threshing floor."

Foreign-speaking lands were yielding no better returns than the efforts four years earlier, but, for some reason, John Stubbs and two associates felt called upon to visit China and the mythical kingdom of Prester John. Why Fox, or anyone else, encouraged them is wholly incomprehensible. No one in England spoke Chinese, only one or two had ever been there and even they many years ago; few had the faintest idea what missionaries would find if ever they arrived. As for Prester John's kingdom, no one really knew just where it was, guesses ranging from Central Asia to Ethiopia; all the legends about the ruler, moreover, were at least three centuries old.

Nevertheless, Fox wrote letters, in English and Latin, to the Chinese Emperor and to the very durable Prester John and gave them to Stubbs to be delivered. Both the English and the Dutch East India Companies very wisely refused to transport the missionaries to their destination—if only because neither at that time had trade relations with either ruler—whereupon Stubbs received a vision that England and the Dutch would soon be fighting. Nevertheless, two members of the expedition reached Smyrna and Constantinople, where they evangelized without success, while Stubbs scattered Quaker pamphlets about the streets of Alexandria. One man died, another had a change of heart, and the British consuls sent back all the missionaries.

The one result was the admission of an ancient friar that there was truth in Quakerism; but, when Stubbs pressed the monk to hand the Holy Father a pamphlet attacking the papacy, the friar clapped his hand to his breast and cried out that he dared not; he would, he said, be burned alive if he attempted it.

Meanwhile, in England, the Breda Declaration proved ineffective. Though personally Charles II held to his promise of religious toleration, Parliament hurried to restore all Anglican clergymen ejected from their pulpits since the start of the Civil War; this, of course, ousted some two thousand Puritans, including William Lampitt and others whom Fox had attacked. Neither Fox nor the King saw in the ousting any violation of the Breda Declaration. To Charles and to his Parliament the restoration was but simple justice; to George it demonstrated once again God's punishment of hirelings and pretenders. But when, in 1662, the government enjoined the Anglican Book of Common Prayer, punished those refusing to take oaths and forbade more than five people to meet for worship other than that set by law, Fox lost confidence in Charles II. The imposition of fines and imprisonment, with transportation to penal colonies overseas in the event of a third conviction, resembled too closely the New England practices.[1]

As usual, local justices outdid in zeal the central government. To thwart counterrevolution they arrested Friends and jailed those who would not take an oath of loyalty.

Sir William Waller, an Oxford magistrate, added a refinement. Three centuries earlier, when England feared papal encroachment in national affairs, a writ called *praemunire* had been invented. This, a species of injunction, forewarned a suspected person not to offend, under penalty of jail without a trial and of forfeiture of estate. Waller revived the writ, issued it against Quakers and, on their refusal to take the oath, committed them for contempt of court. The practice soon spread widely throughout England.

Fox and Hubberthorne wrote a protest to the King, pointing out that thirty-two Quakers still languished in prison for convictions during the Commonwealth and Protectorate and that, since the Restoration, 3,068 other Friends were jailed. Free them, the petitioners implored, and forbid further persecution. Or, if Charles would not release them on the bare word of Fox and Hubberthorne, let the prisoners be brought before the King for a hearing of their case.

Charles did what he could. He had no power to cancel laws

---

[1] George Fox held the King responsible. In common with a majority of his contemporaries, he probably did not realize at the time that the status of Charles II as a monarch differed widely from that of Charles I; he had apparently no concept of Parliamentary supremacy.

nor to make a general jail delivery; but, taking advantage of the arrival in London of his Portuguese bride-to-be, Catherine of Braganza, he gave amnesty to all Friends then in the city jails except—and here his weasel words re-appeared!—those guilty of refusing oaths, of being ringleaders or preaching without proper license. But, only a few days later, new raids upon the Bull and Mouth refilled the cells and all was as repressive as before.

As happened so frequently, hysterical Quakers, in their laudable anxiety to show signs to the people, unintentionally hurt the cause. A woman invaded St. Paul's. Clad in sack-cloth, with sooty face, her hair and clothing thick with clotted blood, she poured blood in sacrifice upon the altar. Solomon Eccles, a recently converted composer, who had given up music as a worldly art to become, like George Fox, a cobbler, advertised his contempt for the official service by starting to mend shoes in the pulpit. He was thrown out, but the next Sunday he returned, jumped from pew to pew to the pulpit steps and resumed his repair of broken boots.

Unfortunately the general public had slight skill in reading symbols. They failed to see that Eccles was demonstrating that constructive labor was more sacred than was empty form. They did not recognise that because they were devoid of righteousness and holiness, the Lord would strip bare their souls until they gave their very blood to Him. Instead, they locked up the demonstrators and branded all the Friends as crazy.

The shock of persecution after all the Breda hopes induced new visions. At Swarthmoor, in 1660, Fox sensed a darkness, which was followed by his arrest; in Lancaster Castle he felt a halter round his neck, and soon thereafter came news of the New England martyrs. There had, however, been no visions for some years; but now he saw in his mind's eye a great mastiff about to bite him. The power of the Lord prevailed. Fox gripped the dog firmly by the muzzle and tore the jaw apart. It was a portent that the Lord would overcome all evil.

Again there were providential escapes from soldiers seeking to arrest George Fox; there was even a minor miracle when Edward Pyott, "a dying man to all appearance," recovered from an ague. Leicestershire constables, however, were insufficiently impressed; they arrested Fox and half a dozen Friends. But, as constables did not wish to take time off from the harvesting, they asked the Quakers to go, unaccompanied, to jail. George and his associates did so, the women carrying their spinning wheels to occupy them in their cells, the men, holding their open Bibles and preaching loudly as they rode to prison.

They arrived at an inn, whose keeper, a justice of the peace, would have freed them, but Fox insisted on arrest; to stay in jail was cheaper, he advised his Friends, than to put up at the inn. The warden of the prison had no desire to admit them; he had trouble enough, he said, with the half-dozen Quakers already there. He also had domestic difficulty; he had a lame, bad-tempered wife who sat all day in her chair swinging her crutches at the man whenever he came within her reach. But George Fox had his way; he bribed the lady to allow the Quakers to come into the jail.

The jailer tried to take revenge upon Friends for the indignities heaped upon him by his wife. He refused Fox permission to bring in beer from the town; they must, he insisted, buy it from him. Fox overreached him; the Quakers, he said, would quench their thirst with water.

Even the prison dog turned against his master. When Quakers held a meeting, the jailer hurried up with a heavy stick and with his mastiff; but every time he raised the stick against a Quaker the dog snatched the stick away. It was a friendly and protective animal and could not have been the

mastiff Fox had visioned; George had not the heart to break
its jaw.

After this, the warden was completely chastened. When, on
Sunday, George Fox invited all the prisoners—debtors, felons
and the rest—to attend a jail-yard meeting, the keeper dared
not put in an appearance.

The trial was, to put the matter mildly, somewhat odd. Fox
and twenty other Quakers would not take the oath, but this the
court passed over; it charged, instead, that the Quakers
gathered in unlawful meeting when no meeting whatever had
been held. The jury found the Fox party guilty of something
or another which it carefully did not clearly state, but a fellow
who busily picked Quaker pockets while the verdict was being
read went off scot-free. The court remanded Fox and his
Friends to jail, whither they walked, preaching all the way,
only to have the jailer let everybody go free.

The warden, however, had learned one lesson which other
keepers had not learned. As the Quakers turned to go, he said,
"There are fees due to me, you know, but I shall leave it to
you to give me what you will."

Fox did not report how much, if anything, the Quakers paid
for their month-long detention. Nor did he reveal until the
incident was over that during the entire time he carried in his
pocket a letter from the Lord Lieutenant of the county ordering the Quakers to be freed.

Swinging through the Midlands, southern England, Cornwall and Wales, George Fox conferred endlessly at Quaker
meetings. The gatherings were glorious and the responses
bounteous, but shadows thickened over Fox's spirit. Constant
travelling and intensive worry over renewed persecution undermined his once-sturdy constitution. Burrough and Hubberthorne died—heavy losses not balanced in the least by the
cutting off of Colonel Hacker, Edward Bowles and a score or

more of other dark spirits. As always happened when his group
was threatened or when trouble mounted, George sensed plots;
when evil did not follow, he never doubted that the Lord
foiled his enemies.

Nor did he doubt that retribution befell his persecutors.
There was, this very year 1663, a certain Colonel Thomas
Robinson, M.P., a wicked justice of the peace, who hated
Quakers. Learning that a jailer allowed imprisoned Friends a
little furlough from their cells to see about their family affairs,
Robinson fined the warden 100 marks—£60 in Charles II's
day!—but, not content with this enormous penalty, he went
out on what he called fanatic hunting to round up the missing
prisoners.

But first he tarried to play bullfighter, poking with his cane
at an unruly animal, stepping aside when the bull rushed upon
him. He enjoyed the sport; it was a common practice for him.
This time, however, the bull, twisting around suddenly, caught
him on his horns and threw him about. A milkmaid ran to
help her master, whereupon the angry bull, as kind to her as
the mastiff was to Quakers, nudged her gently aside, but, when
she was safe, began again to bellow, to gore and to lick up
Robinson's blood.

The man, it must be admitted, had some grains of decency
within him. Though his last words ordered that the bull be
slaughtered, he directed that the meat be given to the poor.

The manifestation refreshed George's confidence. It reassured him at a time when he was discouraged because one
Quaker, taking up astrology, found the stars favorable for
armed rebellion and when another yielded to the seduction of
a Ranter woman.

There was other cause for cheer. Now that matters were
running more smoothly at Swarthmoor Hall, the widowed
Margaret Fell had greater opportunity to increase her work.

When, in 1660, Major Henry Porter invaded her house to arrest George Fox, she wrote to all the magistrates concerned, complaining of the injustice. "If he be guilty, I am, too," she insisted. Twice she visited King Charles to protest persecution; she ventured pleas for Quakers and for the Fifth Monarchy rebels. By 1663, her path was crossing and recrossing that of Fox; she, with her daughters and others of the Swarthmoor household, travelled in company with Fox to various Quaker meetings.

George took great comfort from her presence. Margaret Fell, "the nursing mother" of Quakerism, helped, by her presence and her counsel, to prevent his falling into melancholy and despair.

He unbent sufficiently to chuckle at the dilemma of constables who, in their zeal to keep strict guard, ordered all Friends to assemble in the steeple-house. None went, so the officers arrested many and carted them to the church. The Lord then moved the rest to visit their brethren. All sat quietly, waiting for the spirit; but the spirit was so long delayed that the constables became impatient; and told the Quakers to clear out. Again, they would not move; the Lord had sent them no command. So they lingered, marvelling at priests and officers who first were angry because Quakers would not come and then became offended because they would not leave.

29

Stiff as a Tree

AT SWARTHMOOR THE FELL FAMILY TOLD GEORGE FOX THAT
Colonel Richard Kirkby had searched the house, torn open
trunks and boxes, and had threatened to arrest George.

Fox, even more conscious than usual of his innocence, knew
no good cause for the raid. He put his head, as he would say,
into the dragon's mouth, and rode five miles to Kirkby Hall to
ask the reason.

He found a party in full swing, the Furness gentry gathered
in a send-off for the Colonel, their representative in Parliament. Kirby had stepped out for a moment and the guests gave
Fox a cool reception, no one being moved to speak to him;
nor, for once, had George Fox anything to say. When Kirkby
returned, he denied any intention of arresting Fox; his only
interest, he said, was to persuade Margaret Fell against holding
unlawful religious services at Swarthmoor and, as a patriotic
subject of King Charles, to guard against sedition.

George knew of some minor insurrections, though not by
himself nor by any Quaker; only a few weeks earlier a few misguided plotters demonstrated at nearby Kaber Rigg, but nothing came of it. Kirkby readily admitted that neither George nor
Margaret were implicated, but there had been many strangers

entertained at Swarthmoor. Because some of them might be
suspicious characters, he had made the raid.

Kirby offered Fox perfect freedom provided only that he
kept the Swarthmoor meetings small and that he brought few
strangers into the Furness area.

George Fox made no promises; he argued instead. Kirkby
seemed content, but after he left for London other officials
swore out a warrant and brought Fox before them for a
hearing.

All might have gone well had not George turned the
questioning back upon his inquisitors. They asked if he believed
in God and the church; he replied that indeed he did, but was
not his questioner a papist? He denied that he was a rebel,
pointing out that Cromwell partisans had three times jailed
him for his supposed royalist sympathies, but had not his judges
been on Cromwell's side against the rightful king? Exhibiting
his papers prohibiting Quakers from becoming involved in
plots, he accused his judges of misrepresenting him. When the
Catholic justice proposed putting the anti-papal oath to Fox,
George suggested that he also take it.

They ordered Fox, and Margaret as well, to appear before
the Quarter Sessions court at Lancaster, where other Friends
were also to be tried.

In January, 1664, George and Margaret rode across the
sands to the tribunal over which Judge Fell formerly presided.
They found four justices awaiting them, one of them a gentleman who had offered £5 reward to any one who captured
Fox, another a man so prejudiced against Friends that he
almost choked when speaking of them, a third a nonentity who
did nothing more than sit upon the bench. There was, however, also Colonel William West, an old associate of Judge Fell
and a Fox sympathizer.

The usual hat and oath problems reappeared. There were

also signs and portents. George warned a jurist to beware the judgment of the Lord; when the justice paid no heed, his wife died—somewhat later, to be sure—leaving him with thirteen orphaned children. A wicked countess, who jailed Friends for disobeying her, died suddenly. Wives of some Friends also brought pressure, by threatening, if their husbands were jailed, to demand that the courts pay for their children's care.

Neither arguments, threats, portents nor the intervention of Colonel West availed; George Fox, Margaret Fell and several others went to prison to await their trial. George learned later, probably through West, that all this was prearranged; despite the outward kindliness, the hypocritical Kirkby had induced the judges to teach Fox a lesson.[1]

The final trial was long delayed. Six times, at preliminary proceedings, judges put the oath to George and six times he declined to take it; in the mistaken hope that he might change his mind before *praemunire* was invoked against him, the judges put off the trial.

Lancaster Castle Prison may have been better than Launceston, but it held no comforts for George and Margaret. The cells were larger, possibly, but they were dark, filthy, wet and poorly ventilated; for exercise the prisoners had a four-foot-wide alley that was but fifteen feet in length. Once in a blue moon, the inmates were permitted to go outside, under heavy guard; but, for the most part, they were closely confined. George, however, used the long, slit windows to advantage; he preached at the top of his enormous voice to crowds he hoped had gathered on the grassy slopes that led up to the castle.

According to general belief, the Lancaster Assizes sentenced more defendants to death than did any other court in England; but the justices tried their utmost to spare the

---

[1] If this were so, they paid a grevious penalty; every persecutor died or went bankrupt; Kirkby not only lost his fortune but buried three wives.

Quakers from *praemunire*. When court convened at the
end of August, the judges four times re-enacted the dreary
farce of asking Fox to take the oath. Each time he refused,
usually with a long explanation that the Scriptures forbade it.
The justices—George Fox saw them as dead men sitting on a
bench—had no recourse but to sign the *praemunire*, making
him, and all those following his precedent, liable to indefinite
imprisonment for contempt of court.

Then, as they were required by law, they asked him if he
had anything to say. He answered that indeed he had—a reply
which made them laugh, for they thought it was a sermon
which they might silence as irrelevant.

To their discomfiture, Fox tore the writ to pieces. Doubtless,
he was coached, perhaps indirectly, by William West, for
George never studied law nor, except for his own unhappy
experiences, did he know anything about legal procedure.
That experience, however, drove home the lesson that since
the scales of British justice were weighted heavily against
defendants, every advantage must be taken of technicalities.

This meant that every legal paper, particularly warrants of
arrest and writs of indictment, must be examined with scrupulous attention in order to discover flaws, a process all the
more difficult because, the papers not being seen in advance,
objection must be made extemporaneously, and, in most cases,
without the aid of counsel. Any flaw in the indictment, however petty, any successful quibble about meanings, even a mis-
spelling, could be pounced upon as an excuse to nullify the
writ.

Fox found the flaws he hunted. The paper said that he and
Margaret were indicted on a certain date, but on that day no
court was sitting, hence no writ could have been issued. Moreover, it misstated the year of the King's reign, thus raising
doubt as to just when the events complained of had occurred.

Fox was not properly identified as being a British subject, hence what proof was there that he must swear allegiance to the British crown? Finally, though earlier English kings were entitled to require oaths of allegiance, the indictment did not state that such right was passed on to Charles II.[2]

Fox would have added more objections but the judge interrupted. "Nay," he said, "I have enough."

It was all very clever and, as far as the indictment was concerned, it was effective, but the maneuver was futile; there was still the oath refusal for prosecutors to invoke. Actually, the judges gave George five opportunities to swear; each time he refused. Meanwhile, a new indictment was being drafted and, in due course, was presented. This time the clerk read it so rapidly that George could not understand the words. When he asked time to study it the court readily obliged; the judges locked him up all winter in a wet, cold, smoky cell. Then, suspecting that the new writ was also faulty, the court abandoned the indictment method and, instead, *praemunired* Fox.

Had George known of the action, he might well have protested, but he was not present when the *praemunire* was ordered, nor, for that matter, did he hear of it until much later. But his protest would, in any case, have been ineffective, since courts may issue injunctions at their pleasure. Nor would protest have saved him. In July, 1664, King and Parliament so amended laws that refusal to take an oath of loyalty became a transportable offense. All that would have been necessary was for the prejudiced court to ask once more if Fox would swear and, upon his refusal, to ship him overseas for seven years.

The new regulations, the so-called Conventicle Act, moreover, included serious breaches of the Breda Declaration. It

---

[2] The contention seems frivolous, but it was used, also successfully, seven years later, by another defendant.

was now illegal for more than five people to assemble, under guise of worship, for any service other than that of the Established Church. No jury was required. Any two justices might fine a culprit £5 for a first offense and £10 for a second, the penalties being purposely low in order, it was hoped, to invite a third offense, for which the punishment was transportation overseas to any British colony except America.

Though, to any unprejudiced mind, the Conventicle Act violated Charles' promise made at Breda, the King himself saw no breach of faith. By his somewhat elastic reasoning, an oath of loyalty was a political and not in any sense a religious matter. As the Marylanders told Josiah Coale, punishment for failure to take the oath was for treason to the Throne.

Those opposed to Quakerism thought the Conventicle Act a most convenient law, but clever judges refined its provisions. Obviously, nonconformist services violated the Act, but what of Quaker meetings? How might gatherings where not a word was said or sung be construed to be illegal? The answers were as diabolical as they were unjust. Services need not be verbal. Deaf and dumb persons communicated by sign language; gestures, frowns, nods, shoulder shruggings conveyed meanings, and not one of those methods was included in the Book of Common Prayer. Nor was this all: did not the Anglican service require that certain passages—the collects, the epistles, the first and second lessons—be read to the congregation; were not the people to make certain prescribed responses—the litany, for example, and the prayers? If the passages were unread and the responses not made, was not this a nonconformist meeting?

Silence was as criminal as overt heresy.

Theoretically, the Conventicle Act applied to all Dissenters; practically, it hit Quakers hardest. In five London meetings alone, active law enforcers arrested more than two thousand

Friends. Had all else failed, the Lancaster judges could have applied their new weapon to George and Margaret; the mere matter of *ex post facto* punishment's being illegal would not have bothered them in any way.

Triply locked in that cellar room at Lancaster, George Fox suffered so heavily from illness, disappointment and injustice that the recurrence of visions came as no surprise. He foresaw the Turks' defeat at St. Gothard. Soon afterward the Angel of the Lord appeared, with drawn sword pointing southward. That shining sword foretold the war with Holland that John Stubbs, also, had foreseen; the southward pointing forecast the plague about to ravage London.

Fox was, however, more at peace than were certain of his captors. He had the company of angels and he had leisure, amid that smoke and filth, to write refutations of the claims of rival sects; his judges were discomfited and some must have been embarrassed at keeping their colleague's widow shut up in their cells.

Kirkby had Fox removed from proximity to Margaret. He was much too weak to ride, but soldiers strapped him on a horse and rode him fourteen miles away. Though Fox had little muscular strength, he retained his vocal powers; throughout the journey, he shouted protests at the illegality and the inhumanity of what was happening; he preached mightily to everyone he met, and when, except for the cavalcade, the road was clear, he thundered prayers aloud in that great booming voice.

A young man in the escort would have done well to heed these prayers. Instead, he danced about George's horse, goading the animal into nervous leaps and shyings; as Fox tumbled helplessly about, the fellow, with sham politeness, mockingly inquired, "How do you do, Mr. Fox?"

Soon afterwards, the Lord cut him off.

As none of the escort had any clear idea of the route to follow, it was no wonder that the party lost its way. They came to an inn, put George to bed and then debated what to do. Before long, they started off again, on requisitioned horses, only to stop at a village lockup. Here, since the constables were sound asleep, they hammered on the door, demanded entrance and held a riotous drinking party.

After four days, they came to Scarborough, a 500-year-old fortress on the eastern coast. Outwardly, it was a pleasant castle, standing high above the Yorkshire moors with the sea on three sides and only a narrow isthmus as connection with the mainland. Some score of openings, originally probably portholes for arrow fire, faced the North Sea, from which blew constantly a strong ocean wind.

George was welcomed courteously and was led up a long flight of stone steps to the high arched gateway; but, once he passed the portcullis, the treatment changed. Those portholes, he found, were open windows to cells entered from the interior, cells nine feet by ten, without heat, with no protection against wind, spray or rain.

By spending fifty shillings for repairs, George made his cell somewhat more habitable, but as soon as this was done the warden moved him to another cell where conditions were so bad that streams of water drenched his bed. Fox used a pewter platter to empty some of the pools that formed, as though he were bailing out a leaky boat.

Throughout the rainy summer, he was wet; in cool weather, he was chilled to the bone. He caught a chronic cold and developed painful arthritis; it was miraculous that he escaped pneumonia.

Probably he suffered now from ulcers. He could not eat; it took him three weeks to consume a loaf of bread; he drank little but plain water in which a little wormwood had been steeped. Once he procured a small amount of stomach tonic, a beer made from bitter aromatic herbs, but prison guards stole it from him and drank it up.

To make matters worse, George could not get along either with his jailors or his fellow prisoners. The guards hobnobbed with convicts who would buy them beer; they badgered and insulted Fox because he would not drink with them. One drunken fellow dared Fox to fight; the next day, when the man was sober, George went up to him, hands in his pockets, and offered his head to be punched. He shamed the bully by asking why he picked on a pacifist instead of challenging someone who might hit back.

Scarborough officers were no better than their underlings. Still convinced that George Fox was a rebel, they warned that if any uprising happened anywhere in England they would hang him; often in their rages they bade their soldiers shoot him or run him through. Their bark was far worse than their bite, for nothing of the sort was even attempted, but, none the less, the Lord soon cut off numbers of these people.

Fox's only pleasure was in endless argument. The governor was a Catholic whom Fox disconcerted by showing him the smoky cell and asking if this place were Purgatory. In the vain hope of converting Fox to Catholicism, the governor brought in theologians to debate with him, but when they spoke of papal infallibility, Fox countered with Caton's translations of Eusebius, whereupon they rushed off in a rage. So, too, he discomfited Presbyterians and parliamentarians, various physicians, knights and great men of varied sorts, including old Dr. Cradock of Coventry, the priest who grew so angry when young George stepped on his flowers. None made the faintest impression upon George Fox, nor did he seem to have changed their views, but the arguments gave pleasant relief from the rigors of the jail.

Why did not George Fox complain? Under the unjust contemporary laws, his arrest was entirely legal and prison conditions were no worse at Scarborough—they seem superior to
those at some other jails—but why did he not avail himself of
the King's invitation to call for royal clemency whenever there
was need?

That need had certainly arisen. In the mass hysteria following the Fifth Monarchy uprising, Quakers were crowded
into plague-infested prisons. Some were being transported,
though shipmasters were loath to take them, because, Fox
thought, the Lord sent plagues upon the crews, wrecked the
ships or allowed privateers to capture them.

But when Margaret Fell appealed to Charles, whom Fox
thought tender and loving, she was told that her imprisonment was her own fault; had she held no illegal meetings she
would never have been jailed. George himself might have
fared better, for his powerful friend, Esquire Marsh, was
devoted to him personally; but George would ask no special
favor. Identifying himself with all suffering Quakers, he
refused privileges denied to others, especially from a monarch
who, on the word of a king, assured Friends of safety as long
as they lived peaceably.

Though he would not benefit himself, or Margaret, he did
what he could to aid his enemies. The same governor who
permitted those threats and insults fell into deep trouble. His
ships, sent out as privateers, turned to piracy and there was
fear of punishment. George Fox, he understood, had influential connections at court, among them Esquire Marsh, who
was known to have said he would walk a hundred miles barefoot to help George Fox. Would not the prisoner please
intercede for the unhappy jailor?

It was an astonishing request, particularly from the governor
who, in addition to maltreating Fox, was a brother-in-law of

one of the judges who sent George to prison; but Fox gave him a letter to Marsh. Thus the governor escaped punishment. At the same time, Marsh secured an order releasing Fox.

"The King, being informed that George Fox is a man against all plotting and fighting, and one that is ready at all times to discover plots rather than to make them, and was the instrument of discovering a plot in Yorkshire, orders that he be discharged."

On September 1, 1666, George Fox went free, after sixteen months' imprisonment. The parting was a happy one. The officers and guards who had caused so much discomfort, changed their attitude; they gave George a testimonial. "He is as stiff as a tree and as pure as a bell." George offered to give the governor a present for his civility, but the governor would not accept it; instead he pledged that he would do all he could to help the Friends.

It is not unlikely that the governor interested George Fox in the shipping business, for Fox in later years acquired a partial ownership in two vessels sailing out of Scarborough.

30

The Lord Commands

THE IMPRISONMENTS, TOGETHER WITH THE DEATHS OF SUCH energetic evangelists as Aldam, Caton, Norton and Farnsworth, stripped the Friends of active leadership. Though many new converts were gained, earnest, dedicated and devout people, they were not the passionate missionaries of the earlier years.

Quakerism, in consequence, was settling down. Government regulations against interrupting church meetings only partially explained this development, for neither Fox nor his Publishers of Truth were ever swerved from their duty by any man-made law. The new breed of Quaker ministers, less fiery and less demonstrative than their predecessors, carried their point by reason and example rather than by shock tactics. Quiet men who spoke less about the need of government by saints, saying little about their weapons, spiritual though they were, and keeping aloof from any taint of sedition, they found that their sedateness was security.

But sedateness meant passivity and passivity limited rapid growth. The movement lacked its old vitality; meetings up and down the land sorely needed refreshing. This service only George Fox could inspire. He must reorganize the meetings, start new centers, co-ordinate his people and invigorate them all.

The task well suited him. The cumulative effects of privations in the prisons, the excessive exposure to all sorts of weather and his long continued disregard of his health slowed him physically, but there was no impairment of his mental energy, no loss of persuasive power, no lessened certainty of his authority. His stiff and swollen joints pained him constantly, but, though movement was torture, he continued travelling. He was not as sensational as in the past nor did he shout sermons or warnings as he rode; he was now an executive, forming policy, giving acid tests to the revelations of others, supervising publications and arranging for financing.

He had, in addition, a new advisory responsibility. Margaret Fell's *praemunire* carried with it the possibility of confiscation of her property. Actually, the matter was a problem for Margaret and for the managers of Judge Fell's estate; but all these felt, as did George Fox himself, that he, too, was concerned.

Young George Fell, already estranged from the family because he disapproved of their religious beliefs and they were annoyed with him for his idleness, extravagance and waywardness, challenged the will. Assuring the King that he did not share his mother's Quaker ways but sided with her persecutors, he petitioned Charles to give him Margaret's share of the inheritance.

Charles, already indignant at Margaret for refusing his offer of freedom provided she stayed home and held no meetings, granted the request. George Fell then sent word to Swarthmoor that the place was his and that he intended to reclaim it, its contents and the rentals from the land. His sister Mary, after unsuccessfully visiting the King, hurried back to salvage as much as she could remove from Swarthmoor Hall.

Then, suddenly, the son softened. To all but Fox the change was inexplicable, but Fox knew the power of the Lord came over him.

With all this on his mind, George Fox, sick and suffering though he was, embarked upon a round of visits to Quaker meetings which lengthened into three years of unremitting effort. Enemies derided him; they said that he was growing rich on money offerings. As one critic said, George made more money by his tongue than any other man ever made. They also charged that his increasing bulk was proof that he was eating far too richly and too well.

Nothing could have been further from the truth. The money that he raised—sums far less than his enemies imagined—was never for himself but always for his movement, for Quaker work at home or overseas. Doubtless, Friends with whom he stayed while on his journeys would have pampered him had Fox permitted it, but hard beds and simple foods contented him. His fare was spartan and very badly balanced : a little bread, a bit of cold salt beef no bigger than his fist, a mug of beer in which wormwood, a mild tonic and vermifuge, had been steeped were all that he required.

His tastes were simple, but he had his share of little human vanities. Roundheads raged against the bewigged Cavaliers, St. Paul said that long hair was a shame to man. Bunyan called flowing locks a mark of ruffians and Muggleton refused to listen to unshorn preachers, but Fox delighted in his curls. His dress was plain, but seldom cheap; his leather breeches and his drab grey coat were of good quality, his huge hat of "right special French design."

He was vain about his knowledge and not above exaggerating it. He quoted Hebrew and Latin, spoke words in Welsh and, in collaboration, edited *The Battledore* which cited thirty languages. He made no claim to know these tongues thoroughly, but when asked if he understood them all, he answered, "Sufficiently for myself." The claim incensed an envious opponent, who unjustly quoted Fox as implying that the command of seventy languages was given him in a single night, when, the critic said "'tis so obvious to all the world he understood not his mother tongue."

No mortal was ever more truthful than George Fox nor any more sincerely convinced of the basic equality of all men; but when people of quality accepted Quakerism he enjoyed a warmer glow. An earl who summoned him, a baronet whose family was convinced, "great persons" who attended meetings won special attention; that lackeys, fishermen, watermen and butchers were rude and violent caused no surprise. Yet George never toadied to those of higher worldly rank; he dealt with Cromwell and with Charles II precisely as he treated farm laborers; when plain speech became essential, he spoke more roughly to his betters.

For Fox was forthright and fearless; he hated sham and pretense. When he was right—and he was always right!—he scorned authority not based upon the laws of God. No matter what laws Parliament and King might issue, their enactments had no force if they ran counter to his private revelation.

To others, this was monumental egotism; to Fox, it was submission to the everlasting power of the Lord God. That new word, anarchy, first used in the year of his release, to signify nonrecognition of authority, may well have been coined to describe his attitude toward government.

He had no patience with the timorous who hid their Bibles when officers arrived to break up their unlawful assemblies. He denounced as hypocrites the crafty ones who brought to service bread and cheese and beer so that, if they were raided, they might appear to be at dinner.

"Did you ever read in Scriptures of such practices among the saints?"

For Fox, the example of the saints was always his sure guide. Man's condition had changed mightily since Bible times, but, after all, the Restoration way of life differed less from that of ancient Palestine than moderns might suppose. The rules prescribed for Israel held good in many ways for England under Charles II.

That, despite the national acceptance of the King James version, the Scriptural laws were not unquestioningly followed was, to some degree at least, due to those who, like Fox himself, insisted on individual interpretation of the Scripture passages. Diversity of opinion led to changes, to innovations such as marriage by the priests—a practice for which, as Fox reiterated, the Bible gave no specific warrant. So many sects were following the non-Biblical custom that virtually everyone looked askance at those who lived together, as the Quakers did, without priestly sanction.

Lest his people be accused of "going together like brute beasts," George required Friends contemplating marriage to receive approval both of their near relatives and of the meetings to which the prospective bride and groom belonged; in addition, a widow must also make proper provision for any children by her former marriage. After this was done, the marriage intentions, the banns, were to be published. If no valid objection were raised, the wedding might then take place in the presence of at least twelve Friends.

The regulations were not new; Fox talked of them as early as 1652. But the reiteration, and his evident personal interest in the matter, inspired gossip—George called it a jumble in some minds—that he wished to marry the widowed Margaret Fell. Some thought it undesirable that a 54-year-old widow with six grown daughters, two of them married, should wed a man ten years her junior.

Certainly there was nothing impetuous about the marriage plans. After Judge Fell's death, George was frequently at Swarthmoor, this being convenient for visiting the northern meetings as well as a center for Friends' activities, but their imprisonments prevented meetings. When Margaret was released from Lancaster Castle she did not rejoin Fox, but, with one or two of her daughters, wandered about northern and western meetings for almost six months before going down to London.

Nor, with only George Fox's memoirs as evidence, was the courtship—if so romantic a word may be applied—passionate or even lukewarm; no woman but Margaret would ever have responded favorably. George made no mention of love, nor, for that matter, of any personal feelings; he mentioned casually that "the Lord had opened this thing unto me." Nothing could have been more completely detached from sentiment of any sort, nor could he have been more objective. In this, as in all other matters, he hid whatever personal desires he may have felt; in marriage, as in every other action, he showed no preference, but served only as the puppet of the Lord.

To take Fox's words uncritically would be unjust. Nothing in his nature suggests that he would be an ardent wooer, but no one with his warm affection for his fellows could have been as coldly mechanistic as he presented himself in his memoirs. Over and over again, fellow Quakers testified to his charm and pleasing personality—though they, like George himself, suppressed their evidence. It is decidedly unlikely that his courtship was as unemotional as it has been made to appear.

In any case, Margaret understood; for she, as George declared, "felt the answer of life from God."

She must, however, in conformity with Quaker practice,

discuss the matter with her children, to see if they were satisfied, not only with their share of their father's estate but with George Fox as their stepfather. There was, of course, no doubt concerning their reply—the entire Swarthmoor household was already calling George their father— but, with the children scattered from Lancashire to Cornwall, the consultations would require some time. As the Lord was not requiring an immediate marriage, George and Margaret were content to wait until, in George's phrase, all things were clean and pure and ready to be done in righteousness.

Fox, who did not mention any conversations he may have held with his own relatives—he did not go to Drayton—used the time for conferences with a recent convert, a wellborn 23-year-old Londoner recently arrived from Ireland.

This was William Penn, an admiral's son, who, at sixteen, studied briefly at Oxford until John Owen, the persecutor, expelled him for nonconformity. About the same time that Fox left Scarborough, Penn, soldiering in full armor against the Irish rebels, met an old acquaintance, Thomas Loe, an Oxford tradesman whom John Camm won to Quakerism. Penn, too, became a Friend. He returned to London with Josiah Coale, the Maryland evangelist, eager to preach and write the truth.

Neither Fox nor Penn left memoranda of their talks— indeed, Fox failed to mention Penn until several years later— but both were preoccupied with similar ideas. For at least a decade, George, like many another nonconformist, knew of America as a refuge to which religious dissidents might emigrate, as Pilgrims, forty years before, had fled to Massachusetts.

Penn, fresh from his conversations with Coale, had been told of vast, well-forested lands north of Catholic Maryland, where the soil was fertile, the climate good and where the

Indians were friendly. Access was imperfect, to be sure, for the region had no seacoast and ocean vessels could not sail the Susquehanna; but Maryland was tolerant towards transients and would probably permit the Friends to use the Chesapeake.

Though William Penn was quarrelling with his father, the admiral, over Quakerism, he had access to a royal court that seemed disposed to grant lands to almost anyone willing to settle overseas. If Fox approved an emigration scheme, young Penn might readily obtain a Susquehanna site to found a colony.

Nothing definite was accomplished at the time, but the seed was sown.

While waiting Margaret's answer, Fox decided that he, too, should go to Ireland, a region much upon his mind. William Edmondson, a former Cromwell soldier, broke ground there in 1654 and, in premature missionary movements a year later, Burrough, Howgill and other Friends were active. John Luffe, the martyr of Rome, John Perrot, the hat heretic, and William Ames, successor to Caton in the Netherlands, were all convinced; more recently, John Burnyeat of Cumberland, had begun missionary labors. And, of course, there was Thomas Loe, the convincer of William Penn.

On the whole, however, Ireland seemed rather unpromising. The South was staunchly Catholic, with violent resentments against Cromwell and all his Protestants; it trusted no Englishman. In addition to religious differences and to hatred of military conquerors, there were language difficulties.

It was not surprising, therefore, that when, in May, 1669, Fox set out for Ireland, he went with some forebodings. He took some comfort, however, from the fact that when his ship ran into heavy weather the Quakers, alone among the passengers, escaped seasickness.

But his experience, on landing, did nothing to dispel his

worries. The hosts whom he expected to meet him failed to
arrive, so that the Fox party, lost in the muddy shoreland
which the Irish called slob, wandered for hours. Four times
they were halted by customs officers, which was bad enough;
but it was worse that all the while, the tide being out, the mud
flats gave off what Fox described as "a smell of blood, foulness
and corruption."

Even after his friends rescued him, the troubles did not
cease. Four warrants were issued against him, though, by
daring to ride straight through the heart of town instead of
slinking, as officials thought he would, along the byways, he
escaped capture. An ugly black man appeared in a vision, but
George rode straight at him, the horse leaving a hoof print on
the villain's cheek. George felt evil spirits about, but he was
unafraid. "Let the Devil do his worst," George said, so long as
the power of the Lord prevailed. His enemies, he declared,
were in such rage that they were "ready to eat their own
flesh."

Throughout his entire three months' stay, there were snares
laid for him. Grim black fellows tried to tie his legs together
and constantly the powers of darkness were striking at him, but
the truth prevailed.

After all the Irish suffered at the hands of Cromwell's
troopers, it was no wonder that Englishmen had rough going;
but it is also possible that George's mocking of the mass and
his criticism of the monasteries that, for so many years, had
given comfort, protection and culture, may have contributed
to his difficulties. The trip was not one of his more fruitful
missions, though he did reorganize and reinspire the Irish
meetings. In August, he left the island with the feeling that
the powers of darkness were so vindictive that they chased
him twenty miles out to sea.[1]

[1] The dark spirits pursued him, in fact, much further, mighty storms

In no special haste, Fox made his way from Liverpool to Leicestershire—perhaps, though he did not say so, to tell his mother of his impending marriage. Had he gone to Drayton, he would not have found his old antagonist, Nathaniel Stephens, for that worthy had been ejected from St. Michael's in favor of a Church of England rector. The lame old man had, however, clung to his principles. Though driven seven times from various pulpits, he continued to preach in private houses.

While in his home area, Fox read an astonishing news-book report that he had turned Presbyterian, and that he had created a disturbance in a Wiltshire church. On investigation, he learned that the paper confused him with a scoundrel named John Fox, a wicked fellow who would do anything for money. The news-book would not publish a retraction.

Margaret and her daughters awaited him at Bristol. All declared themselves satisfied with arrangements made for their receiving their full inheritances. Margaret also transferred to them her share in Swarthmoor property which she, by the judge's will, must relinquish upon remarriage. George signed a paper renouncing any rights he might receive, by marriage, to Margaret's ancestral home.

Everyone was now content that "the thing should now be accomplished"; all was in "right ordering." To no one's surprise, George and Margaret announced their engagement. A very few objected, but three separate meetings enthusiastically approved and William Penn declared the union "God's word of life."

On October 27, 1669, George and Margaret married at

tossing the little ship upon the seas for two days. Apparently, the ordeal tried the skipper's temper; for no ascertainable reason he spread reports that George, who had been sleepless the better part of a week, spent the night of his arrival in a drinking bout.

On the return trip, God's just judgment cast away the captain's ship.

Broadmead, the Bristol meeting house, ninety-four Friends signing the wedding certificate.

George described the marriage as a figure of Christ and His Church, a mystic spiritual union, the Church coming from the wilderness, a reconciliation of Heaven and earth. He had no thought of possible children.

"I never thought of any such thing but only in obedience to the power of the Lord. I judged such things below me."

After a week, which could scarcely be called a honeymoon, in Bristol, George resumed his round of visits. Margaret returned to Swarthmoor, where she received a demand from her son that she surrender her property to him. When she refused to do so, if only because she no longer held title to the estate, she was arrested and, in April, 1670, was returned to Lancaster Castle jail.

She stayed there for a year.

Gossip, however. leaped the prison walls. That mystic spiritual union, busybodies said, had been more worldly than George Fox admitted. A Quaker lady, herself a bride of but two weeks, wrote to William Penn that 56-year-old Margaret Fox was about to be a mother.

Enemies of Quakerism blew up the false report into a rumor of fantastic proportions. George and Margaret, they said, were deluding themselves, and trying to delude the world, that they were really Abraham and Sarah. Just as poor, ill-fated John Robins, many years before, awaited a son who would be the Messiah, so reincarnated Abraham and Sarah expected a divine child.

According to these experts in imagination, George and Margaret, who had not even seen each other for almost ten months, were laying in supplies of baby clothes and had a midwife in constant attendance at the jail.

All this on the authority of an anonymous North Country

gentleman who was less skeptical than William Penn about the
Quaker lady's gossip.

31

Persecution and Visions

THE ORTHODOX WERE WORRIED. TRY AS THEY WOULD, THEY could not enforce conformity. Despite four years of fines, imprisonments and threats of transporation, dissent continued; in fact, it mounted steadily. Neither the reactionaries of the far right nor the leftest revolutionaries were controlled, much less crushed.

Charles sat nervously upon an insecure throne. Parliament felt none too certain of itself. Anglicans, though again possessing the cathedrals, the parish churches and all other former privileges, feared the ejected Presbyterians, the Jesuits and the various sectarians.

From here and there came rumors of impending uprisings. In all probability not a single plot was dangerous, and most of the reports were fictional; but spies felt called upon to justify their existence and provincial agents to demonstrate their loyalty to superiors who otherwise would never hear of them. If the court expected trouble, it would be impolitic to rebuke it for trembling at shadows. Better to reassure London by saying that there had been plots but that, by energy and foresight, the wicked were foiled.[1]

---

[1] The John Fox episode was an excellent example. The Wiltshire church disturbance called forth angry words and a prayer book was torn;

A new law, the Second Conventicle Act, effective in May, 1670, tightened controls. Any judge might convict. Transportation was no longer a penalty and fines were reduced insofar as members of a congregation were concerned, but preachers were to pay £20 for a first offense and £40 for a second, fines four times greater than under the earlier act. The owner of a house in which an illegal meeting was held was also to pay £20.

Far more pernicious than the fining system was an incentive to informers, who, for their betrayal of ministers, were to receive a third of the fine, the balance to be divided equally between the Crown and the poor relief fund.

If, next to fear of the Lord, there was any quality which George Fox especially admired it was fearlessness against adversity. He paid no higher tribute to his deceased friends, Hubberthorne and Burrough, than to praise them for never turning their backs. But no one possessed that courage to any greater degree than George Fox himself. He needed no inducement for taking a firm stand, but, had any been required, a challenge of danger would have provided it. On the first Sunday after the Act became effective, no one doubted that he, or, for that matter, any other Quaker minister, would attend a meeting. Characteristically, he chose the meeting in Grace Church Street—he pronounced it "gracious"—which, he expected, would be the first place raided.

George judged correctly. The streets were crowded, the people being, for the most part, friendly, and watchmen and soldiers stood at both the front and back doors of the meeting house. A Friend was speaking when George entered but, when

there was little more to the story. But, by the time the report reached London, it was magnified into a riot wherein George Fox had started a rebellion to make himself the king. Wiltshire being close enough to London to be a source of danger but distant enough to prevent careful checking of the facts, Parliament clamored for stiffer curbs on brawling Quakers.

he finished, Fox rose and likened the oppressors to dogs whose nature was to tear and devour the lambs of God. An informer appeared, with a constable, and, surrounded by soldiers, escorted Fox and two other Quakers towards the Lord Mayor's office.

For the informer, who Fox soon learned was a Catholic, the trip was anything but pleasant. There being three preachers in the Quaker party, he expected a large reward; but, when George repeatedly called out to the crowd that here was a papist informer who opposed not only Friends but all Protestants, the informer began to be afraid that he, and not George Fox, would be a victim. He became worried, bit his nails nervously, and looked about for some way to escape. At the mayor's house, he slipped away, but the crowd manhandled him and the soldiers had to rescue him. Brought back into the mayor's office, he refused to give his name but ran out again and was again attacked and again returned. A third time, by taking off his wig and his coat, he got safely away. The reward remained unclaimed.

There being no informer and no others caring to lodge a charge, the mayor, Sir Samuel Starling, was not unkind. He warned George Fox that the Act applied to all meetings and to all worship differing from the prescribed liturgy and, praising him as an eminent preacher, urged him to dissuade his fellows from gathering illegally.

As soon as George was released, he hurried to Grace Church Meeting House, but he found the building empty. He inquired how this and other meetings had gone and learned that while some few Quakers were arrested all were soon released. "And the Lord's power came over all and a glorious time it was for the Lord's everlasting truth."

The truce was temporary. The genial Lord Mayor was not the first to learn that leniency was no easy road to law observance. Quakers continued to hold meetings. When the government took over various meetinghouses for the use of self-conscious Church of England ministers, the Friends met in the streets. In some areas there were abortive efforts to tear down the meetinghouses, but Quakers rebuilt or repaired them almost as fast as they were damaged; and so that effort was abandoned.

In August, a new crisis developed. William Meade, a recently convinced dry-goods merchant, joined with William Penn to hold a meeting in Grace Church Street. Soldiers and watchmen vainly tried to break through the crowds to arrest the preachers, and scuffles ensued, ending only when Penn and Meade offered to give themselves up as soon as the meeting ended.

There was really no charge against Meade, nor, for that matter, much against Penn, the confusion having been so loud that few could testify to having heard them speak; so, instead of indicting the Friends for illegal preaching, the prosecutors alleged incitement to riot. This, in consequence, changed the nature of the trial; instead of appearing before a one-judge court to be sentenced under the Conventicle Act, the two men, in September, came before a jury, Sir Samuel Starling presiding.

The trial began with a squabble. Penn and Meade appeared at the Old Bailey wearing hats but, before they entered the court room, a bailiff snatched off the headgear, only to clap the hats back on the prisoners' heads as they passed through the door. Starling then fined them £5 each for contempt of court. Penn protested. The restoration was, he said, by Starling's order to the bailiff; if there were any contempt of court it was not shown by him nor by Meade but by Starling himself. As an innocent man, he refused, therefore, to pay the fine; if any fine were to be imposed, Starling should pay it.

The contention was neither well taken nor likely to endear the prisoners to the court, but it did offer an opportunity to the prosecution. Had it been clever, it would have demanded that the prisoners be jailed immediately for contempt, thus ending the case; but, with the usual stupid obstinacy of persecutors, it went forward with the trial. It was a mistake, for Penn now demanded to know what law was broken by worshipping God. "Must I be taken away," he asked, "because I plead for the fundamental rights of England?"

The question was rhetorical but effective. Penn was not on trial for his religion but, justly or unjustly, for unlawful assemblage and for incitement to riot. Nevertheless, his argument confused the jury. Despite Starling's strong charge that Penn and Meade were guilty, it voted eight to four to acquit Meade and to find Penn guilty of nothing but speaking in the street. Starling, dissatisfied with a verdict which he considered contrary to the weight of evidence, ordered the jury to reconsider; when they replied that their decision was unchanged, he ordered them locked up without food, water, fire or toilet necessities until they reached a legal verdict—meaning, of course, one that satisfied him.

It was a complex situation concerning which each of the participants gave different explanations. Penn and Meade felt certain that, despite the kindness to George Fox, the lord mayor was a rabid anti-Quaker. Starling firmly believed the verdict a violation of the jury's obligation to render a true judgment. The jury resented dictation from the bench.

Starling and his assistant, Recorder John Howell, held Edward Bushell responsible for miscarriage of justice. How Bushell became a juryman is a mystery, because, as a well-known character around Old Bailey, he was cordially disliked by both officials. Starling branded him an "impudent, canting fellow" and Howell, who had known him for fourteen years, charged, "You deserve to be indicted more than any man that hath been brought to bar this day." Nevertheless, Bushell was the second juryman chosen; oddly enough, he was allowed to serve without having kissed the Book while taking his oath. It was this Bushell, Starling and Howell believed, who induced the jury to render an illegal verdict.

The jury made Sir Samuel wait two days—one hopes he had withdrawn his prohibitions against food and other necessities. Then, unchastened, it reported agreement upon a different verdict from that rendered before. Starling assumed this was a surrender; but when the jurymen filed back into the courtroom the foreman announced that not only was Meade innocent but so, also, was William Penn. The announcement so shocked Howell that he wished there were a Spanish Inquisition to take care of such fellows as the jurymen. Why not, he shouted, cut off their noses? Starling warned them to think again about their verdict, or he would see to it that the constables kept an eye on every man by day and night. When they refused to change their decision, he invoked a long-unused ancient law which permitted imprisonment of jurors who broke their oaths. He would be lenient, however, he declared. Instead of jailing them, destroying their houses and confiscating their property, as the ancient law permitted, he would fine each man £5, but they must stay in prison until the fine was paid.

There they all remained for a month, Penn and Meade for not removing their hats, the jurors, both the eight recalcitrants and the four who originally voted as Starling wished, for refusing to pay the fines. During this time, Bushell and his fellow jurors sent out more than a hundred demands for freedom before, in November, they secured a writ of habeas corpus. The next year, they were acquitted in what is known as Bushell's Case, a landmark in legal history. Juries, thereafter, were wholly independent of the Bench. A judge might charge the jury, but must not dictate its verdict. Probably the court intended no reference to Howell's angry demand, but its opinion read : "Judges may open the eyes of the jurors but they are not to lead them by the nose."

The victory was not, however, a one-sided triumph. One might have thought that Bushell and his fellows should have some redress for their month's imprisonment, but courts thought otherwise. Four years later, in 1674, the chief justice dismissed Bushell's claim for damages because of false arrest. "An action will not lie against a magistrate for false imprisonment," the high court decreed, "in consequence of acts done by him in the character of a judge."

The court went further. Bushell's bringing suit for false arrest, it said, was a greater offense than what Starling had done to him.

Regardless of Bushell's troubles, the freeing of Meade and Penn, and the subsequent lessening, though not the end, of persecution, cheered George Fox. He moved through the home counties and the midlands, stopping here and there to ease the sufferings of prisoners—at Reading he bribed the jailer into granting favors. His chief concern, however, was to supervise the work of Friends for poor relief and for vocational training.

His idea was extremely simple but only a well-organized movement could put it into operation. Quakerism, alone among nongovernmental agencies, had a national network of meetings; it alone possessed the necessary data. In an epistle circulated several months earlier, in January, 1670, before the enactment of the Second Conventicle Act, Fox proposed to use this network and this data for constructive social purpose.

Let each Quarterly Meeting, he suggested, search out poor children, especially the orphans, to be apprenticed; let it also list employers needing labor. If each meeting selected, every quarter, one such boy and one such master, a steady supply of skilled labor would flow into the building trades, the manufacturing of carts, ploughs and wagons, the leather industry, and into tailoring, weaving and all other manual activities.

After seven years, he pointed out, the apprentice, grown into a journeyman, would support his elders.

Towards this desirable end of training workers, furthering harmony between worker and employer, reducing dependency and providing care for the aged, Fox advised that Quakerism, in all its subdivisions, use such funds as were not needed by the ministry nor earmarked for special use.

There was no objection, he added, to any meeting's increasing the number of apprentices it placed each quarter; the more children who were helped, the more effective the operation of the plan. His practical suggestions were of much different type than his earlier reliance upon good-heartedness, love and fear of God as cures for social ills.

As far as Friends were concerned, most matters seemed moving smoothly, though persecutions had not ceased. But George Fox had deep worries. Margaret was still in jail. Fox sent her two daughters, Sarah and Mary, now the wife of Thomas Lower, of Cornwall, to Charles, but they met difficulties in getting an audience. George Fell, the son, was renewing his claims to Swarthmoor Hall, and this, too, weighed heavily upon the ill and weakened Fox. The undutiful son's death in October, 1670, eased the pressure somewhat, but George Fox still felt himself so laden by the world's spirits that his life was oppressed.

As always, his psychic distress revealed itself in physical ailments. When, in the early autumn, he reached London, his stomach troubles recurred, he slept poorly and he lost both sight and hearing. Pluckily, he made light of his misfortunes, telling Friends that he was now a sign to such as would not see nor hear the truth, and he assured them that, by being blind, he better discerned the honest from the false. But, for all this, he was seriously ill. Friends who were physicians prescribed for him, but he refused their medicine; for several weeks he lay in such suffering that pessimists declared he never would recover. Rumor spread that he had died.

Far from being dead, he was very restless. Various Quaker nurses found him a somewhat difficult patient. As soon as George heard the rumor of his death, he demanded to be dressed and a coach called to carry him twelve miles to another house. The nurses hesitated. Believing him too ill to be moved, they told him to lie still until he gained more strength. When he persisted, they made excuses for not bringing him his clothing; whereupon George said that they were lying. They even went to the extreme of saying that he must be dying because, as people knew, when sick folks asked to have their clothing changed it was a sign that death was near. This, as they might have known, merely increased his determination and, in the end, they had to yield. He groped his way downstairs, insisting all the while that his eyesight was improved. He stumbled into the coach, but, after that hard drive, he lay three weeks so ill that often he could not tell day from night; once he lay a full day in coma.

The experience should have taught him a lesson, but it did not. The notion struck him that he must go to Enfield, eleven miles from London, to visit a dying Friend—and so he did, but the effort took so much out of him that he was ill the entire winter. His daughter-in-law, Margaret Rous, only a month risen from childbed, and the loyal John Stubbs nursed him there.

Probably he had high fever; certainly he became delirious. He warred again with evil spirits; the New Englanders reappeared, with other persecutors, as long-fanged cannibals; he saw his coffin waiting.

There were also happier visions. One day, it seemed, as he

was walking in the fields, he bade his companions dig a deep
hole in the ground. He descended and found there, buried
under earth and rock, a huge vault packed tight with people.
He freed a mighty host. Again, he bade his Friends dig deep
and, when they did, another vaultfull of prisoners came forth.

The symbols were, of course, entirely clear. The Friends
must never tire of carrying the truth to even the most unpromising missionary fields, for, buried under the clods and stones
of ignorance and falsity, lay souls to be recovered for the glory
of the Lord.

Anyone could understand the vision of imprisoned souls
waiting for release, but a further vision was more mystical.
George bade his fellows dig a third hole, and this they did with
zest, anticipating new discovery, for, as they said, "George,
thou seest all things." They unearthed another vault, but this
contained no throng—merely a woman dressed in white,
observing the passage of time. George entered the vault, whereupon a woman, it seems to have been a second woman,
followed him into a treasure chamber. As she laid her hand
upon the treasure, time sped fast, but when George restrained
her, saying, "Touch not the treasure," time slowed.

Those only who are free of earthy, stony nature, George
declared, might understand the vision of the treasure.

"Much I could speak of these things but I leave them to
the right eye and reader to see and read."

Before his recovery, in the spring of 1671, George Fox had
yet another vision. He saw the blessed New Jerusalem, where
all who lived within the light of Christ should dwell. It was a
heavenly city, ten times larger than the earth, unpolluted by
the dogs who scoffed at prophesy, revelation and inspiration,
for these were cast outside the walls, as prey for an ugly,
slobbering hound.

As he recovered strength, Fox resumed active leadership. He
wrote, one mid-April night, a beautiful prayer for justice,

truth and equity, beseeching the Lord to put down cruelty, oppression, falsity and vice. He assured Charles II of loyalty and love, but warned him not to ignore the sufferings of Friends lest torment, misery and destruction fall upon him.

Whether because of the prayer or of the letter to the King, hearts at the royal court suddenly softened. In addition to the stepdaughters, Fox sent other ladies, among them Hannah Stranger Salter, Nayler's adorer, now remarried, to plead for Margaret's release. The petitioners succeeded admirably, the *praemunire* being cancelled and, more remarkably in the Restoration era, the court officials declining to accept the full fees to which they were entitled. One functionary alone, a gentleman who had sent William Penn to jail, waived a claim for £20. The total cost of Margaret's release was only 20 shillings.

Margaret left Lancaster Castle prison in April, 1671. She crossed the sands to Swarthmoor, but soon went down to London, where George Fox was preparing to sail, within three months, for the English settlements in America.

Here, probably, were his close-packed treasure vaults, the hidden multitudes of Indians waiting to be brought into the light. Here were vast areas of fertile pastures, where the lambs of God would live in peace.

Ground was already broken there for the building of a New Jerusalem. Friends who had suffered in Massachusetts, in Virginia and in Maryland had smoothed the pathways. The coming of a band of Quaker missionaries would refresh their hearts; the counsel of the leaders would solidify and strengthen their organization and bring close unity of meetings overseas and in Britain.

As Morgan Llwyd had cried long since, the dawn had broken; the sun had risen. Not in Wales, as Llwyd had thought, but in America, where Quakers soon might live in their own land, governed by the wise and saintly.

George Fox was ready to sail west, where he might see just where a Quaker state could be established.

32

Voyage to the West

IN AUGUST, 1671, THE KETCH "INDUSTRY" SWUNG AT ANCHOR in the Thames. The skipper, Thomas Foster, awaited passengers, fifty in all, among them George Fox and a dozen other Quaker ministers.

Probably Foster was uneasy, for, though himself a Quaker, happy that for ten weeks or so he would have the company of George Fox, John Stubbs, James Lancaster, Elizabeth Hooton, John Rous, Solomon Eccles and other inspirational leaders, he was all too conscious that the voyage would be far from easy. His two-master was a fast sailer, but she leaked badly, so that he would need every hand to man the pumps; but some of these passengers were, like Fox, in poor health and up in years. Two, at least, were aging women, and though one man, George Pattison, was a noted mariner, famous for his recapture of a ship from Moorish pirates, few of the rest were likely to be helpful in emergency.

To make matters worse, the governor and the customs officers took what Foster thought an unnecessary, and costly, interest in his voyage, and the navy sent a press gang to carry off three of his best seamen, a loss not balanced by the transfer in their stead of two of the navy's less desirable men.

Probably the two recruits were more uneasy than was Foster.

They faced a long involuntary journey under difficult conditions. As sailors, they suspected that the Quakers, if not Jonahs or witches, would probably draw storms or other troubles. Seamen as a class were anything but saints, but these passengers were jailbirds and might be madmen. Who knew when Eccles might take it into his head to shed his clothes and run naked through the ship? Who welcomed ten long weeks of steady preaching by a dozen missionaries?

Eventually, all was cleared. The *Industry* weighed anchor. William Penn and his intended bride, with a small knot of other Friends, waved farewell as the ketch stood down the river. Margaret Fox and her sixteen companions sailed as far as the open sea, but there they debarked and the ship was on the way.

Everything went well. Winds blew fresh and fair and the sea was not too rough. But once the vessel lost sight of land some Friends, cooped two by two in tiny cabins, became seasick. One or two cried out that they were dying, but Fox prayed and they were cured. The Quakers felt so much better that a few, including, of course, Pattison, told Foster how better to sail his ship.

Foster willingly took advice from an experienced mariner, but amateurs annoyed him. Other minor matters increased the tension on an overcrowded ship, where people were thrown too much, and too constantly, together. Two weeks after their departure, as the *Industry* cut through the deep blue waters between Madeira and the Azores, a lookout spied a distant ship.

From returned missionaries, Quakers had heard of Moorish pirates. Rich passengers would be held for ransom but poor folk, such as Quakers, would be sold as slaves. This, the Friends insisted, was a pirate, and certain of the seamen, perhaps those who had been pressed, supported them; those distant sails were the same cut as a pirate's ship's.

Foster disagreed; he tried in vain to calm his panic-stricken passengers by advising them to go below for supper. The ketch, he said, would elude the stranger in the darkness. The Quakers had no appetite and, by this time, they had small confidence in Foster's judgment. They rushed to find George Fox, Foster and Pattison following. George asked the skippers their advice, and when they answered that the *Industry* might either try to outrun the ship or lose her by tacking in the darkness, Fox chose the latter course.

Foster may have been pleased that Fox accepted his opinion, though this, of course, was no more than his due, but he resented the interference of landlubbers; he grumbled that the distant ship was not a pirate but a merchantman and that tacking was unnecessary. Nevertheless, at their insistence, he changed his course again and again only to discover, at midnight, that he and the pirate, if it were a pirate, were close to a collision. By dousing all lights and tacking several times, he worked himself free and by morning the *Industry* was alone upon the ocean.

He received no credit for his skill. All that the Quakers said about missing the pirate was: "We saw him no more, which was the almighty hand of God that delivered us. To Him alone be all glory, honor and praise for evermore."

After a month of fair, brisk winds, fresh water supplies ran low, for there had been but two brief showers. Passengers were put on water rations; they were lucky that in these warm latitudes the water had not gone putrid, for, on some voyages it became so polluted that sailors held their noses as they drank and sometimes had to strain the stuff through cloth. Almost always, maggots and weevils infested the hardtack. The Friends could not bring themselves to catch rats for food, as did the hardier sailors, but they ate salt meat fished from the briny harness tubs in bad condition and hacked off at table by their jackknives.

Heat and close quarters began to fray the nerves of all

aboard. The strained relations between professional sailors and their passengers were not eased by the skipper's mutterings that they had run away from an innocent merchantman or by Fox's testy questions why, if this were so, the skipper had bothered everyone about the matter and why all that tacking had been necessary.

But, after all, the captain was considerate. Now and then, when winds dropped off, he managed to harpoon a graceful dolphin or to hook bonito; their flesh was tasty and they made excellent broth. This kind of diet, though usual on shipboard, was insufficient. Scurvy broke out.

The Quakers tried several ways to keep in health. Eccles undertook a seven-day fast, breaking it only by rinsing his mouth with vinegar; at the same time, he insisted on staying awake, though sometimes at night he nodded slightly.

Most of the passengers resorted to exercise. The work was necessary. The *Industry* leaked badly. Water poured in through a long hole along the keel, wide enough for a man's hand to pass. Fish swam about the hold; unfortunately they were too small to eat. Passengers and crew pumped steadily, more than a thousand strokes an hour.

"It was a wonder and amazement that the Lord preserved us."

When Fox was not pumping he was in his cabin studying the mystic significance of the four rivers of Eden or dictating epistles and articles to be sent back to London for publication. He also drafted his plans for his American campaign.

Encouraging reports were plentiful. After Shattuck's delivery of the King's message, Massachusetts established more meetings, as had liberal Rhode Island. Connecticut, with fewer Seekers, remained dark, but John Burnyeat carried the Truth as far north as Piscataqua River, the present site of Portsmouth, New Hampshire.

Farther south, prospects were promising. Charles II's evident loyalty to his Breda promise opened greater opportunity for Quakers in newly acquired New York and New Jersey, as well as in tolerant Maryland. His charter to Carolina colony in 1663 included full liberty of conscience, a freedom reaffirmed in a constitution drawn up by the philosopher John Locke. Virginia's resistance was weakened by the King's toleration policy, though here, as in England itself, local officers acted independently.

Virtually all reports stressed the willingness of Indians to listen to the Quaker message. Much of their friendliness was due, no doubt, to the Quaker method of approach, for evangelists asked for nothing tangible, nor did they come with gun in hand. The Indians reflected Quaker courtesy. True, the missionaries talked at length, but this was also Indian custom. Quaker preaching might be difficult to understand, and probably wholly impossible to translate in exact detail; but when interpreters declared that the English wanted peace, fair dealign and love for all mankind, no Indian would raise the slightest objection.

Fox could not fail to be impressed by Indian readiness to accept the truth; he looked forward eagerly to meeting their leaders and to establishing firm meetings everywhere. Though he may have been a bit cast down by Coale's failure to buy Susquehannock land, a disappointment due to Coale's misunderstanding of tribal custom, he trusted in the basic goodness of the people.

The poor diet, the constant study and the physical labor aboard ship combined to make Fox ill. Exhausted at the outset of the voyage, he gave himself no rest. For three weeks he sweated so heavily that he felt sodden. His legs swelled, he broke out in boils, his bones ached. Scurvy brings muscular pains and heavy hemorrhages; he thought them a recurrence of his many bruises. His stomach rejected the stinking salt meat. Then, for a month, he burned with such high fever that he could not sweat.

On October 3rd, he reached Barbados and was taken to the house of Thomas Rous, John's father and a wealthy planter. Physicians dosed him to make him sweat and gave him ginger water to soothe his stomach; but, for three weeks more, George lay ill; he felt weaker than at any other time he had known.

His spirit remained unbroken. Barbados, the nursery of Truth from which so many evangelists travelled to the main-land, was a Quaker stronghold but there had also been perse-cutions and, what was worse, some serious deviations. Perrot, the hat man, had been here and also Robert Rich, the Lazarus who licked Nayler's sores; they led many into error. Perrot was dead and Rich was gone, but the condition of Barbados remained a heavy burden. Too many Quaker sugar planters held Negro slaves. All this, said Fox, "pointed toward his heart."

While George convalesced, his fellow missioners, "threshing, cutting and hewing up and down the island," cleaned up much of this "filth, dirt and unrighteousness," but the faithful were impatient. "When will George Fox speak?" they asked. "When shall we hear him?"

The anxiety was all the greater because there had been a sign from heaven. Before Fox arrived, a scoffer was heard to say that he would have George burned, but, within a day or so, the wicked man was stricken by a fever that burned his own face black as coal and killed him. When, therefore, Fox announced that he was strong enough to attend Monthly Meet-ing, if it were held at the Rous house, more than three hundred people came. The next day, at a women's meeting, a hundred were present; more throngs came, a third day, at a meeting for the men.

To each of these George brought the same message; they should systematize their work, set up registers of births, marriages and deaths, establish cemeteries, and follow such procedures as were customary back in England.

But, as Barbados was a sugar island where plantation conditions differed widely from British farming practice, there were special injunctions. Friends had not yet opposed Negro slavery, but Fox insisted that, as every soul was equal before God, the Quaker who owned slaves must be humane. He recommended training, if not schooling, and, after thirty years of service, full emancipation. There were immoral practices, of which Quakers doubtless were not guilty, which must be stopped. Ill as Fox was, he was tireless in demanding that masters and overseers treat their workmen kindly and gently.

Stubbs wrote to Margaret that he and Eccles were active in work among the Negroes, but that George Fox did more than either of them.

George campaigned so energetically that non-Quaker slave owners charged that he was stirring up an insurrection. While they were about it, they added that the Friends were non-Christians and atheists; it is astonishing that they failed to bring the timeworn accusations of sorcery and treason.

Fox assured Colonel Christopher Codrington, Governor General of Barbados, that Friends abhorred all wars and rebellions. On an island such as Barbados, where at least half the population were tawny Indians or Negroes, he added in a letter, it was especially important that servants love and obey their masters and that masters return that love with gentleness. Without directly accusing anyone, he took the opportunity to condemn theft, lying, drunkenness and vice.

Codrington believed the letter reflected Quaker views, but Fox reported that the clergy, the justices, the lawyers and the ungodly did not. They raised a great disturbance at a meeting, Paul Gwin, the Bristol heckler, among them; but in the end they tired and left. "And the power of the Lord was over all."

Though no great headway appears to have been made

among the planters, Fox set up, within three months, a system whereby each head of a Quaker family organized his household, white and black, into a patriarchate like that of Abraham. Satisfied that all would then go well, he and four companions took ship, in January, 1672, to cross the Caribbean to Jamaica.

The wind was fair but the ship was leaky, the carpenter on one occasion being obliged to dive overboard to calk the hull; and so, instead of sailing directly, the vessel hugged the shore. The precaution added about two hundred miles to the voyage, but, there being storms, the longer course was wiser. After ten days, the ship came safely into port.

For seven weeks, Fox and his Friends threshed the island of Jamaica. It was a place of special interest, for William Penn's father, the admiral, had won it from the Spaniards only seventeen years before; it had also been a residence for John Perrot. Convincements came easily, and seven meetings were set up. Unlike Barbados, the people were polite—not a single voice was raised against the Quakers.

Yet, it left mournful memories, for it was here that, suddenly, without the slightest warning, Elizabeth Hooton, the first woman Quaker preacher, died. She was well on toward seventy when she died, as Fox said, "in peace like a lamb."

As Stubbs stayed as Quaker leader in Barbados, so Eccles tarried in Jamaica. Fox, with six others, embarked on March 8th for Maryland.

They had a choice of ships—a frigate or a ketch. But the larger vessel asked 10 shillings more per passenger, and so the Quakers took the ketch. It was well they did, for Spaniards captured and looted the frigate, which proved to Fox that those who were covetous fell among the covetous.

Jamaican luck did not accompany the party. First there was no wind, the ketch being for a week unable to lose sight of Jamaica; then winds blew so hard the little vessel could not thread the Windward Passage between Haiti and Cuba. In desperation, the skipper changed his course so as to round the western cape of Cuba, but calm descended, only to be followed by gales that snapped the mainstay, carried away a spar and blew the jib into the sea. They might have landed for repairs but they dared not; the sea was shallow and rocky and filled with sharks; ashore, man-eaters, crocodiles and alligators waited.

George Fox prayed, and all at once the wind was stilled. A week later, in the night, another gale sprang up; this, too, was stilled by prayer. Then came five days of hopelessness; winds blew so hard that the captain lashed the tiller and let the ship drift as it would. When, at last, the storms ceased, the skipper reckoned that the ketch was farther south than when the gale began; but out of the mist and fog he caught sight of the Virginia coast.

"Praised be the Lord who with his mighty hand and power and by faith in it carried us and preserved us ever in it."

On April 18th, after forty-one days at sea, they passed Cape Henry and came into the Chesapeake; they had logged less than thirty-five miles a day. That it had taken almost as long to travel from Jamaica as it had to cross the ocean was bad enough, but, in the more protected Chesapeake, storms so slowed the ketch that it required five days to sail to the mouth of the Patuxent River, just north of the Potomac.

To the great joy of Maryland Friends, Fox debarked just in time for a General Meeting of the Western Shore. It was an important event, called by John Burnyeat to repair damage done to Quakerism by political persecution and by the spread of the hat heresy. Many Marylanders were affected, including Thomas Thurston, the pioneer, who not only ran out with Perrott but who, by worldly ambition and by land speculation,

became what Burnyeat called a spiritual vagabond. Both in
Virginia and in Maryland, Burnyeat warred for several years
to re-establish truth; this gathering, the birth of what is now
Baltimore Yearly Meeting, was designed to restore discipline.

Fox's unexpected arrival made possible greater accomplishment. Maryland and Virginia, more than other colonies,
starved for social contacts. New England was a community of
villages where people saw their neighbors, talked with them
almost daily and worshipped with them twice a week, but the
tobacco colonies possessed few settlements. Maryland's 10,000
people, living in one-story houses strung along the streams,
knew only silent isolation. It was no wonder, therefore, that
when Burnyeat called his meeting everyone within canoeing
distance came to listen. Fox counted half a dozen justices of
the peace, the Speaker of the Assembly and many other "considerable people of the world." They heard the Quaker
message and "a glorious meeting we had."

So glorious that it lasted four days.

33

The Friendly Delawares

As in England, Fox's American life was one long series of meetings. His main purpose, he would have said, was for administrational activity to unify the scattered groups, to organize their methods more efficiently, to see that records were in order, and that everything went well; but, obviously, his presence brought much more than routine and discipline.

Fox smoothed out differences, quelled dissent, and so promoted unity of belief and regularity of group procedure.

The work required much effort. After Patuxent, Fox set forth for a second gathering, at the Cliffs, on the west shore of the Chesapeake. It was a forty-mile trip on a very hot day during which a storm sprang up that cast his sloop ashore. Fox and his companions worked all night, in a driving rain, to get the boat afloat, and did not reach the Cliffs until daybreak. Though none of the party had slept, they held a great meeting where backsliders were retrieved and where many of the world's people were convinced.

The party then split, some Friends going to Virginia to combat the Perrot heresy there, while others took ship for New England. Fox, with a few companions, crossed to the eastern shore of the Chesapeake.

Here was a sturdy Quaker stronghold, with three centers

within a ten-mile radius of what is now the city of Easton. All were small, as was to be expected, but the guiding spirit, John Edmondson, who lived at Tred Avon,, or Third Haven, was a man of mark and influence. One of the largest land-owners of the province and one who, except for his refusal to take oaths, would have been a leading official, he had close business interests with Barbados and, more importantly for Fox's purposes, with Indians.

Fox's knowledge of Indians was not profound, but, from all he heard, he judged them ripe for harvesting. In common with many others of his time, he thought of them not as savages but as kindred spirits wandered from the truth, possibly descendants of the ten lost tribes whom Sargon of Babylonia deported from Israel and who, some supposed, were the common ancestors of both Indians and Britons.

Might not this ancient relationship explain the friendliness of Susquehannocks toward the English? Captain John Smith, moreover, years before, mentioned that Susquehannock voices sounded just like people speaking in a vault; was this corroboration of Fox's vision of imprisoned people?

George invited one Indian chief, whom he thought the emperor, to visit a Quaker meeting and to bring with him two of his kings.

After a tribal council where the invitation was discussed, the emperor and the two kings listened politely to the word of the Lord; they said that it was good. George then asked them to tell their people that God was setting up a tabernacle in the wilderness; they replied that they would come to meetings.

Much of the graciousness, apparently, like that of Sultan Mohammed, was the innate politeness of heathen who had not yet learned Christian intolerance, for Indians failed to frequent the meetings; but the Susquehannocks and their neighbor Indians did send guides to lead the Quakers on their journeys.

Fox was going to New England to inspect the state of Quakerism there, but he had another purpose also. If a colony of Friends were ever to be founded, this was his opportunity to scout a site. A Susquehannock war with the Iroquois rendered Coale's inland area inadvisable for the moment; but what about the lands just taken from the Dutch along the Delaware or the seacoast just below New York?

On May 6th, two guides led the Fox party northwards. The logical route would have been to sail up the bay to the head of navigation, as Coale did, and then to strike out for ten or fifteen miles across level land to the Delaware; but, lacking a sloop big enough to carry his horses, Fox chose to ride.

The guides won no prizes for efficiency. To cross several streams at the narrowest points they led Fox inland, but somehow they lost their way amid the thick black-walnut and chestnut woods. After camping all night in the forest, Fox found himself not at the source but at the mouth of the Sassafras River. To make matters worse, instead of following the waterway upstream, the guides swam the horses over the river while Fox crossed in an unstable canoe.

He was now at World's End, the mansion of one of Maryland's greatest landowners. Apparently he did not stay, which was a pity, for the proprietor of World's End, Thomas Howell, was an influential figure in the government; moreover, he missed meeting a neighbor, Augustine Herrmann, who was even more colorful. Successively a Swedish soldier, a Dutch business man and a pioneer in the English tobacco trade, the Czech-born Baron Herrmann was the best geographer in the colonies. He knew more about the lands lying between the Potomac and the Hudson, the lands available for Quaker settlement, than any other living person.

Three days after leaving Tred Haven, Fox reached New Castle, lately the Dutch provincial capital. Here his Susquehannock guides left him. The Fox party, riding down the crooked narrow Strand, past the steep-roofed houses of the largest town on the Delaware, found ferrymen to take them to New Jersey.

This was land recently bestowed by the King upon two partisans, John, Lord Berkeley and Sir George Carteret, as true and absolute proprietors. Neither beneficiary seemed particularly grateful over the 8500-square-mile windfall. Since neither saw the province, they took five years to decide that Berkeley should control the south and Carteret the north; even then, they drew no boundaries. They knew so little of their grant that they confused their geography, calling Berkeley's south portion West Jersey and Carteret's share East Jersey.

Fox entered West Jersey midway between two former Swedish forts. The first glimpse was attractive. The fields and meadows were fertile and well watered; there was not the slightest hill visible. Nowhere had George Fox seen so much wild life; the river seethed with shad and sturgeon struggling upstream to spawn, and there were oysters at least six inches long.

Though Fox supposed that he was the first white man to ride much beyond the river bank, a few Swedes and Finns lived along the streams. There had once been Englishmen as well, enticed thirty years before by an enthusiastic promoter who promised them an earthly paradise. This land, the promoter assured them, was "the fairest country that a man might see, where angels in the guise of birds sang matins, prime and evensong," and where "it was always day and temperate and neither hot nor cold." These, however, had long since left in disillusion.

Following new and more expensive guides, Delaware Indians who called themselves the Lenape, Fox rode through sandy wastes and wide pine barrens; he floundered through swamps and forded mud-bottomed creeks. He must, the guides warned, be careful where he trod, lest he step upon a rattlesnake; he must not sit beneath a tree unless he first made sure there were no wildcats—the interpreters called them lions and tigers—in the branches.

Some nights, the Fox party slept in the woods—luckily it was before the mosquito season; at other times Indian kings and queens—there were twenty-three Lenape monarchs in this wilderness—entertained him in the bark huts of their Indian encampments. Lenape politeness fitted well with Fox's urge to preach; their practice was to listen without interruption, nodding now and then to show that they were listening, though probably they understood but little that was said. The talking must have been one-sided, for Fox spoke for hours on end, the Indians having little chance to tell him of their Lenape religion.

It was a great pity that his guides apparently knew more Swedish or Dutch than they did English and that they seemed almost wholly unacquainted with words expressing spiritual concepts. George Fox would have been delighted by Lenape beliefs, though—in the light of the Jewish antecedents of these Delawares!—he probably would not have been amazed. Delawares stressed humility of spirit and conduct, dependence upon the benevolence of the divine, insistence upon sincerity and clean behavior; they were altruistic and considerate, believing in what subsequent translators called "concentrated spiritual unity in worship" and in the welfare of all men, regardless of tribe or race.

They hated violence and war. They signed a treaty with the Iroquois, renouncing it. The Delawares, in short, came close to Quakerism.

In the absence of a common language, or of adequate interpretation, Fox knew nothing of their idealism. If, in the

log huts' smoky interiors, their stomachs filled with coarse stew
from the single cooking pot, the Quakers and the Indians
explored each other's minds by signs and simple basic words,
the Friends would have learned nothing more than that other
Indians scoffed at Delaware principles, calling the Lenape
womanly because they did not fight or grandfathers who talked
more than they battled.

Wholly unaware that the people of this hospitable country
were virtually made to order for his harvesting, that here surely
was a treasure vault, George Fox moved north to what was
called East Jersey. Dutchmen lived here, and some Scots and
Puritans came down from Connecticut; a few Friends were
also present. This was better land. Though rather more hilly,
the soil was rich and better drained; instead of pine barrens or
sandy desert, Fox found cornfields and wheat lands and
orchards whose multitudinous blossoms promised heavy crops.

He did not, however, linger. Friends took him to Sandy
Hook Bay and then ferried him, a full day's travel, to Long
Island. Eventually, he reached Oyster Bay and Shelter Island,
that sanctuary set aside for persecuted Friends by Nathaniel
Sylvester and Thomas Rous of the Barbados Quaker family.

Half-Yearly Meeting was about to open, a gathering called
to combat dissension, especially hat heresy. That snare of
Satan, to use Burnyeat's phrase, was not so prevalent in New
England as in the South, but pockets of Perrot disciples persisted. Ranterism, though dying in England, continued in the
colonies. Among Friends loyal to the truth there were, for that
matter, some who complained that private revelation and
individuality were being repressed by rigid disciplines.

After eleven successful days at Oyster Bay, Fox sailed for
Rhode Island, arriving there May 30th. After threading the
wilderness of Maryland, New Jersey and Long Island, exposed
to the "fury of wild beasts"—he was weary.

A familiar face greeted him warmly. Ann Clayton, once a

maid at Swarthmoor, one of the household whom George convinced on his first visit there, later a Quaker preacher who had been whipped and twice jailed, was the First Lady of Rhode Island. She had married only the preceding month and her husband, Nicholas Easton, a 79-year-old widower with nine children, had been chosen governor within a week. Both were happy that George came—Ann because it reminded her of old times, the governor, the first Quaker to hold that office in the colony, though he had been five times deputy, because he sorely needed Fox's counsel.

Easton, who may have been the first Friend to hold executive office anywhere, faced dilemmas. Hostilities were about to be renewed with the Dutch neighbors of New York; he had royal orders to defend the colony, but he detested war. He resolved to treat Indians fairly, even to admitting them as jurors, but tribesmen were hostile.

These matters came before Council meetings, which George Fox attended, and before Friends' meetings. Conflicts arose between principles and duties, whether officials bound to execute the laws of man could break those laws while continuing to hold office. Neither Fox nor Easton revealed the basis for the governor's eventual decision to defend the colony, but the meetings were harmonious. The administrators invited George to suggest measures to improve the government.

Fox readily obliged. The Quaker registration of births, marriages and deaths worked well, so he suggested that Rhode Island keep vital statistics for the colony; he also suggested that each town built a market house for use at least one day a week. Alarmed at the prospect of a steady importation of West Indies molasses for conversion into rum, he urged that laws be passed to control drunkenness and to punish tavern keepers who sold to those who had already drunk enough. He advised that duelling be declared illegal.

Most important, however, was that Rhode Island bend every

effort to preserve its liberties, national and local, but, most especially, the freedom of conscience.

He also pleased the Narragansett Indians; they matched the Marylanders in politeness. A king agreed that, of all the white religions, Quakerism was the best. The admission was, after all, no more than might have been expected out of courtesy. But perhaps the interpreter was not completely accurate, for he quoted an Indian as confessing that the red men had been destroyed because they had mistreated whites.

The Narragansetts would not, however, accept Quakerism. When Fox pressed the king to change his faith, the chief replied that some of the Indians had sampled New England religion, only to become worse people than they were before. If, moreover, Indians should now become convinced, the Massachusetts men would hang them or banish them.

"Therefore, he thought it was best to be as he was."

Towards the end of July, when he had been about two months in Rhode Island, Fox felt called upon to return south. Much good might have been accomplished had he gone northwards into hard-pressed Massachusetts, now slowly recovering under the more tolerant policies, or up to the Piscataque, where Burnyeat had done such good work. These distant areas were, to be sure, participants in Newport's meetings, but the trip across Massachusetts or by sea around Cape Cod was long and difficult, so that most Friends in the northern areas had little opportunity to meet their fellows. Had Fox had time, or physical endurance, to go to them, it would have mightily refreshed them. Those northern areas, however, offered no good sites for Quaker colonies.

Similarly, he missed Connecticut, where neither Seekerism nor Ranterism had won a foothold, nor did he plan on visiting the Dutch settlements of New York.

Fox's announcement of his intended return led Rhode Island to urge him to remain. An ancient justice suggested that he be hired as their paid minister. Fox refused the offer, but, apparently, not as angrily as he would have rejected it twenty years earlier.

None of this pleased Roger Williams. At Fox's arrival in the colony, a six-day General Meeting of Friends from all parts of New England, Piscataqua to Shelter Island, went so well that Quakers found it difficult to end it. Sloops constantly arrived bringing new Friends anxious to participate. The enthusiasm continued; when Fox spoke of leaving, the Rhode Islanders were in the midst of ten glorious meetings in as many days. Williams had attended one of the earlier meetings; he did not forgive Quakers who twice broke off his speaking efforts by being suddenly moved to prayer.

Had Roger Williams met Fox in the decade of the fifties, the apostle of free religion and government might well have been convinced; but, in his seventies, his mind was less receptive than when he had been a Seeker. George, moreover, was allied with that faction which Williams suspected of belief in autocracy and racial injustice. Williams could have made no greater error than to think that George shared that belief. Belatedly he challenged Fox to a series of debates; he sent the invitation by a courier. The day before the arguments were to start, the old reformer rowed thirty miles to face the Quaker, but George did not arrive. Instead, Burnyeat, just back from a Massachusetts visit, appeared with Stubbs and William Edmondson, the Hammer of Ireland. Williams accused Fox of running away—the first and only time anyone ever raised that charge against George Fox! The fact was that the courier had taken so long to deliver the challenge that Fox started south before the invitation came. Williams had no objection, however, against the substitutes, and consequently the debate began—a wrangle first at Providence and then at Newport in which each side hurled slanders and accused the other of deceit. Both sides claimed victory. Fox did not mention the matter in his *Journal* but when Williams published a book with a punning title, *George Fox Digg'd Out of his Burrowes*, George and Burnyeat replied with *A New England Fire-brand Quenched*.

Fox, meanwhile, was sailing south in a small, open boat. At Fisher's Island, off the eastern tip of Long Island, he landed to spend the night, but, by this time, mosquitoes were numerous and he was driven back to sleep upon the sloop. The sea was rough and rain heavy, so that he needed three days to sail eighty miles along the Sound.

At Shelter Island he again courted Indians. Their chief, attending with his council and about a hundred braves, listened lovingly to a two-hour lecture and promised to set up a meeting where Nathaniel Sylvester might read the Scriptures to them and to the Negroes of the neighborhood. Three days later, when Fox held a General Meeting, no Indians appeared.

Small boats were the accepted means of travel, but the Sound was inhospitable. Strong running tides, fogs, gales and heavy rain bedevilled the sloop; at one time, Fox was driven all the way back to Fisher's Island, and then a calm set in. Nevertheless, George completed his round of meetings and, at the end of August, came once more to East Jersey.

He found the province thickly wooded and studded with bad bogs; at one point, near Shrewsbury, he and his horse slithered down a hill so steep and so treacherous that, reaching the foot, the horse had to lie down and pant heavily; they called the place Purgatory. But there were Friends there and thriving meetings; a meeting house was being built.

Near the steep hill of Shrewsbury, Fox amazed his companions by seemingly raising a man from the dead. The feat was not an intentional miracle; in fact, George, neither then nor at any other time, claimed supernatural accomplishment. The special need to demonstrate the power of the Lord had long since passed, nineteen years having elapsed since he healed the deformed eleven-year-old boy. Nor was it necessary, as it might have been in Nayler's day, to match the return to life of Dorcas Erbury.

Actually, George Fox did manipulative bloodless surgery. A Barbados Friend, who was riding with the party, mounted a horse and was thrown. The man lay motionless upon the ground. Bystanders believed him dead and so, after a careful examination, did George Fox. The man's neck, Fox believed, was broken, for the head "turned like a cloth, it was so loose." Just why he thought it desirable to twist the completely relaxed neck muscles back and forth a number of times, Fox did not explain, but he exercised them vigorously. The rough treatment restored the man to consciousness and the neck became rigid. Fox heard a rattle in the man's throat and then he saw him begin to breathe. The season was still warm, but Fox had the man placed by a fire, given warm drinks and put to bed. The only aftermath was a severely strained neck.

Next day, the man rode sixteen miles to attend a meeting.

From Shrewsbury Fox hired Indians to guide him across the waist of New Jersey to the Delaware river. The usual route, a path through oak, hickory and chestnut growths, was about thirty miles of easy travel, interrupted here and there by streams. But either the guides did not know their way or Fox's measurements were inaccurate, for he reported having ridden forty miles one day and fifty the next.

The land along this upper trail seemed rather better than that which Fox had seen farther south; it was a little higher, less sandy, and better suited for settlement. But there were indications that the few white people living here were troubled by the Indians; when Fox reached the Delaware, he saw that one house had been burned and that two others had been abandoned. The misfortune must have heightened Fox's resolve that any Quaker colony must live harmoniously with the aborigines.

34

Scouting a Colony

GEORGE FOX HAD NOW SEEN BOTH LORD BERKELEY'S WEST Jersey and Carteret's East Jersey holdings. Either was attractive as a place to settle if Quakers should be forced out of England, but neither was entirely satisfactory. East Jersey had, perhaps the better land, but much of it was occupied and by people uncongenial to the Friends. West Jersey owned harbors suitable for the vessels of the time and excellent water communications with both England and the hinterland, but much of it was sandy waste. Nor was there, in either section, any guarantee of religious freedom. Berkeley and Carteret both spoke highly of toleration and, being absolute proprietors of New Jersey, they might make what laws they pleased; but both men were staunch Royalists, and if the King permitted persecution, so might they.

Fox was not at all certain that Quakers must move overseas, but if the time arrived when emigration was desirable the site must probably be elsewhere.

Coale's suggestion of lands across the Delaware remained alive. When Fox reached the river bank, he met some Jersey Friends who had explored the region which the Lenape called Sassafras Land. Only a few Swedes lived there, the Quaker explorers reported, together with a small handful of adventurous Jerseymen, some of them Quakers, who found the hunting excellent. As for the Indians, the ten or a dozen "nations" who had difficulty understanding each other's language, all were peaceful and unobtrusive. The more Fox heard of Sassafras Land the more desirable it seemed.

The reality proved as pleasant as the promise. When Fox, with Lenape guides, crossed the Delaware at what is now called Burlington Island, he found wooded, rolling hills, much like those of western England. Tall oaks and silvery beeches, maples and great hickories stood in profusion; dogwood and holly graced the fringes of the forest. Pigeons flew in swarms, often so low that one might knock them down with a walking stick; swans, geese, ducks and forty-pound turkeys mingled with songbirds whose "whistling, noise and chattering" drowned conversation. Elk as big as small oxen were numerous and there were countless deer. Here, as at New Castle, fish were so abundant that a man might net sixty big and succulent, but alas bony, shad at a single haul. There were peaches—so many that boughs broke under their weight—grapes and black-berries—a land of plenty and a wondrous place to colonize.

Nor was it held by any European. Sassafras Land, newly taken from the Dutch, was not yet granted to anyone but the Duke of York, that close friend of William Penn. Half a dozen Swedes and Finns held title to some scraps of land on the west side of the Delaware but not as far north as Fox's crossing point. To all intents and purposes, this Sassafras Land was empty and awaiting colonization.

Moreover, it was easily accessible. No endless chain of shoals barred the river, as they shut off approach at low water from the Jersey seashore; ships out of London could sail as far as the falls of the Delaware, above the crossing point. If Fox, in riding southward, took the shortest and easiest trail, as undoubtedly he did, he would have admired the broad sweep of the Delaware and would have seen how well it fitted trans-portation needs.

He would, in that event, have passed through the site of what was later Philadelphia. No settlement then existed, though a few Swedes lived in log huts close to the sandy beach, where a creek broke through the steep grassy bluffs along the shore. Had he inquired of them, he would have learned that beaver might be trapped along the Sassafras Land waterways, and that Lenape were constantly arriving with furs to barter cheaply.

Fox, however, did not stop; he pushed beyond the Schuyl-kill, "a desperate river of rocks and broad stones very dangerous to us and our horses." Nor did he stop at Upland, now called Chester, where the river trade centered and where an Englishman or two lived in log houses set amid white pines and walnuts.

Avoiding all settlers, Swedes as well as Englishmen, Fox forded the "bad and miry" Christiana Creek, named for the abdicated Swedish queen, and came again to New Castle. In contrast to his first visit, when little notice was taken of him, the town turned out in welcome. Fox gave no reason for the change of attitude, but probably, since he was in less haste than during his journey north, he gave more opportunity for contacts. Strangers, especially those speaking English, were so infrequent that New Castle rolled out the red carpet for any interesting arrival.

Certainly, the Governor, who, meeting Fox upon the Strand, invited him to share the gubernatorial mansion, was no Fox disciple. No man who so thoroughly looted the conquered Dutch, who stripped peaceful, inoffensive Mennonites down "to a very naile," and who traded sixty Negro captives to Maryland in exchange for salted meat would have had but little in common with George Fox. Nor was it likely that the second-in-command, a gentleman who, after impartially serving Dutch and Swedish masters, was now enthusiastically English, would share Quaker principles; he was less well known for his religion than for his peach brandy, a beverage which, he said, surpassed that of his native France.

Nevertheless, the governor offered his house for a Friends meeting, the first ever held in Delaware, and most of the town attended, many of them confessing to the truth of Quakerism. Their conviction could not have been very deep for it did not prevent their almost immediately organizing an armed force of every male between sixteen and sixty for war against the harmless Lenape. The governor, the sheriff and the other leaders warned Fox that the Indians were massed to cut him off; New Castle's vigilance demonstrated itself by the hanging of a redskin for what they said was his intention to commit a crime.

The Delaware Indians did not kill him, but his Maryland guides, if Fox's estimates are correct, doubled the length of his journey back to Tred Avon. He arrived, drenched and dirty, to begin at once another series of successful meetings up and down the bay.

Although, in deference to the legend transplanted overseas, it rained much of September and October, the Marylanders turned out in force to hear Fox speak. One of the many justices exclaimed that never had so many people of the province gathered for any purpose; another compared the numbers of skiffs and canoes to the traffic of the Thames at London. Great men abandoned their public business to attend the meetings; if they could not, they sent representatives to ask when they might hold interviews with Fox. Before George's return, the house in which the meetings were held had been doubled in size, yet the building was too small to hold the thousand people who wished to enter.

"A great convincement there is," Fox said. "The Friends are much established and the world convinced."

Once more, the Indians warmed his spirits. An emperor, apparently not the same ruler he had met previously, brought one of his own great men and a notable from another nàtion. They listened one evening to a long Fox explanation, delivered, of course, through an interpreter, who must himself had had great difficulty in translating; next day, they returned and sat through a meeting.

The emperor declared that George Fox was an honest man.

In the course of these threshings, Fox, travelling mostly by rowboat, reached the mouth of the Susquehanna, the river which Josiah Coale explored. But, though Coale had suggested that the basin of the river might be suitable for Quaker colonization, George did not ascend to any distance; he may have felt that both New Jersey and the valley of the Delaware, being closer to the sea, offered better opportunity. Or, considering the astonishing reception he was receiving in papist Maryland, he may have thought the Chesapeake would suit the Quaker purpose.

His work in Maryland being a complete success, he set off on November 5th to take the truth into Virginia.

Stormy weather, the almost invariable concomitant of George Fox's travel, beset the sloop, but he made fifty miles the first day and, two days later, having passed the site of what is now Norfolk, he landed on Virginia soil.

Since, in March, 1672, the King suspended penal laws against nonconformists and since, in September, he freed all those convicted or *praemunired* for reasons of religion, it seems odd that George did not take the opportunity to do more preaching in Virginia. His landing place, however, was not in the rich, tobacco-planting area but among the sparsely settled coastal swamps, important chiefly as a gateway to the Carolinas.

Ostensibly, Fox was visiting this newly settled area partly to organize meetings and to establish discipline; but he was well aware that Friends were few and that the Carolina Indians, the Tuscaroras, instead of being a treasure vault of people, were but a handful. Nor was their religious spirit strong; a previous missionary reported that when they came to meeting they puffed their pipes. They were, however, receptive; the colony offered bounties to ministers of any denomination who agreed to settle there.

Under such conditions, though Carolina soil was less desirable than that of the Jerseys or of Sassafras Land, it might be suitable for English Friends who might be moved to emigrate, especially as Locke's constitution authorized religious liberty.

Fox entered North Carolina on November 19th, riding through woods and swamps, usually in the rain, and sleeping in the open. For an arthritic, the exposure must have been severe; but George, buoyed by great hopes, reported little suffering.

The Carolinians were hospitable; the coming of a noted visitor may have softened them. A rude, desperate captain, believing that Fox had healing power, asked George to see an invalid whom, the captain said, all physicians abandoned as incurable. Fox did not question the statement, though he must have known that this section of the Carolinas was wholly without medical men; he sent a friend to pray beside the invalid. The sick woman was cured at once and the rude captain was won over.

Fox canoed along the streams and, in the last week of November, came to Edenton, then the capital. The officials received him graciously enough, but one disputatious citizen argued against the Inner Light; it could not possibly exist, he said, among the Indians.

Fox promptly called in a Tuscarora and asked whether, if the Indian told lies or wronged others, anything within him would reprove him. George took the Indian's confession of discomfort as proof of the Quaker argument.

George's technique in winning Indian convincement was extremely simple. He asked but little, not much more than acceptance of principles then professed by all Christians and, in many instances, by Indians as well. God made all things within six days, including Adam and Eve, but when His first people disobeyed His laws, He drowned mankind. Then came Christ, who died for all. There was, of course, much more to Quakerism than this; but, except for silent worship, the Inner Light and the Golden Rule, the rest was difficult to translate to Indian minds; it might be reduced to a simple statement that the evil would be burned but that the good would live in happiness.

It was all very elementary but it was effective. Fox reported that he made "a little entrance for truth." After ten wet days in Carolina, he turned back towards Virginia. Each day, he held glorious meetings, "washing and sweeping those who had spotted themselves by errors," proclaiming the Word to those hungry to receive it. Everything went successfully, even the numerous watchdogs welcoming the Quaker visitor. Each day he was wet, by rain, by a leaky boat or by capsizing, but each night he dried his clothing by a fire and continued his evangelistic campaign. Once or twice he was obliged to sleep outdoors, the wolves howling about him, but he met no harm; he retained enough good humor to remark that Old Point Comfort yielded very little of it.

And this in the face of adversity. He did not reach Maryland until the middle of January, having had six weeks of rough waters, frost and snow; in addition, a house burned, destroying all his clothes except those he wore. He reported, with some astonishment, that, on January 27th, a gust of such unreasonable heat broke out that he could scarcely endure it.

Except for the absence of sunshine, for Fox's *Journal* recorded not a single hour in America when the sun was

visible, all went well. For three months, Fox again threshed
Maryland. Meeting after meeting passed off gloriously. High
personages accepted truth; more than a score of justices and
half a dozen high officials were convinced. There was also a
miracle. Fox met a moping woman who, for two months, had
scarcely spoken and who for all that time had sat in deep
abstraction; he spoke with her and within an hour she was
cured.[1]

Toward the end of March, Fox revisited the Indian rulers.
He went to their capital, where the heathen emperor, the old
empress who sat with him in council, and all the kings and high
officials sat in gravity and soberness throughout a Quaker
meeting. Apparently the taciturn Indians promised nothing,
but they were attentive and on May Day they all met again
in harmony.

With everything so prosperous, with meetings established,
heresy stamped out, discipline introduced and arrangements
made for regular interchange of letters between meetings in
America and those in England, George Fox took ship for home.
On May 21st, he held a meeting aboard the 150-ton *Society
of Bristol* and next day the ship weighed anchor.

As on the voyage from Jamaica, winds and tides delayed the
passage. On the first day, they made but a mile, and only
another mile on the second; the third day they did better,
sailing six miles before head winds caused them to drop anchor.
Ten days passed before the ship gained the open sea.

The crew of the *Society of Bristol* shared Fox's conviction
that the Lord placed the ship in his hands and that divine

---

[1] Other missionaries, too, were reaping harvests. Edmondson, after valiant
work in Carolina and Virginia, had returned to Ireland, but Eccles, after
sailing up to Boston only to be deported, was carrying on the work in
Jamaica. Stubbs, in New Jersey, Lancaster and Pattison were also doing
well. Burnyeat had managed to persuade Thomas Thurston to disentangle
himself from the Perrot heresy, and Fox restored the errant pioneer to
good standing.

protection extended to all aboard. On at least three occasions when they sighted ships which they feared might be pirates George calmed them; his visions, he said, predicted safety. When waves, so high that they stood like mountains in the sea, the like of which sailors had never seen, threatened to engulf the vessel, George soothed their anxieties. Despite the slow start, and later fogs and gales, the ship came to Bristol in only thirty-nine days. Winds were always more favorable for eastward voyages.

Divine protection was not withdrawn when the ship reached harbor. A warship sent a press gang aboard and picked off four men, but Fox invited the naval officers to meeting, where the Lord's power induced them to return two of the men they had selected.

Having thanked and praised the Lord God for carrying him safely through so many perils, man-eaters ashore and storms at sea, Fox returned the *Society of Bristol* to its captain.

He now wrote to Margaret, announcing his arrival. Characteristically, he repressed his personal feelings, nor did he give any hint of what he had seen or done—these matters, as in America, he left to others to report. Happily, she was not a young, incurable romantic, for the only hint of affection lay in his greeting, "Dear Heart," a common Quaker salutation. He said nothing of coming to Swarthmoor nor did he suggest a rendezvous.

"I intend if the Lord will to stay a while thisaway; it may be till the fair. So no more, but my love to all Friends."

As the fair was not to open for a month, Margaret with her daughters Sarah and Rachel, rode two hundred miles to Bristol, where, as it happened, she had business interests. With her came Thomas Lower, who left his wife, the former Mary Fell, to care for Swarthmoor and their new baby. John Rous, whose wife also stayed home to mother their five children, brought the Penns and Gerrard Roberts from London.

It was not merely a family gathering but a meeting of an unofficial executive committee, Roberts being a leading business executive and Fox and Penn the policy makers. Being human, they must have exchanged news items, such matters as Margaret's extensive work in London and Yorkshire, Penn's writings and his prison experiences, the new Test Act imposing oaths and requiring public officials to take the sacrament, as well as what Fox thought about overseas colonization.

Doubtless, Fox dealt a death blow to the Coale idea of peopling the upper Susquehanna; it was too far inland, dependent upon a river that was not navigable the entire distance and which, moreover, emptied into Chesapeake bay, which, however friendly the Indians might be, was capable of being blocked off by Lord Baltimore's Maryland.

The best place for a colony, if ever a Quaker settlement were decided upon, would be, from what Fox saw in America, either in New Jersey, which was flat and fertile, with an equable climate, easy access to the sea and Indians who were few and friendly, or in Sassafras Land, which had all these advantages and, in addition, less waste land and a better river system.

Penn brought up an unexpected, but exciting, possibility. London business circles believed, he said, that Lord Berkeley, to whom, in partnership with Sir George Carteret, New Jersey was granted, was in serious financial difficulty. As neither he nor, for that matter, Carteret ever seriously desired that province, both having sufficient holdings in Carolina, it was quite possible that he might be induced to sell his portion of New Jersey. Carteret, for all his profligacy, was better off as far as money was concerned, but it was not unthinkable that at some future time, he, too, might part with his share of New Jersey.

As all this depended upon what action Berkeley might take, nothing was decided at the Bristol conference, but the idea of a Quaker colony was firmly planted in the minds of Penn and Fox.

35

Worcester and Salem

ONCE MORE UPON HIS ROUNDS, SOMETIMES WITH MARGARET and one or two of his stepdaughters, sometimes alone, George Fox attended many precious meetings. In London he saw the newly knighted Richard Marche; he found Esquire Marsh still loving and tender but on his deathbed. George and Margaret visited the Penns, discussing there, perhaps, the plans for purchasing West Jersey.

Generally speaking, he was moving northward, partly to accompany Margaret and the girls halfway on their return to Swarthmoor, partly to see his widowed mother, now in her seventies; he had not been in Drayton since his marriage. He then intended to return to London.

The plans misfired. One evening as he was eating dinner, he felt a presentiment that he would be arrested. He said nothing of this to Margaret nor to Thomas Lower, their son-in-law from Cornwall. But, apparently, Margaret also was disturbed; she pleaded with him to be careful. This led to conversation which came as close as George and Margaret ever came to argument. She criticized him for indifference to arrest, and he replied that there was a wine press he must tread and that she must be content with what God willed. She then fell silent; but the exchange left a tension in the minds of all, if not a fear of what might happen.

Next day, a week before Christmas, a justice and a priest came into a parlor where George was chatting. They produced a warrant alleging that Fox and Lower were holding large meetings for unauthorized worship prejudicial to the public peace. That very day, the warrant stated, Fox had spoken at an assembly; he and Lower must post bond for trial or go to jail.

As this appeared to be the wine press he must tread, George raised no protest at the time; later, from his cell in Worcester prison, he complained of an illegal arrest.

Though it was not always possible to credit George's recital of events, much less his analysis of the motives of his persecutors, at full face value, in this instance there was ample justification for his protests. The warrant accused him of speaking at a meeting which neither the justice nor the priest attended; they were celebrating a christening and had only hearsay evidence. It said that Fox held many meetings, but this, too, was based on rumor; moreover, any such meetings would have been outside their jurisdiction. But, on the other hand, the parson and the justice of the peace found Fox and Lower at a different meeting and, though Fox insisted he was merely chatting, he never talked of anything except religion, and so, by strict construction of the law, he certainly was guilty, though the warrant did not cite this specific gathering.

The warrant branded Fox and Lower as vagabonds, but, as it went on to give their home addresses, Fox said there was a contradiction which made the writ invalid.

Nevertheless, he trod the wine press, though he wondered what kind of people were these inhumane, unchristian monsters who arrested a peaceful man travelling with his wife and on his way to see a dying mother.

It was no exaggeration. Though, after her son's seven previous imprisonments and after his countless other brushes with the law, news of an arrest must have been familiar to Mary Fox, George said it struck her to the heart. During the past thirty years, it must be confessed, he had spent but little time at Fenny Drayton and, as far as his reminiscences reveal, he had not seen his mother for ten or a dozen years; but, on reading of her death in a letter from her physician—not from a relative—a great weight struck upon his spirit.

Those in the room when George read the letter saw a sudden travail fall upon him. During a full quarter of an hour he sat silent, for, as he said, "I did in verity love her as ever one could a mother." Then his spirit broke through. "I saw her in the resurrection and the life, everlastingly with me over all, and father in the flesh also."

"So those wicked justices God will judge who hindered me from visiting her according to her motherly and tender desire."[1]

Whether because of the prevention of George's visit to his dying mother or because of the illegality of their actions, public opinion ran against the persecutors. Neither justice nor mercy moved them. They did, however, listen to the wishes of the great folk of London.

Richard Lower, a prominent Westminster physician who courted Sarah Fell, asked his associates to write letters calling for his elder brother's release. Their number and the magic of the names of the senders caused the magistrates to offer Thomas freedom.

Thomas, however, refused to take advantage of his oppor-

---

[1] Mary Fox's death cut the last link with Fenny Drayton; George did not again mention his birthplace nor any member of his family. Except for a namesake George, the son of his brother John, no Fox from Fenny Drayton reappears in history; the loss of parish records prevents knowledge even of his sisters' married names.

tunities. Loyal to George Fox, whom he, like the Fells of Swarthmoor, called his father, he would not leave the jail unless George, too, were freed. George Fox's name, unfortunately, was not mentioned in those potent London letters.

Apparently, the justices believed that to offer freedom was enough to satisfy the London letter writers, but there still remained a need to bow to local opinion. They tried the easy way of flattery. Telling Fox that he was a famous man who doubtless spoke the truth, they offered to let him go if only he would take the oath and say nothing more that would provoke them.

Perhaps they did not know that this dodge had been tried before without success. George replied, as almost anyone else in England might have predicted, by earnestly asserting his loyalty to the King and his opposition to the Papacy. This did not satisfy them; they must have the oath and this George would not take.

The refusal angered them. It drove them into telling Thomas Lower, despite that pile of letters, that if he would not leave the jail they would demand the oath from him also and that, if he balked, they would *praemunire* him and his father Fox as well.

If this were a bluff, it did not work. The Quakers stayed in jail. Worcester, evidently, was one of the better prisons, for, though there were no furloughs to go outside to preach, Fox and Lower enjoyed considerable leeway. Apparently, no difficulties rose concerning prison dues—quite possibly the two men paid them or else some one quietly subsidized their stay, for it is unlikely that the wardens fed them free of charge. Certainly there was no hardship inflicted.

Nor was there a dungeon. Fox met those with whom he could talk; they told him that grain prices were soaring and that discontent was rising. He also heard that a ship in which he owned a share was wrecked; the loss caused him no great concern. Margaret sent down £3 in cash, together with a salmon, but George used the money to buy her some black Spanish dress goods—he did not say who bought it for him—while the fish was so long upon the road that it must have been inedible upon arrival. Several times he wrote to Margaret, but, as usual, his letters were impersonal; once, however, he chided her for not writing to those London Friends who supposed that she was sharing his imprisonment.

Six weeks after his arrest, Friends outside the jail, probably those who paid his fees and bought the dress goods for him, secured a writ of habeas corpus ordering the sheriff of Worcestershire to bring or send George Fox before the Kings Bench in London. Normally, this involved assigning a guard to go with Fox, if the sheriff did not choose to attend him, and in this the sheriff saw a solution of a difficulty. Unable to get Lower to quit the prison in any ordinary way, the sheriff appointed him a deputy with orders to escort his father to the city.

Haste was impossible, for roads were either flooded or deep in mud from recent rains. On missions such as this, George Fox was never in a hurry. The two men moved slowly, holding meetings as they went and preaching incessantly. Had George Fox been either a rebel or a Jesuit, he would have had admirable opportunity to spread sedition. No stronger proof could have been offered of the insincerity of his prosecutors than their willingness to turn him loose with only a fellow Quaker prisoner as his guard.

The incongruity must have been apparent to the London court. No one, it seemed at first, could possibly have been more pleasant. The judges, and the king's prosecutor, also, went far out of their way to show their sympathy. But overnight their attitude changed. The Worcester authorities trumped up a charge of seditious plotting, an accusation neither they nor anybody else took seriously but one which could not be ignored. The judges therefore ordered Fox, and with him Thomas Lower, to be tried at Worcester.

Such an order, while it did not free the Quakers, at least would bring them into open court, where the hollowness of the charge would be apparent.

Certainly the Londoners had no fear that Fox and Lower were seditious plotters, else they never would have allowed them to return to Worcester unattended and at their own convenience. The only stipulation imposed was that they cover the seventy-five miles within a month.

Fox stayed in London most of the time—had he really been seditious he could have wrought a great amount of damage!—and then, because he felt unable to endure hard, hurried travel, went slowly toward his jail. Why Thomas Lower's influential connections failed to quash the charges was not explained.

Fox wrote the King about this, but Charles, though he could pardon a prisoner, had no power to intervene while a case was still in the hands of the sheriff or a judge.

Fox appeared in court on April 3, 1674, but, as his case was not called, the jailer let him wander freely about town; when he returned to sleep in his cell, the only watchman was an eleven-year-old boy. Eventually, proceedings began; to his dismay, the judge was the same man who *praemunired* him at Lancaster. The previous experience had been enough for the jurist; after the preliminaries showed that, though Fox upheld the King, he still refused to take an oath or to post bail, the judge postponed the case so that someone else might handle it.

George spent the next four weeks arguing with priests and lawyers, in dictating letters for Thomas Lower to write and in composing half a dozen pamphlets for distribution to all those in authority. He also collected his notes and papers, preparatory to drafting the history of Quakerism.

At the end of the month a new judge, Thomas Street of the Welsh circuit, assuming Fox guilty of everything charged against him, instructed the grand jury that it must find a true bill of indictment. George protested, but to no avail; he was held over for further action. Supposedly, for want of bail, he should have been kept in prison, but he was allowed to leave Worcester to attend Yearly Meeting at London.

It was a glorious meeting, attended by Friends from all Great Britain, with some Hollanders and Norsemen and three men banished for their religion from Danzig. Many inquired about Margaret and her daughters, wondering, it seems, why they had not attended. Some would have tried again to get a writ to bring Fox and Lower before the Kings Bench, but George dissuaded them. There must have been discussion, also, concerning a meetinghouse to be built upon the Strand, for George collected money to repay a woman from whom, at his request, Margaret borrowed for a building fund. Apparently he had enough for the purpose, for he instructed Margaret to borrow no more but to pay off what debts remained.

Then, having reiterated his loyalty and foresworn the Pope, though refusing to take oath to it, he returned to Worcester for trial.

The Lancaster judge should have forewarned Street of what was likely to happen. Fox again tore the indictment apart; it, too, had been deftly sabotaged. It called Fox the King's prisoner but without mentioning the King; this astonished Street, for, as he interjected, "He was in before." The *mittimus* described Fox as a Londoner, but the indictment said he was "of Tredington," a confusion which raised doubt as to which Fox was on trial. As at Lancaster, the indictment failed to specify that, whichever George Fox was meant, he was an English subject.

Street was no stickler for particulars. All he thought necessary was to tender the oath to any George Fox who stood before him and, if it were refused, to jail the individual. But, as Fox objected, how did he know that this George Fox who did not swear was not an alien who did not need to swear?

There were other complications—confusions as to whether the date on which the indictment said an oath had been refused was a day in which the court was sitting, whether George had run away to London or been sent there on a habeas corpus, whether the remanding to prison was or was not a sentence, whether Street was, as he said, merciful or whether he was hypocritical.

All was useless. By July 15th, George Fox was in prison.

The hand of God fell heavily. Street's only daughter, whom he called his idol, died, which "struck a great damp upon people," but only hardened his heart. The son of another persecutor stood trial for murder.

Fox wrote all this, except about the retributions, to the King, "not with particular relation to my own sufferings but for his better information concerning our principle and us as a people." Margaret also went to Charles, asking that her husband be set free. Even the persecutor who had begun the whole train of events asked the jailer to furlough Fox as often as was possible, for the benefit of George's health.

Charles would have granted a pardon promptly. this being his only constitutional way of getting Fox out of jail, but George would not accept it, believing that a pardon carried with it an imputation of guilt; instead, Fox insisted on being cleared by a court. Charles was impatient at the distinction; he said that George need not be disturbed by being pardoned— "There are persons innocent as children new born who are pardoned."

A second habeas corpus returning George Fox to London loosed the deadlock, but then George faced transportation difficulties. Margaret optimistically assumed that he would ride down to the city; his letters, sketchy in personal detail, did not make clear his weakness, his arthritis or the sale of his horse.

A public coach ran the route, but Lower learned that all seats were sold for two weeks to come. Official pressure, however, produced passage for Fox, Lower, the sheriff, the court clerk and several attendants. For other passengers, the journey could not have been enjoyable, for Fox and his persecutors argued loudly all the way to London.

At the trial, Thomas Corbett, a new Welsh lawyer, sprang a surprise. He argued that *praemunire,* which had become the favorite recourse of persecutors, was not a legal reason for imprisonment but merely a summons for a trial; he based his argument on the failure of a statute of 1392 to include an earlier right to imprison on a *praemunire.* Whether or not his reasoning was sound, his argument impressed the court, which noted that, if Corbett were correct, every such imprisonment had been illegal. Rather than face the problem directly, the court quashed the indictment as faulty.[2]

Fox's detention, including his occasional furloughs and the trips to London, lasted more than a year, from November 17, 1673, until February 12, 1675.

He gained his freedom just in time to participate in important London meetings. Lord Berkeley, co-partner with Sir George Carteret in the province of New Jersey, was becoming bankrupt and was ready to negotiate a sale. The Friends were interested, but, largely because of political considerations, were none too anxious to appear upon the center of the scene. No prominent Quaker, therefore, stepped into the limelight, but Fox, Penn and Gerrard Roberts, the administrator, were active in the wings.

Edward Byllinge, the London brewer whose marital affairs Fox cleared in 1657, volunteered as the purchaser of Berkeley's interest. But he, too, had debts; he did not wish his creditors to

---

[2] Although a few imprisonments for *praemunire* occurred later, the device fell into disuse. This Worcester trial, therefore, like the Penn-Meade trial, was a legal landmark.

think that he had cash to spare. He, therefore, asked another Friend, Major John Fenwick, a Berkshire yeoman, to act as straw man, offering, if Fenwick would assist, to give him 10 per cent of the land that Berkeley was about to sell.

No one outside the London circle knew precisely what was happening when, in March, 1675, Berkeley received £1000 in cash for his four thousand square miles of New Jersey land. The price, four square miles for each pound sterling of current money, was a bargain by whatever standard it was judged, but there were difficulties; much of it was swamp, sand or pine barrens, nor was Berkeley's tract, roughly identified as West Jersey, marked off from Carteret's by any boundary lines. Moreover, it was not quite certain whether, in purchasing this land, the Friends acquired the rights of government; Berkeley assured them that, as true and absolute proprietor, he possessed the power to make laws or to veto absolutely any regulations others, except the King, might make; but whether this privilege passed to purchasers was doubtful.

Penn, for one, was sure it did, and Fenwick agreed with him; they were at odds, however, as to what they should do with their acquisition. Penn proposed a colony where all men should be free, a settlement of saints ruled by the spirit of the Scriptures. George Fox certainly agreed with the idea; it was one reason why he sent Josiah Coale to scout the Susquehanna wilderness and why he himself made so careful a study of available American lands. No plans were, however, ready; no Yearly Meeting, nor, for that matter, any Quarterly or Monthly Meeting had discussed the project at any length, if, indeed, at all. Time would be required to study what should best be done.

Fenwick would not wait. Having received his land for no other service than lending his name, he was anxious to reap his benefits; he borrowed money from Friends who must have been extremely gullible, because they lent on the security of a mortgage on Fenwick's acres located, no one knew where, within a tract that had no boundaries.

Scarcely was the deal with Berkeley completed than Fenwick, certainly with the approval of Penn and Fox, sailed for America with a shipload of Quakers. Arriving in November at the first navigable Jersey creek, he began a settlement which he named Salem. It was, for New Jersey, a fairly well-known place. Englishmen once lived here, but their colony had failed, and Swedes had manned a fort here to safeguard their fur trade and their tobacco shipments; the site was some miles below the point where Fox first crossed the Delaware.

Salem prospered, but Fenwick ran into trouble. No one but himself authorized him to occupy the best river port in West Jersey as his personal possession—unless, that is, he had some private understanding with Penn and Fox. Worse, no one thought to tell the English royal governor in New York, the guardian of the Duke of York's interests, of any change in ownership. Assuming that the Quakers were interlopers, the governor sent troops to throw them out.

As soldiers they were inefficient. According to Fenwick, whose reporting was not always accurate, the troopers, standing four yards away, blazed at him with swanshot but missed. Then they moved closer, to within two feet, and fired a pistol; but, incredibly, they missed again. Nevertheless, somehow they subdued him, took him to New York and threw him into prison, where he stayed for twenty-seven months. The settlers were undisturbed.

While these events were happening, Fox, the London meetings concluded, took coach for Swarthmoor, stopping now and then for conferences and, once, to hear a woman thank him for having, through his prayers, cured her daughter of scrofula; she brought the girl with her, to show how healthy she now was.

On June 25th, a day or two after Fenwick's colonists sailed

for Salem, Fox crossed the sands to Swarthmoor, his first visit for a dozen years. Even Colonel Kirkby welcomed him, though he warned George to hold no further meetings. Fox paid no attention to the prohibition.

"The meetings have been quiet ever since and have increased."

36

Sage of Swarthmoor

GEORGE FOX ENTERED UPON A THIRD CAREER. IN YOUTH AN
evangel, in middle age an administrator, he now became an
elder statesman.

Only fifty-one, when he should have been vigorous, he was
prematurely aged by hardship and ill-treatment. He was tired
and ailing. His joints ached, his stomach was ulcered, he
suffered constant headache. He should have rested, but he
could not cease his labors; too much needed to be done.

Nor was Swarthmoor conducive to repose. By contemporary
standards, the mansion was impressive, even luxurious; but,
though from the road it seemed commodious, its chambers,
while generous, were surprisingly few. A spacious living room,
a study and the service quarters filled the ground floor; upstairs, two chambers and an attic provided sleeping space.
Though, in Fox's day, an additional wing, since demolished,
contained one or two more bedrooms, the Hall must have been
oppressively crowded when George lived there with Margaret,
four stepdaughters, a son-in-law and four small grandchildren,
to say nothing of their numerous visitors. Bed space could not
have been available for all; some residents must have slept
upon floor mats, or, like the sixty troopers said to have been

quartered there during the English Civil War, in barracks
fashion in the attic.

George worked, as had Judge Fell, in the little study off the
living room; but distraction was unavoidable. Swarthmoor was
a beehive of activity. A stream of Quaker callers, often arriving
without advance notice, flooded the living room, breaking up
his concentration and taking his time for conference and
exhortation. The poor of Ulverston, and, for that matter, from
everywhere in Furness, appealed for prayer, for sympathy and
for aid; the ill and suffering begged for miracles.

Margaret and her daughters did all they could to relieve
the pressure on George Fox, but they, too, were extremely busy.
At a time when females were supposed to rest content with
their domestic duties, they were businesswomen engrossed with
the iron mines, the smelter, the forge and the shipping business
of the family. How, in the midst of confusion, Sarah, the fourth
daughter, in her early thirties, kept the accounts and handled
the finances of these various enterprises, as well as of the local
Quaker meetings, was as much a major mystery as was Margaret's ability to conduct correspondence and to interview
countless visitors amidst so much distraction.

Simultaneously, household affairs demanded constant attention. No one could estimate how many people would be
present, though it was safe to predict that the house would be
well filled; but supplies had to be laid in, food prepared and
fires kept up for thrice-daily cooking. Time must be found for
cleaning and repairs, for spinning and weaving, dressmaking
and tailoring, furniture making and all the other multitudinous
chores of a seventeenth-century household. Much of this took
place, of course, outside the living quarters, as did the farm
management; but the girls, and Margaret as well, were always
being interrupted to supervise the household staff.

Nor was there opportunity for rest. Quakerism required long
and very frequent meetings. These, in summer, might be held

outdoors, and George could speak from his second-story balcony; but, when weather was cold or inclement, the living room was taken over, so that all business was crowded into George's study or in the congested upstairs chambers. No one at Swarthmoor had much opportunity for privacy or relaxation.

Somehow, while regaining his strength, George managed to complete a vast amount of work. He perfected Quaker organization, tightening and co-ordinating the meeting system and supervising discipline. He spoke incessantly. He read and abstracted hundreds of the letters exchanged between Margaret and the numerous evangelists, edited his own epistles and criticized hundreds of manuscripts, to sift out those suitable for publication.

In addition, he collected and systematized his own thoughts and fugitive writings.

To accomplish all this amid the bustle and confusion of the Swarthmoor beehive bespeaks an almost incredible power of concentration, especially as his chronic arthritis caused intense pain when he was writing.

Towards the end of 1675, Thomas Lower, who now lived at Swarthmoor, came to his assistance. He, too, was overwhelmed with work, for sickness was prevalent in Furness—two of the infant grandchildren died—and patients flocked to Swarthmoor to seek his medical advice; but, nevertheless, Dr. Lower found time to serve as George's secretary.

It was a labor that he himself suggested. While he and George were jailed at Worcester, he had become interested in the origins and early history of the Quaker movement; he urged Fox to write down his experiences. Little could be done in prison, though George spent hours in reminiscing. But, after their release, Fox and Lower went over the memoranda, especially copies of letters and documents that had been kept, to draft a spiritual autobiography.

Fox spent much of the year dictating a *Journal* to his amanuensis.

In large degree, the title was a misnomer. Ordinarily, a journal is a daily record of material occurrences, somewhat more complete, and certainly more objective, than a diary. Fox's story, however, recited, as he said, the steps whereby the Lord prepared him for his lifework as a minister. It covered in detail thirty-two years of spiritual development, from his awakening in 1643, as a lad of nineteen, until his release from Worcester.

Because he did not intend to write a complete autobiography, George rigorously omitted all personal detail except that bearing upon his ministerial career. He suppressed mention of contemporary events that did not directly affect Quakerism, nor did he pass judgment on personalities except in reference to their treatment of the Friends. He travelled extensively, both in Britain and in regions wholly unknown to most of his followers, but without commenting on anything he may have seen or heard. He expressed no private opinion nor did he include any thought or action not directed by the Lord.

Fox was a master propagandist, his 420 epistles being powerful arguments for the principles he taught; but the *Journal* was not primarily intended as a means for converting others. Its purpose, as was that of other Quaker journals, was rather to reassure his fellow missionaries that their strange experiences, their sufferings, and perhaps their visions, were not unique but were shared by the elect. Their youthful doubts, their religious crises, their difficulties at home and with their scoffing neighbors and, above all, their mental and spiritual states, were the common lot of those called to service for the Lord. Such testimony from saintly George Fox went far towards bringing peace to unusual souls who otherwise might have fancied themselves peculiar or perhaps irrational.

Unlike most religious confessors, Fox, though hinting at

early, but certainly nonexistent, lapses, professed no dramatic conversion experience; he had groped for truth long before the Voice said "There is one, even Christ Jesus, that can speak to thy condition." A youth convinced of his perfect purity required no sharp emotional shock.[1]

Any book dictated from memory ten or twenty years after the events occurred would necessarily be inaccurate in minor detail. Even with the aid of the notes, memoranda, letters and documents available at Swarthmoor, errors would creep in; but, even so, the *Journal* has too many careless inaccuracies, especially on dates, which could readily have been checked prior to publication. These faults, however, while primarily due to Fox, reflect also the carelessness of an amanuensis who may have reported him incorrectly, or of the editors who prepared the text for printing.

Nevertheless, the inaccuracies raise at times a doubt whether one or more of the visions wherein Fox foresaw the future may have occurred after, rather than before, an event happened. The question also rises whether the use of too strong language, such as the expressions "strike at the heart," "pack away" or "rage," recurring in scores of passages, does not overstate a situation and so create a false impression.

As the *Journal* was not intended as a literary exercise, none of the criticisms detract from the forcefulness of its impact. The *Journal* radiates sincerity, honesty, faith and power. It carries conviction. Contrary to the current conception of a Quaker as an unemotional pacifist, Fox presents himself as an aggressive, unrelenting, verbally combative crusader for the right.

[1] The volume contained grievous flaws, which, were it not so vital and so earnest, would disqualify it as literature. The writing, except for occasional sharpcut passages and for effective Biblical imagery, lacks style; it is repetitive and sometimes incoherent, and even devoted Quaker commentators admit that it is often dull and tedious. The grammar is not impeccable, words are loosely used and, in at least one portion of the text, twenty consecutive sentences begin with "and."

In later years, the original version dictated by George Fox suffered considerable mutilation, rearrangement and other tampering by more skilled writers who lacked Fox's spiritual strength. But, even at its ebb, the *Journal* retained its vitality. It set the pattern of a special Quaker language, modelled a Quaker literature, strengthened the convictions of thousands of members of the Society of Friends and unified them internationally. And it revealed a personality, the tremendous figure of one of the greatest spiritual leaders of mankind.

Writing chained Fox to a desk, but, the atmosphere being vibrant with constant bustling, confinement, for once, did not bore him. The daily outlet for self-expression made him reasonably content with physical inactivity. That scores of callers consulted him, that Margaret and the girls asked his advice, that groups gathered on the lawn to hear him preach satisfied his hunger to give service. Had Swarthmoor been less stirring, his vigor would have driven him into another Lichfield outburst; but the never ceasing liveliness drained off his excess energy into safer channels.

Better economic circumstances eased his life. His hardships ended; he was cared for. Though not yet able to ride easily, a horse was bought for him, joining the eight riding horses already in the Swarthmoor stables. His clothes were of finer material and provided in increased quantity. His austerities continued, but they were voluntary, not enforced .

Feminine preference defeated some of his whims. At London he ridiculed fashion, but the Fells overruled him. Black was then in vogue, and with this George would have agreed; but Sarah wore reds and blues and Rachel chose sea-green. Margaret and the girls wore ashy- and dove-colored petticoats, but there were also gayer hues. How he must have felt in seeing his womenfolk wear yards and yards of ribbon cannot be conjectured; but his outraged feelings must have been mild in comparison with his emotions when his daughters-in-law wore masks to shield their complexions from the sun.

For the first time since adolescence, George was properly fed. As an itinerant evangelist, he ate when and what he could; primarily a meat-bread-and-beer man, his unbalanced diet was weakening his constitution. But now, in addition to meat, cheese and fish, he ate home-grown fruits and vegetables, both in their season and as preserves. Apparently, he developed a taste for wine, not the gooseberry and currant varieties common in every rural household but the more special vintages which Margaret bought for him. Someone even got him a walking stick, ivory topped and pierced with holes through which tassels could be passed.

In addition to being better fed and better cared for, George Fox may now have had more money at his disposal. Hitherto, he had but little cash. Whatever small inheritance came to him from his parents' estate had been signed over to his brother John and, as he had long since ceased to work at his trade, his modest needs were supplied by voluntary contributions. He needed little pocket money. While at London, he stayed almost always with a son-in-law or at a Friend's house; local Quakers put him up when he went on circuit. Trips abroad were financed by the Kendal Fund or were donated by some wealthy sympathizer.

Following his marriage, his financial status bettered. Though he conscientiously waived any rights that might accrue to him from Judge Fell's estate and though Margaret, with equal carefulness, assigned to her children all her interest in the Swarthmoor property, she had other sources of income. The mines and smelter, the shipping business and the forge prospered; the inheritance from her parents was not inconsiderable. She ventured once or twice to give George money, only to find that he used it to buy presents for her, and so she discontinued that practice. But it is not unthinkable that, in return for managerial advice, she made over to him an interest, large or small, in these commercial enterprises. All this, however, is conjecture, for neither she nor George discussed such matters publicly. There is a record that at one time George Fox owned an interest, worth £144, in the forge, and he mentions a part ownership in ships; but at no time did he explain the source of the money spent for the investment.

Fox, a dedicated servant of the Lord, had no interest in money. Moved to travel abroad preaching the everlasting Gospel and organizing meetings of all sorts—First Day, monthly, quarterly and yearly, meetings for worship and meetings for recording persecutions, men's meetings and women's meetings —he lived in confidence that the Lord would care for him as long as he spread the Truth and kept it clear of error.

There was now no need to protect the Truth against William Lampitt, the gossip monger. That Ulverston pastor, the protégé of Swarthmoor Hall until George branded him a foul priest and an old deceiver, lost his pulpit when the Restoration returned Anglicans to their parishes. Thereafter, Lampitt lived quietly, preaching now and then, still adamant against Quakerism; but in 1677 he died. Whether Mary Lower, who, as an eight-year-old, called down the "plaiges of god" upon him, attended his funeral was not recorded; but, during his last few months, she had been his close neighbor.

With good food and better care, George Fox was regaining health; but recovery was slow. His mind was active and he accomplished much by consultation and paperwork, but, physically, he remained immobile. During his first six months at Swarthmoor, he had been too weak to move about; even through the spring of 1676, he retired frequently to nap in his hammock.

Such was his condition when William Penn paid him a visit. Penn had much to talk about. To no one's surprise, Edward

Byllinge, the London brewer who owned almost all West Jersey, had at last gone bankrupt, and Penn, with two other Quakers, was trustee for the creditors.

As the only important Quaker leader who had ever seen the region, George Fox's opinion was important. There was little question about what the trustees should do : they must sell some land to pay the Byllinge debts, set him back upon his financial feet and arrange, if possible, an amicable division with Sir George Carteret. These arrangements were already in progress, but there were more far-reaching decisions to be made, especially concerning colonization. Many Quakers seemed anxious to settle in the Jerseys, a place they understood to be a new Canaan, flowing with milk and honey. Was the time now ripe to found a Quaker refuge?

This, and its corollary, how to govern if colonization were approved, were problems which George Fox must now face. Because Byllinge's troubles coincided with a rising interest in overseas expansion, with growing official tolerance and with Quakerism's successful progress, Penn and Fox thought constantly about establishing a haven for the Friends.

Their interest reflected the maturity of Quaker leadership. Virtually all the pioneer ministers were gone, by death or by infirmity of age; quieter, more conservative, more meditative replacements guided Quakerism. In Fox's youth, his Publishers of Truth were, for the most part, forceful, dynamic evangels, quick in movement and aggressive in temperament, rebellious against regimes they deemed vicious and oppressive; in his later years, ministers were less flamboyant but far more efficient organizers and administrators whose enthusiasms were restrained.

George Fox, the last link between youthful independence and matured philosophy, still supplied the spark of inspiration; he was one of the very few remaining leaders who combined imagination with authority. He and Penn, working in harmony, could build the framework for a model Christian community in Byllinge's province.

37

Equality for All

TROUBLES WITHIN QUAKERISM DELAYED COLONIZATION. A mild rebellion rose against tightened discipline and increased centralization. Malcontents resented what they considered attempts to limit the acceptance of private revelation. While none of the dissatisfaction was against George Fox personally, he, as the arbiter of discipline and as advocate of the complex meeting system which the dissidents deplored, was very much concerned. Had he taken early action, he could have quelled much of the unrest; but, still convalescent, he was unable to interfere.

Some of the trouble stemmed from the days when he was in Worcester prison. Two Westmorland Friends, John Story and John Wilkinson, were even then complaining of innovations which, they said, were tyrannical. It was not right, they complained, to keep records of persons reprimanded for infractions of Quaker discipline. They disapproved of people who disrupted orderly meetings by groaning, shouting or singing while others were being moved to speak.[1]

[1] Possibly Story was an old acquaintance. Twenty years earlier, a young Ranter of that name pushed a pipe of tobacco into George's hand, inviting him to smoke. Fox thought the forward lad flashy and empty, but, lest the lad consider him not "in unity with the creation," touched the pipe to his lips before returning it.

Though Fox himself no longer interrupted meetings, he defended the practice. "When someone is speaking out of the life," he explained, "the life breathes itself forth for its liberty through groans, sighs and shouts in others and stops him."

Whether or not Story and Wilkinson understood the explanation, they turned their attention to a graver matter—the setting up of separate meetings for the Quaker women. Wilkinson felt strongly on the question; he firmly believed that women should be kept subject. Had not St. Paul enjoined them to obedience? Where in Scripture, he asked in one of Fox's favorite phrases, was there mention of a female apostle?

No one could commit a greater error than to appeal to Scripture when arguing with Fox. For five hours, George bombarded him with Bible passages, citing women who prayed and prophesied; he quoted Moses, Aaron and Jesus Himself, to prove that women should take active part in church affairs. As for St. Paul, there were contradictory passages that nullified his injunctions. When Wilkinson suggested weakly that women should be represented by their husbands, Fox demolished the argument. How, he asked, would this help unmarried girls or widows? What if a Christian wife asked religious guidance from a Moslem husband?

George held such strong views on women's rights to that same equality that Eve enjoyed in Eden that he saw a vision. The "dark power" sent a fierce bull that "did chase me sore and would have devoured me." But Fox was undismayed. Dismounting from his horse, he set on his steed some children who were with him, for safety, and then, grasping a "great hedge-stake," thrust it down the bull's throat to the heart and killed him.

If this were not enough to convince Wilkinson that women were fit to preach and prophesy, as well as to nurse the ill, relieve the suffering and teach the young, he had a further proof.

Once, he recalled, there had been a man in Wiltshire who professed that equality broke the laws of God. It was, the man argued angrily, the will of nature that a man should rule his wife; he, the Wiltshireman told Fox, would certainly insist upon his privilege.

And what had followed? Mark well the sequel, Fox warned. The Wiltshireman stormed from the meeting in great rage; but when he reached the door there stood the angel of the Lord with sword drawn, to cut him off. In terror, he turned back, groping, Fox said, like a dead man, and begged forgiveness, but Fox denied it. The man, he saw, was not yet in the proper spirit.

George had been wise to hesitate. Frightened though he was, the man was insincere; he wrote a paper reiterating his objections. George found it necessary to explain that though there was in worldly matters discrimination against women, it flowed from Eve's transgression, not from the will of God.[2]

When Wilkinson refused to accept these truths, George Fox sent everyone else, except Story, from the Worcester room, and, "standing in the authority of God over them," as Lower phrased it, threatened to fight the dissidents as bitterly as ever he battled priests.

Now, while Fox lay ill at Swarthmoor, the dispute split the Quaker movement. Wilkinson and Story won followers, not because of anti-feminism but because once more the principle of continual revelation seemed at stake. To many sincere Friends, Wilkinson's conviction seemed as valid a revealing of the Inner Light as did a Fox decision. Restriction or censorship of ideas was not, as William Penn proclaimed, "heavenly disciplines" to stop deviation from the Truth but a crystallization of custom that denied the possibility of later revelation.

Independent thinkers, whether or not approving of Wilkin-

[2] Margaret, while still in jail at Lancaster, had written a convincing pamphlet to much the same effect.

son and Story, set up separate meetings, even at Preston Patrick, that early citadel of Quakerism. There was little doctrinal difference, no division of old-liners and progressives, but protest against autocracy and against stifling free expression.

Alarmed at the separation, London Quarterly Meeting, now rapidly becoming the court of last resort, condemned the Wilkinson-Story separation as a running out, as did Fox. Orthodox Quakers suggested a meeting to discuss the deviation, but Wilkinson and Story preferred to settle matters through arbitration, one man to be chosen by each side. This might have been fair enough, though no provision appears to have been made for any decision if the two arbiters should disagree. But, by this time, matters had gone too far. Old-line Quakers were incensed because certain Wilkinson-Story supporters were slandering Margaret Fox for activities which, they said, were male prerogatives, while the two discontented men complained of unfair treatment.

To end the deadlock, a meeting was called. Wilkinson and Story contended that this was unjust; there was no written charge against them nor were they given opportunity to choose representatives. They refused, therefore, to appear for what they contended was a trial before a biassed court.

Nevertheless, a meeting was held, no Westmorland Friends attending. The case was examined and both men were rebuked.

Wilkinson and Story protested that their offer of arbitration had been rejected and that they had been condemned *in absentia;* but when George Fox, confined to Swarthmoor, invited them to visit him, they declined to go. George, considering that everything possible had been done to give the men a proper hearing, then branded them as wilful, heady and unbrotherly; he described their actions as giving forth an evil savor.

As always in Quaker disputes, both dissidents and orthodox

tried earnestly to compose their differences. In April, 1676, they met at Sedburgh, Margaret, Sarah Fell, Lower and Penn with them, though George Fox was absent, being unable to ride the twenty-four mile stretch from Swarthmoor. After four days' discussion, Wilkinson and Story confessed having yielded to temptation; they then visited Fox, who restored them to good standing.

Superficially, all seemed well; but the breach was not closed. The Wilkinson-Story followers, like the Nayler disciples and the Perrot adherents, were more heretical than their leaders. Objecting that too many persons had been at Sedburgh, an indirect attack upon Margaret, and that George Fox was dictatorial, they persuaded Wilkinson and Story to renew the separation.

The deviation caused Fox so much worry that, for the first time in years, he announced a vision. He had seen the spirit of strife rooting out the ancient truth while pretending to protect it. The vision, however, convinced only his own followers, the Wilkinson-Story partisans attacking Fox for couching his imaginations in the guise of visions and for declaring them the work of the Lord.

The controversy grew worse; it lasted many years, until, after Fox's death, it merged into a yet more serious heresy led by a Scotsman named George Keith.

In 1676, however, George Keith was a valiant Quaker advocate. An Aberdeen graduate, convinced, in 1644, by Dewsbury, he was one of the more effective young ministers. Like William Penn and Isaac Penington, he was an able theorist; like Robert Barclay, whom he introduced to Quakerism, he was a powerful propagandist.

Barclay, of the Scottish Gordons, had not always been a writer; in his first flush of conversion he stalked the hilly streets of Aberdeen in sackcloth, as a sign that Scots must repent their evil. Later, armed with a knowledge of Greek, Latin, Hebrew and French, he wrote, in his *Apology for the True Christian Divinity,* what was generally regarded as the first reasoned analysis of Quaker doctrine. The volume, to be sure, had not yet appeared in English, but, having recently been published in Latin in Amsterdam, it was known by Quaker leaders.

Barclay had just been in Holland, doubtless on matters connected with his book, and had gone on to Germany to visit a relative, Princess Elizabeth of the Palatine, a distant cousin on his mother's side.[3]

Fox's inner circle, Penn, Barclay, Keith and Isaac Penington, agreed with George that to recruit the Princess would add exceptional strength and influence to the Quaker cause; if it did nothing else, it would enhance Quaker prestige at Whitehall. For Fox, as for all other Friends, Holland, Germany and Bohemia seemed to extend promise. Amsterdam, that "den of several serpents," that "fair of all the sects where all the peddlers of religion have leave to vend their toys, their ribbons and fanatic rattles," attracted Quaker missionaries who yearned to thresh that ground. Ames had gone to the Rhineland, to Hamburg, to Silesia, to Poland and Bohemia; and Penn, in 1671, to Holland and Germany. All were enthusiastic about the European hunger for the Word.

George Fox had more in mind than foreign missions. He and his circle were managing Quaker affairs admirably, but, with the rise of women's meetings, feminine leadership was less successful. Margaret and her daughters did well, but they were overburdened; to leave feminine matters in their hands not

---

[3] She was a remarkable person. Eldest daughter of England's James I, aunt of Charles II and a former Queen of Bohemia, she renounced court life to become the Protestant Abbess of Herford in Westphalia. Her religious interests were eclectic but she was also interested in secular matters. She was a favorite pupil of Descartes, who dedicated to her his *Principles of Philosophy* and who remarked that she, "a young princess whose charms resemble the Graces," outshone all others in her "thorough and comprehensive knowledge of my works."

only overworked them but encouraged Wilkinson and Story
to attack Quakerism as a family monopoly.

Apparently Fox considered forming a female triumvirate to
advise on women's affairs. Margaret, certainly, would participate, and, he hoped, the Princess Elizabeth would also consent;
the third member might be a lady whom he had not met but
of whom, through George Keith, he had heard much.

This was Anne Conway, soon, because of her husband's
ennobling, to become Viscountess Conway, of Ragley in War-
wickshire. A metaphysician, a mystic, a Boehme disciple and a
connoisseur of the occult, she was in correspondence with
George Fox. Her letters increasingly pressed him to visit
Ragley.

For months, he was too ill to travel even the relatively
short distance; but, had he gone, he would have found
himself thrown into a circle of clever and extraordinarly
engaging eccentrics. Francis Mercury van Helmont, her resident physician, could not cure her chronic violent migraines,
but he diverted Lady Conway and her circle by his absorbing
remarks upon the difficulty of curing sword cuts inflicted in
the dark, on the transmigration of souls and about the oral
traditions handed down from Moses on God's relation with
mankind. Dr. Henry More, a dreamer, poet and recluse who
lived in a college dormitory for seventy-three years, emerged
from time to time to visit his "heroine pupil" and to teach
her what he called Christian Platonism. Valentine Greatrakes,
the Stroker who professed to cure tuberculosis by prayer
and by passing the power of the Lord through his fingers
to the body of his patient, was a Ragley visitor; apparently
Viscountess Conway forgot her indignation at his charging
her £155 for failing to stop her headaches.

Fox would not have listened quietly to any of them, nor, for
that matter, would the Ragley coterie have entirely approved
of him. The recluse More, for instance, after listening to Fox,

professed himself turned into brass because of what he termed George's "crookedness and perverseness."

Nevertheless, the Viscountess Conway accepted Quakerism; van Helmont, the Caballa devotee, came with her.

Without seeing Lady Conway, Fox, again strong enough to ride a few miles daily in a coach, set out, in late March, for London. As always, he faced heavy storms, with snows so deep he could not pass at times. Partly to save strength and partly because of frequent meetings and conferences, his average travel distance was but five miles a day. George often stopped to rest; he broke his journey to call upon such old friends as John Reckless, the Nottingham sheriff, and William Dewsbury.

Riding often in the rain, speaking at many meetings, conferring long into the night, Fox weakened steadily. Daily headaches and troubles with his teeth drained energies he stored at Swarthmoor. After forty days upon the road, he reached London; he was tired and worn, but, happily, there was time for a week's rest—or what only George would term rest— before the opening of Yearly Meeting.

At Yearly Meeting he was his old self. He warned Friends not to relax their opposition to tithing. He drafted a petition to Parliament against fining Quakers who refused to attend Church of England services. He asked visitors from Holland whom to see and where to go if he should travel to the Netherlands.

As usual in these days, West Jersey gave concern. Fenwick was out of prison and, after forgetting his Quaker principles long enough to punch a persecutor in the nose, was accepting Penn's suggestion that he rest content with 150,000 acres of New Jersey land; but his Salem colonists were having trouble with their titles.

Throughout the squabbling, however, one bright spot gleamed. Because Fox insisted that his protégés, the Lenape, be recompensed for lands they lost, all Friends emigrating to the Delaware, in addition to their English deeds, paid Indians for the right to settle. This, to be sure, was not unusual, for other colonies sometimes paid, if only as insurance against raids. But at Salem, when Quakers took land, no Lenape was forced to leave unless he so desired.

Indians and Quakers ratified eternal friendship beneath a giant oak that stood in Salem many decades as a testimonial.

After consultations with Fox at Swarthmoor some months before, Penn produced a charter, "Concessions and Agreements," for West Jersey. The document, probably prepared in co-operation with the now solvent Edward Byllinge, guaranteed religious liberty and authorized an elective assembly whose members must obey the orders of the voters who chose them.

On the basis of this charter, Penn was just about to send 230 Yorkshire and London Quakers to settle on the Delaware. Fox went down with him to Penn's new home in Sussex to talk about the project.

The three-week Sussex conference concerned itself less with colonization schemes than with plans for visiting the European meetings. The objectives were threefold, the projects separate though loosely interdependent. George Fox was to work among the many separatist sects of Holland and North Germany; Keith and Barclay would strive to win the latter's cousin, Princess Elizabeth; Penn, in addition to persuading that lady, would look for possible colonists in the Rhineland and the Palatinate.

The importance attached to the expedition is evident in its personnel. Virtually the entire Quaker leadership participated, excepting Isaac Penington and Margaret Fox, and the latter was represented by her daughter Isabel Yeamans. George Keith's wife, Elizabeth, also went, as did two male secretaries or interpreters.

38

Holland and Germany

AT ONE O'CLOCK IN THE MORNING OF JULY 26TH, THE SHIP weighed anchor for its 150-mile voyage to the Netherlands. The weather was, to say the least, capricious. Throughout the morning a brisk, fair wind drove the vessel to within sight of the Dutch coast; but then a calm set in and the vessel rocked in such choppy seas that some of the Friends, though not George Fox, became seasick. Suddenly, in mid-afternoon, a gale sprang up, but it lasted such a short time that the ship was again becalmed three miles from Brielle, at the mouth of the Maas.

Penn and Barclay, knowing that a welcoming committee awaited them, induced the seamen to set the Friends ashore in a small boat. There may have been some hesitation, for English sailors, conscious that Brielle was the home town of two Dutch admirals, Martin Tromp and his son Cornelius, who, for twenty years, badgered English ships, would not have been too happy to row six miles there and back. Nor, apparently, were the Dutch enthusiastic. They must have seen the English ship lying becalmed in the early evening, but, when the small boat came to land, the town gates were locked. The welcoming committee on the inside could not help the Quakers, who had to spend the rest of the night in a fishing boat.

As soon as the gates swung open in the morning, Benjamin Furly, a former fellow prisoner at Lancaster Castle, came out to greet the Quaker party. He was now a Rotterdam merchant, well acquainted with Dutch customs and with the language; but his chief interest, next to Quakerism, was in mysticism. His house, in the center of the business district, was a storehouse of some four thousand books on unconventional religion. Though, in reading them, he explored unorthodox belief, he avoided heresy and was wholly in Fox's favor.

Furly guided the Quakers through the close questionings to which foreigners without passports were necessarily subjected; he may have been obliged to guarantee that these strangers who would not doff their hats were not Jesuits disguised. Then he explained, as best he could, the confused religious maze reminiscent of that in England during the first years of Quakerism. After long years of hostilities, ending only with the breaching of the dikes—even now peace was not officially declared—Protestants were split, as the English had been divided, into separatist movements. Many of these Seekers, notably a small group known as Labadists, seemed ready for the harvest. George may have met some members of this sect in Maryland; on his trip to the Netherlands six years before, William Penn argued with them. From what Penn and Furly said, George Fox learned that they were quasi-Quakers but would be difficult to convince completely. Barclay could not have been happy to hear that the Labadists had been trying to attract the Princess Elizabeth to their fold.

After a day or so in Rotterdam and a short stay in Amsterdam, therefore, the Quaker party divided, Fox to thresh Amsterdam, the rest of the Netherlands and North Germany, while Barclay, Penn and Keith struck out for Herford, together with Isabel Yeamans, Elizabeth Keith and Gertrude Dericks Nieson, the widowed sister-in-law of William Caton.

The women took with them a long letter, which Fox, overcoming for the moment his prejudice against worldly honors, addressed simply to "Princess Elizabeth." He told the Abbess that he had heard of her tenderness to the Lord, that he was certain that she was not among the all-too-numerous hypocrites, that rejection of the Word of God and of the spirit of the apostles was too prevalent and that, deserting deceitful leaders and false churches, she should follow the same Holy Ghost who inspired the Scriptures.

From Amsterdam, Fox went to Haarlem, where the Spaniards had killed two thousand people, and to Alkmaar, scene of successful defense against the Duke of Alva, who threatened, if he took the town, to murder every living creature. He visited Hoorn and Enkhuisen, home of the great Dutch explorers who opened new areas where Fox might find vaults of people buried under the earth and stone of ignorance. He crossed the Zuyder Zee to Friesland, where a legend, eight hundred years old, recounted how Heaven, when people killed a saint, decreed that for all time every man would be marked by a white tuft of hair and women by a bald spot. Fox failed to report history or legend, neither did he comment on the lace-covered skullcaps nor on the Dutch passion for cleanliness; but he did glory that, wherever he passed, Friends met him, cared for him and summoned neighbors to fruitful meetings.

As Fox spoke little Dutch, Furly, or other Dutch Friends, interpreted for him. The aid was necessary, partly because few Netherlanders understood sufficient English to follow George's long sermons, partly to ease difficulties in dealing with officials. Fox, wholly inexperienced in crossing non-English-speaking frontiers, took border questioning amiss. Accustomed as he was to interference by English authorities on the watch for sedition, he misunderstood the motives of frontier guardsmen. Accusing them of being drunken ruffians trying to overpower the Quaker party, Fox shouted at them to fear the Lord, and they, impressed more by his tone and by his air of authority than by his words, calmed down and listened to the explanations of interpreters.

Travelling chiefly by canalboat, as in Holland, George came to Emden, then a walled Dutch-looking river port. For Quakers, it was not a town of happy memory, for its administrator, the Bishop of Munster, tolerated no Friends; when, at his orders, they moved away from his dominions, his soldiers stole their horses. Nevertheless, the banished returned, again and again, as they had in Massachusetts. One of them, the father-in-law of one of Fox's interpreters, was, at the moment, in Emden; George held there what he called a little meeting.

From Emden, George Fox passed eastward through lowland moors toward Bremen. Apparently, his interpreters, while fluent enough in the local dialects, were rather weak in current history; they told him that he was in Denmark when actually he was in Oldenburg, a protectorate—as a matter of fact, he met the Grand Duke, whom he called the Earl. Unfortunately the "great and famous" city, strictly neutral in the religious wars, was almost wholly levelled by fire.

Though the terrain presented no difficulty for the wagon in which George was now travelling, bands of soldiers constantly harassed the party, halting the journey frequently to inspect credentials. Fox became so annoyed by these interruptions that, at a burgomeister's house, he warned the people that the Lord was soon to punish evildoers.

There were other unpleasantnesses. As usual on George's journeys it was raining. This was dark country where Quakerism was almost unknown. Though little Emden had been holding meetings for three years, despite the persecutions, Bremen, a thriving city, had no meeting. Pausing at Bremen, therefore, only long enough to pass a double inspection, Fox took boat downstream. Wherever he saw knots of people, he declared the way of God and warned of wrath to come. Then he hired another wagon, intending to ride all night toward Hamburg; but the rain was so heavy that the party halted at an inn and slept on straw till daybreak.

Though Hamburg's meeting was eighteen years old, the place remained hard and dark. Fox's arrival encouraged and strengthened the few Friends who lived here; he much impressed a Baptist teacher and a Swede of some importance.

The real goal, however, was Friedrichstadt, a small town of Dutch emigrants in Holstein, where ten Friends had established a meeting in 1663. They had been steadfast in adversity. Unpopular because they kept their shops open on Christmas, New Year's and feast days, they also scandalized their neighbors by their insubordination to authority. For these reasons and because they allowed women to preach the Duke of Schleswig-Holstein once banished them, but then relented and allowed them to return. Fox believed the change of heart was caused by the refusal of local magistrates to enforce the decree of exile.

George, of course, defended his people. Employing the same methods used against Wilkinson and Story at Worcester, he buried the Duke of Holstein under an avalanche of Biblical passages to show that women might preach and prophesy. Compulsory silence, he contended, was imposed by the apostle against unruly women only, not upon the good. As for their remaining silent in the meetings, he inquired whether their singing psalms, when directed to do so by the priests, was not an inconsistency that proved his point.

He was not, however, wholly happy about the women he was helping. Too many were wearing gold and pearls; against the express orders of St. Paul, they were plaiting their hair and wearing embroidered head coverings. Again, as in Cromwell's time, he felt grave concern about the growth of pride, vanity and ostentation. It was bad enough that the Restoration made loose morals fashionable, so that the ladies of a corrupt court were wearing low-cut gowns, but some Quaker women were following the styles; the complexion masks and the red-and-green petticoats of Swarthmoor may have been haunting him. He was thinking quite as much of Britain as of Holstein when he warned the women to be beautified and clothed by salvation, that strong bulwark against wickedness, rather than by costly—and forbidden—garments.

Nothing indicated that the Duke, or the women, listened to George Fox's solemn counsel; he felt obliged to issue precisely the same warnings again upon his return to London. He did, however, refresh and inspire the struggling group of Quakers in their little Friedrichstadt meeting.

Here, apparently for the first time, George Fox met Jews. They showed him their Talmud and other Hebrew books; but, when George argued with the Jews, he found them very dark; because they rejected his interpretations, he declared they did not understand their own prophets.

As at every other place, Fox urged the establishment and maintenance of regular meetings and the observance of Quaker principles of marriage, poor relief and equality. He also advised the erection of a meetinghouse, which the Quaker community at once began. A combination dwelling, preaching room and oat storehouse, it was the first meetinghouse in Germany or Denmark.

Satisfied with what was done at Friedrichstadt, Fox turned back toward Holland. Rain was still falling and streams were swollen, there was much ado about horses being swept off their footing in swift currents and prying bands of soldiers continued to cross-question the Quakers; but two days of hard travel brought them to Hamburg. Again he argued with the eminent Swedish exile and with others. Again he had good service.

Though at Hamburg, Bremen and elsewhere Friends

responded well, the world remained in darkness. By day, as Fox rode by wagon or floated slowly by canalboat, he preached the Truth, proclaimed the coming of the Lord, warned all to flee from evil. As in his first flush of evangelism in England, his first question, on arriving at an inn, was whether there were any people in the town who feared God or had a mind to discourse on religious themes. On seeing soldiers drinking or frivoling at shuffleboard, that vice of Rhys Jones and his Proud Quakers, he exhorted them to turn to the light and Spirit of God. Though most of the Germans and the Netherlanders listened quietly and many with seeming receptiveness, Fox felt burdened with their wickedness.

Upon his return to Friesland, Isabel Yeamans reported that she had delivered his 1400-word letter to Princess Elizabeth; the Princess responded with a note, assuring Fox that she would follow its counsel. A few days later, Penn, coming from Westphalia by way of Amsterdam, confirmed Elizabeth's friendliness. The Quakers placed much store in these assurances; but, unhappily, the Princess died within three years without professing her convincement.

Fox continued his incessant preaching, venturing out of the towns to speak in isolated areas; frequently he spoke so long that he was locked out and had to sleep in the canalboats. He could not have missed hearing of the terror into which the Dutch were being thrown by fear of comets and other astronomical phenomena, nor could he have been so unlucky as not to see Balthasar Bekker, a powerful divine who vigorously attacked the superstitions. It is a pity that we do not have George Fox's memoir of whatever conversation he and Bekker may have had upon the subject, especially in view of George's early diatribes against stargazers.

He now returned to Amsterdam, where, or in the immediate vicinity of the town, he remained six weeks, reorganizing old groups, establishing new meetings, preaching, arguing and writing. He hoped to go to Danzig, where William Ames had done good work among the Mennonites but where the magistrates, tolerant at first, were now increasingly hostile and cruel. His inability to make the trip disturbed him; he partially relieved his feelings by sending a letter filled with love and compassion. He also gave explicit directions as to how, by distributing Quaker writings, by flooding officials with detailed reports of cruelties and persecutions and by bringing personal pressure upon the King and Queen, the Danzig Friends might win support and ease their lot.

He was present at a five-hour debate which Penn and Keith held with Galenus Abrahams, a Dutch Mennonite (Fox called him a Baptist), which, for one reason or another, proved less productive than might have been expected. Abrahams, like Fox and like the English Seekers, denied the existence of a professional ministry, especially that which claimed an Apostolic succession; but, contrary to Quaker principles, he believed that a true minister must be certified by miracles. Uncharacteristically, Fox allowed Penn and Keith to set forth the major portion of the Quaker argument—apparently George was suffering at the time from some sort of bronchial discomfort which led him to withdraw so that his coughing would not disturb the others—but he talked enough, and with such intensity, that Abrahams thought him angry.

Fox equally misjudged Abrahams. "He was very high and shy, so that he would not let me touch nor look upon him," said George. "He bid me keep my eyes off him, for they pierced him."

Nevertheless, Fox admitted, Abrahams became loving and tender, confessing, to some extent at least, the truth, as Quakers saw it.

Fox remained in Holland after most of the party, including

Isabel, returned to England. He wrote incessantly, answering the slanders of false priests, warning citizens of various towns against the consequences of their iniquities, drafting new pamphlets and editing manuscripts. Since, for a considerable length of time, peace envoys had been deadlocked in drafting terms to end a conflict that, though fighting had ceased, was technically continuing, he urged them to renounce war as inconsistent with the spirit of the gospel. Christians, he said, should love one another; it was sad that Turks, Tartars, Jews and heathen should see them biting and devouring their fellows.

A month after the departure of his companions, Fox left Amsterdam and, after a final week at Rotterdam with Furly, he took the packet, on October 21st, from Brielle for Harwich. His usual bad luck at sea recurred. Great storms and contrary winds tossed the sixty passengers about a ship so leaky that the crew pumped day and night. Fox estimated that the vessel took in sufficient water to fill it twice over. Everyone but Fox was sick. As he wrote to "my der frends at roter dam & at harlam & at aneser dam & at harling & at altmar & in all other plases" :

"ther came such great forceable waveses of the seases up the deeke that i was ascard that some of the seamen had been washd over borde . . . . cartrit [Gertrude Nieson] was very sicke and wilam pen soe that hee vmoted blood but all is well . . . ."[1]

Actually, Fox, like most of the passengers and crew feared that all hands would be lost, but he prayed, and a miracle preserved them.

In the early evening of the 23rd, the Quaker party arrived at Harwich, where Friends from several parts of England awaited to hear what had been done upon the Continent. It

[1] In 1670, Fox published a textbook on spelling.

was the first of a large number of meetings which Fox, moving leisurely through eastern England, attended before reaching London more than two weeks later.

"After I had been a little while in London"—in reality, another two weeks—he wrote to Margaret. Because, as he said, he was in haste, he told her nothing of himself nor of his journeys, except that, after many trials and dangers, he was safe. His ten-line note gave no news, except that all was not well at Grace Church Street.

Here, as elsewhere, the Story-Wilkinson controversy raged. Fox found it necessary to attend meeting after meeting in all parts of England, to restore church discipline and order.

39

Again the Gadfly

THE MEDIATION OF DISPUTES WAS NOT A TASK AT WHICH
George Fox excelled. On anything connected with the service
of the Lord, he had no more talent for conciliation than had
the stubborn boy who would not compromise with the
Rev. Nathaniel Stephens. Assured that everything he thought
or did was absolutely right because it sprang from special
revelation, he knew himself infallible on matters of religion.
No more than in his youth did he recognize gradations of
importance in spiritual affairs. Everything was either divinely
proper or wickedly perverse; Fox saw no grays in his moral
spectrum. He had no need for tact, nor, for that matter, of
understanding the position of a rival. Against dissenters, great
or small, he was equally forceful, persistent and implacable;
they were, all of them, to be cut off.

The heavy artillery of George Fox's mighty voice delivering
the Word of God overwhelmed the low murmurs of the discontented but did not solve the questions that they asked.
Rather, the thunder of big guns dignified the unimportant.
Quaker quarrels which began with minor issues—Nayler's
vanity, Perrot's hat, Wilkinson's male pride—swelled into
major crises. Any one of these might have been laughed out
of existence or smoothed away in quiet conversation; except

in Nayler's case, had they been ignored, they probably would have withered into insignificance. But each was treated as though man's fate stood in deadly peril.

Failure to rank matters in their due proportion maneuvered Fox into inconsistences that would have embarrassed any other man. He who went to prison rather than remove his hat excommunicated men who retained their hats. If it were proper to wear head covering when making affirmation before the Lord, should not one do so when praying to Him? If Wilkinson must not protest against those who interrupted testimony, was Fox right in ordering hecklers in meetings to be quiet? If the Inner Light illumined all, why damn the revelations of others as the devil's deceit? If Scriptural authority is final in one instance, why not in others, also?

Margaret's presence would have aided Fox in his campaign against the Story-Wilkinson dissenters. She was devoted to her husband and, though some Friends criticized her for undue activity, she would have eased the tensions without stirring as much antagonism as did George. But, in his ten months spent in visiting most of the English meetings, Fox did not call upon her aid.

The omission, together with the failure to preserve much evidence of communication between George and Margaret, cast a false light upon their relationship; the skeptical wondered if the marriage were a failure. Suspicion was unwarranted. Fox carefully walled off his private life from his ministerial career. The latter took precedence. The work of the Lord was far more important than any selfish preference. That he was tender toward Margaret and considerate both of her and of the family is evident, for she upbraided him, though gently, for buying things for her when he should have spent the money for his personal necessities. All the Fell girls, and their husbands, too, referred to him as father. Little of this tenderness appears in the published writings of George Fox.

In editing his works, he carefully deleted whatever he considered private and of no concern to those outside the family; if, while writing Margaret about the progress of the Friends, he added a supplementary page or two that was distinctly personal, he withheld all mention of it.

The scrupulous omission of anything about himself, which led to the avoidance of mention of Margaret, reduced George's account of his struggle against dissenters to little more than a list of meetings which he visited. Save that "most of their arrows were shot at me," he said little of what took place. Nevertheless, a meeting at Hunger Hill, the home of Thomas Ellwood, stood out, for it was there that Fox successfully opposed two of the stronger Wilkinson-Story advocates—a pretended seer and the prophet's son-in-law, a young man of loose behavior and turbulent spirit.

Ellwood, a friend of the Peningtons and at one time a Latin tutor to their children, eventually became an editor of George Fox's *Journal*. Once an athlete, he later regretted that period of youthful dissipation; he also reproached himself for having run a man through with a rapier for having insulted his father. To expiate his sins, he lived in absolute seclusion; but he then contracted smallpox and, going to London for convalescence, he became a secretary to John Milton, to whom, he said, he suggested writing *Paradise Regained*. He spent much of his time endeavoring, without success, to free the poet from a strong bias against Quakerism.

From Hunger Hill, Fox came at last to Ragley, the home of Viscountess Conway; he found the lady friendly and receptive to the Truth, but, unfortunately, she was too ill to undertake active work. It was a second, and final, blow to George Fox's hopes for a female triumvirate to handle women's affairs, for both Viscountess Conway and Princess Elizabeth died within a few months.

A week later, Parliament being again in session, Fox went

down to London, arriving there March 8, 1678. Once more he protested against fining Quakers because they would not attend Anglican service, and this time he held high hopes that something would be accomplished; but suddenly the King prorogued the Parliament and so everything came to naught.

Nevertheless, things were going well in foreign lands. Fox wrote to Margaret that Quakerism was flourishing in Holland, in Germany, in the West Indies and even in New England. The Polish king, George heard, was taking a personal interest in reducing persecution and, though Friends were being jailed in Danzig, the persecutors were being themselves attacked by Lutherans. As usual, he said not a word about himself, but he ended his letter to Margaret with the phrase, "My love to you and to all Friends."

Whether this marriage which the Lord opened unto them remained as cool and detached as their letters indicated or whether George and Margaret successfully avoided any exhibition of a more earthly love cannot be known. No evidence remains that their relationship was ever closer than that between any other two Friends active in Quaker evangelism; certainly it fell far short of an ecstatic passion. Margaret was at least as devoted, as far as her letters showed, to William Penn; his messages to her were, as she confessed, "sweet and blessed," and they seemed to tell more of Fox's movements than did the more bloodless epistles George sent to Swarthmoor.

Obviously, she was lonesome for her husband. Again and again she wrote to tell him how eagerly he was awaited—"thy company would be more and better to us than all the world or than all the earth can afford"—but she was resigned to separation, since this was the Lord's will.

It also was the will of George Fox, whose submission to the Lord's requirements betrayed none of the unhappiness that Margaret unconsciously displayed. Had circumstances been different, with Margaret instead of George being summoned to service, he probably could never have written, as she wrote, "Though the Lord had provided an outward habitation for him, yet he was not willing to stay at it because it was so remote and far from London where his service must lay."

Larger shares of that service were being claimed by questions of American emigration. Word was reaching London that the better lands were filling up. To escape persecution on Long Island, Friends were moving down into East Jersey. Barbados businessmen, finding iron ore in the hills, or even, it was said, in swamps, were importing gangs of slaves, sixty or seventy at a time, to man forges and furnaces. Unless Quakers moved quickly, a golden opportunity might be lost. Perhaps, in fact, the best opportunity was already lost in Carteret's East Jersey.

Though Fox wrote little about those problems, and nothing whatever about them to Margaret, he and Penn consulted constantly not only on what should be done in East Jersey but about the Byllinge and Fenwick enterprises.

West Jersey continued to present problems. Penn's ship, the *Kent,* bound for Salem in 1677, found all the best land occupied by Swedes or by Fenwick's people. Moving farther up the river to the place, just below the head of navigation, where Fox crossed on his return from Rhode Island, the 230 Yorkshiremen and Londoners started a settlement which they called Burlington, after a Yorkshire town which claimed to be a nest of prophets.

The location was good enough, but it was very close to the ill-defined line separating the Carteret and Byllinge properties; some settlers,, it appeared, were crossing into East Jersey. Others, among them the tempestuous Hannah Stranger Salter, saw better prospects across the Delaware in Sassafras Land; she was setting herself up as a land dealer and as a prophetess, and, it was reported, was having difficulties with two rival prophetesses.

As though this were not enough, some colonists were charging fraud. They came out, they said, on the understanding that the Concessions and Agreements would govern their relationships, but now they found that Byllinge, or his agents, refused to honor the promise of democracy.

The charge was true, but Byllinge was blameless. James, Duke of York, who granted him the land, withdrew the right of governance from him; the Concessions and Agreement charter was never operative. Fox, whom both Byllinge and his colonists accepted as their arbiter, cleared Byllinge of responsibility.

There was, moreover, yet another possibility of conflict. A second emigrant vessel, the *Shield,* took Friends to Burlington, but only after a proposed secession from the ship. While beating up the river, the ship drifted so close to the west bank, in Sassafras Land, that the spars and sails struck a tree. While the crew worked her clear, a passenger, admiring the good land that lay at the confluence of the Schuylkill and the Delaware, cried out, "What a fine place for a town." Some Friends would have debarked, but the captain, fearful of the few Swedes and the handful of Marylanders already there, refused permission to land.

Had they gone ashore to take up land, there would have been confusion. The land was English, to be sure, but Charles II, with his customary disregard for accurate map drawing, had already granted it, so claimants alleged, to both Lord Baltimore and the colony of Connecticut. The claims were certainly disputed and their bases may have been wholly imaginary, but the arguments were real and the presence of Quakers with titles from Byllinge would have led to trouble.

The conflicts were, in fact, already under way. Some of Byllinge's people, such as Hannah Salter, had moved into the northern reaches of the river, and some of Fenwick's friends were living farther south at Upland. None had clear title but none would move out voluntarily.

Unbeknown to Fox and the other London leaders, certainly without their approval, the settlers of the Jerseys were moving towards a far larger Quaker colony than anyone had planned. True, some Friends, among them William Penn, anticipated that, in time, Carteret might be induced to give up his dominions, but no one imagined that the time was ripe to add Sassafras Land to the Quaker holdings.

George Fox, the best informed of all the Friends, the only Quaker who was intimately familiar with the territory, did not then envision this. Though he, by his knowledge of the migration movement, as arbiter between Fenwick and Byllinge, and as a logical consultant on the nonoperative Concessions and Agreements, knew more than any other Quaker except William Penn about the workings of the Quaker scheme, he thought of Sassafras Land only as a substitute for, not as an addition to, New Jersey.

In September, 1678, nearly a year after his return from Holland, George returned to Swarthmoor Hall. Though this, apparently, was his first glimpse of Margaret in seventeen months, his only comment which has survived was that he arrived just in time for meeting.

Fox was now fifty-four, but hardships and the cumulative effects of his seven years in prison—one-fifth of his ministerial life—aged him beyond his years. By sheer will power, he could summon strength to combat crises facing his people and he could prolong a spurt until the need was past; but long-continued routine labors were impossible. The bursts of energy were, however, costly; he needed long periods of recuperation.

The relaxation was purely physical; while Margaret and the rest of the Swarthmoor household coddled him as much as he would tolerate, he kept active in counselling, in preaching at Swarthmoor meeting and in writing.

His manuscripts, his frequent circular letters "to all Friends everywhere" and his special missives to the Grand Turk, the ruler of Algiers and to other dignitaries revealed his weariness. They reflected a deep concern for humanity and justice, and when there was outstanding grievance, as in the treatment of Quakers captured by Barbary pirates, they were pointed and specific. But, for the most part, they repeated earlier exhortations to fear God and to hold to Truth. Zeal still burned within George Fox, but his youthful originality was spent. Even in his early vigor, he had never been a scholar; while his insight was sure and sharp, his written words seldom struck deep. In those days, however, what was missing in his writing was more than supplied by the power of his personality; his intensity and fire, his warmth and sympathy produced conviction. In semiretirement at Swarthmoor, in sounding the same strains, he could not convey the former magic; those who knew him in his prime would certainly be moved—but by their memories rather than by his repetitions.

Because personnal appeal was always his major weapon, those who knew him personally, though they might not be convinced, invariably testified to his great power, while those who knew him only by his letters were less impressed.

For an active man, the stay at Swarthmoor was frustrating. Much as George Fox appreciated the loving care of Margaret and her daughters, he could not be wholly happy without constant movement. Probably he could not have phrased the matter clearly; but, subconsciously, Fox realized that his most effective service lay in visiting the meetings where his presence would inspire the Friends and wipe away what differences arose.

Possibly he sensed that control of Quakerism was slowly slipping from his hands. At best, management of the movement could not be completely conducted from a rural retreat days distant from the capital. But remoteness was not the only threat to the old dictatorship. As Quaker problems multiplied and grew more technical, with greater stress on elaborate financing, colonization and statecraft overseas, leadership relied less upon inspiration and improvisation than upon informed technology. Younger hands, better educated and with wider worldly interests, were assuming powers once handled by evangels. Though, both from a real need and from common courtesy, they carefully consulted Fox on all important moves, it was they and not he who initiated and directed what was done.

After a year and a half of semi-isolation, George Fox, in March, 1680, left Swarthmoor for the last time. In his first eleven years of marriage, he spent, all told, only about forty months at home, while Margaret was with him twice in London.

At meeting after meeting while on his way to London, George Fox set forth "the outward state of the church, how each member ought to walk and act, according to its place in the body," which meant the discipline to be pursued and errors to be avoided. He visited prisoners for the Truth, met old Friends, collected details of sufferings, both that justice might be rendered and that the mounting totals would impress judges and lawmakers into granting mercy. Eventually, he came to London, in time for Yearly Meeting; he spent five weeks writing letters to Friends in Britain, Holland, the West Indies and America.

Letter writing was important; together with the circulation of approved books and pamphlets, it unified the Quaker movement. However widely Friends might be dispersed, the interchange of thoughts and principles knitted them into a compact community. No contemporary group was more culturally homogeneous.

But letter writing, however effective, could not transmit the personal touch that was George Fox's greatest gift, nor could it satisfy his restless spirit. He was an active man, happiest when moving here and there to sow the Quaker seed, most serviceable when, as a Public Friend, a travelling missionary, he furthered the sense of brotherhood and fellowship.

In this service, he accomplished much; but, because his work was more by inspiration than by deed, the credit fell to others. Scores of British meetings traced their beginnings, or their effective organization, to his prompting; in America, at least a hundred Quaker communities date from his visit.

But organization was not his only contribution. When, as in America, his continued presence was impossible, he held the meetings together through his numerous epistles. Throughout the early colonial period, no other influence was as effective in binding scattered colonists into unity, no other force gave them consciousness of solidarity.

His concern for American development led him to assign to London and Bristol meetings the responsibility for overseas correspondence that overtaxed his time and energy. He made them clearinghouses for ideas and centers of guidance, and so linked colonists with the mother country. He gave direction to the emigration movement.

London headquarters, accordingly, buzzed with business concerning Quaker colonies. Burlington and, for all its difficulties, Salem, too, were flourishing; ships were being fitted out to take more settlers and more supplies. Numerous details of government were being worked out and plans were being discussed for wider expansion of Quaker interests.

40

Holy Experiment

EXCITING PROSPECTS LOOMED. THE CROWN OWED THE LATE
Admiral William Penn a considerable amount of back salary.
Nor was this all; the admiral had not only worked for nothing
but promises but he had also lent King Charles II sizeable
sums from his own pocket. Since Charles, as usual, had no cash
with which to pay, the suggestion was made that the debt,
some £16,000, be cancelled by the transfer of some of his
empty colonial lands.

Friends discussed the matter at the 1660 Yearly Meeting.
On the strength of the enthusiastic reports from Burlington and
Salem about the Delaware Valley, of what Fox had seen of
Sassafras Land and of Coale's experience with the Susquehannocks, Penn asked the King to cede this land to him.
Cheerfully disregarding protests that much of the land was
already granted to Maryland or Connecticut, Charles gladly
agreed. On March 4, 1681, he gave Penn title to a tract only
slightly smaller than all of England.

The monarch was so happy that, when Penn named the
region Sylvania, Charles added Penn's name as a prefix. Penn
protested, even to the point of trying to bribe the clerk to omit
the prefix; when this effort failed—itself an astonishing event
in Restoration history!—he tried to explain the name away

by saying that in Welsh the word "pen" meant a hill, and so Pennsylvania meant hilly forests. No one but William Penn himself believed the explanation.[1]

No evidence remains that George Fox participated in the negotiations, but it is unthinkable that, when he and Penn were both attending London meeting, the two men were not in steady, close consultation. The scheme to settle the debt by ceding land may not have been Fox's idea, but certainly his words carried weight in choosing the tract for which Penn petitioned. Since George was an exhorter rather than a planner of detail, an enthusiast when statecraft was essential, his suggestions must have been more inspirational than practical; nevertheless, he played an important role in building the new province.

The important concept of fair treatment of the Indians stemmed straight from Fox. Europeans generally had no thought that those of different color, race or culture should have equal rights, and Englishmen were no exception. But, as early as 1657, Fox was insisting that all men were equal under God and that all subject peoples must be treated kindly and humanely. Under this guidance, Fenwick scrupulously observed Indian claims to land and Penn was following the precedent. The emigrants whom he sent out to Burlington were under orders to pay Lenapes for tracts that white men settled; Penn accepted the same Fox principles for Pennsylvania.

Penn, extraordinarily busy now in planning his colony's settlement and government, dropped out of West Jersey affairs. His work as Byllinge's trustee was, as it happened,

[1] The bargain was as good as that of West Jersey, for, in exchange for an otherwise uncollectible debt, Penn received 45,000 square miles—approximately eight acres per penny. Penn was not a greedy man, but, like Charles, he had sketchy geographical knowledge; his original request was for land "as far north as was plantable." This, if, granted, would have given him most of New York and much of eastern Canada.

complete, the brewer being out of debt and, by virtue of a grant from the Duke of York, restored to his governing power.

Again, probably after consultation with George Fox, Penn drafted a set of "Conditions and Agreements" for his colonists, avoiding this time the ultrademocratic passages which displeased the Crown. As guidance for treatment of the Indians, he prescribed the Golden Rule. No one must cheat or defraud Indians; there must be no restriction on their right to move freely within the province; and both Indians and white men should have equal freedom to establish homesteads.

If Fox proposed, as doubtless he did, that Pennsylvania's administrators be guided by the spirit, along patterns set by Scripture, he was overruled. However workable this theory of government may have been in ancient Israel, Penn deemed it ill-advised for seventeenth-century America. He was a devout Fox partisan, but, in erecting what he termed his Holy Experiment, with its capital at a city to be called Philadelphia, or Brotherly Love, he relied upon more practical advice.

Significantly, in drafting his second American constitution, the Frame of Government for Pennsylvania, Penn, while granting wide powers to an elective Assembly, reserved more control for the Proprietor than was provided in the cancelled New Jersey Concessions and Agreements. He did not, however, abandon the provision for religious liberty for all who professed the Christian God. He retained his firm belief in democratic government.

"Any government is free," wrote Penn, "where the laws rule and the people are a party to those laws."

Penn's preference for a more workable colonial government than George Fox would have preferred implied no hint of any breach with Fox; he gave George more than a thousand acres of Pennsylvania, some of it in the heart of the future Philadelphia.

In autumn, 1681, new settlers appeared upon the Delaware. The number was less than was expected, for one ship froze up in the river and held its passengers aboard all winter, while another was blown so far off course that it did not come to Pennsylvania until spring. More, however, were imminently awaited. Penn's agents, active both in England and on the Continent, were selling land at less than 5 pence an acre or, if bought in larger quantity, at a discount. The price was cheap, but, had Penn been fortunate enough to sell his holdings even at the lowest rate, he would have reaped a tremendous profit.

He met competition, however. Byllinge, who, for all his opportunism, was a loyal Quaker, followed, in November, 1681, a Fox suggestion for the relief of the poor. He sent a circular to Quaker meetings throughout England offering one-hundred acres of West Jersey free to each of a hundred poor Quaker families who would emigrate. Well, not entirely free; they must pay a yearly rent—one grain of wheat per family.

In the absence of complete documentary evidence, especially that dealing with personalities and motives, it is difficult to grasp just what Fox, Penn and Byllinge had in mind concerning Quaker colonies.

On receiving his Pennsylvania grant, William Penn surrendered his interest in West Jersey; but when, after George Carteret's death, East Jersey was put up at auction in February, 1682, Penn and eleven other associates bought the province. The price, £3,100, was three times as much as was paid for West Jersey, but the land was neither so sandy nor so barren; it was, by any yardstick, a great bargain.

The purchase brought all land between New York and Maryland into the hands of owners all but one of whom were Quakers. The ownership was inter-locking; more than half of the proprietors held title in two of the three provinces and some had interests in all of them.

There was, however, something of a difference. Pennsylvania was designed primarily for Englishmen, but also for Friends from Wales and the German Palatinate, while West Jersey cared for Londoners, North Countrymen, Yorkshiremen and the Irish; the lines, however, were not tightly drawn. East Jersey, more heavily settled, with 5,500 people in seven towns, was less a Quaker center, though Robert Barclay believed that he and his influential Scottish relatives could build it into an asylum for religious and political freedom.

Whatever the original purpose of taking up so large a portion in the very center of the English colonies, Fox's role in America steadily diminished. As a spiritual leader he remained revered, but, practically, he wielded little influence save as a father figure. Nor, though three provinces were held in interlocking control, was little effort made to govern them as one co-ordinated colony; each went its separate way until, at last the two Jerseys joined as one, and Delaware, in time, split off from Pennsylvania.

Perhaps Fox's last direct connection with the American settlements followed Penn's landing at Upland in 1682 and the convening of the first Assembly. Penn presented a set of sixty-one draft laws, drawn up in England after consultation with Fox.

The first, and most important, the Great Law of Pennsylvania, was almost wholly William Penn's conception, although he must have listened to suggestions from his patron, the Duke of York. Some of the rest, however, bore Fox's stamp; they forbade the drinking of healths—was this an echo of George's teen-age drinking bout?—made the spreading of false news illegal and threatened punishment for clamorous persons, ranters and scolders. The code, moreover, proposed that these laws be used as reading lessons in the schools, replacing Aesop's Fables.

Two proposals, however, the Assembly very wisely rejected; they would have obliged young men to marry before they reached a certain age and would have limited Pennsylvanians to two suits of clothes, one for winter and the other for summer wear.[2]

William Penn was very pleased. He wrote to English Friends : "I must, without vanity, say that I have led the greatest colony in America that ever any man did upon a private credit and the most prosperous beginnings that ever were in it are to be found among us."

While Penn wrestled with colonization problems, George Fox went by river barge to Thomas Lower's house at Kingston-on-Thames, where years ago the Diggers planted carrots. As usual he kept busy; but, as always, he chafed in physical idleness. Again and again, from Kingston as his base, he frequented meetings in the neighborhood.

Ten days of this were quite enough; he went back to London, crossed the city and visited the boys' school he established in 1668.

Changes had occurred. The school was no longer at Waltham, its original location, but was now at Edmonton, some seven miles from London. Though Christopher Taylor, brother of Thomas Taylor, Seeker leader of Preston Patrick, remained as headmaster, he was anxious to leave for Pennsylvania; there was much talk of asking George Keith, Fox's companion on the Netherlands trip, to fill the position about to be vacated. The curriculum was modified. Instead of training apprentices, George's method of safeguarding Friends against old-age dependency, the school was teaching law and Latin, the better,

[2] On the other hand, the Assembly accepted the Duke of York's decree that beer be sold at a penny a pint.

it was thought, to protect young Quakers against legal writs they otherwise would not understand. Fox, who had disapproved the teaching of foreign languages, was appeased upon learning that though two Silesian Friends were teaching Greek, Latin, and Hebrew, they were using the Scriptures as their texts.

Other schools, at Bull and Mouth, at Southwark, and the London school for the free instruction of the children of poor Friends, were following the Edmonton example. Because they abandoned the "old, corrupt, heathenish books and grammars," George Fox approved of them, though he must have disliked the practice followed here and there of placing what he considered too great stress upon his personal accomplishments.

His intention of teaching students "whatsoever things were civil and useful," his instructions for Shacklewell school for girls, remained strong.In conjunction with Penn and Thomas Lawson, the former priest whom George had known for thirty years, Fox planned a special course in botany and agriculture, using a garden in which every plant, foreign or domestic, that could be grown in England would be available for study; a Latin text would teach their properties. For once, a university professor commended a George Fox project, but too many difficulties were met and the project was abandoned.

Fox, however, did not forget the plan. If the botanical garden were not possible in Britain, it might be feasible in the New World. As part of his gift from Penn of Pennsylvania land was a sixteen-acre tract in Philadelphia, George began to think of devoting it to a meetinghouse, a school and a garden plot.

The fact was that, while Quakers revered George Fox and studiously sought his opinions, the active movement was bypassing him. His evangelistic talents remained unimpaired, but, rightly or wrongly, Friends no longer considered them as vitally essential, as in the past, when Quakerism struggled for acceptance. New business managers were rising, efficient men who laid less stress upon the letter of the Scriptures. Reluctantly, George Fox conceded that the dramatic and exciting overseas adventures lay beyond his failing powers; his temperament did not fit him for selling Pennsylvania land to the Welsh and English or for recruiting Germans to settle in America.

Nor was it possible to repeat his earlier exploits. Quaker meetings were illegal, but when Fox revived his former protest methods, officers would not co-operate. Under orders, they entered Grace Church Street meeting, but they contented themselves with pleading with George to sit down and hold his tongue; when he persisted in speaking, the constables pretended not to hear. He went so far as to invite a constable to arrest him but, reminding the latter that it was Sunday, inquired all too politely whether an arrest on the Lord's Day would be legal. The constable, perplexed whether he would be praised for vigilance or punished for violating Sunday, went off and did not come again.

None but George Fox wished to see the situation changed. Magistrates shrank from bringing matters to a head. Soldiers kept Friends from entering the meetinghouses, but helped carry chairs and benches outside, so that Quakers could hold their meetings in the streets. Constables took part in the service, removing hats if prayer was going on, tugging gently at a speaker's hand at intervals to urge him to cease talking, but making no real effort to enforce the laws. Once Fox asked a guard if he were not weary of the game, and the soldier answered with deep feeling that indeed he was, but that Quakers never tired.

Once or twice, a touch of gentle humor enlivened the dull routine. An informer, eager for his £20, urged a judge to find

Fox guilty, only to have the justice turn angrily against him and demand to know if the informer was trying to teach him how to run a court. Another justice threatened mightily to send George Fox to prison, but, after eating a good dinner, he thought better of the idea—jail would give Fox too good an opportunity to preach before a captive congregation—and so he set George free. One justice went so far as to impose a fine of £20; but when no one came forward with the money, he sighed, and forgot the whole affair.

Fox, for his part, broke the monotony by performing what some Friends thought a miracle. A certain man was suffering sharp pains from gallstones. Fox spoke to him, laid his hand upon him and prayed the Lord to "rebuke the infirmity." Suddenly the stone passed and the man was so relieved that next day he rode twenty-five miles.

George was not so successful when an eight-year-old step-granddaughter came down with smallpox. She called for him, and he rushed up to Kingston-on-Thames, to be with her. He felt the Lord's power run through the child, but, to the un-- happiness of Thomas and Mary Lower, the power had come not to raise their little girl but to carry her away; that night she died.

It was one of a series of misfortunes afflicting the Fell family. Things were not going too well as Swarthmoor. Gossipy neighbors were chattering about Margaret's living apart from her husband. Outwardly, she professed herself content; by God's will, George must serve the Lord in London while she ordered and governed her children and her household. "If any judged hard of us because of that, the Lord will judge them for we were innocent," she said.

Doubtless, Margaret, now almost seventy and losing her sight, must have known that she was manufacturing excuses. It was, of course, true that, after the efficient Sarah married William Meade in 1681, more business duties fell upon her shoulders; but the forge was already sold and Rachel was doing much of the work. With most of her daughters, all but Rachel and Susannah, married and moved away, Swarthmoor needed less attention.

Gossip was not her only concern. In common with many other careful mothers, she criticized the men who courted her daughters. She disapproved at first of Mary's marrying Thomas Lower—he was too poor—but later she was reconciled to the union. The widowed Isabel fell in love with a man whom Margaret thought unsuitable—the match fell through. Then Rachel, in her thirties, announced her intention of marrying Daniel Abrahams, eight years her junior. Though Margaret was eleven years older than George Fox, she did not think her daughter should wed a man younger than she. Nevertheless, the wedding took place and, in due course, Abrahams bought Swarthmoor, which meant that Rachel took over even more of the household responsibilities.

Grandchildren galore offered solace. Mary Lower had ten children, Margaret Rous eight, Rachel and Isabel Yeamans each four. But most of them lived far from Swarthmoor, some as distant as London or Barbados, so that Margaret was unable to see them as often as she would have liked. Death, too, was frequent. Seventeenth-century knowledge of hygiene, medicine and child care being inadequate, fifteen of the children died young, many of them in infancy.

As though loneliness, criticism and death were not enough to bear, she suffered persecution. She and the Abrahams were arrested in 1683 for failure to attend Episcopalian services. The warrant against her was insulting; it was drawn against Margaret Fell, widow, as though she was never married to George Fox. Margaret believed the purpose was to fine her as a widow, whose fine would be twice that of a married woman. More likely, the Episcopalian authorities refused to recognize that marriage without a priest was legal.

George Fox, increasingly weak, weary and unwell, joined William Meade and Thomas Lower's brother—Thomas was in Launceston jail—in petitioning the King and the courts on Margaret's behalf. Unfortunately, Esquire Marsh was dead and Penn was in America, so release was slow. When it came belatedly, Daniel Abrahams was almost immediately rearrested on the same charge of refusing to attend the Anglican church.

Nor was Margaret out of danger. Both she and, for the first time in his life, George Fox, faced trouble over tithes. In 1684, Ulverston authorities, who never before assessed tithes against the Swarthmoor property, accused George and Margaret of tax evasion.

Whether the former omission of tax levies by Ulverston parish was due, as at Fenny Drayton, to its possession of glebe lands in lieu of tithing rights or to an exemption because of Judge Fell's official position was not made clear; but, whatever the circumstances, Margaret, who no longer owned the land, was certainly not liable. Nor, since he owned neither land nor other taxable property, was George Fox. Even less excuse existed for preferring a demand for tithes in London, where a parallel suit was started.

George believed the London demand was a pretext for requiring him to take an oath in answering the charge and, on his refusal, for committing him in contempt of court. If so, the plaintiff, whom George did not identify, failed of his purpose, for the law-enforcement officers were very lax. Though Fox attended meetings openly, lodged at his usual haunts and made no effort to avoid service of the warrant, no one moved a finger to arrest him.

Fox was no man to accept a favor. As soon as Yearly Meeting ended, following his usual custom of thrusting his head into the dragon's mouth, he hunted up the justices to tell them why he would neither pay the tithes nor take an oath.

None of the judges had any strong desire to press the charges. They told Fox that they were too busy to listen; when George insisted upon a trial, they postponed the case. One justice only was bitter about the delay; "a little time after he died."

His fate did not deter the other persecutors. Constables descended upon Swarthmoor, broke into the barns and led away six cows, two steers, a fat ox and some calves. Soon after, they came again and took all the other animals; not even a milch cow was left for Margaret.

To make life easier in what everyone supposed were her last years, friends suggested that she leave Swarthmoor and join George in London; but Margaret would not agree. Too much needed to be done at Swarthmoor, she insisted; this was her field of service.

George, moreover, was about to leave the city; he was being drawn again to Holland, and she had not the strength to go with him.

41

Thou Excellest All

FEW MAJOR PROPHETS LIVED TO SEE MORE OF THEIR MAJOR aims attained. With the Word spread far and wide, a tight Friends organization running smoothly and efficiently, doctrinal dissension reduced both in numbers and intensity, and with freedom of worship guaranteed throughout the English-speaking world, George Fox, in much less than half a century, fulfilled the visions of his youth.

He spent himself completely. Aged before his time, a victim, not, as he believed, of his early exposures and beatings but of the relentless pace at which he always drove himself, he was worn out at sixty.

His body was weak, but his will to work remained as strong as ever. So tired that he must lie down at frequent intervals, exhausted by summer heat, susceptible to winter cold, sickly, as he diagnosed, because of stuffy and ill-smelling London air, he needed long periods of recuperation. He did not know, however, how to rest. His stays at the Rous or Meade country houses gave him the change of air he thought he needed, but not the relaxation that was essential. A hobby would have helped him, but he had none; recreation he considered sinful. Mere muscular quiescence, in the rare moments when he succumbed to it, was of little value, when his mind was overladen

424

with the burdens of the world. A country sojourn was no vacation to a man who, when only slightly refreshed by a night's fitful sleep, dashed off to meetings, wrote feverishly and voluminously and preached with passionate conviction to swarms of callers who broke through his privacy.

For, despite his battery of clever young executives working through a hierarchy of meetings, George Fox remained busy. Other leaders might initiate action and carry out decisions, as did Penn in colonization work, but, however, independent, they considered his judgment infallible.

Fox, of course, credited his wisdom and discernment to divine direction, but the guidance focussed upon an unmatched knowledge. Because he scrupulously avoided almost all comment upon current happenings, it was all too easy to suppose that he was ignorant of them; actually few contemporaries had greater opportunity than he to know what was occurring. The close-knit Quaker system poured more news into headquarters than any other organization, except possibly the government, enjoyed; by personal experience, George Fox knew more of Britain, and probably more people in every corner of the nation, than any other private citizen. Men in public life received official reports that might be colored or distorted in the interests of governmental policy; but Fox was told of moods and aspirations, as well as of deeds and dry administration.

He might have made a greater use of his unparalleled resources had he been able to adjust himself to the world in which he lived. A practical man with exceptional managerial skill, he saw both Britain and all other lands not as seventeenth-century nations but as early Christian communities whose basic principles and current laws had been laid down immutably by prophets and apostles. These precepts were a constitution against which to test the worth of new ideas; legislation or conduct out of harmony with what was written in ancient

Palestine had no validity to him. To George Fox, there was nothing amiss in citing Scripture to convince the Turk of error, nothing unusual in expecting the Chinese or the American Indian to accept the Hebrew Bible as their code. No English king or Parliament possessed the right to make George Fox conform to any order not specifically expressed in Scripture nor to deny him any privilege conferred by Biblical authority. Fox adopted an attitude of almost complete isolation from mundane events, assuming that his godly life would lead "the world" to follow his example.[1]

Scripture gave him guidance for his stubborn nature. Basically, he was an individualist who followed his own whim. No man controlled him, no government existed, past or present, to whose dictates he pledged complete obedience. He warred against mundane authority in every field; no man-made laws or doctrines commanded his support.

Yet, as far as carnal weapons were concerned, he was in no sense a rebel. No matter how strongly he detested what he wrongly named the "filth" of Puritanism or the Restoration's frivolity and vice, he made no physical gesture against the governments permitting the abuses. However violently priests raged or magistrates abused him, George Fox returned no blows.

It would have been easier for his enemies had he replied in kind. By jailing Fox, they could have quelled his insurrection. But a rebel at heart whose roots were in the Scriptural Holy Land could neither be put down nor persuaded.

To manage one who fashioned his own rules as he needed them was wholly impossible. Fox lived by the Scriptures, but he chose his passages selectively and he interpreted them as he

---

[1] Sometimes a quite opposite effect resulted. As late as November, 1962, *The Friend*, the most important Quaker journal, warned that "inward withdrawal" betrayed "appalling arrogance." "We have been foxed too long," the editor remarked.

alone saw fit. Nothing could be clearer than the Scriptural injunction of rendering unto Caesar those things which were Caesar's, but Fox found nothing that was exclusively man's own. From the standpoint of constituted authority, he was worse than a revolutionist; he was an anarchist.

Legally, also, he was, as laws were then written and interpreted, a blasphemer. True, the courts either acquitted him or, at worst, let him off with minimum sentences; but, had the judges been as hostile as Fox accounted them, he might easily have been transported or sent to his execution. The invariable defense that he knew everything because the Lord revealed all things to him by a secret Inner Light was, to his judges, convincing proof that Fox claimed to be one with Christ. His brash contention that those who spurned the Word of the Lord God as he spoke it would be forthwith cut off intensified their conviction.

His rigid construction of the letter of the Bible, as he interpreted those words, did not endear him to rivals who were less bound by them or who read different meanings into the passages. His inflexibility sharpened their indignation.

Fox's fundamentalism was firm, but the tide was running against him. Theology and strict construction of the Scriptures no longer gripped the English. Reaction was setting in against Puritanism. Though the nation professed to deplore the excesses of the early Restoration years, it welcomed the relaxation or abolition of Cromwellian strictness. To George Fox, these were symptoms of decay; sensing a widening gap between the virtuous and the lost, he saw Britain rushing into error.

In the hope that perhaps the Dutch were more consistent Christians he went again to the Netherlands. Ostensibly the visit was to attend a five-day Yearly Meeting of the Dutch and German Friends; in reality he was seeking to rediscover the enthusiastic responses of his youth. He found the people eager and receptive but undemonstrative; he was pleased, however, to see that Galenus Abrahams, no longer high and shy and mighty, was loving and tender. Doubtless, he would have reaped better results had he not rushed so rapidly; on this 1684 visit he travelled 420 miles. The mileage was slightly less than on his first visit but it was covered in one-third the time taken in 1677.

When George Fox returned to England in July, Gulielma Maria Penn advised Margaret to join him in London but she delayed until November. Then, largely because she wished to petition the King against persecutions, she went down to get his help, and that of William Meade, in drafting her appeal.

The time was ill-chosen. Charles II was only 55 but, like Fox, he was worn-out, tired and ill. Margaret, making no allowance for his failing health, upbraided him for his anger and roughness in receiving her. Actually he was dying. A day or two later he was stricken. Four days later he died.

Immediately upon the accession of James II Fox and other leaders conferred five hours on how to obtain the release of 1,460 Friends from prison and how to gain toleration for dissenters.

They placed more faith in James II than circumstances warranted. Charles had been a secret Catholic and of elastic conscience, but James was openly Papist and stubborn against religious dissidents. As Duke of York he had been promising and pleasant for then he bore no responsibility, but as king he was unbending. At the very moment that Quakers trusted in his help he was writing "I have not great reason to be well satisfied with Quakers in general."

James admitted individual exceptions—William Penn and Robert Barclay for example; but of others he was not so sure. For half a dozen years, Protestants in the West and in Scotland had been plotting to put James, Duke of Monmouth, illegitimate son of Charles II, on the throne, and, despite continual denials by Fox and other Friends, the Quakers, chiefly because they refused to swear allegiance, were supposed to be participants in the conspiracies. James may have shared these fears, but, if so, he held his tongue, his idea being that he could buy off all dissenters by treating them with kindness.

When Margaret called upon him, begging relief against oppression, he suggested that she go home to Swarthmoor; he gave her what she considered a hint that persecutions would be checked.

In April, 1685, Margaret returned to Swarthmoor; she was not to see George again for more than five years.

In Furness, Justice William Kirkby entertained no such thought as toleration. For twenty years or more, he and his relatives had been persecuting the Fell family. Because of them, Daniel Abrahams was serving yet another term in jail for not attending Anglican church; it was with them that her undutiful son George had conspired to take her home from her. When she held meetings in her great hall, Kirkby fined and imprisoned her; he now announced that she might "expect the same again."

His only assurance was that the local justices would not kill Margaret or her family, "but whilst you have anything we will take it."

After the capture of the rebel Monmouth and his execution in the summer of 1685, danger to the throne, while still existent, appeared less imminent. Perhaps, as Margaret believed, in answer to her letter of complaint, more likely as a gesture to appease dissidents, James announced his intention of freeing all imprisoned Friends, of halting the iniquitous custom of rewarding informers for espionage and of stopping the practice of fining those who would not attend official worship. In the following March, he issued a general pardon.

Whether he took the action because of real belief in freedom of conscience or because, by helping Quakers, he was giving even greater aid to his fellow Catholics, the pardon failed to win the great approbation it deserved. Some of his more rabid opponents were convinced that, by linking Friends and Catholics, James was disclosing that the Quakers were allied with Jesuits if, indeed, they were not themselves Papists in disguise. When, in the following spring, he ended all religious persecution by his Declaration of Indulgence, his enemies strengthened their opposition to him; the decrees, which should have been applauded, became strong reasons for urging his expulsion.

Meanwhile, with Margaret in the north, living with the Abrahams, who now owned Swarthmoor Hall, George drove himself unsparingly. During most summers, he lived at the Rous home at Kingston-on-Thames or with the Meades in Essex, where Susannah Fell was also staying; for shorter stays, especially when business detained him in the city, he lodged at various Friends' houses. One Quaker family kept his riding things, another a trunk, a hammock and about £200 he kept on hand for his emergency expenses; the Meades cared for his box of business papers and his 335-volume library. At one or another of these places he was busy, often beginning conferences or committee meetings at daybreak and continuing them, with intermissions when he lay down and rested, until late in the evenings.

Though holding no official position in any of the meetings, he was a welcomed and a valued participant in all. He inspired, if he did not organize and direct, groups of various sorts, especially those which might be best described as Quaker clubs of men and women of similar trades and professions. He arbitrated differences, advised and counselled leaders in all Quaker activities, and visited the sick.

Above all, he wrote—a virtually endless stream of letters circulated far and wide. Most of those that went to Friends were sermons, couched in such manner as to seem general exhortations towards a righteous life but cleverly contrived to carry strong warnings against some deviation which was threatening; almost invariably they cited Scripture pertinent to the purpose.

George, however, continued weak, a condition he ascribed, at least in part, to the fact that England was governed by politicians, priests and soldiers, instead of, as Scriptural example suggested, by farmers and shepherds. Abel was a shepherd, as were Moses and David, he pointed out; Noah and Jacob and Elisha were husbandmen, while Abraham and Isaac were both. If these rural folk were wise enough to rule Israel, if they found favor in the eyes of the Lord, why should not their counterparts rule England?

Fox's emphasis on rural rather than city virtues was not surprising at a time of moral decadence and general revulsion against Puritan regimes, but seemed at odds with recent Quaker trends. A movement which arose on northern farms and in the villages was now drawing strength from the trades-men and other city dwellers who once were the backbone of Puritanism. The more important leaders were no longer coming from the fields nor from small-town pulpits, but from the same cultured or aristocratic circles which produced the statesmen whom George Fox decried. Keith and Barclay were both city men, and William Penn was born on Tower Hill; Fox, alone among the Quaker chiefs, was country bred.

Fox seemed, indeed, in these later years, to be reverting towards his early interests. He, too, had been a shepherd, and possibly a farm hand, who may have stood, with straw in mouth, at a Nottinghamshire hiring fair. The country people he had met in those first years of wandering had not been rakes and rascals; unlike the London wastrels of the 1680 decade they had been earnestly concerned about religion. Many professed misguided, even filthy and wicked, views about proper ways to worship; but, as George looked back, he saw that they were blindly seeking God; they were not as lost as Londoners who scoffed at all religion.

He was, in other ways, returning to his youth. Again, as when he was a boy, he was appalled at seeing old men "cleaving to the earth" and was shocked at the loose behavior of young people "running into the fashion of the world." Doubtless, had he possessed the strength, he would have made evangelistic tours to bring the errant back into the Truth, but, frail and exhausted as he was, he could do no more than visit all the meetings within easy distance; after exhortations, sometimes in the midst of meetings, he withdrew to lie down and rest.

Much work fell upon his shoulders. With virtually all the seasoned Quaker Publishers dead or broken in health, with theoreticians such as Penington and Barclay dead or dying, Fox assumed their literary and evangelistic tasks. Supposedly, William Penn was to carry on the circuit-riding tasks, but Penn simply did not have the time. Preoccupied with his Holy Experiment and, latterly, with defending himself against those who, because of his close friendship with the deposed James II, considered him a Jesuit in disguise, Penn left the responsibility to the ailing Fox. Moreover, as George Keith was in Philadelphia heading the boys' school Penn had chartered there, Fox felt obliged to supervise Friends' education in Great Britain.

Yet, with all this activity, he found time to reprimand delinquent rulers. Hearing that Danzig Quakers were imprisoned on a bread-and-water diet, Fox wrote to King John III of Poland, who called himself "Defender of the City," asking how he, the King, would feel if someone, the Turks perhaps, treated him in such a fashion; he sent a copy to the Danzig magistrates. Where in the Bible, George demanded, was there evidence that either Jesus or the apostles arrested those who worshipped in unchristian fashion, much less fed them starvation rations?[2]

Fox paid special attention to the tightening of bonds between the English Friends and the Quakers of the colonies. He urged the American meetings, now stretched in scattered settlements from Maine to Carolina, to maintain close communication with Bristol and London. To both American and West Indian Quakers he pleaded for fair treatment of Negroes and Indians. In his last important letter overseas, written in mid-December, 1690, he urged Americans to foster Negro meetings and to act in harmony with the Indian kings, their councils and their tribesmen.[3]

In February, he returned from the country to resume his busy schedule of activities. Happy that all things were going well, that Friends everywhere—in America, in Holland and in Germany, as well as in Britain—were at one in love and peace, he preached lengthily and effectively at Grace Church Street meeting.

Perhaps he overstrained himself. As he was leaving the meeting cold struck to his heart; at the same moment he felt his life work was complete. While walking with his friends to his lodgings in adjacent White Hart Court, he said, contentedly, "I am glad that I was there. Now I am clear. I am fully clear."

As soon as his companions left him, George lay down, but, unable to be still, he tried to rise to do a little more work. The effort was too much for his depleted strength. He lay down again, complaining of the cold. For rest and warmth, he put himself to bed, weary and exhausted but untroubled and serene. He was not to rise again.

[2] It was typical of George Fox's provincialism that he referred to the Danzig jail as Bridewell. Incidentally, neither the King nor the magistrates bothered to reply.

[3] Yet somehow the rumor spread, especially in Maryland, that George Fox, who, above all men, believed in freedom and equality, owned a Negro slave! Some people will believe anything provided only that it is incredible.

Realizing that he was on his deathbed, he summoned various Friends, to counsel them to exalt the righteous, to publish Quaker writings and to spread the Truth to all nations and all peoples.

"All is well," he assured them. "The Seed of God reigns over all, over death itself."

On Tuesday, February 13, 1691, two days after the cold struck to his heart, George Fox died. He was in his sixty-seventh year.

William Penn wrote the unhappy news to Margaret at Swarthmoor. The distance was, of course, too great for the letter to reach her before the funeral, much less for her to make the trip to London. But a large gathering assembled on Saturday to hear testimonies to George Fox's labors. After a two-hour service, his body was borne to the Friends' burial ground at Chequers Alley, near Bunhill Fields.

The next Yearly Meeting listened to a farewell message, written by George Fox for delivery after his death. He urged Friends to stand steadfast in Christ Jesus, to dwell in the pure, peaceable, heavenly wisdom of God, and to live not for self but for the Lord. He told them, also, to avoid schism and strife, for the Lord blasts the loose and the unruly, and to maintain the true church government.

Fox left no formal will, but, instead, a series of instructions to guide those who survived him. Some years before 1685, he had paid Susannah and Rachel Fell £72 for a three-acre tithe-free property, with cottage, barn and outbuildings; he directed that the main buildings be converted into a slate-roofed meeting house, with well-paved approaches and a porch with seats. Conscious of his infirmities, he thought of others who might need to rest; he gave the meetinghouse an ebony four-poster, a large chair and a chest fitted out with bottles, "so that Friends may have a bed to lie on, a chair to sit in and a bottle to hold a little water to drink." He proposed that a stable be made over into a house for some poor, honest Friend who would act as caretaker. Over and above all this, he contributed £20 for maintenance.[4]

This, as Fox explained, was "all the house and land I have in England," but in America he owned a city lot in Philadelphia, a sixteen-acre plot in what was then the city suburbs and 1,250 acres in the undeveloped hinterland of Pennsylvania. For all this property, he had given Penn, in 1681, a token payment of £25, but nothing further had been done to perfect the title. Fox assigned his rights to his sons-in-law, with the understanding that the city land be used for a meetinghouse, a schoolhouse and an enclosed garden; whatever space remained could be fitted out with hitching posts, where horses would stand while their owners were in meeting.

Not until some years after George Fox's death was action taken to carry out his wishes. When Thomas Lower asked about the status of the land, he was informed that a squatter had built upon the city plot. Rather than disturb the man, who had acted in good faith, Penn offered a twenty-acre tract in exchange, but three-quarters of a century elapsed before satisfactory adjustments were complete. By that time, meetinghouses were built and a school established, and much of the land was used as a burial place.

In addition to his land, Fox possessed investments and other assets worth about £700. Some of this, he directed, should be distributed among a number of Friends, especially to those at whose homes he was accustomed to stay; he left nothing to his surviving brother John nor to his sister Katharine. Nor

[4] Thus, whoever in the future might own Swarthmoor Hall, the Friends of Ulverston and its vicinity would have a meetinghouse in perpetuity. The building, with its rare Coverdale Treacle Bible, its burial ground, its shed for horses and its mounting block, is still in use. Swarthmoor Hall, also, after many years of private ownership, is once more in Quaker hands, a permanent memorial to George Fox and to Margaret, the nursing mother of Quakerism.

was Margaret mentioned in his testamentary papers, for she possessed ample independent income, as did, through marriage or in their own right, the daughters of Judge Fell. In addition, the girls shared the bequests left their husbands.

The remainder of his wealth, Fox anticipated, would be used to print his *Journal* and perhaps three volumes of his epistles, letters and doctrinal comments. This task Thomas Ellwood undertook through the Monday Morning Meeting of Quaker ministers, which had general supervision over the publication of approved manuscripts; upon completion of the *Journal*, in 1694, each Monthly Meeting received a copy of the folio volume.

After George's death, Margaret, her daughters and their husbands testified to the memory of the man they called their father. "He was one of the Lord's worthies, valiant for the Truth upon earth." William Penn, in his preface to the *Journal*, described George Fox as "a new and heavenly-minded man, a divine and a naturalist and all of God Almighty's making," who triumphed over death.

"I have done," said Penn, "when I have left this short epitaph to his name. Many sons have done virtuously in this day, but, dear George, thou excellest them all."

Bibliography

Any biography of George Fox necessarily rests upon his *Journal,* first printed in 1694 and since republished in numerous editions. The dozen "lives" written before Rufus Jones' tercentennial volume were little more than rewrites of these reminiscences.

Though Fox—a man of strong bias and intense feeling—dictated his memoirs to unscholarly secretaries long after most of the events occurred, few disciples questioned the *Journal's* authenticity. Obvious inaccuracies escaped discovery; no one mentioned the sharp style contrasts within the *Journal's* pages. Not until well within the present century, when Norman Penney began work on a revised edition, was notice taken that Thomas Ellwood, in piecing together the original text, took exceptional liberties with his materials.

Only comparatively recently have highly qualified men like William Braithwaite, Neave Bradshaw and Henry Cadbury reconstructed Quaker history. In their laudable zeal to give a balanced picture, they sometimes laid undue stress upon unimportant facets of Fox's personality, but they restored to him the charm, humanity and vigor that previously idolators had chilled.

Because Fox's dictated manuscript ended in 1675, only slight attention has been given to his later years; the impression was left that he lived in almost fruitless retirement. This was unfortunate because George Fox exerted a great and very direct influence, especially upon the growth of Quakerism in America.

Prior to William Hull and Rufus Jones, most important historians of the Friends were British to whom overseas development seemed less important than domestic progress. Since Fox himself wrote little about the colonies, they underestimated his contributions. Happily, the American researchers Frederick Tolles, Thomas Drake, John Pomfret, Kenneth Carroll and others are actively presenting more complete data in this field.

The time has come to soften some of Fox's harsher judgments. A victim of contemporary intolerance, his indignation induced false impressions of a bitterness and a spirit of detraction out of keeping with his character. Quaker writers are discovering that not all his adversaries were venal hypocrites who served their bellies or the Devil.

The Journal

Ellwood, Thomas (ed.). London, 1694.

Nickalls, John L. (ed.). Cambridge, England, 1952.

Penney, Norman (ed.). 2 vols. (Incorporates Fox's manuscript journal of travels in Ireland, 1669, John Hull's journal of the voyage to Barbados and Fox's manuscript journal of travels in America.) Cambridge, England, 1911.

———. *Short Journal.* (Covers the period 1647–1664.) Cambridge, England, 1925.

Biographies of George Fox

Backhouse, Edward. *Life of George Fox.* Sunderland, England, 1912.

Bickley, A. C. *George Fox and the Early Quakers.* London, 1884.

Bownes, Samuel. *Life of George Fox.* London, 1756.

Brayshaw, A. Neave. *Personality of George Fox.* London, 1919.

Evans, William. *Memoir of the Life, Travels and Labors of George Fox.* Philadelphia, 1829.

Hodgkin, Thomas. *George Fox*. London, 1896.

Janney, Samuel McPherson. *Life of George Fox*. 2 vols. Philadelphia, 1853.

Jones, Rufus Matthew. *George Fox: Seeker and Friend*. New York, 1930.

———. *Life and Message of George Fox*. New York, 1924.

———. *The Story of George Fox*. New York, 1904.

Knight, Rachel. *The Founder of Quakerism*. London, 1922.

Marsh, Josiah. *Popular Life of George Fox*. London, 1847.

Noble, Wilfred Vernon. *The Man in Leather Breeches*. New York, 1953.

Post, Jacob. *Brief Memoir of the Life of George Fox*. London, 1854.

Rowntree, John Stephenson. *Life and Works*. London, 1908.

Spurgeon, Charles H. *Life and Character of George Fox*. An address. London, 1866.

Taylor, Ernest E. *Cameos from the Life of George Fox*. London, 1907.

Tuke, William. *Memoirs of the Life of George Fox*. Philadelphia, 1815.

van Etten, Henry. *George Fox: Fondateur de la Societe des Amis*. Paris, 1923.

Watson, John Selby. *George Fox*. London, 1860.

Wigham, John. *Memoirs of His Life*. London, 1842.

Books and Pamphlets

Barclay, John. *Memoirs of the Rise—in Scotland*. London, 1833.

Barclay John (ed.). *Letters of Early Friends*. London, 1841.

Barclay, Robert. *An Apology for the True Christian Divinity*. Philadelphia, 1789.

Belasco, Philip S. *Authority in Church and State*. London, 1925.

Berens, Lewis Henry. *The Digger Movement in the Days of the Commonwealth*. London, 1906.

Besse, Joseph. *Abstract of the Sufferings—of Quakers*. 2 vols. London, 1733.

Bowden, Thomas. *History of the Society of Friends in America.* London, 1850, 1854.

Brailsford, Mabel Richmond. *A Quaker from Cromwell's Army: James Nayler.* New York, 1927.

———. *Quaker Women,* 1650–1690. London, n.d.

Braithwaite, William C. *The Beginnings of Quakerism.* London, 1912, 1923.

———. *The Second Period of Quakerism.* London, 1919.

Brown, L. F. *Political Activities of the Baptists and the Fifth Monarchy Men.* London, 1912.

Burnet, George B. *The Story of Quakerism in Scotland.* London, 1952.

Cadbury, Henry Joel. *George Fox's Book of Miracles.* Cambridge, 1948.

———. *The Swarthmoor Documents in America.* Supplement 20, JFHS, 1940.

Cadzow, Donald A. *Archeological Studies of the Susquehannock Indians of Pennsylvania.* Harrisburg, 1936.

Calamy, Edmund. *Account of the Ministers—Ejected* in A. G. Matthews' *Calamy Revisited.* Oxford, 1934.

Coate, Mary. *Cornwall and the Great Civil War.* Oxford, 1933.

Cole, W. Alan. *The Development of Quaker Political and Social Ideals,* 1647–1660. Typescript, Swarthmore Pa., College Library.

Croese, Gerardus. *Historia Quakeriana.* Amsterdam, 1696.

Crosfield, Helen G. *Margaret Fell of Swarthmoor Hall.* London, 1913.

Dankaerts, Jasper. *Journal.* New York, 1913.

Edwards, Rev. Jenkyn. *Fenny Drayton: Its History and Legends.* Nuneaton, England, 1924.

Fell, Sarah House. *Account Book of Swarthmoor Hall.* Cambridge, 1920.

Firth, J. B. *Highways and Byways of Derbyshire.* London, 1905.

Fogelklou, Emilie. *James Nayler: Rebel Saint.* London, 1931.

Foulds, Elfrida Vipont. *The Birthplace of Quakerism.* London, 1952.

Glynne, Sir Stephen R. *Notes on the Churches of Lancashire.* Manchester, 1893.

Gough, John. *History of the People Called Quakers.* Dublin, 1790.

Gummere, Amelia Mott. *Witchcraft and Quakerism.* Philadelphia, 1908.

Hallowell, R. P. *The Quaker Invasion of Massachusetts.* Boston, 1883.

Harvey, T. Edmund. *Quaker Language.* Supplement 13, JFHS, 1928.

Hazard, Samuel. *Annals of Pennsylvania.* Philadelphia, 1850.

Henderson, Charles. *Essays in Cornish History.* Oxford, 1935.

Hodgkin, Lucy Violet (Mrs. John Holdsworth). *A Book of Quaker Saints.* London, 1922.

Holder, Charles Frederick. *Quakers in Great Britain and America.* New York, 1913.

Homan, Walter Joseph. *Children and Quakerism.* Berkeley, Calif., 1939.

Hull, William Isaac. *Quakerism in the American Colonies.* London, 1911.

———. *Rise of Quakerism in Amsterdam.* Swarthmore, Pa., 1938.

———. *William Penn and Early Quaker Migration to Pennsylvania.* Swarthmore, Pa., 1935.

Janney, Samuel McPherson. *Rise of the Religious Society of Friends.* Philadelphia, 1867.

Jones, Rufus Matthew. *Quakerism in the American Colonies.* London, 1911.

———. *Spiritual Reformers of the 16th and 17th Centuries.* London, 1914.

———. *Studies in Mystical Religion.* London, 1909.

Jones, T. L. *Launceston Castle.* London, 1959.

Jorns, Auguste. *Quakers as Pioneers in Social Work.* New York, 1931.

King, Rachel Hadley. *George Fox and the Light Within.* Philadelphia, 1940.

Knight, Rachel. *The Psychology of George Fox*. New York, 1923.

Laycock, Bettina. *Quaker Missions to Europe and the Near East*. Mss (1950) Euston House.

Lloyd, Arnold. *Quaker Social History, 1669–1738*. New York, 1950.

Locker-Lampson. Sophy Felicitede Rodes, *A Quaker Post-Bag*. New York, 1910.

Longshore. Thomas Ellwood, *George Fox Interpreted*. Philadelphia, 1881.

Manners, Emily. *Elizabeth Hooten*. London, 1914.

Marshall, J. D. *Furness and the Industrial Revolution*. Barrow-in-Furness, England, 1958.

Maxwell, Ezra K. *Quakerism and English Literature 1650–1750*. Mss at Harvard University Library.

Mortimer, Russell S. *Quakerism in 17th Century Bristol*. Bristol University, 1946.

Nightingale, Rev. Benjamin. *Early Stages of Quaker Movement in Lancashire*. London, 1921.

———. *The Ejected of 1662 in Cumberland and Westmorland*. Manchester, 1911.

Nokes, G. D. *History of the Crime of Blasphemy*. London, 1928.

Norway, Arthur H. *Highways and Byways in Devon and Cornwall*. London, 1911.

Nuttall, Geoffrey F. *James Nayler: A Fresh Approach*. Supplement 26, JFHS, 1954.

———. *The Welsh Saints, 1650–1660*. Cardiff, 1911.

Petegorsky, David W. *Left-Wing Democracy in the English Civil War*. London, 1940.

Pickworth, Henry. *Charge of Error—*. London, 1716.

Rees, Rev. T. Hardy. *A History of the Quakers in Wales*. Carmarthen, 1925.

Roper, William Oliver. *Materials for the History of Lancaster*. Manchester, 1907.

Ross, Isabel. *Margaret Fell*. London, 1949.

———. *Swarthmoor Hall*. London, 1960.

Rowntree, Joshua. *Social Service: Its Place in the Society of Friends.* London, 1913.

Sabine, George H. (ed.). *Works of Gerrard Winstanley.* Ithaca, 1941.

Sewel, William. *History of the Rise—of Quakers.* Burlington, N.J., 1774.

Smith, Charlotte Fell. *Extracts from State Papers Relating to Friends,* 1654–1672. London, 1913.

Smith, Samuel. *History of New Jersey.* Burlington, 1877.

Speck, Frank G. *A Study of the Delaware Big-House Ceremony.* Harrisburg, Pa., 1931.

Steiner, Bernard C. *Description of Maryland.* Baltimore, 1904.

Stewart, Frank H. *Major John Fenwick.* Woodbury, N.J., 1939.

Sykes, John. *The Quakers.* Philadelphia, 1959.

Taylor, Ernest E. *Cameos from the Life of George Fox.* London, 1907.

———. *The Valiant Sixty.* London, 1951.

Thomas, Allen C., and Thomas, Richard H. *History of the Friends in America.* 2 vols. London, 1850, 1854.

Tolles, Frederick B. *Quakers and the Atlantic Culture.* New York, 1960.

Trevelyan, George T. *England Under the Stuarts.* London, 1907.

Turner, P. Storrs. *The Quakers.* London, 1889.

Vulliamy, C. E. *William Penn.* London, 1933.

Wagstaff, W. A. *History of the Society of Friends.* New York, 1845.

Watson, John Fanning. *Annals of Philadelphia and Pennsylvania.* Philadelphia, 1884.

Webb, Maria. *The Fells of Swarthmoor Hall.* London, 1897.

Wight, Thomas. *History of the Rise—of Quakers in Ireland.* London, 1811.

Wildes, Harry Emerson. *The Delaware.* New York, 1940.

———. *Twin Rivers.* New York, 1943.

Wise, Jennings Cropper. *Ye Kingdom of Accomache on the Eastern Shore of Virginia in the 17th Century.* Richmond, Va., 1913.

Wood, Anthony A. *Athenae Oxoniensis.* London, 1813, 1920.

Wright, Louella M. *Literary Life of the Early Friends.* New York, 1932.

PERIODICALS

Abbreviations :

BHP   *Bulletin,* Friends Historical Association, Philadelphia

Fr. Intell.   The *Friends Intelligencer,* Philadelphia

JFHS   *Journal,* Friends Historical Society, London

MdHS   *Maryland Historical Society*

"alpha." "George Fox and Tolstoi," *Manchester Guardian,* Nov. 24, 1910.

Anderson, J. R. "George Fox and the Early Quakers," 5 *National Magazine,* 32.

Aydelotte, Frank. "George Fox's Style," 13 *BHP* (1924), 69–78.

Belasco, Philip S. "George Fox," *Encyclopaedia of Social Sciences,* VI, 406–7.

Bickley, A. C. "Fenny Drayton, Birthplace of George Fox," 13 *Antiquary* (1886), 22–8.

Boison, Anton T. "George Fox Among the Doctors," 101 *Fr. Intell.* June 8, 1944, 359–60.

Braithwaite, Alfred W. "Early Tithe Persecutions of Friends as Outlaws," 49 *JFHS* (1960), 148–55.

———. "Errors in the Indictment and Pardons in the Case of Theophilus Green," 49 *JFHS* (1959), 1.

Braithwaite, William C. "Westmorland and Swansdale Seekers, 1651," 6 *JFHS* (1908), 3.

Brockbank, Elizabeth. "Story of Quakerism in the Lancashire District," 36 *JFHS* (1939), 3.

Burr, Nelson R. "The Quakers in Connecticut," 31 *BHP* (1942), 11–23.

Cadbury, Henry Joel. "Early Quakerism and Uncanonical Lore," 40 *Harvard Theological Review* (1947), 177–205.

————. "George Fox's 'Openings'," *Friends Quarterly* (Jan., 1955), 44–7.

————. "Intercolonial Solidarity of American Quakerism," 60 *PMHB* (1936), 362–74.

————. "Recording the Rise of Truth," 41 *BHP* (1952), 3–11.

Carroll, Kenneth L. "Maryland Quakers in the 17th Century," 47 *MdHS* (1952), 297–313.

————. "Talbot County Quakers in the Colonial Period," 53 *MdHS* (1958), 326–70.

Cole, W. Alan. "Social Origins of the English Friends," 48 *JFHS* (1957), 99–118.

Corder, Anna. "Quakerism in Friedrichstadt, 1663–74," 39 *JFHS* (1947).

Douglas, John M. "Early Quakerism in Ireland," 48 *JFHS* (1956).

Drake, Thomas E. "William Penn's Experiment in Race Relations," 68 *PMHB* (1944), 372–87.

Dudley, Albert Cassell. "Non-Conformity Under the Clarendon Code," *American Historical Review* (1912); 10 *JFHS* (1913).

Edmundson, Frank B., and Roberts, Emerson B. "John Edmondson, Large Merchant of Tred Haven Creek," 50 *MdHS* (1955), 219–33.

Edwards, George W. "The Bull and Mouth Meeting," *Fr. Intell.*, April 2, 1955, 192–4.

Evans, E. Lewis. "Morgan Llwyd and the Early Friends," *Friends Quarterly* (Jan., 1954), 48–57.

Ewart, Henry C. "George Fox and the Inner Light," 171 *Living Age* (1886), 491–3.

Goerke, Edmund. "First Quakers in Pennsylvania and New Jersey," *Friends Journal,* February 8, 1958.

Goodbody, Olive C. "Presidential Address," 49 *JFHS* (1961), 4.

Graham, John W. "The Inspiration of George Fox," *Spectator,* June 27, 1925.

Grubb, Edward. "George Fox as a Social Reformer," 118 *Nation* (June, 1924), 732–4.

Grubb, Isabel. "George Fox in Ireland," 45 *JFHS* (1953), 75–80.

Gummere, Amelia B. "William Penn's Trip to Holland and Germany, 1677," 4 *BHP* (1912).

Haistwell, Edward. "Diary of the Travels of George Fox, 1677–8," 19 *JFHS* (1922), 61.

Harvey, T. Edmund. "Young George Fox and Nathaniel Stephens," 80 *Friends Quarterly Examiner* (1946), 69.

Hobhouse, Stephen. "Jacob Boehme's Influence in England," 33 *JFHS* (1936), 34.

Holcomb, Cmdr. Richmond C. "George Fox's Sea Voyage to America," 13 *BHP* (1924), 64–9.

Holder, Charles Frederick. "The Quaker and the Puritan," 33 *Arena* (1905), 382–92.

Hudson, Winthrop S. "A Suppressed Chapter in Quaker History," 24 *Journal of Religion* (1947), 108–18; Cadbury reply, *ibid*, 201–12.

Hull, William Isaac. "Dutch and Quaker Peacemakers," 23 *BHP* (1934), 40.

———. "Egbert van Heemskill's Quaker Meeting," 27 *BHP* (1938), 17.

———. "Quakerism in Danzig," 41 *BHP* (1952), 81–92.

Hyde, James. "The Muggletonians and the Document of 1729," 7 *New Church Review* (1900), 215–27.

Jackson, J. W. "George Fox, Founder of Quakerism," 113 *Zoist* (January, 1856), 361–6.

Lewis, Martha Serene. "Lavendar and the Grand Turk," 102 *Fr. Intell.* (June 7, 1945), 366–8.

Lowenhertz, Robert J. "Roger Williams and the Great Quaker Debate of 1672," 9 *American Quarterly* (1959), 157–65.

Mackey, Lydia Miller. "The England of George Fox's Journal," 190 *Blackwoods* (1911), 557–66.

Maclear, James F. "Quakerism and the End of the Interregnum," 19 *Church History* (1950), 240–70.

Martin, Robert Edmund. "Legends, Folklore and Dialect of Leicestershire," 17 *Transactions,* Leicestershire Archeological Society (1933), 174–95.

Middleton, W. C. "George Fox, A Practical Mystic," *London Quarterly Review* (1932).

Mortimer, Russell S. "Allegations Against George Fox in Lancashire," 39 *JFHS* (1947), 15.

Nightingale, Rev. Benjamin. "Lancashire : Its Puritanism and Nonconformity," *Preston Guardian,* March 10, 1906.

Nuttall, Geoffrey F. "Early Quakerism in the Netherlands," 44 *BHP* (1955).

————. "The Dating of George Fox's Journey from Launceston to London in the Autumn of 1656," *Friends Quarterly Examiner* (1946) 117–24.

Penney, Norman. "George Fell and the Story of Swarthmoor Hall," 31 *JFHS* (1934), 27; 29 *JFHS* (1932), 67.

Perkins, Hugh. "George Fox's Cottage," letter, March 22, 1892, Euston House.

Pickvance, T. Joseph. "George Fox and His Use of the Word 'Seed'," 41 *JFHS* (1949).

————. "Healing and Spiritual Regeneration," *Friends Quarterly,* 1957.

Pomfret, John E. "Edward Byllinge's Proposed Gift of Land to Indigent Friends, 1681," 61 *PMHB* (1937), 88–92.

————. "Proprietors of the Province of East New Jersey, 1682–1702," 77 *PMHB* (1953), 251–93.

————. "Proprietors of the Province of West New Jersey, 1674–1702," 75 *PMHB* (1951), 117–46.

————. "Thomas Budd's True and Perfect Account of Byllinge's Proprietaries in West New Jersey, 1685," 61 *PMHB* (1937), 325–9.

Robbins, Alfred. "Launceston's Doomsdale," *Launceston Weekly News,* Nov. 15, 1924.

Robinson, George. "Jerusalem Journey, 1687," *Fr. Intell.,* July 17, 1948.

Royce, Josiah. "George Fox as a Mystic," 6 *Harvard Theological Review* (1913), 31–59.

Simpson, Margaret H. "Bristol Friends and the Friends Meeting Houses," 47 *JFHS* (1955).

Snell, Beatrice Saxon. "George Fox's Leicestershire Training," 41 *JFHS* (1949).

——. "The Lichfield Vision," 41 *JFHS* (1949).

Stephens, Francis J. "George Fox and the Early Quakers of Cornwall," *Cornish Post,* May 16, 1925.

Stites, Raymond. "George Fox and the Beliefs of the Indians," 101 *Fr. Intell.* (August 5, 1944), 511–2.

Strachey, J. St. Loe. Review of Fox's *Journal, Spectator,* June 13, 1925.

——. "The Christianity of Christ," 73 *Forum* (March 5, 1925), 342–9.

Taylor, Ernest E. "From Prison to Prison," 72 *Gentleman's Magazine* (1904), 132–9.

Thomas, Gilbert. "George Fox and the Quakers," 122 *Fortnightly* (1924), 170–81.

——. "The First Quaker," 126 *Contemporary Review* (1924), 63–8.

Thornbury, Delmar Leon. "The Society of Friends in Maryland," 29 *MdHS* (1934), 101–15.

Tolles, Frederick B. "George Fox and the Spires of Lichfield," 104 *Fr. Intell.* (May 10, 1947), 239–40.

——. "A Quaker's Curse : H. Norton to J. Endecott, 1658," 14 *Huntington Library Quarterly* (1951), 415–21.

——. "The Trans-Atlantic Quaker Community in the 17th Century," 14 *Huntington Library Quarterly* (1951), 239–58.

Vann, Richard C. "From Radicalism to Quakerism: Gerrard Winstanley and .Friends," 49 *JFHS* (1959).

Walker, J. "The Yorkshire Plot," 3 *Journal,* Yorkshire Archeological Society (1934), 348–59.

Watkins, Owen. "Some Early Quaker Autobiographies," 45 *JFHS* (1954).

UNSIGNED ARTICLES

"An Account of Ministering Friends Who Visited America, 1658–1793," 10 *JFHS* (1913), 147.

"American Journal of George Fox," Bodleian Manuscript. 9 *JFHS* (1912), 5–52.

"Anne Gargill," 4 *BHP* (1912).

"Benjamin Furly," 11 *JFHS* (1914).

"Biddle, Hester and the Grand Turk," 47 *JFHS* (1958).

"Character of George Fox," 65 *Academy* (August 15, 1903), 151–2.

"Coale, Josiah, and the Susquehannocks," 6 *BHP* (1914).

"Fenny Drayton," *Birmingham Post Weekly,* July 5, 1924.

"Fenny Drayton Monument," 17 *JFHS* (1920).

"Firbank Fell," *Westmorland Gazette,* August 9, 1924.

"George Fox and His Salvation Army," *Salvation Army* (London, 1881).

"George Fox and the Early Quakers," 63 *London Quarterly Review* (October, 1884), 97–112.

"George Fox and the Wreckers," *Fr. Intell.,* January 8, 1955.

"The George Fox Lot in Philadelphia," 1 *BHP* (1904); 3 *BHP* (1904).

"George Fox's Humor," *Friend* (London, 1926), 141.

"John Perrot," *Fr. Intell.,* May 21, 1955.

Review of *Journal, Current Opinion* (September, 1924), 346; *London Times,* July 9, 1925.

"Sir Peter Lely's Portrait," 10 *JFHS* (1913).

"Women Writers Among Friends in the 17th Century and Later," 10 *JFHS* (1913), 93–5.

Notes

No trace remains of the grass-thatched Fox cottage in the Dog Yard. True, some seventy years ago, when a Pennsylvanian came searching for the birthplace of George Fox, a canny real estate salesman obligingly showed a house where, he solemnly asserted, the Quaker founder had been born. It was neither in the Dog Yard, nor, for that matter, near the church, but it looked antique and was vouched for by the salesman's guarantee. The American was on the point of buying when the horrified rector of St. Michael's joined with the resident of Hartshill in revealing the fraud. The real Fox house, they explained, was torn down early in the 19th century.

The fact should have been well known to the real estate man. Almost a hundred years ago, a neighbor from across the fens, a man with the Washington Irving name of Bracebridge set up a small but unmarked pyramid near the fruit trees in commemoration of George Fox, but when Bracebridge died no one continued to pay the rental of two-and-six yearly for the site and so rank weeds overran the little monument.

Thus an antiquarian searching in 1885 for house or monument found neither. Inquiry at the best source of local history revealed that no one remembered such remains. The informant added, surely most incorrectly, "It only shows that Quakers nowadays care nothing for George Fox."

Actually, the rector of St. Michael's, Rev. Jenkyn Edwards, proposed in 1936 that a new monument to Fox be erected within the church but two neighborhood Monthly Meetings decided against the proposal, preferring to maintain the Bracebridge memorial. Reverend Henry Baylis, rector of St. Michael's in 1962, professed some doubt whether Fenny Drayton actually was the George Fox birthplace.

Contemporary source material treating of the life, rather than of the teachings, of George Fox is so rare that little more than his own *Journal* is available. Though, in the more than two and a half centuries since his death, more than a score of formal biographies were attempted

451

—virtually all published prior to 1924 were mere rewritings of the *Journal.*

More recently, Quaker scholars—writing with an astonishing objectivity—have, without adding greatly to the detailed incidents of Fox's life, analyzed the forces acting upon him and have interpreted the effects of Fox's activities. The works of Braithwaite, Brayshaw, Cadbury, Penney and Jones so underlie every chapter of the present book that detailed citations are impossible.

For specific individuals mentioned in the text, Besse, Calamy and the various entries in the *Dictionary of National Biography* are authorities except where special reference is given.

Preface, Chapter 1 and Chapter 2. Drayton is described by Bickley, Edwards and Martin. In addition, Friends House in Euston, London, has letters reporting research by Alexander Gordon (1889) and Hugh Perkins (1892). For the monument, in addition to Edwards, there are letters at Friends House from J. Douglas Maynard (1926) and Norman Ellis (1939); see also *Birmingham Post* July 5, 1924. Other letters, from William A. Rippon (1924), A. C. F. Davies (1913) and W. T. Hall (1931) trace the Fox and Lago ancestry. The Drayton legends are from Edwards and the *Birmingham Post* and the dialect from Martin. The identification of Gee, ascribed by Henry Pickworth (1736) to William Rogers in "The Christian Quaker" (London 1690) is reported in 31 *JFHS* (1934), 141.; there are other notes in *JFHS* vols. 4, 6 and 7. Cadbury, 21 *JFHS* (1924), 3, identifies the Fox Bible and a note in 22 *JFHS* (1925), 14 suggests, on the authority of Henry Pickworth's *"True and Faithful Relation . . ."* (1736) the presence of a Ranter, one Hicks a shepherd, at Drayton. Harvey has an article on Nathaniel Stephens and Cadbury on Fox's "openings."

Chapter 3. Hobhouse, in a review in 33 *JFHS* (1936), 52, describes Boehme's influence on England. Petegorsky discusses the political and economic impact of the radicals. A. C. Thomas, "The Family of Love," 12 *Haverford College Studies* (1893) deals with the Familists. Jones writes of the mystics and reformers and King explains the Inner Light. Uncle Pickering is identified in 7 *JFHS* (1910), 34.

Chapter 4. A. W. Braithwaite examines tithing as it affected Quakers and Edwards reveals the Drayton situation. Aydelotte comments on the probable sources of Fox's finances.

Chapter 5. Knight and Royce do best with Fox's psychology. Berens, Harvey, Hudson, Sabine, Tolles and Winstanley discuss various aspects of the Digger movement. Manners has a life of Elizabeth Hooton. An odd, and certainly incorrect, identification of Prophet Brown appears in 2 *JFHS* (1905), 69. A note in 19 *JFHS* (1922), 101 quotes a Fox contemporary as using the nickname "Leathercoat."

Cadbury in 49 *JFHS* (1960), 3 reports an alleged early portrait of Fox, but Nickalls says that identification is impossible. Hull, in 27 *BFP* (1938), 19 mentions a number of possibly Quaker paintings, including Egbert van Heemskerk's so-called "Quaker Meeting." The Lely portrait, early mentioned by 10 *Friends Quarterly Examiner* (1879), 58 and by *The Friend* (Philadelphia) May 1892, was questioned by 10 *JFHS* (1913), 96–7. Tolles, in a letter to Isabel Ross, October 20, 1948, cites three leading American art critics as denying its authenticity.

Chapter 6. For a discussion of steeple-house interruptions see 68 *Macmillans Magazine* (1893), 372, 2574 *Living Age* (November 4, 1893), 259 and Russell S. Mortimer in 44 *JFHS* (1952).

Chapter 7. Firth sets the Derbyshire stage. Nokes is the best authority on the legal aspects of blasphemy. The Moslem ladies are from Burnet. Rhys Jones (Rice Jones or Johns) and his Proud Quakers are in 7 *JFHS* (1910), 50. The first appearance of the name "Quaker" in print may have been in Thomas Hall's "The Pulpit Guarded" (1651), but Cadbury, 49 *JFHS* (1959), found it in manuscript as early as November 4, 1647.

Chapter 8. Royce and Knight explain the Lichfield episode psychologically; see also Tolles. Snell, in 41 *JFHS* (1948) tells of a local legend of a pool of blood. For Winstanley see notes to Chapter 5. The carrot planting is in Petegorsky and in Vann 49 *JFHS* (1959). Berens and Hyde discuss the Muggletonians, as does 68 *Macmillans Magazine* and the *Times Literary Supplement,* August 15, 1903. W. C. Braithwaite, in 6 *JFHS* (1908), 3, reports on the Westmorland Seekers.

Chapter 9. Brailsford, Fogelklou and Nuttall have excellent biographies of Nayler. The comments on Fox's oratory were made by William Penn in his preface to the *Journal.*

Chapter 10. Nightingale and Calamy report on ejected preachers; there is a second Thomas Taylor in 6 *JFHS* (1909), 23. The Evangelists are well covered in Penney, while Cole, in 46 *JFHS* (1953) and 48 *JFHS* (1957), as well as in his dissertation, has analyzed their social and economic composition; see, also, 19 *JFHS* (1922), 66. Taylor's "The Valiant Sixty" is standard. Firbank Fell is described by Lucy Violet Hodgkin as well as in *Westmorland Gazette* August 9, 1924. Witchcraft as it affected Quakers is discussed by Roper, Gummere and by Brockbank in 36 *JFHS* (1939), 3. The general situation in Lancashire is based on Foulds, Glynne, Marshall, Mackey, Nightingale and Roper.

Chapter 11. The official American spelling is, of course, swarthmore, but Swarthmoor is authentic British. Ross and Foulds well describe Swarthmoor Hall; there is an account of its ruin in 20 *JFHS* (1923), 31. Crosfield, Ross and Webb have written biographies of Margaret Fell.

Penney writes of both the Judge and his son in 29 *JFHS* (1932), 67 and 31 *JFHS* (1934), 27. Hull tells of Caton and Nightingale, in *Preston Guardian* March 10, 1906, comments on Hawkshead education. A sketch of Bridget Fell appears in 35 *JFHS* (1938), 43.

Chapter 12. Roper and Mortimer, in 39 *JFHS* (1947), 15, comment on the charges against Fox. Nightingale and Brocklebank report the trial. The Milner case is in Penney, 29 *JFHS* (1932), 67. Cadbury is by far the best authority on the "cures" and "miracles"; his book is reviewed in 40 *JFHS* (1948), 20. Later "cures" are discussed in 19 *JFHS* (1922), 58 and of a man "broken in his belly for four years" in 19 *JFHS* (1922), 58.

Chapter 13. All blasphemy material is from Nokes. The Simpson affair is in Besse.

Chapter 14. For the Fell family see Chapter 11 notes; for Nayler, chapter 9. The adulation, which grew progressively worse, is noted in 26 *JFHS* (1929), 41; and 32 *JFHS* (1935), 59. Hudson attacked it in 24 *Journal of Religion* (1944), 106; there is, in the same issue, a point by point reply by Cadbury.

Chapter 15. For the Apocrypha see Cadbury; for Bristol see Mortimer and Simpson. The Oxford-Cambridge outrages are in Besse, Braithwaite and "First Publishers of Truth."

Chapter 16. All persecution cases are drawn from Besse. For Fox on fashions see 7 *JFHS* (1910), 39.

Chapter 17. The Bull and Mouth, which may be the scene pictured in Van Heemskerk's "Quaker Meeting" (Hull: 27 *BFP* 38), is described by George Edwards, 12 *JFHS* (1915), 30. Stubbs' relationship to Uncle Pickering is suggested in 7 *JFHS* (1910). Cadbury discerned a Fox reference to Dutch possibilities in 47 *BFP* (1958), 30. Ann Gargill is mentioned in 4 *BFP* (1912), 105.

For early Massachusetts meetings see *Friend* (Philadelphia) April 24, 1953 and Gummere 11 *BFP* (1924); also Hallowell and Holder. Elizabeth Harris, Hester Biddle and other early missioners to America appear in Bowden, Hull, Jones and Thomas. The Massachusetts witchcraft charges are discussed by Gummere. Connecticut is in Burr.

The closing rhyme is taken from Petegorsky.

Chapters 18 and 19. For Cornwall, see Coate, Henderson and Norway. Fox's criticism of Launceston, republished in the tercentenary edition of the *Journal,* led to a flood of newspaper rebuttal. Among the newspapers commenting were *Cornish and Devonshire Post,* May 16, 1925 and September 5, 1925; *West Briton and Cornwall Advertiser,* September 17, 1925; and *Launceston Weekly News,* November 15, 1924 and October 17, 1925. For more detailed reports on Launceston see T. L. Jones, Alfred Robbins, "Launceston, Past and Present" and de R. and O. B. Peters "Histories of Launceston and Dunhavin." The Fenner identification rests on a note at Friends House referring to *Friend* (London, 1861), 307 and (1892), 634.

Chapter 20. For Nayler, see notes to Chapter 9. Nuttall dates Fox's return to London in *Friends Quarterly Examiner* (1906), 117. The Fifth Monarchy Uprising is described in Brown.

Chapter 21. For adulation see notes to Chapter 14, but for Nayler see Brailsford.

Chapter 22. The Quaker women writers are mentioned in 10 *JFHS* (1913), 93, and the autobiographers in Watkins. Early censorship (1653) is reported in 6 *JFHS* (1909), 60 and the later, with Robert Drings of London as censor and Calvert and Simonds as publishers in 21 *JFHS* (1924), 12. Hudson, of course, goes to extremes.

Chapter 23. Nuttall and Rees are best for Wales, Barclay and Burnet for Scotland. E. L. Evans and Southall, in *Friends Quarterly Examiner* (1919) treat of Llwyd while ap John is discussed in 10 *JFHS* (1913), 192.

Chapter 24. Fox's learning has always been a matter for debate. Croese says he had memorized the Bible, and George Whitehead (1691) credited him with understanding, reading and writing Hebrew; but Francis Bugg, a notorious anti-Quaker, charged that the Friends, especially Gerrard Roberts, paid a literary ghost "£80 of milled money and a dozen bottles of wine" for the Hebrew references supposedly supplied by Fox, 6 *JFHS* (1909), 41 and 15 *JFHS* (1919), 31. An article in *The Friend* (Philadelphia, 1831), 3 says that Fox knew some Hebrew and there were Hebrew volumes in Fox's library 28 *JFHS* (1931), 3. Apparently he knew only a few words of Dutch 3 *BHP* (1904), 156, but Furly, a close associate, was learned in that language, 11 *JFHS* (1914), 62; and 17 *BHP* (1928), 38.

Maclear has material on Vane as has 4 *JFHS* (1907), 68. The election appeal is in 21 *JFHS* (1924), 22. Tolles has a monograph on the Atlantic culture. In addition to the references in Chapter 17, Hester Biddle's adventures, especially in the Near East, are covered by Laycock, Lewis and Robinson, also in 47 *JFHS* (1955).

Chapter 25. Coale's missionary work appears in 3 *Maryland Archives* (1885), 348; and 41 *Maryland Archives* (1922), 104, and Steiner describes the Maryland scene. Gummere summarizes the Maryland work in 11 *BHP* (1924). The Susquehannocks are discussed in 6 *BHP* (1914) and Cadzow reports their ceremonies. Tolles reports the Norton curse on Governor Endecott and Gummere is authority for stating that Massachusetts alone executed Quakers, 11 *BHP* (1924). Perrot's Roman troubles appear in *Friends Intelligencer* (May 21, 1955), 246.

Chapter 26. For Restoration laws affecting persecution see Dudley;

for estimates on the number of sufferers see Taylor "From Prison to
Prison" and, of course, Besse. Maclear writes about Heselrige, and
George Fell's references are in notes on Chapter 16. For Fox's charges
against wreckers see Coate and *Friends Intelligencer,* January 8, 1955.

Chapter 27. Roper describes Lancaster Castle. Pepys reports the
Fifth Monarchy uprising of January 7, 1661. Esquire Marsh is identified in 3 *JFHS* (1906), 147.

Chapter 28. Alexander Gordon, in a letter dated February 19, 1902,
to J. S. Rowntree, now at Friends House, has a detailed explanation of
the hat controversy, as does Jones in "Life and Message . . ."; Pepys,
under date of July 29, 1667, comments on Eccles.

Chapter 29. L. V. Hodgkin describes Scarborough Castle, and
Nickalls in 28 *JFHS* (1931), 3 mentions the ship ownership. A. W.
Braithwaite explains the indictment flaws.

Chapter 30. Wight, Douglas and Grubb, the last named in 45 *JFHS*
(1953), 75, tell of the Irish mission. John Wigan's jibe about Fox's
wealth in *Anti-Christ's Strongest Hold Overturned* (1665) is reported
in 7 *JFHS* (1910), 86, while Pickworth (1736) in a wholesale denunciation of Fox's comments, denied that George knew either Latin or
English. Wright treats of the "Battledore,'" written in collaboration
with Furly (see Notes to Chapter 24). The biographers of Margaret
Fell describe the marriage. Elizabeth Bailey, in 70 *PMHB* (1946), 354,
traces the legend of the supposed child.

Chapter 31. Bushell's Case is reported in 86 *English Reports,* King's
Bench Division 15, Easter Term, 26 Carolus II, with an aftermath in
89 *English Reports* and 6 *Howell's State Trials,* 189. The Quaker case
is presented in *The People's Ancient and Just Liberties Asserted in the
Tryal of William Penn and William Mead,* London, 1670. Thomas
Lower's ancestry and his biography are in 20 *JFHS* (1923),˙28. (For
Penney's accounts of George Fell see Notes to Chapter 11.) The calls
of Margarett Fell and her daughters upon Charles II are in Crosfield,
Ross and Webb.

Chapter 32. Margaret Fell's letters to her daughters describe the
sailing of the *Industry* (Haverford College Library) 40 *JFHS* (1948), 25.
Holcombe gives detailed log of the voyage.

Chapter 33. Fox's adventures in America are recounted in a contemporary journal at the Bodleian, 9 *JFHS* (1912), 5, and are sum-
marized by Gummere in 11 *BHP* (1924). The unity of American
Quakerism is shown by Cadbury. For a report on the Fox mission, as
well as other visiting Friends, 1658–1673, see 10 *JFHS* (1913), 147.
Maryland is covered by Carroll, Edmonson and Thornbury. New Jersey
is based on Smith, Dankaerts, Pomfret and Goerke. Burr treats of Connecticut. Rhode Island, especially the Roger Williams debates, rests on

Lowenhertz, as well as on articles in 1 *BHP* and *Friends Journal,*
London, August 1, 1924. A physician's explanation of the "cure"
appears in 14 *JFHS* (1917), 87. The Indian lore is from Cadzow, Speck
and Stites, but Stewart makes the link to the Ten Lost Tribes. Penn
once thought they were ancient Welsh.

Chapter 34. Pennsylvania material comes from Goerke, Hazard and
Watson. Additional Indian material is available in Drake. Wise presents
the early Virginia story.

Chapter 35. The death of Mary Fox is related in 7 *JFHS* (1910), 79;
and 16 *JFHS* (1919), 61. The New Jersey events are drawn from
Pomfret, Smith and Stewart.

Chapter 36. Life at Swarthmoor is from Crosfield, Fell, Ross and
Webb. Cadbury, 41 *BHP* (1952), 3 speaks of the Fox work in preserving
a historic record. Wright and Watkins discuss Quaker autobiographies.
Byllinge's work is from Pomfret.

Chapter 37. Fox's vision, reported in a Mss. at Friends House, is
published in 4 *JFHS* (1907), 65.

Chapter 38. The journey to Europe has been far better covered than
the mission to America. The situation in the Netherlands is by Hull
and Nuttall, the dates of the Holland meetings established in 40 *JFHS*
(1948) and by Cadbury in 44 *JFHS* (1952). The possession of a Dutch
testament is mentioned in 3 *BHP* (1904), 156 but with the additional
statement that Fox needed interpreters. Both Janney and Watson speak
of the Abrahams debate. Quakerism in Denmark is ascribed to John
Hall by *Friends Journal,* January 12, 1957, and Corder shows the
growth in Friedrichstadt. Both Cadbury, 44 *JFHS* (1952) and Gummere, 4 *BHP* (1912), 97, treat of the Princess Elizabeth; the same
articles deal with Quakerism in Germany. Hull's research into Danzig
and Poland is reported in 10 *JFHS* (1913), 149 and 11 *BHP,* 81. There
is a copy of Fox's letter, in Dutch, at Friends House. His *Primmer and
Catechism for Children on a Plaine and easie way for Children to learn
to Spell and Read properly in a little time* . . . was published in 1670.
It is not unthinkable that the misspelled letter in English, dated August
23, 1677, and also at Friends House, is an unfortunate copy. (See notes
on Chapter 24.)

Chapter 39. For the unity of the American colonies see Cadbury
and Tolles. New Jersey material from Pomfret, "Thomas Budd . . ."
and Dankaerts; Pennsylvania is from Watson. Both Watson and Dankaerts mention Hannah Salter.

Chapter 40. Drake and Vulliamy are excellent for the Holy Experiment. George Vaux in "Settlers in Merion," 13 *PMHB* (1889), 147,
speaks of a Maryland migration to Pennsylvania. The Silesian teachers
are described in 10 *JFHS* (1913), 149.

Chapter 41. Fox's estate is inventoried, as far as is possible, by Aydelotte, Brayshaw and, with especial attention to the library, Nickalls in 28 *JFHS* (1931), 3. The gift of an Ulverston building as a meeting house, dated February 15, 1684, is noted at Friends House. The donation of the Philadelphia land, and the aftermath, are in 1 *BHP* (1904), 89; and 3 *BHP* (1904), 100. The story of the alleged slave seems to have arisen out of a 1683 case of a contested will. According to 30 *JFHS* (1933), 27, the story alleged that Fox died "possessed of a slave," but since the contested will occurred seven years before Fox's death the authority is doubtful.

Index

459